Card Games

ALL-IN-ONE

for
dummies®
A Wiley Brand

by Kevin Blackwood,
Chris Derossi,
Mark "The Red" Harlan,
Richard D. Harroch,
Lou Krieger,
and Barry Rigal

for
dummies®
A Wiley Brand

Card Games All-in-One For Dummies®

Published by:
John Wiley & Sons, Inc.
111 River Street
Hoboken, NJ 07030-5774
www.wiley.com

Copyright © 2017 by John Wiley & Sons, Inc., Hoboken, New Jersey

Published simultaneously in Canada

For general information on our other products and services, please contact our Customer Care Department within the U.S. at 877-762-2974, outside the U.S. at 317-572-3993, or fax 317-572-4002. For technical support, please visit https://hub.wiley.com/community/support/dummies.

Wiley publishes in a variety of print and electronic formats and by print-on-demand. Some material included with standard print versions of this book may not be included in e-books or in print-on-demand. If this book refers to media such as a CD or DVD that is not included in the version you purchased, you may download this material at http://booksupport.wiley.com. For more information about Wiley products, visit www.wiley.com.

Library of Congress Control Number: 2016951043

ISBN 978-1-119- 27571-8 (pbk); ISBN 978-1-119- 27572-5 (ebk); ISBN 978-1-119- 27574-9 (ebk)

Manufactured in the United States of America

10 9 8 7 6 5 4 3 2 1

Contents at a Glance

Table of Contents

Introduction

Card games offer the most fascinating challenges that you may ever encounter. In most games, you can manipulate the 52 pieces of pasteboard into infinite permutations and combinations. Working out those combinations is the fun part of cards — in almost every game, you don't know what the other players have in their hands. During the course of play, you use strategy, memory, cunning, and a whole host of other qualities to put together the best hand possible (or to bluff with the worst hand out there).

All in all, figuring out the fundamentals of a new card game can bring untold satisfaction. At the same time, you don't have to play cards all that well to enjoy yourself. Card games allow you to make friends with the people you play with and against.

If you've never played a card game before, you may wonder why you need to buy a book about the subject. All your friends say the games are easy to pick up, so can't you just sit down and start playing, picking up a few rules here and there? Well, no.

Many card games have been in circulation for hundreds of years, generating scores of variations. A reference book not only explains the core rules of a game but also lists the main variations to let you choose the rules you and your friends want to play by.

Regardless of how much experience you've had with card games, you'll find something here for you. Absolute beginners will appreciate that we discuss each game in this book starting at the very beginning, before a card hits the table. If you've played a few card games before, you can try out a new game or pick up a variation on one of your favorites.

Throughout this book, we talk about specific cards. Instead of constantly saying "the king of hearts" or "the 7 of spades" every time we refer to those cards, we abbreviate the cards and suits by using the following symbols:

>> **The suits:** We represent each of the four suits in a standard deck of cards with spade ♠, heart ♥, diamond ♦, and club ♣ symbols. (However, these symbols are also used when bidding for tricks in Bridge. More on that in Book 5.)

>> **The card values:** We use the following abbreviations to refer to specific card values: ace (A), king (K), queen (Q), jack (J), 10, 9, 8, 7, 6, 5, 4, 3, and 2.

Foolish Assumptions

We haven't assumed that you have all that much technical knowledge. The book is aimed at serving as an introduction to many card games (and a few popular non-card casino games like Roulette and Craps). If you get hooked on a game after reading about it, you can access many other Dummies titles (all published by John Wiley & Sons, Inc.) that can provide more knowledge of the games. For example, if you want to focus on Bridge, check out *Bridge For Dummies* by Eddie Kantar. You Poker fiends can find more information in *Poker For Dummies* by Richard D. Harroch and Lou Krieger, and *Texas Hold'em For Dummies* by Mark "The Red" Harlan. If playing card games (as well as a few other bonus chapters on games, such as roulette, craps, and slots) in a casino is your thing, get a copy of *Casino Gambling For Dummies* by Kevin Blackwood.

Icons Used in This Book

In each chapter, we place icons in the margin to emphasize certain types of information.

WARNING

This icon points out the wrong way to play a game. Pay special attention to these icons so you avoid finding things out the hard way.

REMEMBER

This reinforces a point that may be less obvious (or intuitively right) than meets the eye. You should keep these points in mind as you play the game.

TIP

These icons emphasize some insights born of our experience that will help make you a sharper player.

Where to Go from Here

Clear your calendar for the next few days because you're going to be busy playing new card games and trying out smart strategies. If you want to play a variety of (mostly) quick and easy card games, head to Book 1. If you're curious about Poker, check out Book 2; Texas Hold'em gets its own coverage in Book 3. Perhaps you've heard an older relative talk about her Bridge club; Book 5 introduces you to this fun but tricky game. Finally, if you're enamored with casinos and want to try your hand at the table games, flip to Book 6. You can also go to www.dummies.com and search for "Card Games All-In-One For Dummies Cheat Sheet" in the Search box."

1

Taking a Stab at Card Games

Contents at a Glance

Chapter 1

Getting Familiar with Card Game Basics

I f you've ever played cards, you don't need us to explain what fun 52 pieces of pasteboard can be. But just in case, here goes . . .

Because you don't know what the other players have in their hands in almost every card game, playing cards combines the opportunity for strategy, bluffing, memory, and cunning. At the same time, you don't have to play cards all that well to enjoy yourself. Cards allow you to make friends with the people you play with and against. A deck of cards opens up a pastime where the ability to communicate is often of paramount importance, and you get to meet new faces and talk to them without having to make the effort to do so.

If you want to take the plunge and start playing cards, you encounter a bewildering range of options to choose from. Cards have been played in Europe for the last 800 years, and as a result, you have plenty of new games to test out and new rules to add to existing games.

We can't hope to list *all* the rules of every card game in this book, so this chapter discusses the general rules that apply to *most* card games. Get these basics under your belt so you can jump in to any of the games we describe in detail later in the book.

Talking the Talk

Card gamers have a language all their own. This section covers the most common and useful lingo you encounter as you get to know various card games.

REMEMBER

When card games come together, the players arrange themselves in a circle around the card-playing surface, which is normally a table. We describe it as such for the rest of this section.

Getting all decked out

You play card games with a *deck* of cards intended for that game, also referred to as a *pack* in the United Kingdom. The cards should all be exactly the same size and shape and should have identical backs. The front of the cards should be immediately identifiable and distinguishable.

A deck of cards has subdivisions of four separate subgroups. Each one of these subgroups has 13 cards, although the standard deck in France and Germany may have only eight cards in each subgroup. The four subgroups each have a separate identifiable marking, and in American and English decks, you see two sets of black markings (spades and clubs) and two sets of red markings (hearts and diamonds). Each of these sets is referred to as a *suit*.

Ranking card order

Each suit in the United States and UK decks has 13 cards, and the rankings of the 13 vary from game to game. The most traditional order in card games today is ace, king, queen, jack, and then 10 down to 2.

As you find throughout this book, the ranking order changes for different games. You see numerous games where 10s or perhaps jacks get promoted in the ranking order (such as in Pinochle and Euchre respectively), and many games have jacks gambol joyfully from one suit to another, becoming extra trumps (as in Euchre).

Also, Gin Rummy and several other games such as Cribbage treat the ace exclusively as the low card, below the two.

Preparing to Play

Before you can start any card game, you need to ration out the cards. Furthermore, in almost every game, you don't want any other players to know what cards you've been dealt. That's where the shuffle and deal come into play.

Shuffling off

Before the dealer distributes the cards to the players, a player must randomize, or *shuffle,* them in such a way that no one knows what anyone else receives. (Shuffling is particularly relevant when the cards have all been played out on the previous hand.)

The shuffler, not necessarily the player who must distribute the cards, mixes up the cards by holding them face-down and interleaving them a sufficient number of times so the order of all the cards becomes random and unpredictable. When one player completes the task, another player (frequently in European games, the player to the right of the dealer) rearranges the deck by splitting it into two halves and reassembles the two halves, putting the lower half on top of the other portion. This is called *cutting the deck.*

Getting a square deal

In most games, one player is responsible for distributing the cards to the players — this player is the *dealer.* For the first hand, you often select the dealer by having each player draw a card from the deck; the lowest card (or, perhaps, the highest) gets to deal. After the first hand is complete, the rules of most games dictate that the player to the dealer's left deals the next hand, with the deal rotating clockwise.

REMEMBER

Before the deal for the first hand, a process may take place to determine where the players sit. In games in which your position at the table is important, such as Poker or Hearts, you often deal out a card to each player and then seat the players clockwise in order from highest to lowest.

The player to the dealer's left, frequently the first person to play a card after the deal, is known as the *elder* or *eldest hand.* The *younger hand* is the player to the dealer's right. These players may also be known as the *left hand opponent* and *right hand opponent* (which you sometimes see abbreviated as *LHO* and *RHO*). The player sitting opposite the dealer (his partner in a partnership game) may be referred to as the CHO or *center hand opponent.*

The due process of a deal involves the dealer taking the deck in one hand and passing a single card from the top of the deck to the player on his left, in such a way that nobody can see the face of the card. The dealer then does the same for the next player, and so on around the table. The process continues until everyone receives their due number of cards.

Players generally consider it bad form for any player to look at his cards until the deal has been completed.

In several games, only some of the cards are dealt out. In such games, you put a parcel of undealt cards in a pile in the middle of the table. This pile is known as the *stock* or *talon.* Frequently, the dealer turns the top card of the stock face-up for one reason or another, and this card is known as the *up-card.*

The cards dealt out to a player, taken as a whole, constitute a *hand.* It's normal practice to pick up your hand at the conclusion of the deal and to arrange the hand in an overlapping fan shape; if you like, you can sort the cards out by suit and rank, as appropriate for the game you're playing, to make your decision making easier. Make sure, however, to take care that no one but you can see your cards. Similarly, you shouldn't make any undue efforts to look at any one else's hand.

Most card games need not only a dealer (a job that changes from hand to hand) but also a scorekeeper — not normally a sought-after task. The least innumerate mathematician may be landed with the task. The good news is that scientific studies have shown that the scorer generally wins the game.

Exposing yourself (or someone else)

In general, any irregularity in a deal that leads to a card or cards being turned over invalidates the whole deal, and the normal procedure is for the dealer to collect all the cards and start over.

However, some minor exceptions to this principle exist, and these tend to result in the dealer getting the worst penalty if he exposes cards from his own hand. But most casual games call for leniency.

Bidding fair

Some, but by no means all, of the games in this book include another preparatory phase of gameplay during which players have to estimate how much their hands will be worth in the latter stages of the game. The game may call for a silent estimate (as in Ninety Nine), an announcement (Oh Hell!), or an *auction* (Euchre or Bridge), in which whoever makes the highest bid wins a right to form a prediction.

The process may offer the option to make a single call (Euchre) or a competitive auction (Bridge). Either way, these phases of the game are known as the *bidding*.

Frequently, a contested auction results in one player or partnership winning the chance to determine the boss, or trump, suit. This right is also known as *determining the contract*. One player or side essentially promises to achieve something in the play of the cards in exchange for being allowed to determine which suit has special powers.

REMEMBER

The bidding at games such as Euchre or Bridge should be distinguished from the *betting* at Poker or Blackjack. At Bridge, players must predict how many points or tricks respectively they can take, with penalties if they overestimate their hands' values. In games such as Spades or Oh Hell!, underestimation is similarly penalized. However, at Blackjack, you have to pay to play, without seeing your hand. At Poker, by contrast, although you must put up a stake in order to stay in the game and receive cards, the real expenditure comes after the initial bet, when you have to pay to stay in the game.

Making a Declaration

Are you the impatient type? Want to score points even before the gameplay begins? Well, some games have a *declaration* phase, in which you score points for combinations of cards that are worth certain amounts based on a predetermined table of values unique to the game. You can accumulate these points in a game like Pinochle, and sometimes an exchange of cards is permitted to improve your score on the hand.

REMEMBER

Having a number of consecutive cards in the same suit is called a *run* or *sequence*. Having three or four cards of the same rank (obviously in different suits, unless you have more than one deck of cards in play, in which case there are no such restrictions) is called a *set* or *book*.

Playing the Game

The most important phase of most card games resides in the *play* of the hand. In many of the games in this book, the objective is to try to accumulate points — or, in a game like Hearts, to try to *avoid* accumulating points.

The standard way of accumulating or avoiding points derives from the concept that a game is made up of several distinct phases; in each phase (except for certain games like Poker and Blackjack), players detach cards from their hands and put them face-up on the table in order. Whoever plays the highest card in the suit led usually gets to collect all those cards and stack them face-down in front of him. This unit of playing cards is called a *trick* — your success in many competitive card games hinges on how many tricks you win during the course of play. (Again, however, some games feature trying to win specific valuable cards rather than simply trying to obtain the majority of the tricks.)

So the high card takes the trick. But how do you get to that point? Here are the steps that get you there:

1. **The first player to act makes the *opening lead*, or the lead to the very first trick.**

   Depending on the rules of the game, the elder hand (the player to the dealer's left), the dealer, or the player who selected the contract during the bidding process makes the opening lead.

2. **The player who wins the trick generally leads to the next trick and so on throughout the hand, until everyone plays all their cards.**

   The order of play nearly always follows a clockwise or occasionally counter-clockwise pattern in relation to the deal or the winner of the trick.

The player who wins the trick makes the next lead and scores or avoids points. But it doesn't always take the high card to win the trick, and sometimes you make mistakes during the course of a hand. The following sections detail tricks and penalizing treats.

Winning with high cards or trump

The concept that the highest card played on a trick wins the trick is a simple one, but it doesn't do justice to the rules of most games in this book. Each has more complex rules than that. For example, in most games, it isn't simply the high card that wins the trick; it's the highest card in the *suit led*.

The point is that most games (but not all!) state that when a player leads a suit — say, spades — all subsequent players must play spades if they still have one in their hands. This concept is called *following suit*.

So what happens if you can't follow suit? Well, here is where the concept of the trump suit comes in. Many of the trick-taking games have a trump suit, which has special powers. You may like to think of this as the "boss" suit, which outranks all the other suits. In games such as Whist, you select the boss suit at random. In other games, such as Euchre, the initial suit is random, but the players have a chance to select another suit if they want to. And in some games, such as Bridge, the choice is entirely up to the players playing individually or acting in a partnership.

REMEMBER

So, what do trumps do? Well, if you have no cards in the suit led, you can put a trump on the lead (or *trump it*). This action is also called *ruffing the trick.* Consequently, the importance of the trump suit lies in the fact that the smallest trump can beat even the ace of any other suit. So, if a trick doesn't have any trumps in it, the highest card of the suit led takes the trick; however, if one or more trumps hit the table on a trick, the highest trump takes the trick.

Failing to follow suit

Most games have rules that require you to play a card in the suit led if you can; and indeed, that is your ethical requirement. However, if you can follow suit but don't, you incur no penalty — you only face a penalty for being *caught* failing to follow suit! The penalty varies from game to game but is generally a pretty severe one.

In failing to follow suit, you have three terms to bear in mind:

>> **Revoke:** The sinful failure to follow suit when you're able is known as *revoking* or *reneging.* (The latter term seems to be exclusive to the United States and is now synonymous with the revoke.)

>> **Trump:** Putting a card from the trump suit down when a suit is led, in which you have no cards. If you play a trump, you stand to win the trick — so long as no one else subsequently plays a higher trump.

>> **Discard:** The laying down of an off-suit card when you're unable to follow suit is called a *discard* or *renounce,* although the former term is more common these days. Discarding implies that you're letting go a card in a plain, non-trump suit rather than trumping.

Say your hand consists solely of clubs, diamonds, and hearts, and you're playing out a hand where hearts are trump:

>> If another player leads a club and you play a diamond or a heart on the lead, you revoke.

>> If a player leads a spade and you play a heart, you trump the spade.

>> If you play a diamond on the lead of a spade, you discard.

Playing out of turn

For one reason or another, players occasionally lose track of who won the previous trick. If a player neglects to remember that she's supposed to lead, a potentially long and embarrassing pause ensues until someone plucks up enough courage to ask her whether she's thinking about what to do next or if she's spacing out.

More frequently, however, somebody *leads out of turn,* under the false impression that the action is on her. If this happens, the general rule is that the next player can accept that lead by following to the trick, if he wants to do so. Alternatively, he may be so hypnotized by the sight of the card that he may genuinely think it's his turn to play, so he follows suit innocently.

Either way, the general rule is that the next player's following legitimizes the original mistake. However, some games state that up until the faulty trick is completed, if anyone spots the error, you still have time to pick the whole trick up and correct the error.

Exposing yourself to public ridicule

The rules about *exposed cards* (accidentally dropping a card on the table as opposed to playing it) tend to vary, depending on whether you're playing a partnership game or playing on your own:

>> In an individual game, the rules tend to be fairly lax; you can normally pick up your exposed cards, and the game continues. (Of course, your opponent benefits from seeing part of your hand, which is considered punishment enough for the error.)

>> In a partnership game, the consequences of exposing a card are much more severe because you simultaneously give unauthorized information to both your partner and your opponents. Often, the rules of a game require you to play the exposed cards at the first opportunity, or your partner may be forbidden from playing the suit you let slip.

MISS MANNER'S GUIDE TO CARD-GAME ETIQUETTE

Some elements of card-game etiquette relate to basic good manners and polite behavior, and some deal with areas that come perilously close to cheating. On the etiquette front, for example, you shouldn't pick up your cards until the deal is finished — if for no other reason than that you may cause the dealer to expose a card if your fingers get in the way.

After you pick up your hand, avoid indicating in any way whether you're pleased or unhappy with its contents. This is particularly important in a partnership game where you can't divulge such potentially useful information.

The idea that you should play card games in silence may give the impression that you can't enjoy yourself — that you should focus on winning to the exclusion of having fun. That isn't the case, but you should avoid conversation if it gives away information that you're not entitled to pass on or if the sole purpose of your remarks is to upset or irritate your partner or opponents. (The rules in Poker are a little different. Conversation during a Poker game is one way for players to influence their opponents.)

The tempo of the way you play your cards can also be very revealing. You can make it clear by the way you play your card that you have doubt or no doubt at all as to what to do. You can't eliminate doubt altogether, but you can try to make your mind up before playing a card so you avoid conveying information by your tempo to your partner and opponents.

Chapter 2

Going Solo with Solitaire

You see many different versions of Solitaire in this chapter. The different games don't have all that much in common, except that you can play them with a single deck of cards. Some Solitaires need more than one deck, but not the ones included in this chapter. These games range from *automatic* Solitaires, where you can make every move immediately without thought or forethought, to Solitaires where you can plan your game strategy for at least 10 minutes if you want to. These games aren't easy, so if you win any of them, you'll feel a sense of achievement.

To play Solitaire, you need the following:

>> **One player**

>> **One standard 52-card deck of cards** (you usually don't need jokers in games of Solitaire)

>> **Space to spread out the cards**

Acquainting Yourself with Solitaire Terms

Before you start enjoying the various games of Solitaire, you need to know a little technical vocabulary:

» When you initially deal the cards, the pattern is known as a *layout* or *tableau*. The layout can consist of *rows* (horizontal lines of cards), *columns* (vertical lines), or *piles* of cards (a compact heap, frequently of face-down cards, sometimes with the top card face-up). Sometimes the pile of cards is all face-up, but overlapping. Accordingly, you can see all the cards in the pile, even if you can only access the top, uncovered card. You can move tableaus under the correct circumstances, which are dictated by the rules of the particular Solitaire you're playing.

» *Building* involves placing one card on top of another in a legal move. The definition of a *legal move* varies according to the individual rules of the Solitaire.

» In games where the objective is to build up cards on some of the original cards, the base cards are known as *foundations*. As a general rule, after you place cards on a foundation pile, you can't move them. You may build on a tableau in some cases.

The tableau and the foundation may sound like very similar items, but they differ in a few important ways. The object of a Solitaire is to build up the foundation; a tableau is just an intermediary home for the cards as they make their way to the final destination: the foundation. You use tableaus to get the cards in the right order to build on the foundation.

» When you move a complete row or column, you create a *space* or *gap* into which you can often move whatever card(s) you like.

» Frequently, you don't use all the cards in the initial layout; the remaining cards are called the *stock*. You go through the stock to advance the Solitaire.

» When working through the stock, you frequently have cards that you can't legally put into the layout. In such cases, the unused cards go to the *waste-pile*.

» *Redeals* take place in the middle of a Solitaire when you've exhausted all legal moves. The rules of the Solitaire may allow you to redeal by shuffling and redistributing the unused cards in an attempt to advance the game.

» Many Solitaires permit one cheat — you can move an obstructing card or otherwise advance the game. This process is also known as a *merci*.

After you build your own foundation of Solitaire knowledge, you can begin to explore the many variations of the game. The following sections detail some of the specific types of Solitaires.

Putting the Squeeze on Accordion

The game Accordion is also known as Methuselah, Tower of Babel, or Idle Year (presumably because of the amount of time you need to keep playing the game to win it).

Accordion is a charmingly straightforward game that can easily seduce you into assuming that it must be easy to solve. Be warned — we've never known anyone who has completed a game of Accordion! This challenge makes success at the game doubly pleasurable.

Accordion also takes up very little space — a major benefit because you tend to play Solitaire in a cramped space, such as while waiting in a bus station or an airport gate.

The objective of Accordion is to finish up with a single pile of 52 cards. Relative success is reducing the number of piles to four or fewer. Your chances of complete victory may be less than 1 in 1,000, but don't let that deter you from giving this game a try! The fact that it is a very fast game to play means that you can abandon unpromising hands and move on to another without wasting much time.

Looking at the layout

The layout for Accordion is simple. Follow these steps to begin your long journey:

1. **Shuffle the deck well, and then turn over the top card in your deck and put it to your left to start your layout.**

2. **Turn over the next card.**

   If the card is either the same suit (both clubs, for example) or the same rank (both jacks) as the first card, put the second card on top of the first. If you don't have a match, use the card to start a new pile.

3. **Turn over the third card and compare it to the second card.**

   Again, if the suits or ranks of the cards match, put the third card on top of the second card; if not, start a third pile with the third card. You can't match the third card with the first card. However, when matching cards (of suit or rank) are three cards apart, you can combine them as if the cards were adjacent. In other words, you can build the fourth card on the first one.

4. **Continue by going through every card in the deck in this way.**

   We told you it was easy! The game ends after you turn over the last card. To win, you must assemble all the cards into one pile.

Shuffling the deck well is important because you work your way through the deck one card at a time, so you don't want to make the game too easy by having all the diamonds coming together, for example. That would spoil your sense of achievement, wouldn't it?

Your initial cards may look like one of the examples in Figure 2-1 after you lay out three cards.

FIGURE 2-1:
At the start of Accordion, your cards may fall in this manner.

© John Wiley & Sons, Inc.

In the first example, you must create three different piles because the cards are unrelated in rank or suit. In the middle example, you can put the ♦4 on top of the ♦Q (because they share the same suit), leaving you with only two piles. In the last example, you can put the ♦7 on top of the ♦Q, which allows you to combine the two 7s, resulting in a single pile.

To see how you can combine cards placed three piles away from each other, look at Figure 2-2.

FIGURE 2-2:
You can match cards that are three places away from each other to further your game progress.

© John Wiley & Sons, Inc.

After you turn up the ♣Q, you can place it on the ♦Q (because they're three apart and match in rank) and then put the ♣K on the ♣Q (same suit). The ♥J then moves to the first row.

Laying the cards out in lines of three helps ensure that you properly identify the cards that are three piles apart.

Choosing between moves

When moving the cards, you frequently have to be careful to make the plays in the correct order to set up more plays. You may have a choice of moves, but you may not be sure which move to execute first. Look at a possible scenario in Figure 2-3.

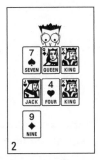

FIGURE 2-3:
Look ahead to see which move to make first.

After you turn up the ♥4, you can place it on the ♥9, which opens up a series of moves that you can play. The best option is to move the ♥4 onto the ♠4 and then move the rest of the cards into their new spaces.

Because the ♠K is three cards away from the ♣K, you can combine the two cards and then move the ♥4 onto the ♥J. Now the ♦9 is three cards away from the ♦Q, so you can combine those two cards.

WARNING

If you move the ♥4 before you move the ♠K, you miss out on two possible moves.

REMEMBER

Making an available play isn't always mandatory. When you can choose between possible moves, play a couple more cards to help you decide which move is superior. Figure 2-4 shows you how waiting can help you make up your mind when you have a choice.

At this point, you may not know whether to put the ♠A on the ♣A or on the ♠K because your piles don't indicate whether you should keep aces or kings on top of your piles.

TIP

If several piles have kings on the top, you may want to avoid hiding the ♠K. Instead of jumping the gun, you turn over another card to see what happens, which turns out to be the ♠J.

FIGURE 2-4:
Playing the
waiting game can
help you make up
your mind.

Now you can see daylight: Put the ♠J on the ♠A and then on the ♠K, and then you put the ♠J on the ♥J. Now you can combine the 9s. Next, put the ♠4 on the ♠J, allowing the ♣A to go on the ♣K and the ♦9 to go on the ♦Q. Put the ♠4 on the ♠7 to move down to three piles. Wasn't that fun? Getting a series of moves to come together like that makes up for the hundreds of unexciting plays you go through.

Play continues until you end up with one pile of cards — good luck!

Piling It On in Calculation

Different people have different criteria for what makes a good game of Solitaire. The version called Calculation should satisfy most tests, because you can solve it in a fair amount of the time (so long as you work at it), it takes up little space, and you can devote your full attention to it or play without thinking — depending on your mood. However, unless you plan your plays carefully, the game will likely stymie you fairly early on.

In this game, only the card rankings matter — the suits of the cards are irrelevant. The object of the game is to build up four piles of cards on the foundation, from the ace on up to the king.

You begin by taking out an ace, 2, 3, and 4 from the deck and putting the four cards in a row from left to right, horizontally. These cards are the foundation on which you build — you hope — using the rest of the cards in the deck. Underneath those four foundations are precisely four waste piles, where you put cards that do not immediately fit on the foundation. Determining which pile to put those cards on is the challenging part of the game.

You build on each of the foundation piles one card at a time; however, you build up each pile in different sequences:

>> On the ace pile, you can only put the next ranking card — that is, the play sequence must go A, 2, 3, and so on.

>> On the 2 pile, you go up in pairs: 4, 6, 8, and so on.

>> On the 3 pile, you go up in intervals of three: 6, 9, Q, 2, 5, and so on.

>> And you shouldn't be surprised that on the 4 pile, you go up in fours: 8, Q, 3, 7, J, 2, and so on.

For each of the four piles, you have 13 moves available. After the last move, you reach the king, and your piles are complete.

You turn up cards from the stock one at a time. If the card you turn over has no legal place, you put it directly on top of one of the four waste piles that you create below the foundation. As soon as the card becomes a legal play on a foundation pile, you may take the card from the top of the waste-pile (but not from the middle of the waste-pile) and move it up.

TIP

When you have a legal move (you can put a card on one of the foundation piles), go ahead and make it. Don't wait to see what other cards you may turn up, because you may end up burying a card you could have played.

REMEMBER

You can't move cards from one waste-pile to another. After a card is on one pile, you can move it only to the foundation. And just because a waste-pile is empty doesn't entitle you to move cards from another waste-pile into the gap.

You arrange the waste-piles so you can see all the lower cards in them to maximize your strategic planning.

Kings are exceptionally bad news in Calculation. They're always the last cards to go on each of the foundation piles, and when you put them on the waste-pile, they can easily block everything beneath them. In a strange way, it's good to turn up kings at the beginning of the game — you can put them on the bottom of each of the waste-piles or put them all together in one pile.

TIP

As a general rule, try to keep one waste-pile reserved for the kings. However, if two or three kings appear early, it's a reasonable gamble to use all four piles and not keep one for the kings.

Figure 2-5 shows an example of the start of a game. Having selected your ace, 2, 3, and 4 from the deck, you start turning over the cards one at a time.

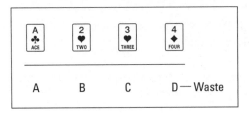

FIGURE 2-5:
A sample game of
Calculation.

© John Wiley & Sons, Inc.

TIP

Try to construct lines in the waste-piles in reverse. For example, if your 4 pile is lagging because you're waiting for a queen, and you put a 7 on a jack on a waste-pile, put a 3 on top of the 7 if it comes up. You hope that when the queen emerges, you can put the 3, 7, and jack on at one time and advance matters efficiently.

Reserving Your Time for Canfield

Canfield is one of the most commonly played Solitaires in the Western world. People often erroneously refer to this game as Klondike, which also appears in this chapter (see the section "Striking Gold with Klondike" later in this chapter). To further complicate matters, Canfield is also known as Demon Thirteen in the United Kingdom.

To set up Canfield, follow these simple steps:

1. **Place 13 cards in a pile with only the top card face-up; this pile is called the *reserve* or the *heel*.**

2. **To the right of the reserve, spread out four cards, called a *tableau,* on which you can build by using the cards from the reserve or the *stock* (the remaining 34 cards in the deck).**

3. **Above the tableau, place a single face-up card, which acts as the base-card of a foundation from which each suit will be built up.**

The object of Canfield is to get rid of all 13 cards in the reserve pile. You get rid of these cards by placing them in legal positions in the tableau.

REMEMBER

You build on the tableau by placing a card that's one rank lower and of the opposite color of the uppermost card. For example, you can legally put the ♣2 on either the ♥3 or ♦3. After the ♣2 is on the top of the pile, you can place either the ♥A or ♦A on it. If you place the ♦A on the ♣2, you can place either the ♣K or the ♠K on the ♦A, and so on.

Take the remaining 34 cards, the stock, and work your way through them in threes, taking the top three cards at a time and flipping them over into a waste-pile (make sure you preserve the order of the three cards). You have access to only the top card in the three, but if you use the top card — that is, you put it on the tableau or foundation — you gain access to the second card, and so on. After you go through the stock in threes, you turn up the last card out of the 34; this card is accessible. When the stock comes out in threes, you treat the last three cards as a regular group of three. If you have two cards left over at the end of the stock, you get to look at and use them both separately.

After you work your way through the stock, pick it up and start again; continue until you either finish the game or get stuck and can't move any further.

As soon as a card equivalent in rank to the foundation base-card emerges from either the reserve pile or the stock, pick the card up and put it in a separate pile in the foundation, above the tableau. You can build only the next higher card of the matching suit, and no other card, onto the foundation.

TIP

The cards (even a whole pile of cards) in the tableau can be moved onto other cards in the tableau, so long as you observe the opposite-color rule, and also onto gaps in the tableau. And you have the option of placing the top card in the reserve pile on the foundation or in the tableau.

Take a look at an example layout of the start of a game in Figure 2-6.

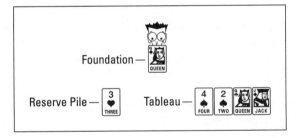

FIGURE 2-6:
Starting a game of Canfield.

© John Wiley & Sons, Inc.

You're in luck! This layout is a very promising start. The ♣Q joins the ♦Q at the top of the foundation, in a separate pile. This move creates a gap in the tableau where you can place a card from the reserve pile.

The red 3 goes on the black 4, and the black 2 goes on the red 3. Another card from the reserve pile fills the gap in the tableau left by the black 2.

One variation that makes Canfield more difficult is to build up the foundation from the ace, meaning that you don't give yourself a random foundation card to start with. To compensate, some players use a reserve pile of only 11 cards.

Striking Gold with Klondike

Klondike, frequently misnamed Canfield (see the previous section), is by far the most frequently played Solitaire. You need only a little time and a little space. In addition, you have a good chance of winning at Klondike — you may find yourself winning half the games you play.

Klondike requires little tactics or strategy. It's an ideal game for children, perhaps for that very reason. Klondike is also an ideal Solitaire for a spectator, who can lean over the player's shoulder and say things like "Put the red 7 on the black 8" until the player loses patience and punches him in the shoulder.

The object of Klondike is to build up piles of the four suits from the ace (the lowest card) to the king on the foundation. You don't start with any cards in the foundation; you collect cards for it during the course of play.

To build the initial layout, or *tableau*, you deal seven piles, with one card in the first pile, two in the second pile, three in the third, and so on. Turn over the top card of each pile as you deal out the cards.

REMEMBER

When dealing out the piles, place seven cards face-down to form the seven piles; deal the next six cards to form the second layer of each row (except the row on the far left), and then the next five cards to form the third layer, and so on. If you lay out the cards in this way, you avoid any problems caused by imperfect shuffling.

You build on the top cards of each pile by putting the next-lower numbered cards of the opposite color on the top cards. Your building cards come from the stock.

To start the game, you play the cards in the stock, which should consist of 24 cards. Go through the stock three cards at a time, putting the cards into a waste-pile, while preserving the order of the cards in that pile. You have access to only the top card of each set of three. If you use that top card, you gain access to the card below it, and so on. When you finish going through the stock, gather it up and go through it again.

You may go through the stock only three times. If you can't persuade the Solitaire to work out after the three turns, you lose the game. However, most people ignore the three-times rule and continue with the Solitaire until it works out, which it does a fair percentage of the time.

As an alternative, you can go through the stock one card at a time and only one time. We haven't concluded whether you're more likely to get the Solitaire to work out with this rule or not, but instinctively, we feel that it must help. Some people go through the deck one card at a time on three separate occasions before calling the whole thing off.

You can move the turned-up cards around (leaving the face-down cards in place), and whenever you move all the face-up cards from one pile of the tableau, you turn over the new top card.

When you use all the cards in a pile, you create a space. You can move any king, or pile headed by a king — but only one headed by a king — into the space, and then you turn another face-down card over on the pile from which you moved the king pile.

Whenever you turn up an ace in the tableau (or in the stock), move that card to the foundation and start a new foundation pile. You may then take any top card from the tableau and move it onto the foundation, where appropriate. For example, after you put the ♦A in the foundation, you can take the ♦2 when it becomes available to start building up the diamonds.

Living La Belle Lucie

In La Belle Lucie (which is also known as Midnight Oil, Clover Leaf, the Fan, or Alexander the Great), every move is critical. The game requires great planning and forethought and rewards the player with a healthy chance of success.

One of the authors has been known to take more than 10 minutes to make a move while he plans the intricacies of competing strategies. It's certainly not unusual for players to take a few minutes at a time to plan a move.

The objective of La Belle Lucie is to build up all four suits from a foundation of the ace through to the king.

Getting started

You start by dealing all the cards face-up in piles of threes, making sure that each card in every trio is visible (you fan each trio so you can see a top, middle, and bottom card, hence its alias Fan). The last four cards go in two piles of two. Your aim is to move cards around the tableau to free up cards that can build up the foundation.

Whenever you expose an ace on the top of a pile, you move it to start a foundation pile, and can start building the suit up from there. The next card to go on the ace is the 2 of that suit, and you keep going up to the king of the suit. If you don't expose an ace, you have to uncover one by moving the cards around.

You get three tries (or *cycles*) to move all the cards into suits. At the end of each cycle, you pick up all the cards off the foundations, shuffle them well, and distribute them in trios again.

Making your moves

You can move cards in the tableau onto the card of the same suit one higher in rank, but beware! You can move each card only once, and you can only move one card at a time, which is critical. For example, as soon as the ♦7 goes on the ♦8, you can't move the ♦8 again unless both cards go onto the foundation in the diamond suit. You can't move the ♦7 and ♦8 onto the ♦9 because of the one-card-at-a-time rule. You have thus "buried" the ♦8. You can't move this card until the next redeal, unless the ♦A through the ♦6 go into the foundation, whereupon the ♦7 and ♦8 can also go onto the foundation.

However, this rule doesn't matter if the ♦8 is at the bottom of a pile; no cards are trapped by the move. The rule does matter if the ♦8 covers something else. Note that kings never move; therefore, you want them at the bottom of piles.

TIP

Bear in mind that the purpose of the game is to build up all the suits in order, starting with the ace, so you try to get the aces out from their piles. If the aces are at the top of their piles already, so much the better. If not, you have to excavate them, but at the same time, you have to plan the sequence of moves that brings the cards to the top. It isn't a good idea to play five moves to get out the ♦A and then discover that the ♦2 got permanently buried in the process. Of course, sometimes burying a card may prove inevitable. The skill of the game is to bury as few cards as possible by making your moves in the right order and to bury only cards that seem less relevant at the moment, such as jacks and queens. Kings automatically trap everything below them, so if you're worried about burying the ♦J by putting the ♦10 on it, and the ♦Q is below the ♥K, relax! You cost yourself nothing — you were never going to get to move the ♦J anyway.

Another example of a potentially bad holding is seeing something along the lines of the ♦Q ♦10. Even if you get to put the ♦10 on the jack, doing so freezes the jack. You can't move the ♦J again, because you can't move the ♦10 and the ♦J onto the ♦Q.

Sometimes you get mutually impossible moves, as shown in Figure 2-7. With the base shown, you can't move the ♦6 until you clear the ♥2, and you can't move the ♥2 until you free the ♦6 to get at the ♥3. Neither card moves until the ♥A is free, when the ♥2 can go to the foundation.

FIGURE 2-7:
Only one series of moves can get you out of this mess.

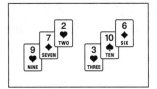

Certain moves are risk-free at the start of the game:

>> You can always move any queen onto the king of the same suit (because kings are stuck anyway).

>> After you move the top two cards of a pile of three and expose the card at the bottom of a pile, you can put the relevant card on top of it without worrying about the consequences. (When a card is at the bottom of a pile, it stands to reason that you can't trap anything underneath it if you should render it unable to move.)

>> Whenever a card is stuck (for example, if you put the ♦7 on the ♦8, you make both cards immobile), you can build more cards, such as the ♦6 and ♦5, on top of it. In fact, doing so can only help your chances of getting more cards out.

The initial layout for a sample hand appears in Figure 2-8 (the top card in each trio appears on the right).

The figure layout has some encouraging features: All the kings are reasonably placed (they either appear at the bottoms of their piles or at least don't trap too many cards), and three of the aces are immediately accessible — a very fortunate combination of events. The bad news is that the ♥J and ♥9 are on top of one another, ensuring that the ♥10 (which traps the fourth ace) won't move this cycle.

Start by making the automatic moves:

1. **Take off the ♠A and start a foundation pile for spades.**

2. **Put the ♦9 on the ♦10 (because the ♥10 can't move, and the ♦J can't come free, so you may as well build on the ♦10).**

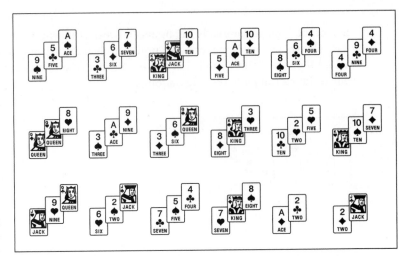

FIGURE 2-8:
Starting a game
of La Belle Lucie.

3. Take off the ♣A, the ♣2, and the ♦A.

4. The next card to go for is the ♠2; you can get it easily by putting the ♠J on the ♠Q.

But before you do that, can you put the ♠Q on the ♠K? To make that move, you need to put the ♥3 on the ♥4, and to do that, you need to move the ♦4 onto the ♦5. That last move is impossible, because the ♦5 is trapped below the ♥A, so put the ♠J on the ♠Q and take up the ♠2, ♠3, and ♠4.

Figure 2-9 shows an interesting combination of piles.

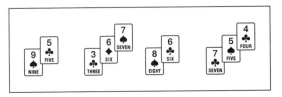

FIGURE 2-9:
Your game begins
to take shape
after you make
the automatic
moves.

You want to clear the ♣4 away to get the ♠5 out, and you want to clear the ♠7 away to get the ♣3 out. Should you put the ♣4 on the ♠5, or should you put the ♠5 on the ♣6 and then put the ♣4 on the ♠5? The answer is that you need to keep the ♠8 (below the ♣6) free. Here's how to progress:

1. **Put the ♣4 on the ♣5 and free the ♠5 for the foundation.**

2. **Now put the ♣6 on the ♣7, the ♠7 on the ♠8, and the ♦6 on the ♦7.**

   (Because the ♦8 is under a king, it's stuck for the duration, so you can't move the ♦7.)

3. **The ♦3 is now free, which allows you to move it through the ♣8 onto the foundation.**

The preceding example shows a relatively simple problem, but the degree of interaction can get considerably more convoluted. This element of trading off one move against another is what makes La Belle Lucie such good fun.

The ♣9 is stuck (you can't move the ♦4), the ♠6 is stuck, and the ♥A is stuck, which leaves only diamonds. The ♦2 comes out easily enough by putting the ♣J on the queen. However, the ♦3 is under the ♠Q and the ♠J, so you take the ♦2 out, which ends the first cycle.

Starting the next cycle and ending the game

You keep your foundations, but now you pick up the cards left in the tableau, shuffle them well (they were in sequence, so an imperfect shuffle can restrict your mobility), and deal them out in threes again. If you have two cards left over, make one pair; if one card is left over after you put the cards out in threes, as at the start, make two pairs out of the last four cards.

You have three cycles to get out, and if you fail at the last turn, you're allowed one cheat, or *merci*, by moving a single card in the tableau; whether you want to pull one card up or push one card down is up to you.

Practicing Poker Patience

Poker Patience is, in theory, an undemanding Solitaire. It takes only a minute or two to play, and you can approach the game frivolously or seriously. We do both in this section.

To start, you need to know the ranks of Poker hands (in other words, what beats what). In ascending order, the ranks are as follows:

>> **One pair:** Two of a kind

>> **Two pair:** Such as two 5s and two 10s

>> **Three of a kind:** Also known as trips

>> **Straight:** Five cards in consecutive order; for example, ace through 5 or 7 to jack

>> **Flush:** Five cards of the same suit

>> **Full house:** Combination of three of a kind and a pair

>> **Four of a kind:** Also known as quads

>> **Straight flush:** A straight with all the cards in the same suit

REMEMBER

Aces can be either high or low — your choice.

The objective of the game is to lay out 25 cards to form a square, five cards by five cards. In the process, you want to make ten Poker hands (five across and five down) and score as many points as possible.

Scoring 200 points (using co-author Barry's scoring system) counts as a win. Various scoring systems are shown in Table 2-1.

TABLE 2-1   ## Scoring Systems for Poker Patience

Poker Hand	US Scoring	UK Scoring	Barry's Scoring
A pair	2	1	2
Two pair	5	3	5
Three of a kind	10	6	10
Straight	15	12	25
Flush	20	5	15
Full house	50	10	50
Four of a kind	70	16	70
Straight flush	100	30	100

The US scoring system has a major flaw (which has been corrected in the UK scoring method), based on the fact that although flushes are rarer in Poker, they're considerably easier to play for in Poker Patience than straights. To fix this problem, you can reverse the scoring table, as in the version that Barry recommends.

To start, turn over one card face-up and then go on to the next, building your grid in any direction you like — up and down or right and left.

REMEMBER Although you can put any card anywhere you like in the grid, and you can expand the cards out in any direction you like, each card must touch another card. Whether you put it adjacent to another card or link it diagonally by touching the corner of another card is up to you.

TIP The best way to play (particularly when using Barry's scoring table) is for straights to be set out in one direction (vertically or horizontally) and full houses or four of a kinds in the other direction. If you take this advice and decide for straights to go in the horizontal rows, you have excellent reasons to put the cards in columns either with themselves or with numbers five less than or five more than themselves. By making this separation, you help the formation of straights.

When playing Poker Patience, sooner or later you run into a useless or unplayable card. When this happens, don't panic; all you have to do is start a junk row or junk column. Inevitably, at least one row or column won't score as much as you want it to.

Look at the layout in Figure 2-10 to see the game theory at work. The matrix is updated after every two cards, although each card is turned over individually. After ten cards, the basic structure is going well. The nucleus of the straights is fine on the horizontal lines, and all the pairs are matched up.

In Figure 2-11, you can put the ♠9 on the bottom row, but completing the straight and collecting points always produces a warm, fuzzy feeling.

Play continues in Figure 2-12. The ♥8 could've gone under the ♣3, but it seems premature to abandon the right-hand column. The ♠Q scores the full house, so abandon the straight in the fourth row.

In Figure 2-13, the bottom row has become a junk pile. One row or column normally does.

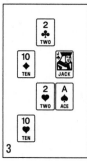

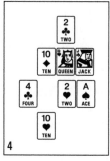

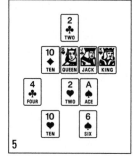

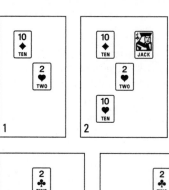

FIGURE 2-10:
A hand of Poker
Patience after ten
cards.

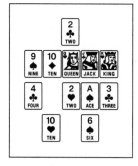

FIGURE 2-11:
Don't be tempted
by the bottom
row. Go for the
points!

FIGURE 2-12:
Dumping a straight to go for the higher-scoring full house.

© John Wiley & Sons, Inc.

FIGURE 2-13:
Creating a junk pile is a normal thing for Poker Patience.

© John Wiley & Sons, Inc.

In Figure 2-14, a lucky last card allows you to scramble to respectability; two straights, two full houses, and a three of a kind are 160, and having three pairs takes you to 166.

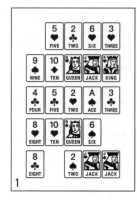

FIGURE 2-14:
Sometimes you have to get lucky to make something out of this big mess.

After you finish playing, you can further exercise your mental agility by trying to rearrange the cards to score as many points as possible. A rearrangement is really only worth doing, however, if you have a straight flush so you can rack up big numbers. Using all the cards in high-scoring combinations (flushes or higher) is a real coup.

Some people also count the long diagonals (from top right to bottom left and vice versa) in the scoring. Planning the scores on the diagonals too carefully is pretty difficult, but it can be done — or you can just regard any score on them as a bonus. You can also play Poker Patience as a competitive game for two players or more. One player calls out the cards he draws at random, and then both players try to arrange their own grids to maximize the scores. The highest score wins.

Chapter 3

Creating Combinations in Rummy

Although the word *Rummy* may conjure up some beverage-related memories — some of them possibly involving headaches — we can assure you that in this book, Rummy refers to a variety of fun games that you don't have to be over 21 to play.

In this chapter, we show you how to play Rummy and a popular Rummy variation, Gin Rummy. After you get the basics under your belt, feel free to call up some friends, throw a party, play some Rummy, and drink the beverage of your choice (gin or not). And before the party, pick up a few rum-based beverage recipes in *Bartending For Dummies* by Ray Foley (John Wiley & Sons, Inc.). Enough with the shameless promotion. Time to play some cards.

Rummy: Throw a Combo and Go

In this section, you master the basics of Rummy and discover some playing tactics, including how to go for your opponent's jugular, when to minimize the risk of getting caught with a number of cards left in your hand, and how to take advantage of other players' strategies.

To play Rummy, you need the following:

>> **Two or more players:** For six or more players, you need a second deck of cards. You can play with up to 12 players with a second deck.

>> **A standard deck of 52 cards:** Jokers are optional, depending on whether you want to play with wild cards (see the section "Rummying with wild cards" later in this chapter for information).

>> **Paper and pencil for scoring:** You can use a pen or computer, too.

Setting up and laying out the objective

Rummy is a card game in which you try to improve the hand that you're originally dealt. You can do this whenever it's your turn to play, either by drawing cards from the undealt pile (or *stock*) or by picking up the card thrown away by your opponent, and then throwing away (or *discarding*) a card from your hand. Your aim is to put (or *meld*) your cards into two types of combinations:

>> **Runs:** Consecutive sequences of three or more cards of the same suit.

>> **Sets:** Three or four cards of the same rank (also known as a *group* or *book* in North America). If you're using two decks, a set may include two identical cards of the same rank and suit.

Figure 3-1 shows some legitimate Rummy combinations.

Figure 3-2 shows an unacceptable combination. This run is illegal because all cards in a run must be of the same suit.

REMEMBER

In most Rummy games, unlike the majority of other card games, aces can be high or low, but not both. So runs involving the ace must take the form A-2-3 or A-K-Q but not K-A-2. For example, you can't put down ♣2-♣A-♣K. You have to wait until you pick up the ♣Q in order to combine the ♣A and ♣K in a legitimate run.

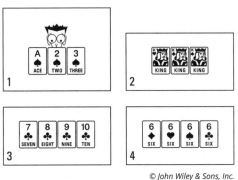

FIGURE 3-1:
Legal runs follow
the same suit;
legal sets consist
of the same rank.

© John Wiley & Sons, Inc.

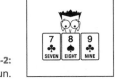

FIGURE 3-2:
An illegal run.

© John Wiley & Sons, Inc.

The first person who manages to make his whole hand into combinations — also called *melds* — one way or another, with one card remaining to discard, wins the game.

Dealing the cards and starting the Rummy

When playing Rummy with two, three, or four players, each player gets ten cards; when playing with five players, each player gets six cards. With more than five players, you must use two decks of cards and a hand of seven cards. The two-player game can also be played with seven cards each.

Designate a scorer and a dealer at the start of the game. To determine who should be the scorer, just volunteer the person closest to the pencil and score card. Try always to be on the other side of the room when someone asks, "Do you have a pencil?"

To decide who should be the dealer, each player takes a card, and the person who draws the lowest card is the dealer for the first hand. The deal rotates clockwise for each following hand.

Deal each player a card, starting with the player on the dealer's left and moving clockwise. When each hand is complete, put the undealt cards face-down on the center of the table as the stock and place the top card, turned upward, beside the stock as the first card of the discard pile.

Pick up your cards slowly; you don't need to play Rummy with excessive haste, so give yourself time to think about all your possible card combinations before starting play.

Misdeals — accidents during the deal, such as a card getting turned face-up or too many or too few cards dealt out — generally result in another deal with no penalties attached.

The player to the left of the dealer plays first. She can do one of two things: She can either pick up the card on the discard pile or the top card from the stock. If she can put some or all of her hand into combinations, she may do so (see the section "Putting down and adding to combinations" later in this chapter). If not, she discards one card from her hand, face-up onto the discard pile, and the turn of play moves to the next player.

The next player can either pick up the last card the previous player discarded or the top card from the stock. He can then meld some or all of his cards down in combinations, if he wants to. The play continues clockwise around the table. When the stock runs out, shuffle the discard pile and set it up again.

You can't pick up the top discard and then throw the card back onto the pile.

If you pick up two cards from the stock by accident and see either of them, you must put the bottom card back, which gives the next player an additional option. She can look at the returned card and take it if she wants it. If she doesn't want it, she puts it back into the middle of the stock and continues with her turn by taking the next card from the stock.

When you pick up a card from the stock that you don't want, don't throw it away immediately. Put the card into your hand and then extract it. No player, regardless of skill level, needs to give gratuitous information away.

During the play, you work your way through the stock, taking one card from it (or the discard pile) and discarding a card from your hand. If you completely use up the stock, the dealer reshuffles the discard pile and turns over a new upcard, and play continues.

Putting down and adding to combinations

You can only put down a combination during your turn. The correct timing is to pick up a card from the stock or discard pile, put down your meld, and then make your discard. The advantage of putting down a combination before you're ready to go out completely is that you reduce your exposure if you lose the game (for the details on scoring, see the section "Going out and tallying your score" later in this chapter). However, you do run a few risks by putting down a run or meld.

The disadvantage of putting your cards on the table is that any player can now add to your meld of three of a kind (by adding the fourth card) or extend your runs. Although adding to your combinations proves very beneficial to your opponents, the longer the game goes on, the more wary you should be of keeping melds in your hand.

Conversely, you can add to your opponents' combinations — or, if you draw the right card, you can add an additional card to your own melds. If you want to add a card to an existing combination, put down any combinations you have, add to the existing set or run, and then make a discard. Your turn finishes with the discard, so make sure you don't mix up the order of events. If you do, you can't put down any combinations you may have until your next turn.

WARNING

If you put down an imperfect run, you simply pick up the cards and put them back in your hand. But by revealing the cards in your hand to everyone else at the table, your chances of getting anything useful from the other players decrease. Better put on your glasses and double-check before laying any cards on the table.

When you have a set of four of a kind, no card can add to the combination, if you are playing with a single deck of cards, so you're safe to put these sets down immediately. The only reason to hold them is if you're close to going out and you want to play for the extra score (see the section "Going out and tallying your score" later in this chapter for more information). Additionally, if you can possibly use a card in the set for a run, you may want to retain the combination in your hand until you know how you want to use the cards. For example, you may want to hold some of the cards in Figure 3-3 until you get some more information.

In Figure 3-3, you could use the ♥9 both in the set and in a run with the ♥10 and ♥J. Holding the cards for a turn gives you a chance to pick up the ♥Q or ♥8, which would improve the run.

FIGURE 3-3:
Waiting for the
right cards.

© John Wiley & Sons, Inc.

Rummying with wild cards

You can also play Rummy with wild cards, or cards that can represent any card you like. You can add the jokers that come with the cards to the deck, treating them as wild cards, or you can make the 2s wild, for example.

You can substitute the card represented by a wild card when it's your turn to play. So if a combination including a joker, standing in for the ♥4 is put on the table, the next player can put in the ♥4 and pick up the joker for use elsewhere.

If you put down two eights and a joker, you don't have to announce which eight the joker represents, but with a run such as 5-6-joker, the assumption is that the joker represents the 7.

TIP

When playing with wild cards, you may not want to put combinations containing wild cards down immediately; you don't want to give another player the use of a wild card by way of the substitution. Of course, if you feel obliged to put down the set or run, try to ensure that the card your wild card replaces has already been played in some other set or run.

Going out and tallying your score

The first player to be able to put seven of the eight cards in her hand into combinations (including the card that she picks up in her current turn), or ten of her 11 cards as the case may be, *goes out* (places all her cards on the table) and wins. You discard your remaining card as you go out, usually having made the others into one combination of four and one combination of three. You don't have to make the plays at one turn; you may have put down some cards into sets already, of course. If your last two cards are two sevens, and you pick up a third seven, most people play that you can go out by making a set, without needing a final discard.

The winner collects points from all the other players. She bases her point total on the remaining cards in the other players' hands, regardless of whether the cards make up completed combinations — which is a good reason to put down melds as soon as you get them.

The players put their cards face-up on the table and call out how many points they have left for the winner. You score the cards according to the following scale:

>> **2s through 10s** get their face value, meaning that a 5 is worth 5 points.

>> **Jacks, queens, and kings** receive 10 points apiece.

>> **Wild cards** cost you 15 points each, if you are playing with them.

>> **Aces,** in keeping with their lowly status during the game, charge you 1 point only.

For example, if you're left holding ♠K, ♦K, ♦Q, and ♣A at the end of the game, the winner of the game scores 31 points. With more than two players, the winner cumulates the points from all the other players.

REMEMBER

Laying all your cards down in one turn is called *going Rummy,* which doubles your score; obviously, the availability of this bonus affects your decision to put down combinations earlier rather than later. If you think you can claim this bonus, you may want to delay putting down your combinations.

The first player to score 100 points is the winner. For a longer game, you can play to 250 points.

Simple Rummy strategy

When you first start playing Rummy, you may find that putting your cards into combinations is quite challenging. The best strategy is to aim for melds that have the best chance for completion.

The cards in your hand and on the table give you information about your chances for completing certain combinations. For example, if you can keep only two cards from the ♠7, ♠8, and ♣8, and you've already used the ♦8 in another run, you should keep the spades because you have two chances for success this way — the ♠6 or the ♠9. Keeping the two 8s gives you only one possible draw, the ♥8.

Another typical problem is knowing when to break up a pair in order to increase your chances elsewhere. For example, imagine that you have to discard from a collection such as the one shown in Figure 3-4.

FIGURE 3-4:
Time to choose
or lose.

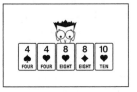

© John Wiley & Sons, Inc.

The solution to this problem is to throw the ♥10 away. Keeping your two pairs gives you a reasonable chance to make three of a kind, and the ♥10 gives you only a single chance of making a combination — by drawing the ♥9.

In general, you don't want to split up your pairs. But life (or at least Rummy) isn't always so simple. Suppose that you have the cards shown in Figure 3-5.

If you need to throw out one card, throw a 4 away. The ♠7 is a useful building card, meaning that it fits well with the ♠8; mathematics says that the nest of 7s and 8s gives you four possible cards with which to make a combination (the ♠9, ♠6, ♣8, and ♥8). You have the same number of options if you throw the ♠7 away and keep the two pairs. But the real merit in throwing away one of the 4s is the degree of freedom you attain for a future discard. By throwing one 4 away, you allow yourself to pick up another potentially useful building card (such as the ♦7) at your next turn, and then you can throw away the other 4. By contrast, throwing away the ♠7 fixes your hand and gives you no flexibility.

The odds favor your draw to the run rather than your hopes for a set. When you make a run, you can build on it at either end. A set, on the other hand, has only one possible draw. For this reason, be careful about which cards you discard. If you must give your opponent a useful card, try to let her have the sets of three or four of a kind instead of helping her build her runs.

Keeping your eye on the discard pile

You can't go through a game of Rummy thinking only about the cards in your hand — you also need to watch the cards thrown into the discard pile. Monitoring the discard pile helps you keep track of whether the cards you're hoping to pick up have already been thrown away. For example, if you have to keep two cards from the ♠7, ♠8, and ♣8, consider whether the ♠6, ♠9, or ♥8 has already been discarded. If both spades have already gone, you have no chance of picking them up — at least not until you work your way through the entire stock, at which point you may get a second chance at the cards when the deck is reshuffled. In such a stuck position, you should settle for a realistic chance, however slim, of picking up the last 8 by discarding the ♠7.

Try to avoid *drawing to an inside run* — keeping, for example, a 3 and a 5 in the hopes of drawing the 4. Holding onto *builders* (cards that may be helpful elsewhere) is better than relying on a single card.

You can't review the discard pile for clues. You have to remember which cards were thrown away — or be very adept at taking stealthy peeks at the discarded evidence!

Thinking about your opponents' hands

Contemplating what your opponent has in his hand helps you make smarter choices about what cards you should discard. After all, you don't want to throw away that ♥K if your opponent can use it to complete a run with the ♥Q and ♥J.

You compile a picture of your opponent's hand by reading the negative and positive messages you get from his plays. For example, if you see your opponent throw away the ♥Q, you can be sure that he isn't collecting queens. That information in itself doesn't make discarding any queen safe, however, because he may be collecting high diamonds. But if do you subsequently throw down the ♦Q, and he picks it up, his action provides you with an informative message; you can safely infer that he's collecting high diamonds.

Making a good discard

TIP

Early in the game, try to avoid discarding exactly the same rank of card as your opponent; he may be trapping you. For example, if you hold the ♣J, ♦Q, and ♦10, you may be able to persuade your opponent to let his jacks go by tossing your ♣J at the first opportunity. This trick is good strategy — so try it yourself, but be aware that your opponents may be on the ball, too.

REMEMBER

Kings are the most attractive discard, followed by queens, because fewer runs involve kings and queens than involve jacks or 10s. (Kings can only appear in K-Q-J runs, but jacks can appear in runs of K-Q-J, Q-J-10, and J-10-9.) Of course, discarding court cards reduces your potential exposure if you lose the game. The higher the card, the more points you may present to the player going out.

Picking up cards from the discard pile

Another critical strategy dilemma in Rummy is whether to pick up *builder cards* — cards that lend themselves well to combinations — from the discard pile. Say, for example, that you start the hand with the ♠Q and ♦J, and early in the game an opponent throws away the ♦Q. Should you pick it up?

You would automatically keep the ♦Q if you picked it up from the stock, of course — doing so doesn't give your opponent any clues as to which cards you may find helpful. But if you take a card from the discard pile, you tip off your opponent to part of your hand. If you're playing against a good player who carefully watches cards, you probably shouldn't take the builder card. On the other hand, picking up a card that multiplies your options, such as the ♥7 with the ♠7, ♠8, and ♥8 in your hand, is definitely a good idea because the ♥7 gives you some flexibility in two directions.

TIP

Along with your opponents, you should watch the discard pile like a hawk. Technically, the cards should be arranged one on top of another, but in reality, you can generally see many cards below the top card. Crafty opponents keep a sharp eye on the pile; so should you.

Try to remember the cards that haven't been discarded as well as the ones that do appear on the discard pile. If you've almost worked your way through the entire deck and you see your first 5, assume that your opponent is collecting them — if your opponent isn't interested in collecting 5s, you probably would've seen a 5 before reaching the end of the deck.

Assume that your opponents are honest until they prove you wrong. If they hesitate on your discard, assume that they want to pick it up; their possible need for that card may affect your future discards. If you subsequently discover that they simply paused for effect, say nothing, but remember that they may do the same thing next time. You should be able to draw the right inferences after observing the first performance!

Gin Rummy: Knocking Down Your Foe

Gin Rummy is very similar in aim to regular Rummy (see the previous section), but Gin has some additional wrinkles that make it a more interesting and challenging game.

To play Gin Rummy, you need the following:

>> **Two players:** If more than two people want to play, you may want to send the extras out for ice cream or a walk.

>> **A standard deck of 52 cards:** No jokers allowed in the Gin house.

>> **Paper and pencil for scoring:** For more on scoring, head to the section "Boxing up the scoring system" later in this chapter.

Getting a fair deal

Both players get ten cards. The dealer turns the rest of the cards into the stock by placing them in the center of the table and turning over the first card. The upcard is offered to the nondealer first. If he doesn't want the upcard, the dealer may take it, and then play continues. Gin Rummy play resembles regular Rummy, except for how you go out, and the fact that you don't put down combinations mid-hand. (For more information on how to play Rummy, see the section "Rummy: Throw a Combination and Go" earlier in this chapter.)

TIP

The first upcard is a free card; be prepared to take it, even if it has no relevance to your hand because the option reverts to your opponent if you don't take advantage of it. If nothing else, taking the card misleads your opponent about the combinations in your hand. You can't take up the discard and then immediately put it down — just as at Rummy.

Going Gin and tallying your score

The most difficult (and therefore rewarding) way to go out and win the game is to put all your cards into melds, which is called *going Gin.* If you go Gin, you score 25 points, plus the sum of whatever your opponent fails to make into complete combinations — her unconnected cards, or *deadwood.*

You must pick up a card, either from the stock or the discard pile, before you go Gin.

To better understand how to score points after you win (and we assume you'll win because you're reading this great book), take a look at the cards in Figure 3-6.

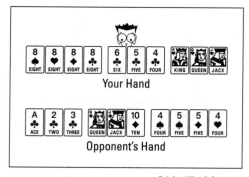

FIGURE 3-6:
The winner collects points from the deadwood in the loser's hand.

© John Wiley & Sons, Inc.

The example opponent has 18 points left: two 4s and two 5s add up to 18 points; no calculators allowed! Together with the 25 points you get for going Gin, you score 43 points.

You can play to 100 or 250 points, depending on how long you want the contest to last. (For more on scoring, see the section "Boxing up the scoring system" later in this chapter.)

Knock, knock! Another way to go out

The most intriguing facet of the rules of Gin Rummy, compared to the standard Rummy rules, is that you have more than one way to go out. Instead of forming all your cards into combinations, you have the option to *knock* (which involves literally tapping the table).

You knock when

>> You've put almost all your cards into combinations.

>> The cards that don't make melds total less than or equal to 10 points.

If you meet these criteria, you can knock (just once will do — no matter how happy it makes you feel) and then put your cards down on the table.

After you knock, play stops, and the tallying begins. Your score comes from the deadwood — the cards that aren't part of combinations. If your opponent's deadwood exceeds yours, you pick up the difference between your total and his. If your opponent's deadwood doesn't exceed yours, you must face the consequences.

WARNING

Sometimes your opponent can outdo you when you knock because he has an additional way to get rid of his deadwood. He can put down his melds, and those cards don't count toward his score. He can also add his loose cards to your combinations. After your opponent adds any loose cards, only his remaining cards count.

Take a look at the cards in Figure 3-7 to get an idea of how to score after you knock.

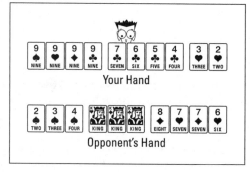

FIGURE 3-7:
Someone's knocking at the door; someone's racking up some points.

Your Hand

Opponent's Hand

© John Wiley & Sons, Inc.

If you count up all the cards in Figure 3-7, you see that your 5 points against his 28 leaves you with 23 points.

REMEMBER

If you knock, you don't get 25 points for going out.

Glance at the cards in Figure 3-8 for another example of how scoring can work after a player knocks. Your opponent knocks with 6 points, and you appear to have 11. But you can add your ♦J to his run, reducing your total to 1. You now undercut him by 5. You score 25 points plus the difference (5), so you get 30 points.

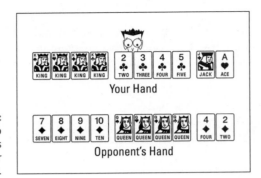

FIGURE 3-8:
Add cards to combinations after your opponent knocks.

Your Hand

Opponent's Hand

© John Wiley & Sons, Inc.

TIP

Always knock if you can do so early in the game, unless your hand is highly suitable for going Gin. For example, if you can knock early in the game with the cards shown in Figure 3-9, go ahead and knock away; only three cards allow you to go Gin, so your chances are below the average expectation. If five or more cards allow you to go Gin, play for Gin instead. The longer the game goes on, the more wary you should be of knocking because your opponent likely has less deadwood and will be able to undercut you.

FIGURE 3-9:
Go ahead and knock with this hand.

© John Wiley & Sons, Inc.

REMEMBER

In Gin Rummy, the hand doesn't have to be played to conclusion. If the stock gets down to two cards, the hand comes to an end. The player who draws the third-last card can knock or go Gin. If he doesn't do so and discards, the other player can pick up that discard and go out as well. If not, the game is over. Just throw in the cards and start all over.

Boxing up the scoring system

When you reach your game-winning target, you get 100 points simply for winning. In addition, you're awarded bonuses based on the number of hands you win compared to the number of hands your opponent wins. The bonus comes in the form of a box, which is 25 points added to your score for each hand you win minus the number of hands your opponent wins. For example, if you play six hands and each player wins three, the winner doesn't get a bonus. But if the winner wins more hands, the bonus comes into play.

Say that Player A and Player B go through six hands in a game. If Player A wins four hands to Player B's two, Player A scores a 50-point bonus. Table 3-1 shows the scoring of a sample game between bitter rivals Harry and Sandy.

TABLE 3-1   **Hand-by-Hand Score of a Sample Gin Rummy Game**

Harry's Score	Sandy's Score	Notes
52	—	Harry went Gin, and Sandy had 27 points in her hand.
—	26	Harry knocked with 6, but Sandy undercut with only 5 points.
11	—	Harry knocked with 3, and Sandy had 14 points.
28	—	Harry went Gin and caught Sandy with 3 points.
—	27	Sandy knocked with 6 and caught Harry with 33 points.
41	—	Harry went Gin, and Sandy had 16 points.

Table 3-2 shows the after-game totals.

TABLE 3-2   **Harry and Sandy's Final Scores**

Harry's Score	Sandy's Score	Notes
124	53	Total scores
–53	—	Harry subtracts Sandy's score
71	—	Harry's margin of victory
+100	—	Harry's bonus for winning
+50	—	Harry's box bonus
221	—	Harry's total winning score

If you're fortunate enough to reach the winning post — be it 100 or 250 points — without allowing your opponent to win a single hand, you *blitz, schneider,* or *skunk* him, and your final winning score is doubled.

Chapter 4

Working toward a Run with Fan Tan

You can get along just fine playing Fan Tan with remarkably little grasp of the underlying strategy. However, to be really good at Fan Tan, you can't rely solely upon the luck of the hand you're originally dealt. To play well requires a fair degree of skill and an understanding of the mechanics of the game. We tell you everything you need to know about this exciting game in this chapter.

And for those of you who require a little money action with your card games, Fan Tan works very well as a gambling game, and I fill you in on how to bring the monetary element into the game in this chapter, too.

To play Fan Tan, you need the following:

>> **Four players:** Three, five, or six players work, but four are ideal.

>> **A standard deck of 52 cards:** No jokers required.

>> **A pencil and paper for scoring.**

A typical contest at Fan Tan consists of playing to a set score, the objective being to avoid scoring points by leaving your opponents with cards in their hands. When you win a hand of Fan Tan, you score zero, but each opponent scores the number of points equal to the number of cards left in his hand at the end of the game. Playing to 11 or 15 points means a game likely to last half an hour or so.

Accepting Your Fan Tan Mission

The objective of Fan Tan is relatively uncomplicated. You deal out the entire deck of cards among the players, and you spend the game trying to get rid of all your cards before the other players can manage the feat.

You get rid of cards by adding them to an already existing *run,* or sequence of cards in a suit, which builds up during the play. You can play a single card whenever it's your turn. You have to build the cards up and down in consecutive order, starting from the 7 in each suit. After someone plays the 7 of a suit, the next player can legally put on the 6 or 8 of the suit. If the 6 hits the table, the next player has the choice of adding the 5 or 8. If he plays the 8 on the 7, the next player can put down the 6 or the 9, and so on.

After the first 7 is played, if the next player has no 7 or can't add to the cards on the table, he passes. You must play if you can.

Wheeling and dealing

To determine who gets to deal first, pick someone to deal a card face-up to each player until someone receives a jack; the lucky prince gets to deal the first hand. For subsequent hands, the deal passes one place clockwise.

If you play the game for money, everyone puts in an initial *ante* — a fixed unit — before the start of the hand. (You can make the stakes whatever you like; it only takes a small stake to get the blood racing. Because additional bets can be made, a nickel may be quite enough for the ante!)

After shuffling and offering a cut to the player on his right, the dealer gives out all the cards, facedown and clockwise. If you're playing with four people, everyone gets the same number of cards. If you're playing with three, five, or six players, some people get more cards than others (you just can't divide 52 evenly by 3, 5, or 6). This imbalance gets corrected over the course of a round of Fan Tan because everyone deals a hand and gets extra cards on some hands during play.

If you play the game for stakes, you can make it that the players with fewer cards put in an extra unit to compensate for starting the game with such an advantage.

Letting the cards hit the fan

The player to the left of the dealer has the first opportunity to play. If she has a 7 in any suit, she must play it by placing it face-up in the center of the table. If she doesn't have a 7, she passes.

TIP

If you have more than one 7, do not automatically put down the one in the suit in which you have more cards. Put down the 7 where you have more awkward end-cards such as aces and kings, or 2s and queens.

If you're playing for money, any player who passes must put an additional unit into the pot. Fan Tan's original name, Play or Pay, was very much to the point.

After someone starts the game with a 7, the next player can make one of the following plays:

>> You can play a 7 in another suit if you have one. If you want to play another 7, you place it directly above or below the other 7.

You don't have to play another 7 if you have a different legal move that you would prefer to make.

>> You can build up or down on any 7. If you have an 8 or a 6 in the appropriate suit, you put it down to the right or left of the 7.

>> If you can't make any other move, you pass.

Similarly, the next player can either build up or down from the existing structures or pass.

REMEMBER

In Fan Tan, aces can only be low, and you can only play an ace after a 2, not after a king.

If you can play, you must do so, however tactically unwelcome it may be to release a card that you'd rather keep in your hand. Often, you find that you don't want to play a card that simply makes other people's lives easier — but that's Fan Tan life. A player who's caught holding back in a stakes game can't win the hand on which the offense occurs.

After a few turns around the table, the cards form into piles on both sides of the 7s that may look like the ones shown in Figure 4-1. In the spade suit, for example, the ♠8, ♠9, and ♠10 are nestled beneath the ♠J, and the ♠6 and ♠5 are invisible below the ♠4.

FIGURE 4-1:
Running high and low in all the suits.

© John Wiley & Sons, Inc.

In Figure 4-1, the next legal cards to play would be the ♠Q or ♠3, the ♥9 or ♥2, the ♦10 or ♦4, and the ♣9 or ♣6. The player with the action can play any one of these cards or pass if he can't.

When a pile comes to the end of its natural life (when an ace or king stops the sequence from advancing any further), turn over the pile to indicate that fact.

The first person to get rid of all his cards wins, and play immediately stops. He takes the pot (which consists of the antes plus any additional contributions made during the hand) if you're playing the game with stakes, but before he does that, all the other players put in one unit for every card left in their hands.

Expanding your Fan Tan smarts

To play Fan Tan well, you need to familiarize yourself with a few essential elements of strategy. First and foremost, if you only have one card that you can play, you don't have much choice but to play it. Your Fan Tan strategy starts when you have more than one card you can play.

Assuming you have more than one playable card, look first at the suits in which you hold *end cards* — the aces and kings in each suit. End cards pose all kinds of problems because you can't get rid of them until every other card in the suit has been played, usually close to the end of the game. Your strategy should revolve around persuading people to play cards in the suit in which you hold end cards. You give persuasion by playing cards in that suit, and if you have the choice of leading or playing different 7s, look at the suits with the end cards.

Choosing between 7s

Starting at the beginning of a hand, your first idea is to play as quickly as possible any 7 in a suit in which you have an end card. Similarly, if you have 2s or queens, think about playing the 7s in those suits right away. If you're playing in a four-player game and you hold back a 7 in a suit filled with end cards, you may increase your chances of not finishing last, but you reduce your chances of winning.

For example, pretend that you get the cards shown in Figure 4-2.

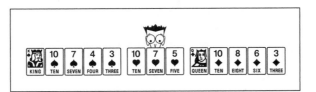
You want to play the ♠7 as soon as possible to encourage others to play on the suit. You have both a high (♠K) and a low (♠3) card in spades — time to get cracking on the suit at once!

With your mid-range cards in hearts, you may keep the ♥7 back for as long as possible, because it's to your advantage to keep players from being able to play hearts for the time being. If hearts are the last suit played, you're more likely to win the game.

REMEMBER

Given the choice, you should start with suits in which you have end cards (aces, 2s, kings, and queens) rather than suits in which you're comfortably placed with middle cards (between the 3 and the jack).

Playing your end cards through sequences

In general, you want to minimize your opponents' opportunities to play — and thus restrict their freedom of action so they have to release cards they want to retain in their hands. Following that logic, playing an end card (an ace or a king) whenever it is legal to do so is generally a good idea. The end card gives no new opportunity for play. Make the other players release cards they're reluctant to let go, which in turn allows you to play your other cards.

For the same reason that end cards are potentially attractive plays, you often find that you can use a run in your hand to force others to play. A run occurs when you hold something like the ♠Q-♠J-♠10-♠9; playing the 9, 10, or jack gives no other player an additional opportunity and thus forces your opponents to make moves that they would rather not do. With any luck, those moves will help you get your end cards out.

Think carefully about whether you want to release a card in a suit to give other players opportunities to play, rather than play an end card or work on a sequence. The answer depends on whether you want your opponents to play on the suit in which you have that card in the middle of a suit, or whether you want to hold that card back to inconvenience them and make their lives more difficult. If you hold, say, a 9 and also the Q of a suit, you may want to put the 9 down quickly to encourage play on that suit. With a 9 and no card higher than it, keep the 9 for as long as you can. Why help others to play their end-cards if you don't have to?

Break out your sequences only after you've made all your plays in the suits where you have end cards.

Playing Double-Deck Fan Tan

All your friends will want to join in when you play Fan Tan, which is where Double-Deck Fan Tan comes in — it's a great game for large groups, when a single deck leaves you with too small a hand to start with.

To play Double-Deck Fan Tan, you need the following:

>> **Seven or more players**

>> **Two standard decks of 52 cards without jokers**

>> **A pencil and paper for scoring**

>> **A big table and plenty of chairs**

You play Double-Deck Fan Tan just as you play Fan Tan (see the section "Accepting Your Fan Tan Mission" earlier in this chapter). The most glaring difference is that you have eight rows of cards in Double-Deck Fan Tan rather than the four rows in traditional Fan Tan (eight 7s compared to four).

With two of each card circulating in the double-deck, you have no assurance that you'll be able to put down a card when a space arises because someone else may fill in the vacancy first. More 7s are around, but you still don't know exactly when you can get your cards out. When the player on your left puts down the ♦J, will you be able to get your ♦Q out, or will someone with the other ♦Q beat you to it?

Double-Deck Fan Tan is more random than standard Fan Tan, and thus less strategic, which you may view as a disadvantage. At the same time, Double-Deck Fan Tan equals out skill levels, so it's appropriate for adults and children playing together, and the longer game fits well in social atmospheres.

The scoring works as in regular Fan Tan, with players playing to a specific target, or for stakes.

Chapter 5

Nailing Bids with Oh Hell! and Romanian Whist

O h Hell! (the exclamation point always accompanies the title) is ideal both for children and adults, in that it requires sufficient skill to make it an enjoyable challenge and involves just enough luck that everyone has a reasonable chance to win — or at least a chance to not lose by too much. (If you lose to your children, you can emphasize the luck factor; if you win, you can console them with the thought that when they get older, they may finally beat you.)

Oh Hell! goes by a wide variety of other names. You may know the game as Pshaw, Blackout, Up the Creek without a Paddle, and the rather boring Nomination Whist.

To play Oh Hell!, you don't need to bring any satanic paraphernalia with you. Just have the following on hand:

>> **At least three players:** Oh Hell! is best played with four players, but you can play it with up to eight players.

>> **One standard deck of 52 cards:** No jokers allowed.

The Lowdown on Oh Hell!

Oh Hell! is based on taking *tricks.* During gameplay, players take turns putting a card face-up on the table. The person who plays the highest card wins and collects all the played cards — one trick. The winner of the trick plays the first card to start the next trick. The process continues until all the cards play out.

Like in most games that involve taking tricks, the players in Oh Hell! score points for winning tricks. However, winning is more than just a matter of taking tricks. Before the actual play of the hand, you must estimate *precisely* how many tricks you think you'll win in the hand (see the section "Placing your bid" later in this chapter).

The importance of accurately predicting your trick total far outweighs the reward for actually winning tricks, so picking up a bad hand isn't necessarily a problem. Indeed, a terrible hand may be easier to judge than a great one. Making accurate estimates about your hand determines your success at the game, which is a very satisfying ingredient for a card game.

Dealing the cards

You give a card to each player to determine the dealer. The player who draws the lowest card deals the first hand.

The dealer deals out every card in the deck, starting with the player on his left, as long as everyone gets the same number of cards. You deal the cards face-down. You put down the remaining cards and turn over the top card to determine the trump suit (see the next section for more information) for that hand; the other undealt cards play no further part in the game. For a four-player game, in which all the cards go out, cut the deck to determine the trump suit before you deal out the first hand.

After a hand ends and you tally the scores, the deal passes clockwise for the next hand, and that player deals out the cards. For the subsequent deal, however, you deal one fewer card to every player, and the reduction continues for each subsequent hand until each player receives only one card. Following the single-card hand, the number of cards goes *up* by one each hand. The sequence progresses until you reach the maximum again. The game ends after the second maximum hand, and the winner is the player who finishes with the highest total.

You can also start with one card, work your way up to the maximum, and then come back down to one card. Either way works, and the variation you choose really doesn't matter.

If two players tie for the lead at the end of the game, the deal passes on, and everybody plays one more hand with the maximum number of cards. Additional deals with the maximum number of cards continue until you determine a winner.

Taking tricks with the trump suit

You must play a card in the suit led, or *follow suit,* if you can. If you don't have a card in the suit led, you can play a card from the *trump suit,* which automatically wins the trick — unless an opponent plays a higher trump card. You can also let go (or *discard)* a card from any other suit — in which case you can't win the trick. The smallest trump card beats even the ace of a *side-suit* (any non-trump suit).

Placing your bid

After you look at your hand, you swallow your pride and place a realistic bid. Your bid represents the number of tricks you intend to take during the course of the hand. The *bidding* starts with the player to the left of the dealer, who can bid any number of tricks that she likes up to the maximum, which is the number of cards received by each player.

How much you bid depends on your high cards, your trump cards, and by what the other players bid around you. The more the players around you seem to be bidding, the less you should rate your hand to be worth — and vice versa. Additionally, if you can gauge that the players with good hands are to your immediate right (so you play after them and capture their honors), you may again up your bid by a trick.

The bidding continues clockwise until it comes back to the dealer, who has the final bid. Nothing stops the players from bidding, as a group, for too many tricks or too few tricks, and any player can try for no tricks at all.

Everyone but the dealer can bid for as many tricks as they think they can take, up to the number of cards dealt to each player. One of the little peculiarities of Oh Hell! that can lead to pleasurable aggravation (if you aren't the unfortunate dealer) is that the total number of tricks the players are going to go for can't equal the number of tricks available. For example, if five cards go to each person, the total number of tricks bid can't be five; therefore, if the first three players bid 1, 2, and 1, respectively, the dealer can't contract for one trick because doing so makes the total five.

Why this stipulation, you ask? Allowing the number of tricks contracted for equal the number of tricks available presents the possibility that everyone could nail their bids — a situation that's inherently unsatisfying. And the smaller the number of cards you deal, the more potentially arduous this rule can be, and on the round when only one card is dealt, it can produce particularly irritating results for the dealer, who bids last.

Note: It isn't universal to play the rule that dealer is restricted by the number of tricks available. We think it spices the game up, but not everybody sees it the same way.

The designated scorer writes down the bids on the score sheet as players call them out so he can check the accuracy of the bids afterwards and tell the dealer what bid (or *call*) is forbidden.

If you make a bid out of turn, the bid stands, and the other players can take advantage of it by having more information. However, if the dealer makes a bid out of turn, it doesn't stand because the disadvantage of bidding last must go to the dealer.

WARNING

Don't bid too high; when in doubt, playing to lose a trick is generally much easier than playing to win it. Look at the hand in Figure 5-1 to see what I mean.

FIGURE 5-1:
A hand with plenty of potential — but no guarantees!

© John Wiley & Sons, Inc.

Suppose that four people are playing, and you hold this hand as first to bid. If hearts are trump, you may, on a very good day, win all four tricks — you're virtually certain to win at least one, if not two. The odds are in your favor; however, it may be smarter to bid two rather than three and then listen carefully to the rest of the bidding to determine your play strategy.

Playing for your bids

The player on the dealer's left leads to the first trick, and play continues clockwise. Cards rank in the standard order, with aces high, and you have to follow suit (play a card in the suit led) if you can. If you can't follow suit, you have the choice of discarding (playing a card in a non-trump suit) or trumping with the trump suit.

In the early phases of the game, when you have plenty of cards, leading a suit in which you have only one card (a *singleton*) can be a good idea. Depending on whether you win or lose that trick, you can be more flexible in your strategy with other suits. If you win a trick unexpectedly, you go out of your way to lose another trick that you may have won (by undertrumping say). If you lose a trick that you expected to win, you know to go all out to make up for it elsewhere.

TIP

When leading, if you don't have any singletons, consider leading a high honor such as a queen or a king. That way you find out early whether the card is destined to win a trick, which may affect your strategy for the play of other suits. Similarly, if you're going to lead from an ace-king, play the king first. Other players won't be quite so sure that you really want to win the trick.

At the end of a hand, all players announce how many tricks they took, and the scorer writes down the scores for each player. For every trick that you get on each hand, you score 1 point. If you make your bid, you get an additional 10 points. The player with the highest total after the second maximum-card hand wins the game (see the section "Dealing the cards" earlier in this chapter for more dealing information).

If you expose a card by playing it out of turn or by dropping it, it becomes a *penalty card*, and you must play it at the first legal opportunity. If you err by failing to follow suit, you may correct your mistake before the next trick starts. Your *revoke card* (the card that you played by mistake) becomes a penalty card to be played on your next turn, and all the other players who played after you on the previous trick can change their cards if they want. If they don't spot the revoke in time, the deal is canceled, and the revoker suffers a 10-point penalty.

Eyeing the Basics of Romanian Whist

One of the main variations on Oh Hell! (see the previous section) is called Romanian Whist, for the surprisingly good reason that it comes from Romania. In fact, the game is called plain old Whist in that country.

To play Romanian Whist, you need the following:

>> **At least three players:** You can play with up to eight players.

>> **One standard deck of 52 cards:** At the start of the game, pare down the deck so you have eight cards per player in the deck, using only the highest-ranking cards. For three players, prepare the deck so it has only the aces through 9s in it; in other words, a 24-card deck. If you have six players, use a 48-card deck. With seven or eight players, you play a six-card game.

>> **Paper and pencil for scoring:** You may want to construct a score sheet set out in columns, with a column for each player.

Dealing the cards

You cut the deck to determine the dealer. The dealer gives each player the appropriate number of cards, dealing clockwise. The appropriate number depends on what stage of the game you're currently in (see the section "Dealing the cards" earlier in this chapter).

Romanian Whist differs from Oh Hell! in that you start with one card for the first trick, work your way up to eight cards, and then work your way down again. But the differences don't end there. The progression of Romanian Whist is a rather labored one because instead of going up one card at a time, every player takes a turn to deal a hand with one card each (thereby eliminating the dealer disadvantage discussed earlier). After each one-card trick, the deal progresses normally until you get to the round of eight cards. At that point, everyone takes a turn at dealing eight cards, and then the progression retreats back down to one again for another complete round.

Choosing your trump suit, making your bids, and playing your tricks

Determine the trump suit by turning over the top card of the undealt-card pile. When you play the eight-card round, you play the hands with no trump suit at all (refer to the section "Taking tricks with the trump suit" earlier in this chapter for the details on trump suits).

All the normal Oh Hell! rules apply to the bidding (see the section "Placing your bid" earlier in this chapter) and to the playing of the tricks (refer to the section "Playing for your bids") — with one exception.

The exception is that at Romanian Whist you are forced to play a card from the trump suit if you have no cards in the suit led. In Oh Hell!, you can discard anything you like; if you have no trumps, you can throw anything you like.

Scoring the tricks

If you make your contract, you score 5 points, plus 1 point for each of the tricks you take. If you take fewer tricks than you contract for, you lose the value of your bid. If you take more tricks than you bid for, you lose the value equivalent to the tricks you took.

The scoring routine sounds complicated, but it really isn't. Look at how the scoring may apply to the four-handed game shown in Figure 5-2. Each player has three cards, and clubs are trump. North player deals.

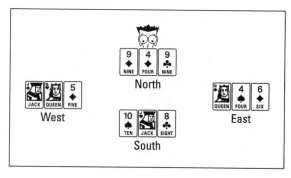

FIGURE 5-2: With clubs as the trump suit, the bidding and scoring for this hand may get ugly!

© John Wiley & Sons, Inc.

East bids zero, South bids one, West bids one, and North bids zero — rather unhappily. A bid of two by the dealer is a valid option here, but the diamond suit just seems too unlikely to generate two tricks (hey, you can see the other players' cards — North can't!).

East leads the ♠4, and South plays the ♠10. West wins the trick with the ♠J, and North discards the ♦9.

For the second trick, West leads the ♦5, North plays the ♦4, and East plays the ♦6, which creates a problem for South. If South trumps this trick and leads the ♥J, the lead may well win the last trick. Because discarding brings the bonus of defeating East's contract, South throws away the ♥J, giving East an unwanted trick. North wins the last trick with the ♣9, the highest trump card left.

The scoring goes like this:

>> **West** nails the bid of 1 and scores 6 points.

>> **East** underbid and loses the single trick, or 1 point.

>> **South** overbid by one trick and loses 1 point.

>> **North** underbid and loses 1 point.

One highly entertaining variation to the last one-card hand is to hold your card on your forehead so everyone but you can see your card. You have to make your bid in the usual fashion, without knowing your card, based on the bids that everyone else makes and the cards you can see.

Chapter 6

Bowing to Trump in Euchre

E uchre is an excellent social card game, simple in concept but with a high degree of subtlety in the play. The game offers myriad variations because you can play it with any number of players and as a long or short game.

To play Euchre, you need the following:

>> **Four players:** Two teams, two players to a team.

>> **A standard deck of 52 cards:** Take out the ace through the 9 in each suit, making a deck of 24 cards for the game.

>> **Paper and pencil for scoring:** You can also keep score with some of the remaining playing cards. See the section "Tallying Your Score" at the end of this chapter for more information.

Acquainting Yourself with Euchre

Euchre is a trick-taking game at heart. Each player receives five cards, and you play one card at a time; the player who lays the highest card in the suit of the first card played — unless someone contributes a trump, in which case it is whoever lays the highest trump card (see the section "Determining the Trump Suit" later in this chapter) — collects all four cards and stacks them in front of him, thus taking the *trick.*

In Euchre, you win a hand and score points for taking the majority of the tricks in a hand, which means winning three or more of the five tricks available. You get more points if you take all five tricks (see the section "Tallying Your Score" at the end of this chapter). But to summarize: You score points for bidding and making a contract or defeating the opponents when they are trying to make their contracts. The first to a specified total of points, generally 10, wins the match.

You play the game with partners, but under special circumstances, one member of a partnership can elect to go solo — if he thinks that going alone is worthwhile. See the section "Playing for Bigger Stakes Alone" later in this chapter for the details.

Picking Partners

You play Euchre with two teams of two players, either with prearranged partnerships or with partners selected by cutting the deck. If you cut the deck for partners, the two highest cards take on the two lowest cards.

Make sure the partners sit opposite each other. In partnership games, you almost always sit across from your partner, probably to keep you off each other's throats.

Striking a Fair Deal

You can select the dealer at random, or you can deal out the cards until a jack appears. Whoever gets the jack becomes the dealer.

The dealer shuffles the cards and offers them to the player on his left to cut. That player can cut the deck or tap (*bump*) the cards to indicate that no cut is necessary.

You deal the cards clockwise. Just to make the game interesting, the dealer deals out five cards, face-down, in packets of two to each player and then three to each player (or three then two if you absolutely insist). Go figure. After dealing the cards, you turn over one card and place it in the middle of the table on top of the other three unused cards. These three cards, or the *kitty*, play no further part in the hand. The upturned card represents the trump suit (see the section "Determining the Trump Suit" later in this chapter).

At the end of each hand, the deal rotates clockwise.

WARNING

A *misdeal* can occur in several ways, but, for the most part, no serious consequences arise from a misdeal. If the deal is flawed for whatever reason — because a card turns over on the table, the deck has a face-up card in it, or the deck contains the wrong number of cards — you cancel the deal and redeal the hand.

REMEMBER

If a player deals out of turn and someone notices before he turns the top card over, you cancel the deal. However, if the player turns the top card up before anyone notices, the deal stands, and whoever misses her deal simply loses out. (As you see later, in the section "Determining the Trump Suit," dealing carries an advantage, so you don't want to skip your deal.)

If a player receives the wrong number of cards and discovers it before the first trick starts, a redeal takes place with no penalties. If the error isn't corrected in time, however, play continues, and whichever team has the player with the wrong number of cards can't score on that hand. The moral of the story is: Count your cards!

Determining the Trump Suit

After the deal is complete, the dealer turns over the top card of the four remaining cards. This is called the upcard, and it determines what the *trump suit* is for the current hand. The remaining three cards play no part in the current hand.

REMEMBER

The trump suit represents the boss suit, meaning that a trump card beats any card in any other suit. In Euchre, you have to *follow* the suit that the first player leads (play a card in the same suit), but if you can't follow suit, you can play a trump card and win the trick (unless someone plays a higher trump card).

The dealer can add the turned-up card to his hand and discard an unwanted card of his choice — under certain circumstances (we explain those circumstances in the section "Bidding for Tricks").

Jacking Up the Card Rankings

When you pick up your hand, you can sort it into suits. The standard ranking order applies — within each suit, the ace is high, and the values descend to the lowly 9.

The only exception to the normal ranking rules lies in the trump suit, which ranks as follows:

>> The highest trump card is the jack of the trump suit, often referred to as the *right bower* (rhyming with "flower" and deriving from the German word *bauer*, which means "jack" — surprise, surprise!).

   In England, you play the game with a joker, which ranks as the master trump. The joker is known as the *Benny,* or the Best Bower.

>> The second-highest trump card is the other jack of the same-color suit, often called the *left bower.* The jack deserts its own suit and becomes a trump card for the hand; for example, the ♠J ceases to be a spade when clubs are the trump suit — it becomes a club.

>> The remaining five cards in the trump suit are the ace, king, queen, 10, and 9, ranking from highest to lowest in that order.

For example, if clubs are the trump suit, the cards rank in the order shown in Figure 6-1. Diamonds and hearts rank from the ace through 9 in the normal fashion.

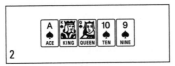

FIGURE 6-1:
Card ranks when clubs are the trump suit.

© John Wiley & Sons, Inc.

Bidding for Tricks

After you pick and sort your cards, you get a chance to make your bid. Everyone sees what card gets turned over for the trump suit; the question is whether anyone wants to bid to take three or more tricks with that suit as the trump suit. Each player gets the chance to take on that assignment or refuse the invitation. If all players refuse, the bidding goes into its second phase. To make your decision, you need to value your hand for play in the trump suit.

Because the second phase of the game involves playing with the trump suit of your choice, you also have to look at your hand and value it for play in a different trump suit.

Starting the bidding

Each player in turn, starting with the player on the dealer's left, can agree to play the suit of the upcard in the middle of the table as trump on behalf of his or her partnership, or each player can pass. If any player accepts the suit of the upcard as the trump suit, the dealer adds the upcard to his hand and throws one card away face-down.

The partnership that makes the decision to take three or more tricks (as opposed to passing) is referred to as the *makers*, and the other players are the *defenders*. You follow these protocols during the first round of bidding:

1. The first player either plays with the predetermined trump suit, called *ordering it up* (meaning that he asks the dealer to pick up the upcard), or he passes by saying "I pass."

2. The second player, the dealer's partner, can pass, or she can accept the current trump suit by saying "Partner, I assist," "I'll help you," or "Pick it up."

3. The third player follows the pattern for the first hand by ordering the trump up or passing.

4. The dealer accepts the choice of the trump suit by saying "I pick it up" and taking up the card to add it to his hand, or he rejects the card by saying "Over" or "I turn it down."

   If he rejects the trump suit, he takes the upcard and puts it face-up at a right angle to the deck below the other three cards to indicate what suit isn't acceptable as the trump suit for the second round of bidding (see the later section "Entering the second phase of bidding" for more information).

Knowing what to bid

The most delicate strategy in the game hinges on your decision to accept the trump suit and make a bid or not. As a general rule, you should expect your partner to help you get one trick. If you look at the tricks you think you can take from your hand and see two sure tricks, you have enough to consider bidding. If you hold three good trump cards, you definitely have enough to make a bid.

You must also consider whether a different trump suit may work better for you and your partner. If no one wants to play in the initial trump suit, each player has a chance to select a different trump suit, so evaluating your hand for both purposes is important.

The state of the score is also critical. Euchre is played to a set target; if you (or your opponent) are close to winning, consider whether your hand plays better in the specified trump suit than another suit. Picking that suit as trump may be your best chance to win — or stop your opponents from winning.

You get rewarded if you succeed in your bid and penalized if you fail, so you want to get your decision right if you can. If you fail to get the required three tricks, you get *euchred* — hence the name of the game. (See the section "Tallying Your Score" later in this chapter for all the scoring information.)

Each member of the partnership who didn't deal the hand — with the member to the dealer's left being the first to speak on both the first and second rounds of bidding — needs a relatively good hand to accept the trump suit on the first round. You shouldn't accept the trump suit without at least three probable tricks in the early phases of the game (and thus before tactical considerations of the state of the match enter into the equation). The non-dealing partnership gets first crack at selecting the trump suit on the second round of bidding if everyone passes, which is an advantage. In addition, the fact that the dealer picks up a trump card tilts the odds in his favor and pushes his side toward making an aggressive bid to select the trump suit in the first round.

Keep in mind that the left bower (the second-highest jack) may be of more use to you during the second round of bidding, particularly if you aren't the dealer. If you have the left bower, consider passing the trump suit on the first round and then selecting the suit of the same color on the second round. The dealer doesn't get to take the upcard to improve his hand, and your left bower becomes the boss trump card, the right bower. Of course, you won't enjoy a second round of bidding if another player accepts the initial trump suit, but that's a risk you have to take if you don't have a good enough hand to order up the trump suit.

A variation to the bidding is played widely in Australia, England, and Canada. If the partner of the dealer accepts the trump suit, she must accept on her own (thereby playing solo; see the section "Playing for Bigger Stakes Alone" later in this chapter) instead of accepting for the partnership.

Entering the second phase of bidding

If all four players pass on the trump suit, you turn the top card down, thereby eliminating the dealer's inherent advantage. On the second round of bidding, players may again accept the responsibility of going for three tricks, naming any other suit as the trump suit. You can't bid the suit of the original upturned card during the second bidding stage. That suit is only a possible trump suit for the first round.

WARNING

If a player on the second round calls the same trump suit as the upturned card, her side can't participate in the bidding.

Again, the bidding goes around the table, starting with the player on the dealer's left, who can pass or name the trump suit. If she passes, the next player has the same choices, and so on around the table. Whoever selects a trump suit wins the bidding — now all the partnership has to do is make the bid good. If all four players pass, you throw the hand in, and the next player deals a new hand.

In a variation called "stick the dealer," the dealer *must* call trump at his second turn if no one else has taken on the responsibility. The penalty for failure remains the same for him as if he had voluntarily taken on the task.

REMEMBER

Don't forget your jacks; they become very valuable when trump is up in the air. Also remember to value the jack in the suit of the same color as the trump suit. As soon as you or someone else nominates a new trump suit, a previously irrelevant jack may suddenly become very powerful.

TIP

If the dealer doesn't accept the original trump card, it normally implies that he doesn't hold a bower (jack) in the trump suit or in the same color. (If he does, he may well have gone for the original suit as the trump suit.) If you don't know whether to bid and what suit to select as the trump suit, the nondealers should go for the suit of the same color as the initial trump suit, and the dealer's partner should go for a trump suit of the other color.

At the end of the bidding, both sides go for at least three tricks. If the bid comes on the first round, the dealer picks up the upcard and puts it in his hand. If you make trump on the second round, whoever chooses the trump suit announces it, and the dealer leaves the upcard alone. Is that all there is to the game? Not quite.

Tallying Your Score

The team that chooses the trump suit and then wins three or four tricks scores 1 point. If the side that makes trump gets all five tricks, it *marches* or *sweeps* the hand, and the team scores 2 points.

REMEMBER

Three tricks are necessary to fulfill the obligations you assume when you determine the trump suit.

If the makers fail to fulfill the trick obligation, the defenders score 2 points (whether they get three, four, or five tricks) — they have *euchred* the makers. However, the biggest score comes if you go solo (see below) and make all five tricks: 4 points.

The first team to 10 points *reaches game* and wins. You can also play to 5 points for a shorter game.

TIP

You don't need to write down the scores to keep track of the running totals. Serious Euchre players often use playing cards, placed one on top of the other, to keep their totals. Specifically, you need an extra 2 and 3 to keep score with playing cards. To indicate one point, you turn up the 3 and put the 2 face-down to cover all but one spot. Showing 2 and 3 are easy, of course. For 4, you put both cards face-up with the 3 partly over the 2. If you play to 10 points, some people use a 6 and a 4.

Playing for Bigger Stakes Alone

A player with a particularly good hand can raise the stakes by opting to play the hand *alone.* The player who selects the trump suit has this option. As soon as you indicate your intention of going alone, your partner puts his cards face-down, for this hand alone, and the game becomes three-handed.

A hand with the top three trump cards (♠J, ♣J, ♠A, for example) is often a sure thing for going alone, especially if you have an off-suit ace. Two of the top three trumps and an ace on the side may be enough, but you may want a little more for insurance.

Why would you want to play alone? The only reason for doing so is if you have a guaranteed three tricks with a serious chance of making five tricks with your hand alone. If you make three or four tricks, you score the game the same as you do in partnership situations (see the section "Tallying Your Score" earlier in this chapter for details). But if you make all five tricks, as maker, you score 4 points.

Another game version states that the penalty for getting euchred when a defender goes alone is doubled. This provides the incentive for a defender going alone.

Going alone has no real advantage unless you have a good chance to make five tricks on your own; otherwise, you simply increase the chance of a penalty without any chance of increasing the rewards. With three sure winners in your hand, you must ponder whether your remaining cards give you a chance for a clean sweep. If not, play in your partnership and hope that your partner can come through with the goods for your feeble cards.

For example, say that your partner is the dealer, the ♣9 is the upcard, and you have the hand in Figure 6-2.

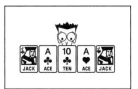
This hand isn't assured of winning you three tricks, although it's heavily favored to do so. However, if the ♠J is in your partner's hand, is one of the three cards in the muck, or is in one of your opponents' hands without any other trump cards accompanying it (and you see three trump cards out of the seven already), you stand a fair chance of making five tricks. Still, the odds of your partner making the vital difference are almost nonexistent because you can either win the tricks on your own or not at all. The hand in Figure 6-2 is an excellent hand to go solo on.

TIP

Before deciding whether to go alone, here are two factors that may influence you. If the score is such that getting four points may be critical (your opponents are close to winning and you are three or four points away), that may tempt you to go for the bigger gamble. Additionally your chances of going alone and getting all five tricks are rather better on a two-suited hand than a one-suiter. With three high trumps and the A-10 in a side suit you may well find yourself taking the last two tricks, whereas the bare 10 in a side-suit is far less likely to win the last trick.

Tricking for Points, Not Treats

After the opening lead is made (typically by the player to the dealer's left but not always), the play goes clockwise around the table. You must *follow suit* (play a card in the suit led) if you can, but if you can't, throw off any card or play a trump card as you see fit. Whoever plays the highest card of the suit led, or the highest trump card if one or more trumps have been played on the trick, wins that trick.

When a player goes alone, the hand on her left leads to the first trick. If both a defender and a maker go alone, the defender leads.

Failure to follow suit when you can do so is called a *revoke* or *renege*. You must correct a revoke before the winner gathers the trick. If another player identifies a revoke, the innocent side may add 2 points to its score or deduct 2 points from the guilty side. If your side is going alone and one of the opponents revokes, the penalty is 4 points.

We can offer only limited advice in the play of the cards. Part of the game lies in memorizing the cards played. You have to think about who may have what cards left to determine what to lead and what to throw away, when you have a choice. For example, the original trump card is one that you want to remember; if the dealer adds it to his hand, don't forget it.

If you have the opening lead and you have two or more trump cards, consider leading them. You should certainly lead a high trump if your partner called the trump suit because it helps your partner locate the missing cards. Otherwise, lead from a sequence if you have one. Start with high cards to help out your partner so he doesn't waste his high cards unnecessarily. For example, if hearts are trump, you could lead the ♠A or ♣A to try to win a trick.

TIP

Unlike some other card games, saving a winner for a rainy day in Euchre generally has no advantage. Take your tricks when you can, or you may never get them.

Chapter 7

Following Suit with Spades

C ard gamers the world over are exercising great amounts of creative energy on harnessing the rules of Spades — an all-American card game created in the United States in the 1930s — which, in turn, implies that the game is likely to improve as players test these modifications and incorporate or discard them. However, because the rules are so fluid and no rules are *official*, everybody seems to have a unique version, and the scoring system is a nightmare.

So you must bear with us. The rules that we set out in this chapter may not correspond exactly to the rules that your friends play by, but they do cover the basics of the game and allow you to play along with others or even teach your friends to play by "your" rules.

To play Spades, you need the following:

>> **Four players:** No more, no less.

>> **One standard deck of 52 cards:** In some variations, you need the jokers, too.

>> **An efficient scorer with pencil and paper:** Don't select the guy on his cellphone in between deals.

Grasping the Basics of Spades

Spades is traditionally a game for exactly four players, played in partnership (with the partners sitting opposite each other). The players take turns playing out one card from their hands clockwise around the table. You must play a card in whichever suit is played first (or *led*) if you can, which is called *following suit*. The four cards played constitute a unit of play called a *trick*. The objective of Spades is for your partnership to accurately estimate the strength of your hands in the bidding, and then in the play to take as close to your estimate of tricks as you can.

Choosing partners

The partnerships in Spades are frequently fixed in advance, but you can alternate lineups at the end of a contest, or *rubber* (a predetermined amount of games you set; for example, a best-of-three contest constitutes a rubber; see the later section "Finishing the game" for more information about rubbers).

Reviewing the card ranks

The cards rank from ace (high) down to 2 (low). If you decide to play without adding in any wrinkles, ranking the cards is no big deal.

However, if you like wrinkles, you can use a number of variations when ranking the cards. One common variation is to add two jokers to the deck, making sure they have separate markings to distinguish the big and little jokers. The two jokers become additional trump cards, and big cards at that: They rank as the highest and second-highest trump cards. Because it makes the most sense to play the game with each player having 13 cards, you can either remove ♥2 and ♦2 or deal 15 cards to the dealer. The dealer then removes two cards from his hand and discards them face-down so they play no further part in the game.

Making the deal

You select the dealer at random by cutting the deck; the person who draws the highest card deals. The traditional Bridge custom of having the player on the dealer's left shuffle the cards and the player on the dealer's right cut them is as good as any.

Starting with the player to his left, the dealer distributes the deck card by card, face-down to each player, so everyone has a 13-card hand (with two discards if you play with the joker variation; see the previous section). The deal progresses one place clockwise after each hand.

The object is to win as many tricks as possible. However, each of the four players must estimate in advance of the start of play how many tricks he or she will win. This estimate is called a *bid,* and your bid can include opting for no tricks or up to 13 tricks.

However, the peculiarity of Spades is that, although both sides join freely in the bidding, this auction isn't competitive — both sides get to make a bid and then pursue their targets (unlike some games, in which only one side gets to make a bid, and the other side is totally occupied with stopping them).

Each player independently names a number, and then each side chases its own specific number of tricks, the total of the two players' bids. If your side succeeds, you're generously rewarded; if you fail to meet your target, you're referred to as *set* (a phrase you will hear a lot of in this chapter) and heavily punished. But that isn't the end of the story. Spades is an *exact trick* game: If you make more tricks than you bid during the auction, you're also punished rather severely, though not as seriously as you are if you fail to meet your side's target. In fact, overtricks are known as *bags* because of the tie-in to being "sandbagged" (see the section "Getting sandbagged with overtricks" later in the chapter; bags will also crop up a fair amount in this chapter!). The trade-off between valuing your hand correctly in the bidding and making your contract exactly (rather than making too many tricks or making too few tricks) is a very fine line indeed. All these factors make Spades a fascinating game.

Your first duty for the partnership is to try to make at least as many tricks as you bid. As a secondary objective, provided you secure the first one, you try to avoid making too many overtricks. However, in most cases, you are happy to make overtricks if doing so sets your opponents.

The winner of the game is the first partnership that arrives at a set target — 500 or 250 points is a normal target — or the pair leading after a set number of deals — such as 10.

Bidding your hand accurately

In turn (around the table from the left of the dealer), each player can opt to bid any number of tricks between 0 and 13. After your opponent bids, your partner makes an estimate, and the combined total for each side is the number of tricks that the partnership needs to take to fulfill its *contract* for the hand.

Bidding nil (going for no tricks at all) is different from any other bid. I discuss this bid in the later section "Bidding for nil."

MANY MISDEAL RULES

Some variations of Spades allow a player to call for a misdeal before the bidding if his hand satisfies certain conditions. For example, a player may call for a misdeal if he holds one or no spades, holds a *side-suit* (that is, not spades) of seven or more cards, or doesn't hold any court cards (the ace, king, queen, and jack). In these situations, the player should ask his partner if he wants a misdeal before the bidding commences; however, his partner's reply isn't binding.

In the constantly evolving world of Spades, even the question of who bids first generates controversy. Some people say that the dealer is the first to speak, but the standard game calls for the bidding to start with the player to the left of the dealer, or the *elder hand*.

REMEMBER

Each partnership registers its tricks as a unit — it doesn't matter whether you or your partner takes the tricks unless a bid for nil has been made by one of the players; the important thing is that your side gets them. For example, if you bid two and your partner bids three, whether you get five or your partner gets five is irrelevant; if you get five tricks between you, you make your contract.

A different school of bidding is much more lax about the restrictions on communications between the partners. Starting with the nondealer's side, the two players can have a brief and non-specific conversation about their trick-taking capabilities. The first player of each partnership may provide clues along the following lines: "I have a hand with three sure tricks and the possibility for up to five or even six tricks."

When you pick up a hand, consider your high cards and your trump length to try to estimate the value of the hand. There will be imponderables, of course, but the initial calculation is linked to those two factors.

For example, with the hand shown in Figure 7-1, you bid two, counting one trick for the ♥A and one for the spades. Note that the ♥A is probably a trick you don't have to win; you have enough hearts to be able to refrain from playing that card on a heart lead. So you have some flexibility as to whether you want to bid one or two with the example hand. With the ♣K, you would bid three tricks. If you take this basic starting hand and change the ♣9 to the ♠K, the hand is worth four tricks: three in spades and the ♥A.

FIGURE 7-1:
Deciding what
to bid.

© John Wiley & Sons, Inc.

Basking in the dealer's choice

Being the dealer (or the fourth seat) in Spades is a significant advantage because you get to hear the other players commit themselves to a number of tricks before you have to decide on a bid.

As a player in fourth seat, you hear the three players suggest a combined total. As a general rule, you shouldn't take the total to more than 13. At an early stage in the game, consider, for example, that your opponents have jointly contracted for six tricks, and your partner has bid for three. If you make five tricks and your partner makes his three, then you have already combined to set your opponents by stopping them from making their announced target of six. Because you have already achieved a major target on the hand, you're better off bidding four and settling for an overtrick if it accrues. Yes, your side takes a small hit, but you administer a bigger blow to the opponents in the process. Conversely, if you really need to set the opponents to have a chance to win the game, you may bid five if you're truly confident — however, the penalty of the overtrick may be too severe — see the later section "Getting sandbagged with overtricks."

TIP

As a general rule, if you have a strong hand and the player to your left bids strongly, you should go low because that player will be in a position to capture your kings and queens if he so desires. If the player to your right bids strongly, the reverse applies; you're in the catbird seat.

Figuring the value of your high cards

Your success at bidding rests largely on knowing how to value your cards:

>> You count all aces as being worth a trick to start. No surprise there.

>> Count kings as worth about two-thirds of a trick, unless you also have the ace in that suit. Obviously, you can't bid for fractions of a trick, but the point is to add on something to your sure tricks for each king. If you have the ace and king together, treat the pair as two full tricks. However, be aware that the ace-king in a *side-suit* (a suit that isn't spades) of more than five cards is potentially extremely vulnerable because the danger of your opponents

trumping a high card increases. In fact, you should mentally devalue any ace or king in a side-suit.

» Queens are difficult to value unless other court cards support them. Queens are worth something — but not much. With an ace, treat the combination as one-and-a-half tricks; with a king, treat the combination as worth a full trick. Otherwise, treating a queen as about one-third of a trick is about right, unless it's in a side-suit of more than five cards, in which case you may discount it altogether.

WARNING

» Valuing jacks, unless they're combined with other high court cards, is very risky business. Because a jack is unlikely to win the first or second round of a suit, and because someone may be out of the suit by then and be able to trump your winner, counting jacks at all is pretty optimistic.

» Trump cards (any spades) are all valuable; count any trump card after your first three as worth a full trick. You should value all significant trump court cards, such as the ace, king, or queen of spades, at a full trick.

» Whatever the suit they're in, all high court cards (A, K, Q, J) in a very short suit (meaning you don't have many in the suit) become less valuable because your flexibility is impaired. A king on its own (also called a *singleton*) and a *doubleton* queen (one in a two-card holding) can both be wiped out very easily. For example, when someone leads out an ace in that suit, you have no choice but to play your king under it if you have only one card in the suit.

» If you have a void in spades, take off something from your hand valuation — your side-suit court cards are now more likely to be trumped.

TIP

PAINTING YOUR BIDDING PICTURE

One of the most testing areas of Spades is evaluating your hand correctly for the bidding. The consequences for a miscalculation in the bidding are almost equally severe whether you overestimate or underestimate your call. Having said that, the penalty for underbidding is less painful because the ax does not fall immediately. Still, getting your bid right and drawing the right inferences from other people's bids can gain you a large number of points — not to mention your partner's undying affection.

As soon as the bidding begins, each subsequent bidder can build up more and more of the picture, and using your judgment becomes easier as the bidding proceeds.

Depending on whether you believe them or not, your opponents' bids and comments should factor into your calculations. Those clues can help you work out just how good your hand really is and can help you make an accurate assessment of its worth.

WARNING

Hands generally fall into one of two categories: *balanced hands,* which have two to four cards in each suit, or *unbalanced* or *distributional hands,* which have some suits with plenty of cards in them (a *long suit*) and some suits where you have very few cards (a *short suit*). The more distributional your hand, the higher the danger that your high cards in the side-suits won't score tricks. For example, if you have ♥A and only one other card in the suit, everybody else is likely to have at least one heart. But, if you have five clubs, including ♣A and ♣K, counting both as sure tricks is dangerous because one of your opponents may have only one club and trump your winner by playing a spade on it.

Bidding for nil

You can bid for zero tricks if you think your hand really stinks. A bid of *nil* (also known as *nill, null,* or *nillo*) carries additional benefits and liabilities. The concept is to make no tricks at all, and you get a generous bonus for success — 50-point bonus — with an equally heavy penalty for failure.

REMEMBER

Normally, the two players on a team combine their bids to form a total contract for their side. If you bid nil, however, your success or failure depends on your own personal performance. Although your partner does his best to help you by overtaking any high cards that you play, making the contract is up to you and you alone.

It may also be worth emphasizing that when one player bids nil, his partner's bid still stands. That player must make his bid good in the usual fashion, with the standard bonuses and penalties applying.

A more unlikely option is to *blind nil,* which carries with it the same concept of not taking any tricks, but you make the bid without looking at your hand. The rewards and penalties are doubled (so the consequence is plus or minus 100 points). You can only attempt the blind nil option if your side is 100 or more points behind. Because bidding blind nil is a highly risky strategy, you should attempt it only as a last resort. It's also helpful to remember that it may be better for your side to be down 100 rather than 90 points because of this option.

In some forms of scoring, nil is worth 100, and the score for blind nil is 200, and it is only allowed if you are at least 200 points behind.

Because going blind is such a difficult feat to achieve, the player making the call can exchange two cards with his partner to improve both players' hands for their various purposes. The cards are passed face-down, and the bidder passes his two cards first, letting his partner look at the cards and select two from his own hand in exchange.

Bidding blind is a good way to randomize the proceedings if you're losing the game heavily; desperate situations demand desperate remedies. In fact, after you get 100 points down, you should seriously consider bidding blind immediately.

Bidding blind nil is a gamble, but fun. Even potentially unpromising hands apparently with too many high cards can turn out well. Check out the potentially unpromising hand in Figure 7-2, which turns out to be quite suitable for the blind nil bid.

FIGURE 7-2:
With a hand like this, bid nil.

© John Wiley & Sons, Inc.

You can exchange the high trump cards and hope to pick up low cards in the other suits from your partner to protect you from the danger of winning a trick with your high cards in diamonds or clubs.

Turning the tables, your partner may bid blind nil when you have the hand shown in Figure 7-3.

FIGURE 7-3:
Adjust your bid if your partner bids blind nil.

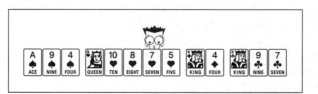

© John Wiley & Sons, Inc.

You probably intended to bid for three tricks because of your aces, kings, and queens. But if your partner bids blind nil, you should increase your bid because you expect to receive at least one sure trick from your partner. Say, for example, that you bid five tricks and receive the ♣A and ♠J. Getting those cards argues for passing the ♦4 and ♥5 because you can be pretty sure that your hearts can overtake any high card that your partner has in the suit.

TIP

When your partner bids blind nil, you should protect it, even at the potential cost of not making your contract. When you lead to the first trick, start with high cards from your long suits, which lets him discard on later rounds of the suit. Consider not overtaking your opponent's high cards, even if you think you may need the trick to make your bid, to make sure you're left with enough high cards to protect your partner. If you lead to the first trick on your own nil, consider starting with a middle card in a short suit — the odds are that your partner will be able to overtake.

See the section "Going for your scores" for the details on scoring successful and unsuccessful nil bids.

Playing to the score

The scorer writes down the bids after the auction ends. A single digit for the team's score is usually sufficient, unless a nil or a blind nil bid has been made, in which case the scorer notes that element as well. When the bids hit the paper, the play starts.

TIP

Before you start, however, take time to consider whether the combined total bids by both sides mean that the players will be trying to create extra tricks or lose them. If the total is 10 or less, both sides will be trying to lose tricks, where possible, to avoid overtricks, or bags. Consider overtaking your partner's winners or even trumping them if you feel confident you can make your bid even after combining your honors in this way. By doing so, you avoid potentially costly overtricks later on. If the total is 13 or more, the likelihood is that both sides will be risking getting set, so make sure you get the most out of your cards. Don't interfere with your partner's tricks and try to win them twice! With the bid in the middle at 11 or 12, play normally, but try to preserve low cards and use up your middle cards for maximum flexibility. That way you can go high or low as the case demands.

Leading and play conventions

The play of the cards goes clockwise, starting with the player to the dealer's left. He puts a card face-up in the middle of the table, and then all other players contribute a card in turn.

If you have no cards in the suit led, you can play anything you like; if you play a spade on the lead of a heart, diamond, or club, you win the trick because spades are the master (or *trump*) suit. Even the smallest spade is higher than the ace in any other suit. The person who plays the highest card in the led suit or the highest spade collects up the four cards played and wins the trick.

REMEMBER

At every trick, the player who won the previous trick can lead anything she likes — with the exception of spades. You can't lead spades at any point in the game until the suit is *broken*. The *breaking spades* rule means that the suit is off-limits until someone trumps the lead of a side-suit or until a player on lead is down to only spades in his hand. After trump is broken, you may lead spades at any time.

Some play that the opening lead has significant restrictions; in fact, the play has no flexibility at all: Everyone must play his or her lowest club. If you can't follow suit, you must discard a heart or a diamond — no trumping allowed. Some authorities allow a player to trump the first trick if she has no clubs. Yet another variation is that if the ♣2 is led, all players can then play any clubs they want, not just their lowest clubs.

Most variations require you to put in some mental-homework time before you can make a successful lead.

Opening with the other players in mind

Some of the conventions more commonly used in Bridge (see Book V) can also be used in Spades. To start with, when leading with an ace-king, lead the king rather than the ace to let your partner know you have that sequence (because your partner knows that you know an opponent would surely have taken the trick). If you follow on your partner's lead of a side-suit with a high card and then a low card, you're suggesting that you have only two cards in the suit. Conversely, playing low and then high suggests you have three or more cards.

As a general rule, early on in the play when the opponent on your right leads a suit in which you have a king, queen, or jack, together with some small cards, but no touching honor, don't put up that court card. Save it for later. Conversely, when you're in the third seat on your partner's lead, you should generally try to win the trick by putting up a high card.

TIP

When your partner shows out of a suit by trumping it, try to lead to your partner to let him do it again — unless your partner led out trumps earlier in the hand, a sure sign he didn't want you to lead a suit to force him to trump. Conversely, when your opponents start ruffing in, you should consider leading trumps — or at least not leading that suit again.

Along with your partner, you have to always keep your opponents in mind when leading. When the total of the two side's bids is 10 or less, don't allow your opponents to win easy tricks at the start. Aggressive play at the start of the hand causes your opponents to worry about making their bid, which may cause them to wind up with the overtricks themselves. In practice, weak players worry far more about bags than strong players. It may be more rewarding to look for the set, and to not worry about taking an extra bag or two, if you have any possibility of setting your opponents. Lead an ace from a long suit as soon in the play as you can. This prevents anyone discarding from the suit and trumping your ace.

Leading trump

After leading trump becomes legal, you often have a tough decision as to whether to play spades or not. Bear in mind that a long spade suit's value doesn't solely come from using a trump to capture an opponent's high card. It comes primarily from the ability to take out or "draw" the opponents' trumps and stop them from scoring trump tricks.

Consider leading trump when you have a long spade suit, unless the lead itself is dangerous (from a holding such as ace-queen or king-jack) and your partner has bid very low. By contrast, when your partner bids high, lead trump when you can.

When you know your partner has long spades, don't weaken his trumps by forcing him to trump in on a losing card of yours.

Going for your scores

Those of you familiar with Bridge (see Book V) may think the scoring for Spades follows a predictable path — but beware the sting in the tail that comes from getting set, or from underbidding, and racking up the overtricks!

Dealing with undertricks

If you fall short in your bid, no matter by how many tricks, you lose ten times the value of your bid. For example, if you bid 10 and fail, you lose 100 points.

A less popular version of the scoring treats the overbidding penalty as 10 points for every trick that you overbid. So calling 10 and making 8 tricks costs you 20 points, not 100.

Scoring nil bids

If you bid nil and make it, you score 50 points, but bidding nil and failing costs you 50 points. (See the earlier section "Bidding for nil" for the details.) Bidding blind nil gains you or costs you 100 points, depending on whether you succeed. Win or lose on a nil bid, these points do not affect your partner's bid, which is scored in the normal fashion.

If you fail in a bid of nil, the rules vary as to what happens to your tricks. Some versions play that your tricks count toward helping your partner make his bid; other variations say that you ignore your tricks for that purpose. The more standard position is to allow your tricks to count toward your partner's target.

Getting sandbagged with overtricks

If you bid and make your contract, either exactly or with *overtricks* (tricks over your bid), you multiply your bid by 10 and score that total. Any overtricks you accrue count 1 point each. For example, bidding seven and collecting nine tricks scores 72 points — not all that much different, you may think, from bidding eight and scoring nine tricks for 81 points or actually hitting the nail on the head with a bid of nine for 90 points.

You may see little reason to be cautious in the bidding — because a slight under-bid hardly seems to matter — but that's before you experience the true joy of overtricks.

Here's a shock for your system: When you accumulate 10 overtricks, you automatically get 100 points deducted from your total, and the clock starts again. In the standard version of the scoring, the 10 overtrick points you gathered during the course of play are also canceled out, although some versions allow you to rack up your 10 as you lose 100. But the mainstream approach dictates that if you're at 458 points, for example, and you bid five tricks and make seven after racking up eight overtricks, your score becomes 400, not 410 (458 + 52 − 100 − the 10-point overtrick deduction = 400).

You can also play without the overtrick rule altogether, or you can just take off 1 point for each overtrick, but that approach defeats the main purpose of the game, in our opinion. You can achieve the same negative values for overtricks by counting each of them as −10. This accounting method simply gives you an immediate deduction for the sandbags rather than a delayed impact. (*Bags on* or *bags off* is the "in" way of referring to whether the overtrick rule applies.)

Time for some strategy. You can consider overtaking your partner's trick or even trumping it if you seem to be making your contract with ease. This may well be a sensible strategy to reduce your side's trick-taking potential, particularly when the combined number of tricks contracted for by both sides is less than 10.

If you know you can defeat, or *set*, your opponents, don't make it too obvious too soon! Otherwise, both opponents will sacrifice tricks to give you bags. Take this hypothetical situation for an example: If your opponents bid eight and you bid five, your opponents are far better off taking four tricks — giving you nine and thus four bags (which could be deemed to have a real value of −40) — than they are taking six tricks. Getting set, no matter by how many tricks, still loses them the same 80 points while you collect your 50, but it only costs you two bags, and thus a notional 20 points.

TIP

When either your team or the other team is sitting at eight or nine bags, go for the set; if you know you're to lose that 100 points, you may as well get a set out of it if you can. (Remember that if your opponents bid five and get set, it costs them 100 points, in a sense, because they lose 50 instead of gaining that number.) If your opponents are getting close to losing 100, they're more likely to overbid their hands and are more likely to overtake their winners. In turn, this makes them perfect targets for a set.

Some people play that you get an additional bonus for making your contract exactly by winning the last trick with a high trump card (a spade higher than the 9). In fact, if you win the last two or three tricks with high trump cards, you get a bonus of 20 or 30 points. This situation happens surprisingly often because the prohibition on playing spades before they're broken often results in the high spades remaining until the end of the game.

Scoring revokes

WARNING

The failure to follow suit (or the failure to follow with your lowest club on the first trick if playing that variation) is a serious crime. Such *revoking* or *reneging* carries varying consequences. One rather kind possibility is to award the non-offending side a 15-point bonus and abandon the hand. This approach is too lax, in our opinion. The more severe penalty is that the offenders are deemed to have failed in their contract(s), and the other side scores their contract. This may be generous to the innocent parties, but it does help to remind the guilty players of the gravity of their offense.

Finishing the game

You play until someone wins the *rubber*. Each rubber is made up of several hands, on which either side can record a positive or negative score. Usually, the first side to get to 500 points wins the rubber. If both sides go past the winning post of 500 points on the same hand, the higher score wins. You can also play the game to 250 or even to 300 or 400 points. Make sure you agree in advance!

Digging Spades for Fewer Than Four

Spades is primarily a four-person game, but what happens if you have less than a full quorum? Fortunately, you have a couple of variants that allow you to have an entertaining contest with either two or three players.

Spades for two

In Spades for two players, instead of dealing out the cards, you place the deck between both players, and you take turns drawing cards.

When you draw the top card, you decide whether you want to keep it. If you keep it, you draw the next card, look at it, and discard it face-down. If you don't keep it, you discard it face-down and then draw the next card, which you must put in your hand.

The other player repeats the process until you exhaust the stock of cards. You each have a hand of 13 cards, and you've looked at and discarded 13 cards each. Now, each player bids an appropriate number of tricks, and you play and score according to the same rules as for four players (refer to the beginning of this chapter).

Spades for three

When playing with three players, you have no partnerships; each player plays for himself. You use one standard 52-card deck, and you deal 17 cards to each player. Toss the remaining card out of play for that particular game (face-down, of course).

You can play with a 54-card deck, including big and little jokers as the top two trumps (see the section "Grasping the Basics of Spades" for joker explanation). In that case, you deal 18 cards to each player.

Unlike the two-player version, playing with three requires some rule changes.

Differences in betting

Each player, starting with the player to the dealer's left, names a number (called a *bet*). Each player's object is to win that number of tricks. Some people play that the total of the three bets can't be 17 tricks so not everyone can make his or her bets exactly.

Differences in play

The player who has the ♣2 must lead it to the first trick. In the rare occasion that the ♣2 is out of play, the player with the ♣3 must lead it.

As in the regular game, you can't lead spades until someone breaks trump by playing a spade on an off-suit. The exception is when a player has nothing left but spades.

Differences in scoring

Scoring is similar to the four-player game. You play to a set number, usually 300, 400, 500, or some other round number. When multiple players pass that number at the same time, the player with the highest score wins.

In the three-person game, you score the overtricks as −10 each rather than waiting to get to 10 overtricks and penalizing 100 points.

Check out these scoring variations: If you take the very last trick with a high spade (9 or above), and with that trick you make *exactly* what you bet, you gain a 10-point bonus. If you win an unbroken sequence of tricks at the end (2, 3, 4, or more tricks), all with high spades (9 or above), and you get exactly what you bet, you get a bonus of 10 points per trick (for example, if you take the last five tricks with high spades to make your bet, the bonus would be 50 points).

For successful bids of seven or more, you get an extra 10 points for each trick bid above six. For example, if you make a seven-trick bid exactly, you gain 80 points. Eight tricks exactly gains you 100 points, 9 gains you 120 points, and so on. This rewards the more daring players.

Making a bet of exactly two, one, or zero is very difficult, and is therefore rewarded as follows: Anyone who bets two and gets two wins 40 points (instead of 20). If you get three, you still get 20 points (one bag penalty). Four tricks gets you nothing, and every additional bag is −10 each (per usual). Anyone who bets one and gets exactly one wins 60 points. If you get two, you get nothing, and each additional bag counts −10 each. Anyone who bets zero and gets it gains 100 points. Otherwise, you subtract 10 for every trick taken (just like regular bags).

You may decide to not look at your cards and bet blind. This doubles your score on the hand — be it good or bad! Only attempt this if you're significantly behind in the game (although no score restrictions stop you from doing it at any time). The best time to bet blind is when you're the dealer, and thus third to speak, at which point you may have an idea of what the other players believe they can get. But it is an even bigger gamble than in the four player game — you have two enemies and no friends, and no exchange of cards to improve the odds for you.

Chapter 8

Handling a Heaping Helping of Hearts

Hearts is a game of skill — to a certain extent. You're under the sway of whether you receive helpful or unhelpful cards, but good card sense and a good memory make an enormous difference in this game. Keeping track of the cards played in each suit helps you to master this game, and practice and experience have no substitute.

To play Hearts, you need the following:

>> **Three or more players:** Four are ideal, but you can play sensibly with any number up to seven.

>> **A standard deck of 52 cards:** No jokers or wild cards come in to play.

>> **A pencil and paper for scoring:** Make a column for each player.

Getting to the Heart of the Matter

Hearts is a cutthroat game, meaning that you normally don't play in partnerships, no matter the number of players involved. The game we discuss here focuses on the four-player game, where all the cards are distributed evenly, 13 to a player. Later in the chapter, we discuss how to cope with fewer, or more, players.

The game revolves around *tricks*. In a trick, everyone takes turns playing one card. Whoever plays the highest card in the suit led (the suit of the first card played) picks up all the cards played. The person who wins the trick leads a card to the next trick (he can lead anything he likes — with one exception, which we discuss in a moment), and the process repeats itself until all the cards have hit the table.

Unlike most competitive games, the object of Hearts is to avoid scoring points. More specifically, the aim is not to win tricks that contain certain cards that score you points.

The name of the game holds the clue: The problem suit in this game is hearts. However, the ♠Q has a particularly unpleasant role in the game, too. Whoever wins a trick that includes one of the 14 *danger cards* picks up a penalty in the process; I discuss the scoring details in the section "Scoring: The time of reckoning" later in this chapter, but bear in mind that the ♠Q is as bad as all the hearts put together.

You play Hearts to a set score, and the winner of the game is the player who has the lowest score when another player goes over the top. Alternatively, you can play a set number of hands and stop the game at that point with the lowest score winning.

Dealing the cards

At the start of the game, you cut for seating rather than just for the deal because the seating positions matter in Hearts. Arrange the seating from the highest card to the lowest, with the player who cut the lowest card dealing the first hand. You stay in the same seats for the whole game. The dealer shuffles and passes the cards to the opponent on his right to cut.

Deal all the cards out in the traditional fashion — one card at a time, face-down, and clockwise. At the end of every hand, the deal passes to the left to the next player.

WARNING

Misdeals can arise in a number of ways. If a card appears face-up in the deck, the dealer gives out the wrong number of cards, or the dealer turns over anyone else's cards, the hand is immediately redealt with no penalties. If the dealer manages to turn over one of her own cards, the deal stands, with the only consequence being that the other players have a little extra information about her hand.

If no player spots that some players have the wrong number of cards before play begins, the deal stands, but the penalties are very severe. Play continues until the last possible valid trick, when the players with the wrong number of cards pick up the penalties for the unplayed heart cards as if they had won the tricks with those cards in them.

Passing your cards left, right, and center

After you pick up and sort your cards, you get to pass three of your cards to another opponent. The passing stage of the game gives you a chance to get rid of some cards that you think may score points or to get rid of a particular suit, thereby strengthening your chances of dumping high-scoring cards on someone else, or of discarding danger cards in another suit at the appropriate moment.

Passing methods

Getting rid of your bad cards involves a cycle of four passes:

>> **1st hand:** You pass three cards to the opponent on your left.

>> **2nd hand:** You pass three cards to the opponent on your right.

>> **3rd hand:** You pass three cards to the opponent across the table.

>> **4th hand:** You retain your hand without a pass.

To pass your cards properly, select your three cards, put them face-down in front of you, and then pass those cards before looking at the cards that you're about to pick up.

Two common additions to the cycle of passing on cards (making it a cycle of six deals rather than of four) are to pass one card to everybody — the *scatter* — and for each player to put three cards into the middle of the table, shuffle the cards, and then redistribute them at random — the *smoosh*. With the scatter, each player puts three cards face-down and passes on the cards without looking at what cards they receive. With the smoosh, all 12 discards are mixed together before redistribution.

Another alternative rule allows you to pass along the cards that you receive to the next player, as long as you don't look at the cards first. This procedure can result in getting back the cards you passed on, particularly if you switch with the player opposite you.

Passing strategies

TIP

When passing on cards, think carefully about the nature of your hand before making your move. You may assume that because hearts and the ♠Q score the points (and, by extension, the ♠K and ♠A, because they're likely candidates to capture the ♠Q), these cards are the hot potatoes that you want to pass on immediately; but this assumption isn't necessarily so.

On some occasions you want to pass your hearts and your top spades, of course; for example, if you're short in either suit, you want to unload the high spades (♠A, ♠K, or ♠Q) and your top hearts. However, if you have plenty of spades — say, at least five in the four-player game or four spades other than the queen — you can safely hold on to your high spades. If you do pass on the ♠Q, remember to whom you passed it. Doing so sometimes allows you to unload the ace or king of spades safely when a spade is led.

Similarly, if you have a series of low hearts, you don't need to pass any of them on. Instead, throw away all the cards in a side-suit so you can play whatever you like when another player leads the suit — however unpleasant it may be for your opponents. (You call the act of dumping an unwelcome present on an opponent *painting* a trick.)

REMEMBER

By the third or fourth time diamonds or clubs are led, you're just as likely to collect the ♠Q or a bunch of hearts by winning a trick as you are from leading hearts or spades. A side-suit containing the J, 10, 9, 8, 7 is a strong candidate to fetch the ♠Q, whereas a suit such as A, Q, 10, 9, 6, 4, 2 presents virtually no danger at all. Why? The answer is the control of those nice low cards. You should do your best to ensure that after the pass you don't saddle yourself with a long minor suit holding, unless you have small cards to protect yourself from being dumped on. The high cards in the minor suits don't cause problems as much as the lack of low cards in a long suit. Any suit (other than spades) in which you can't duck a trick leaves you exposed to collecting the ♠Q, or the *Black Maria*, at a critical moment.

Even the 3 may be a danger card; in a five-card suit such as K, J, 9, 6, 3, don't be surprised to discover that on the third round of the suit someone leads the 2, and you get showered with hearts from the other two players.

For an example, look at the hand in Figure 8-1. The spades are dangerous, but the hearts are useful because you have so many of them. You should get rid of the ♠A, the ♠Q, and the ♣J in the pass. (If you are playing the variation that demands clubs be led to the first trick, being short of clubs can be good news.)

FIGURE 8-1:
Keeping your
hearts may
be the wisest
decision.

© John Wiley & Sons, Inc.

Alternatively, check out the hand in Figure 8-2. The spades look safe enough, but you may want to get rid of all your hearts. Or you may keep the hearts and throw the ♦A, ♦Q, and ♣10 to create suits in which you have no or few cards.

FIGURE 8-2:
Saving your
spades may
spell safety.

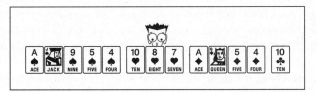

© John Wiley & Sons, Inc.

REMEMBER

Focus on what cards you get from your opponent. Doing so may help you guess what sort of hand she has by virtue of what she let go — and thus what her intentions are for the hand. You can usually infer what her possible danger suits are, too.

As soon as the cards have been appropriately passed, the play of the hand starts.

Starting the trick play

Whoever has the ♣2 leads it to start play. Having only a few clubs or even passing all your clubs before play begins may allow you to discard critical cards early in the game when a club is led. You're also not allowed to play any penalty cards on the first trick, which makes this a good moment to dump your ♣A!

REMEMBER

In Hearts, the cards rank in regular fashion, from ace to 2, with the ace being high. You must *follow suit* (play a card in the suit led) if you can, and if you can't, you can play whatever you want.

Each player throws in a card, and whoever plays the highest card in the suit led wins the trick. You stack the tricks you take in front of you to facilitate the scoring at the end of the hand, and you leave the penalty cards you unwillingly garner face-up in front of you (see the section "Scoring: The time of reckoning" later in this chapter).

After the opening lead, where a club lead may be compulsory in some variations of the game, you have only one other vital restriction — and this condition is much more restrictive. Unless the heart suit has been *broken* — that is, a player discards a heart on a trick — you can't lead a heart unless it's the only suit you have left in your hand.

Some play that the discard of the ♠Q allows you to lead hearts thereafter, and some versions of the game allow you to lead hearts at any time.

If you have the ♠Q, you may want to get rid of it as quickly as possible, or you may want to pass it on to the opponent who's winning the game, to the closest pursuer behind you, or even to someone whose attitude you don't like! Whichever approach you choose with respect to playing the ♠Q is fine. It is up to you what you do, unless you play that you have no choice, and must pass on the ♠Q as quickly as possible. This version of the rule makes sense if playing Hearts for money.

TIP

As a general rule, the right approach in Hearts is judicious self-preservation first, spite and malice next. Throw the dangerous cards in your hand away first before painting tricks that your opponents win. If you never score any points, you're pretty sure to win, so try for that goal first and wait to upset your opponents until you feel safe.

REMEMBER

We can't emphasize how important it is to try to remember, if not all the cards, the cards in the suits that matter to you because your hand suggests they may be dangerous. You may not have to remember the diamonds if you have only the Q, 8, and 3 (you can be fairly sure your 3 won't win the third round), but with the Q, 8, 5, and 4, you need to keep a count of the suit and note if the 3 and 2 have put in an appearance. Otherwise, the third and fourth round of the suit may be more painful than you expect!

We suggest you don't try to count the hearts — players normally leave them visible on the table in front of you within taken tricks. Focus on the spades and whichever of the diamonds or clubs look worrying to you. Start by counting the number of times the suit has been led (assuming each time that four cards were played, that is unless you have noted someone show out). Far trickier is remembering to add one to your count of the cards played in a suit every time a player discards in that specific suit. After you feel confident you can keep count of the suit, try to expand your record keeping to remembering which small cards are still missing.

Say you have the Q, 8, 5, and 4 of diamonds that we mention earlier in this section. If the ♦K is led, you throw your ♦Q, and the ♦J and ♦9 show up. On the next diamond trick, your ♦8 comes in under the ♦A, and the ♦10 puts in an appearance along with the ♦3. When you see the ♦7 discarded, you know that two rounds of diamonds represent eight cards in the suit. The discard of the ♦7 makes nine, and your two remaining diamonds make 11. Two diamonds still out — one being the ♦2, which you're watching for, the other being a higher one than your ♦5 (you don't actually care what card it is, although just for the record, it's the ♦6). The point: If one player has both diamonds, you might lose the next trick, but you would then be able to lead your last diamond and know the player with the diamonds will take the trick. Of course, it may be too late — someone may have passed you the ♠Q already! And note that the player with the ♦6 and ♦2 might win the first diamond trick with the 6 and lead back the 2, letting you win the second diamond trick not the first.

If the missing diamonds are split, you can lead a diamond now and leave yourself with a safe card in diamonds. Playing a diamond yourself, as soon as you can, may be a better strategy than letting someone else discard that ♦6.

TIP

Leave yourself with low cards in each suit for the later tricks — the third and even the second round of a suit. Doing so allows you to lose tricks late in the game when everyone wants to unload their hearts and the ♠Q. Avoid playing on your safe suits (the ones where you have 2s and 3s that won't win tricks) until the end of the hand, but be aware that your opponents want to do the same thing. For example, when you have the Q, 9, and 3 of diamonds, lead the queen and follow with the 9, keeping the 3 for the third (more dangerous) round — unless someone has already discarded a scoring card on one of the first two rounds.

TIP

When you receive three cards in a suit from the player on your right, avoid leading a high card in that suit yourself. You can be fairly sure that something nasty may happen to you — unless the player in question was unlucky enough to pick up some cards in this suit from the player to *his* right!

WARNING

Hearts may not have the complex rules that other games have, but it does have rules. Keep yourself out of trouble by following these guidelines:

>> Playing out of turn has no formal penalty. If you finish and turn over a trick in which someone led or played out of turn, the game simply continues, but a player who still has to play on a tainted trick can demand that the lead and all the other cards played to that trick be taken back.

>> Failure to follow suit is called a *revoke*. A player may correct a revoke at any point until the trick ends. After that point, if someone draws attention to a revoke, the player who didn't follow suit takes all the penalty points on that deal.

Scoring: The time of reckoning

At the end of the hand, each player collects all the cards in the taken tricks, and the arithmetic begins. The simple version of the game doesn't tax your math skills unduly. Each player gets 1 point per heart, for a total of 13 penalty points possible in each hand. However, not many people play that way anymore, and when the ♠Q is involved, Hearts becomes more expensive.

The ♠Q, which has many names (the Black Lady, Black Maria, Black Widow, Slippery Anne, or Calamity Jane, to name a few), costs you 13 points on her own. Not surprisingly, therefore, you need to gear your strategy of both passing and playing to avoid taking this card. For that reason, you may want to pass the ♠A and ♠K, and also the ♠Q, before play begins if you have only a few spades. Conversely, if you have length in spades (particularly with some of the low cards), spades don't propose a danger to you.

You play to 100 points when 26 points are at stake. At that point, whoever has the fewest points wins. Or if gambling for stakes, you can play that you settle up with everybody paying or receiving the differences in score.

WARNING

Passing on low spades before play starts is almost certainly a tactical blunder because you help a player guard the ♠Q.

TIP

Because the penalty associated with the ♠Q outweighs that of the individual heart cards, leading spades early (if you can afford to, and as long as you don't lead the ace or king) often ensures that someone else takes in this card — not you. By leading spades early, you hope to flush out the ♠Q, and with the ♠Q out of the way, you can't be too badly hurt on a hand, even if you do win a number of hearts. So long as you don't leave either the ♠A or ♠K insufficiently protected by small cards, leading spades early is usually safe.

You do have one challenging escape if you get a really terrible hand stuffed full of high cards. If you manage to take all the penalty cards and thus collect 26 points, you finish up doing remarkably well: You have the option of reducing your own score by 26 points or charging everyone else 26 points. This accomplishment is called *shooting the moon,* and just like becoming an astronaut, it's a great deal easier to do in theory than in practice. The right hand rarely comes along for it, and if your opponents see you trying to take all the tricks, they'll save a heart or two for the end to take a couple penalty points and prevent you from achieving your aim.

WARNING

Shooting the moon is more dangerous than it may seem; you usually lose more points in unsuccessful attempts to shoot the moon than you gain by making it. If you have a very good hand, you may choose to take an early trick with one or two points in it just to stop anyone else from trying to shoot the moon. Alternatively, you can give hearts to two different players to accomplish the same result with less discomfort to yourself.

Scoring variations in Hearts flourish as thickly as weeds on a lawn. Here, listed in descending order of frequency, are some of the most common additional scoring rules (you can play them simultaneously or not at all):

» Shooting the sun, as opposed to the moon, involves taking all the tricks as well as all the penalty points. You get a 52-point bonus for shooting the sun.

» Counting the ♦J — or, in some circles, the ♦10 — as a bonus card is quite common. Winning the trick with that card in it has real merit because it reduces your penalty points by 11 (or 10, in the case of the ♦10). If you have fewer penalty points than 10, you can even finish up being plus for the hand.

TIP

If you allow shooting the moon, you generally don't need to take the ♦J to shoot the moon, but some versions of the game require that you win this card, too.

Implementing the rule about the ♦J influences which cards you decide to pass on. You may want to keep the top diamonds in order to try for the prize. However, you may find capturing the ♦J is easier if you pass it on. In high-level games, you're unlikely to find players winning tricks in diamonds early on with this card. In practice, because players rarely get the chance to take an early diamond trick with this card, it tends to get discarded at the end of the hand.

» If you manage to score exactly 100 points, your score is immediately halved to 50 points. Some versions play that if you avoid scoring any points on the next hand, you further reduce your score to zero.

» The ♣10 can be a potentially lethal card if you play the rule, common in some circles, that the card doubles the value of the penalty points for whoever takes it. For example, capturing the ♣10 and three heart cards costs you 6 points, not 3.

» The ♥A may be charged at 5 points, not 1.

» Occasionally, the ♠Q carries a penalty of only 5 points, not 13.

» Anyone who avoids winning a trick in a hand may be credited with –5 points.

» In Spot Hearts, all the heart cards are charged at face value rather than at 1 point apiece. The ♥A ♥K, ♥Q, and ♥J are 15 (or according to some, 14), 13, 12, and 11 points, respectively, meaning that the deck contains 130 penalty points if the ♠Q counts for 25 points. Playing this game to a score of 500 or so is sensible.

Hearts with Three or Five-Plus Players

The rules of Hearts for three players or for more than five players differ from the four-handed rules because you can't divide the deck equally (refer to the section "Getting to the Heart of the Matter" for more information about playing with four people). But you can correct this problem by removing one or two surplus cards. For example, take out the ♣2 — clubs are traditionally the lowest suit — in the game for three players (which leaves 17 cards for each player), and remove the ♣2 and the ♦2 in the game for five players to even out the deck at 50 cards (at 10 cards apiece).

More interesting, however, is to start the deal with a full deck, giving an even number to each player. You leave the extra cards face-down on the table as a *kitty*. Whoever wins the first trick has to add the points in the kitty to his total at the end of the hand. The trick winner can look at the cards without showing anyone else until the end of the hand. This rule makes losing the first trick a very good idea!

A more generous alternative is to permit whoever wins the first trick to add the cards in the kitty to his hand and then discard an equivalent number of cards. Because this version can result in some significant cards playing no part in the hand, this rule seems unnecessarily generous to us.

The rule about forming a kitty has occasionally been extended to the four-player game — where it isn't strictly necessary. The idea is that you deal each player only 12 cards, with the remaining four cards forming the kitty.

The rules about passing cards change depending on the number of participants. The cycle of possible ways to pass and receive cards must expand with every additional player added into the game. You can add additional passes so you exchange cards once with each of the other players — whatever takes your fancy.

After the Wedding: Honeymoon Hearts

In Honeymoon Hearts, you play with two players, and each player gets 13 cards. You put the remaining stock of cards in a pile and turn the top card over. The nondealer leads a card, the dealer (who must follow suit if he can) plays a card in turn, the winner takes the face-up card, and the loser takes the top face-down card. You turn the new top card over, and the sequence continues for 13 rounds until you use the stock up.

At the end, when the stock is exhausted, both players play out their remaining cards and score them up as you do in a regular game of Hearts (refer to the section "Scoring: The time of reckoning" earlier in this chapter).

REMEMBER

Only the last 13 cards count for this game; the first 13 tricks are just an attempt to build up the hand.

TIP

Because the leader gets to dictate strategy, retaining the lead for the last few tricks is a good idea. That means getting rid of your middle cards early and retaining low cards for the last 13 tricks. Plan to lead with high cards for the last few tricks.

If the game appears to be going well, retain your penalty cards to try to dump them on your opponent. If it is going badly, do a damage-limitation exercise and get rid of your potentially expensive cards as soon as possible.

Chapter 9

Trying Some Children's Games

Just because this chapter refers to children, adults shouldn't skip it. The games in this chapter are suitable for a range of players — younger players, new players, adults playing with younger players, or players who just like fast-action card games that are easy to pick up and fun to play. So whoever you are, you're sure to find a game in this chapter to enjoy.

Outdoing Your Friends: Beggar My Neighbor

Beggar My Neighbor, also known as Beat Your Neighbor Out of Doors and Strip Jack Naked, requires no strategy or planning at all, making it a great game for kids and for social situations. The objective of the game is to win all the cards from the other players.

To play Beggar My Neighbor, you need the following:

>> **Two to six players:** You can play with more than six players in a pinch.

>> **A standard deck of 52 cards:** With four or more players, add a second deck of cards. A great advantage of this game is that you don't really need a complete deck of cards — a card or two gone missing is almost irrelevant. Don't forget to remove the jokers!

To begin, one player deals out the whole deck in a clockwise rotation, dealing the cards face-down and one at a time so each player gets about the same number of cards. You don't look at your cards; you form them into a neat pile, face-down in front of you.

The player to the left of the dealer turns over the top card from his pile and places it in the center of the table (or floor, if you want to sprawl out).

Different things can happen now, depending on what card the first player turns over:

>> If the value of the card is between 2 and 10, it has no special significance, and the play goes on to the next player.

>> If the card is a *court card* (an ace, king, queen, or jack), the game becomes a little more exciting. The next player has to pay a *forfeit,* meaning she has to turn over some of her cards and place them onto the central pile:

● If the first card up is an ace, the second player must turn over four cards one by one onto the middle pile.

● If the first card is a king, the next player has to pay three cards.

● If the first card is a queen, the second player must pay two cards.

● If the first card is a jack, the second player turns up only one card.

If all the cards the second player turns over are between 2 and 10, the first player who turned over the court card takes up the whole pile and puts it under his personal pile, face-down. If the second player turns over another court card during the course of the forfeit, she pays the debt off, and the second player doesn't have to turn over any more cards. Instead, the third player must pay the forfeit dictated by the second court card and either turn over a court card in the process, or allow the second player to pick up the whole central pile if no court card comes.

When you have no more cards left, you're out, and the game continues without you. If you run out of cards in the middle of paying a forfeit for an ace, king, or queen, you are out of the game. In games of more than two players, the previous player picks up the pile of cards, and the next player starts afresh. The last player in the game — the one who accumulates the whole deck — wins.

KIDS AND CARD GAMES

These days, most children seem to be born with a remote or video-game controller in their hands. However, some children are lucky enough to receive decks of cards when they're young.

Teaching children how to play cards is fun — both for them and for you! Children get an opportunity to interact with others, revel in the challenge of a game, and enjoy a sense of mastery. Card games also foster a strong sense of belonging and a connection to the family or social group.

In a more tangible sense, card games can enhance a child's skills. To play card games, children must master rules, develop mental strategies, understand objectives, evaluate their (and their opponents') strengths and weaknesses, and make plans. The games also force them to respond quickly and to deal socially with others.

Some studies suggest that card players develop better problem-solving and lateral-thinking skills (the ability to "think outside the box"). Developing competence in one field can improve a child's self-confidence to learn in other areas. Therefore, cards can increase a child's scores in math and critical thinking, as well as improve his social skills.

Finally, card games — like other cognitively engaging activities, including chess, back-gammon, and crossword puzzles — are cited as excellent activities for keeping the brain supple and engaged throughout life, potentially delaying the onset of Alzheimer's disease and other memory disabilities.

REMEMBER

Your success at Beggar My Neighbor depends on the luck of the draw; if you get a good smattering of court cards, you have a good chance to win. If someone feels bad because he lost, you may want to remind him of the luck factor. But don't forget to congratulate him if he wins!

TIP

Because Beggar My Neighbor can go on for a long time — making it ideal for long car journeys, waiting for planes, or similar situations — you can agree that the player with the most cards at a certain predefined time is the winner.

Snap, Animals, and Slapjack, Oh My

Snap, Animals, and Slapjack are close cousins in the family of games that focus on acquiring your opponents' cards (such as Beggar My Neighbor; see the previous section). For these games, speed is the key to victory. The player with the quickest reactions wins. Snap, Animals, and Slapjack are among the few card games that depend almost entirely on physical dexterity.

Snap

Get ready for a fast and furious game! Snap is all about mental reaction time, and one of the few games in which luck plays no part at all.

To play Snap, you need the following:

>> **Two or more players.** There is no formal upper limit, but if you play with more than six players, the neighbors may complain about the noise.

>> **A standard deck of 52 cards.** Play Snap with a single deck of cards if you have fewer than four players; add a second deck if more players compete. Playing this game with a used deck is a good idea — the cards can take a beating (literally).

You don't need a full deck of cards — a card or two can be missing from the deck. You can also play Snap with special cards designed for another game (such as an Old Maid deck), as long as most of the cards have backs identical to other cards in the deck.

The dealer deals out the whole deck of cards face-down, one card at a time to each player, in a clockwise rotation. It doesn't matter if some players get more cards than others. What does matter, however, is that you don't look at the cards you get.

Each player, starting with the player to the left of the dealer, takes a turn flipping over the top card of his pile and putting it face-up in front of him. After a few turns, each player has a little pile of face-up cards.

When you turn over all the cards into the pile in front of you, you pick up the pile and use it again without shuffling the cards.

The flipping process continues until one player turns over a card of the same rank as the top card on another player's pile. As soon as the matching card is revealed, the first person to call out "Snap!" takes the two piles with matching cards and puts them face down under his own pile.

Frequently, two players make the Snap call simultaneously. In this case, you put the two piles with the same card together, face-up, in middle of the table. Everyone continues to turn over the top cards on their piles until someone turns over a card that matches the card on the pile in the middle of the table. The first person to shout "Snap pool!" wins the middle pile. The new piles that are being created are still up for grabs in the usual way, of course. Whenever a pairing is created, the first to shout "Snap" wins them.

WARNING

When a player mistakenly calls out "Snap!" her pile goes into the center of the table; the first player to call "Snap pool!" at the relevant moment gets her pile. You have to operate with what you have left, and if you run out of cards, you're out of the game.

The player who ends up with all the cards wins the game.

For some reason, Snap brings out the worst competitive instincts in people. Establishing several informal rules can avoid Snap-induced bloodshed:

>> **Set rules about the proper way to turn over your card.** You can't turn over the card so you see it first, which means you must flip over the card in a continuous, fast motion onto your pile.

>> **Get an impartial witness to decide on all close calls.** If you can, choose someone who isn't playing the game, preferably an authority figure such as an adult.

TIP

A cunning player remembers the order of her pile (or of another player's pile) when the pile gets small, so she gains a big edge in the calling. Keep an eye on the cards as the game draws to a close; if you don't, you put yourself at a disadvantage. If you want to avoid this situation, you can agree to shuffle your pile when you've worked your way through it.

A variation on Snap, Speed Snap, provides a challenge, which makes it better for older players. All players turn over their cards at the same moment so the reaction process speeds up. To make sure all the players turn over their cards simultaneously, the umpire (or one of the players) must say "One, two, three!" with all players turning over the cards on three.

Animals

Animals is a much louder version of Snap. To understand the basics of Animals, see the preceding section, "Snap." The major difference between Snap and Animals is the way you call out for the cards.

Make sure you have the following items to play Animals:

>> **Two or more players**

>> **A standard deck of 52 cards**

>> **Pencils and scraps of paper**

At the start of the game, each player selects an animal, preferably one with a long and complicated name, such as *duck-billed platypus* or *Tyrannosaurus Rex*. Each player writes the name on a piece of paper and puts it in the middle of the table.

You shuffle the papers around, and every player takes one and then announces the name of the animal. Play can then begin.

When two players turn up matching cards, those players are the only ones who can win the cards. They must each try to call out the other person's animal name first, and whoever succeeds wins both piles.

If you call out a name at the wrong moment, you concede all your played cards to the player with the animal you call out. Making the wrong call or naming the wrong animal at the appropriate moment costs you nothing but loss because the other player is likely to beat you to the punch.

Slapjack

Slapjack involves physical agility rather than verbal dexterity and memory, so make sure the players involved are active and eager. Young children can play this game if they can tell the difference between a jack and a king or queen.

Assemble the following items to play Slapjack:

>> **Two or more players.** A maximum of six is probably sensible or too many collisions may result at home plate.

>> **A standard deck of 52 cards:** Slapjack can totally wreck a deck of cards, so don't break out the collector cards you bought in Las Vegas.

The dealer deals out the entire deck, face-down and one card at a time, to each player in a clockwise rotation. At the end of the deal, each player should have a neat stack of cards in front of him. Make sure you don't look at your cards.

Beginning on the dealer's left, each player takes a turn playing a card face-up onto a single stack in the center of the table.

Play continues peacefully until someone plays a jack. Whoever slaps the jack first wins all the cards in the middle of the table and adds them to the bottom of the pile in front of her. The player to the slapper's left starts the next pile by placing a card face-up in the center of the table.

Spirits run high in Slapjack, so you may need to define some rules before the game starts:

» You turn over a card by turning it away from you so you can't peek at it in advance. (This puts the turner at a slight disadvantage, but the luck evens out things eventually.)

» Rest your slapping hand on the table. Make the player who puts out the card slap with her other hand, which must also rest on the table.

» When you can't decide who slapped first, the hand closest to the jack always wins the day.

WARNING

If you slap the wrong card, you must give a card from your face-down pile to the person who played the card you slapped.

After all your cards are gone, you aren't automatically out of the game; you stay in for one more chance, lying in ambush and waiting to slap the next jack that gets turned over. At that point, if you fail to slap the jack, you're out. The first player to get all the cards wins.

Declaring War

War is a great game for young children. The object is to acquire all the cards, which you can do in different ways.

To play War, you need the following:

» **Two players**

» **A standard deck of 52 cards**

Start by dealing out the deck one card at a time, face-down, so each player gets 26 cards. Keep your cards in a pile and don't look at them. Each player turns over one card simultaneously; whoever turns over the highest card picks up the two cards and puts them face-down at the bottom of his pile.

The cards have the normal rank from highest to lowest: ace, king, queen, jack, and then 10 through 2 (see Book 1, Chapter 1 for card-playing basics).

The game continues in this manner until both players turn over a card of the same rank, at which point you enter a *war*. A war can progress in one of three ways. We start with the most benevolent version and work up to the most brutal:

» Each player puts a card face-down on top of the tied card and then one face-up. Whoever has the higher face-up card takes all six cards.

» Each player puts three face-down cards on the table and one face-up card, so the competition is for ten cards. This option speeds up the game, which often drags a little — especially for children!

» Each player puts down cards depending on the rank of the tied cards. If the equal cards are 7s, you each count off seven face-down cards before turning a card over. If the equal cards are kings, queens, or jacks, you turn down ten cards before flipping one up and squaring off. For an ace, count out 11 face-down cards.

» If another tie results, repeat the process until someone achieves a decisive victory.

If a player runs out of cards in the middle of a war, you have two possible solutions: You lose the war and are out of the game, or you turn your last card face up, and these count as your played card in the war.

Whoever wins the cards gathers them up and puts them at the bottom of her pile. The first person to get all the other player's cards wins.

You can play War with three players. The dealer gives out 17 cards to each player, face-down. The remaining card goes to the winner of the first war. The players simultaneously flip over one card each. The highest card of the three takes all three cards. If two players tie for the high card, they each place three cards face-down and then place one face-up, and the highest card collects all the cards in the pile. If you have another draw at this point, you fight another war. If all three players turn over the same card, a double war takes place; each player turns down six cards and flips one up, and the winner takes all.

Playing Fish and Friends

The Fish family features Go Fish and Authors. Both games have the same aim: Each player tries to make as many complete *sets* of four of a kind as possible.

Go Fish

Get out yer fishin' pole and head to the waterin' hole — you're about to go fishin' fer sets (four cards of the same kind).

To play Go Fish, you need the following:

>> **At least three players**

>> **A standard deck of 52 cards**

Each player gets ten cards from the dealer. You pretend as you deal out the full deck that you have one more player than you really do. With four players, for example, you deal out ten cards (one by one, face-down, in a clockwise rotation) in five piles. Add the two leftover cards to the pretend pile and leave those 12 cards as the *stock* in the middle of the table. With three players, you have three hands of 13 cards and a stock of the remaining 13.

Everyone picks up the cards they've been dealt. Starting with the player to the left of the dealer, each player asks any other player at the table a question. This must be in the form of "Do you have any *Xs*?" (X is the rank of card; 4s or queens, for example.) The player asking the question must have at least one X to pose the question.

If the person asked has an X or two, she must hand them over, and the questioner's turn continues. The questioner can then ask the same player or any other player if he has a card in a particular set. As soon as the questioner completes a set of four cards, she puts the set down on the table in front of her and continues her turn.

If the person asked has no cards of the rank specified in the question, he replies "Go Fish," and the questioner takes a card from the stock. The questioner's go ends, whether she picks up the card she was looking for or not. If the card that she draws from the stock completes a set, she must wait until her next turn to put the set down on the table. The turn passes to the player who sends his rival fishing.

Some play a variation that if the card you draw from the stock completes any set in your hand, or if you pick up the card you were unsuccessfully asking for, your turn continues.

At the end of the game — which almost always occurs when all the cards are in everybody's hands and the stock has been used up — you count the sets. The player who collects the most sets wins. However, if one player puts all her cards into sets before the stock gets used up, she wins.

Authors

Authors resembles Go Fish in many ways, with a few interesting exceptions that make it a far more subtle game.

TIP

At one time, people played Authors with special decks of cards bearing the pictures of famous authors. These decks are coming back into fashion; try www.thehouseofcards.com/kids/authors.html.

The big difference between Authors and Go Fish is that the questions you ask other players must relate to specific cards rather than to a type of card. For example, you ask, "Do you have the ♠7?" instead of asking for 7s in general.

The other rules on asking questions are also quite specific:

>> You can't ask for a card if you already have that card in your hand.

>> You can't ask for a card unless you have at least one card of that set in your hand.

TIP

If you have two cards of a set in your hand, hearing someone else ask for a third card in the set may pinpoint who has the cards you need. If player A successfully asks player B for the ♦Q, for example, he now has two queens, so you can collect them from him at your next turn if you get the chance.

An unsuccessful question means that the turn passes to the left rather than to the player who was unable to provide a card. Just as in Go Fish, when you complete a set, you place it on the table.

WARNING

If you ask for a card when you have nothing in that set, if you fail to provide a card when you're asked for it, or if you fail to put down a set as soon as you can, you must give one set to the player to your left — a pretty severe charge!

When you run out of cards — because other players picked your hand clean or because you've made your hand into sets — you're out, and the game continues without you until all the sets have been completed and no one has any cards left. Whoever has the most sets at the end wins.

When Lying Is Okay: Cheat

Children love Cheat (which is also called I Doubt It) because it gives them the opportunity to develop their deceptive powers in a way that their parents approve of. Most children master the art of lying convincingly and looking guilty when telling the truth very early on.

You need the following to play Cheat:

>> **Three or more players:** You can play with up to 12.

>> **A standard deck of 52 cards:** You normally play Cheat with a single deck of cards for up to five players. With 6 to 12 players, use two decks.

The object of Cheat is to get rid of all your cards as quickly as possible. To do that, you play your cards face-down, announcing what you put down — but you don't have to tell the truth.

The dealer deals out all the cards one at a time, face-down and clockwise, and the players pick up and look at their cards. The player to the left of the dealer is first to play.

The first player puts down cards onto a central pile on the table, squaring the cards up so other players can't see precisely how many cards he put down. He then makes an announcement about his play, along the lines of "three 6s." The first player must start with aces.

The player's statement about what he has played can be false in more than one way. He may put down more or fewer cards than he claims, or he may put down cards unrelated to what he claims. The players who follow put their cards on top of his.

To make a challenge (anyone can do so), someone calls out "Cheat," and the player accused has two options:

>> He can concede (gracefully or otherwise) by picking up the entire pile.

>> He can turn over the cards he just put down to demonstrate that he was telling the truth, in which case the challenger must pick up the whole pile.

The player who picks up the pile from the center gets to start the next round with whatever number he wants.

REMEMBER

If you have a dispute over who called out "Cheat" first, the player nearest to the left of the accused has priority.

If no one has called "Cheat," then the next player has to pick up from the last set put down. He has three choices as to what to play:

>> **He can claim to be playing the same rank as the previous player:** If the first player claims to lay three 6s, the next player can take this choice by putting down a number of 6s.

>> **He can claim to be playing cards of one rank higher:** If the first claims to put down 6s, "cards of one rank higher" means as many 7s as he wants.

>> **He can claim to be playing cards of one rank lower than the previous move:** If the first player claims 6s, any number of 5s works for the next player.

The second player can't pass. He puts his cards face-down on the table, on top of the previous play. Of course, he may be lying!

The next player has exactly the same set of options (play the same rank as the previous player or one higher or one lower), and play continues until someone makes a challenge.

The winner of the game is the person who succeeds in playing all his cards first. A player can go out by withstanding a challenge on his final turn or by going unchallenged before the next player makes a play. In practice, someone always challenges a player going out, but if you can conceal that you have no cards left on your last play (not easy to do!), you may avoid a challenge.

Steering Clear of the Old Maid

Old Maid allows you to keep card strategy and psychology simple, making it an ideal game for younger children.

All you need to play Old Maid is the following:

>> **At least three players:** There is no real upper limit, if you have enough decks of cards.

>> **One or more standard decks of 52 cards, with three queens removed:** Use a single deck of cards for up to six players. For seven or more players, use two decks, but take care that the decks have the same markings. You can play the game with special commercial decks, too, with animal faces on the cards and just one Donkey in the deck. You can also play with a special Old Maid deck, with one ugly Old Maid card.

The object of Old Maid is to get rid of all the cards in your hand without being left with the one unmatched card, the solitary queen, or *Old Maid*.

The dealer deals out all the cards, one by one and face-down in a clockwise rotation. You start by removing every pair of cards that you have (a pair can be two 5s or two kings, for example). You set these cards aside face-up on the table so everyone can see how many pairs you have.

Take care not to remove any three of a kind — only remove pairs from your hand.

After the removal of pairs, the player to the left of the dealer fans out her cards face-down on the table, and the player to her left takes one card. The player who's offered the cards must take one of them, and then he looks at it to see whether it forms a pair with another card in his hand. If it does, he discards the pair onto the tabletop.

Whether the card he draws forms a pair or not, the second player spreads his cards face-down and offers his hand to the player on his left, who must then choose a card.

The game continues with players dropping out as they get rid of all their cards. Eventually, one player gets left with the lone queen, and other players torment him with taunts of "Old Maid!" until a new hand starts.

TIP

You can use a certain element of psychology or reverse psychology to persuade people to take the lone queen away from you. If you arrange your cards with some paired up and more prominently positioned than others, the next player may think that you want to pass off the prominent cards. Make sure the prominent cards are "safe" ones, so you increase the chance that the player takes one of the other cards — perhaps the queen.

2

The Lowdown on Poker

Contents at a Glance

Chapter 1

Warming Up with Poker Basics

Poker is America's national card game, and its popularity continues to grow. From Mississippi and Michigan to New Mexico and North Dakota, you can find a game in progress everywhere. If you want to play, you can find Poker played on replicas of 19th-century paddle wheel riverboat or on Native American tribal lands. You can play Poker in two-table, no-frills cardrooms and elegant Los Angeles County megaclubs where 150 games (with betting limits ranging from $1–$2 to $200–$400) are in progress 'round the clock.

Poker looks like such a simple game. Anyone, it seems, can play it well — though nothing, of course, is further from the truth. Figuring out the rules can be quick work, but becoming a winning player takes considerably longer. Still, anyone willing to make the effort can become a fairly good player. You can succeed in Poker the way you succeed in life: by facing it squarely, getting up earlier than the next person, and working harder and smarter than the competition.

Book 2 targets readers who are new to Poker. If you've played in home games but have never played in a casino, this book can help you too. Even if you consider yourself to have a pretty good hand at the game, this book is bound to improve it.

Establishing the Groundwork: Before You Put on Your Poker Face

Like a house, Poker requires a foundation. Only when that foundation is solidly in place can you proceed to build on it. When all the structural elements are in place, you can then add flourishes and decorative touches. But you can't begin embellishing it until the foundation has been poured, the building framed, and all the other elements that come before it are in place. That's our purpose here: to put first things first — to give you a basic understanding of what you need before you begin to play.

Planning and discipline

Some Poker players, and it's no more than a handful, really do have a genius for the game — an inexplicable, Picasso-like talent that isn't easily defined and usually has to be seen to be believed. But even in the absence of genius — and most winning players certainly are not Poker savants — Poker is an eminently learnable skill. Inherent ability helps, and while you need some talent, you really don't need all that much. After all, you don't have to be Van Cliburn to play the piano, Picasso to paint, or LeBron James to play basketball. What you do need to become a winning player are a solid plan to learn the game and discipline.

>> **Plotting a strategy:** If you aspire to play winning Poker, you need a plan to learn the game. While the school of hard knocks might have sufficed as the educational institution of choice 20 or 30 years ago, most of today's better Poker players have added a solid grounding in Poker theory to their over-the-table experiences.

>> **Discipline:** All the strategic knowledge in the world doesn't guarantee success to any Poker player. Personal characteristics are equally important. Success demands a certain quality of character in addition to strategic know-how. Players lacking self-discipline, for example, have a hard time ever winning consistently regardless of how strategically sophisticated they might be. If one lacks the discipline to throw away poor starting hands, then all the knowledge in the world can't overcome this flaw.

Knowledge without discipline is merely unrealized potential. Playing with discipline is a key to avoiding losing your shirt.

REMEMBER

If you can figure out how to play Poker at a level akin to that of a journeyman musician, a work-a-day commercial artist, you'll be good enough to win consistently. You don't have to be a world champion like Doyle Brunson, Phil Hellmuth,

Johnny Chan, or Tom McEvoy to earn money playing Poker. The skills of a good journeyman Poker player enable you to supplement your income. If you go on to become the very best Poker player you can be, that should be more than enough to ensure that you will be a lifelong winning player.

REMEMBER

Your challenge for as long as you aspire to win at Poker is this: Be willing to examine and analyze your character and game. If you do this, and have even a modicum of talent, you can become a winning Poker player.

The object of the game

The objective of Poker is to win money by capturing the pot, which contains bets made by various players during the hand. A player wagers a bet in hopes that he has the best hand, or to give the impression that he holds a strong hand and thus convince his opponents to *fold* (abandon) their hands. Because money saved is just as valuable as money won, knowing when to release a hand that appears to be beaten is just as important as knowing when to bet. In most Poker games, the top combination of five cards is the best hand.

Number of players

Any number of players, typically from two to ten, can play, depending on the game. Most casino games are set up with eight players for a seven-card game like Stud Poker or Razz, and nine or ten players for Texas Hold'em. (Refer to Book 3 for the lowdown on Texas Hold'em.)

The deck

Most forms of Poker involve a standard 52-card deck. For Draw Poker and Low-ball, a joker, or *bug,* is sometimes added to the deck. It's not a wild card per se, but can be used in Draw Poker as an additional ace, or to complete a straight or flush. In Lowball, the joker is used as the lowest card that doesn't pair your hand. For example, if you held 7-6-2-A-joker, it would be the same as if you held 7-6-3-2-A.

Poker chips

Whether you use pennies, pretzels, or peanuts to bet with at home, nothing beats the feel of real Poker chips. Originally made of clay, chips now come in a durable composite or plastic.

Chips are available in a wide range of colors and patterns. The designs and "edge spots" you see on casino chips vary because of security reasons, but the colors generally follow a set of traditional dollar values:

$1	White
$5	Red
$25	Green
$100	Black
$500	Purple or Lavender

If you want to add a dose of Vegas-style playing to your home game, then try using real chips. Following is a list of the number of chips you'll need:

3 to 4 players	300 chips
5 to 6 players	400 chips
7 to 8 players	500 chips
Large games or multiple games	1,000 chips

Understanding the Basics of Play

Poker is a simple game to learn, although one can spend a lifetime trying to master it. You win money by winning pots — the money or chips wagered during the play of each hand (or round) of Poker, from the first cards dealt until the showdown. A hand also refers to five cards in the possession of a player.

You win hands in one of two ways:

» You *show down* (reveal) the best hand at the conclusion of all the betting rounds. When two or more players are still active when all the betting rounds are done, they turn their hands face up. The pot goes to the player who holds the highest hand during this showdown.

» All your opponents fold their hands. No, this doesn't mean they politely clasp their fingers on the table in front of them. Folding a hand (or, more simply, folding) means that a player relinquishes his or her claim to the pot by not matching an opponent's bet.

In this case, you may have had the best hand or you may have been bluffing — it doesn't matter. When opponents surrender their claim to the pot, it's yours.

In games like Seven-Card Stud and Texas Hold'em, the best hand is a high hand. (For more detail about high hands, see the section titled, "Hand Rankings" in this chapter.) In other games, like Lowball and Razz, the best hand is a low hand. (The best possible low hand is 5-4-3-2-A; the next best is 6-4-3-2-A.)

In split-pot games, two winners split the pot. For example, in Seven-Card Stud, High-Low Split, Eight-or-Better (mercifully abbreviated as Seven-Stud/8) and Omaha High-Low Split, Eight-or-Better (or just Omaha/8), the best high hand and the best low hand split the pot (provided that someone makes a low hand composed of five unpaired cards with a rank of 8 or lower). The worst possible low hand would consist of 8-7-6-5-4. The best of all low hands is 5-4-3-2-A (known as a *wheel* or *bicycle*). Although a high hand always will be made in split-pot games, there won't necessarily be a low hand. And when there's no low hand, the high hand wins the entire pot.

Most games require ante or blind bets. If *antes* are used, each player must post a token amount of money in order to receive cards. As for *blinds,* one or two players are required to make a bet or portion of a bet *before* the hand is dealt. This requirement rotates around the table so each player pays his fair share.

Each time a round of cards is dealt, players have an opportunity to check, bet, fold, call, or raise. Any time a player decides to forfeit his interest in the pot, he may release his hand when it is his turn *to act* (to do something related to betting: raise, fold, check, or call). When a player folds a hand, he isn't required to place any more money in the pot. If a player bets or raises and no one calls, the pot belongs to that player, the cards are collected and shuffled, and the next hand is dealt. If there are two or more players still active at the end of the hand, the best hand wins the pot.

Although there are different rules for each specific version, Poker really is this simple. Yet within its simplicity lies a wonderfully textured game structure that is always fascinating, frequently enjoyable, and, for some, a lifelong source of pleasure.

Grasping Who Wins: Hand Rankings

Seven-Card Stud and Texas Hold'em are the two most popular forms of Poker in which the highest ranking hand wins. These games are played with a 52-card deck — there is no joker — composed of four suits: spades, hearts, diamonds, and clubs. Each suit is equal in value, and there are 13 ranks in each suit. The ace is the highest ranking card in a suit, followed by king, queen, jack, and 10 through 2 (or deuce), in descending order. An ace may also be used as the lowest ranking card in a 5-high straight (5-4-3-2-A), which is also called a *wheel* or *bicycle*.

Although Stud and Hold'em are played with seven cards, the best hand refers to the best five-card hand. Hand rankings are a function of probability. The rarer the hand, the more valuable it is. See Figure 1-1 for an at-a-glance look at hand ranking in descending value.

Royal flush; straight flush

A *royal flush* is simply an ace-high straight flush and is the best possible hand in Poker. There are only four of them: A♠K♠Q♠J♠10♠; A♥K♥Q♥J♥10♥; A♦K♦Q♦J♦10♦; and A♣K♣Q♣J♣10♣.

A *straight flush* is five cards of the same suit in sequence, such as 9♥8♥7♥6♥5♥ or Q♦J♦10♦9♦8♦.

Four-of-a-kind

Four-of-a-kind, or *quads*, is a five-card hand composed of all the cards of one rank, plus one unrelated card, such as J♥J♠J♦J♣5♣. The higher the rank, the better the hand. For example, four kings beats four jacks.

Full house

Three cards of one rank and a pair of another make a *full house*. The rank of the full house is determined by the three-card grouping, not the pair. A hand like 9♥9♠9♦5♦5♣ is referred to as "nines full of fives."

Flush

A *flush* is any five cards of the same suit. The cards are not in sequence. If they were in sequence, it would be a *straight flush*. If there is more than one flush, the winning hand is determined by the rank order of the highest card, or cards, in the flush. A flush composed of A♥Q♥J♥6♥5♥ is higher than A♣Q♣J♣4♣3♣.

Straight

Five sequenced cards, not all of the same suit, compose a *straight*. If more than one straight is present, the highest card in the sequence determines the winning hand. A jack-high straight J♥10♠9♦8♦7♣ will beat this 9♠8♠7♦6♦5♣ nine-high straight.

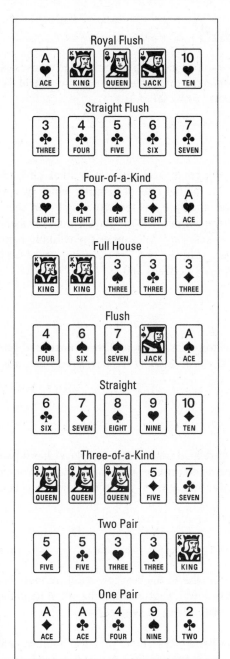

FIGURE 1-1:
Poker hands in descending value, with royal flush as the best hand.

Warming Up with Poker Basics

Three-of-a-kind

Three cards of the same rank, along with two unrelated cards is called *three-of-a-kind*. This hand is also referred to as *trips*, or a *set*. If you held 8♣8♥8♠K♦4♣ you could refer to it as "trip 8s" or "a set of 8s."

Two pair

Two cards of one rank along with two cards of another rank and one unrelated card composes *two pair*. The higher rank determines which two pair is superior. If two players hold two pair and each has the same high pair, then the rank of the second pair determines the winner. If both players hold the same two pair, then the rank of the unrelated side card determines the winning hand. If the hand is identical, then the players split the pot. For example, Q♣Q♥8♠8♦4♣ queens and 8s is superior to Q♠Q♦5♣5♠K♦ queens and 5s.

One pair

One pair is simply two cards of one rank and three unrelated cards. If two players hold the same pair, then the value of the unrelated side cards determines the winning hand.

No pair

No pair consists of five unrelated cards. When no player has a pair, then the rank order of the unrelated cards determines the winning hand. For example, if Harry has A-Q-9-6-3 and Adrien has A-J-10-3-2, then Harry wins because A-Q ranks higher than A-J.

Low hands

In split-pot games, like Omaha/8, the best low hand composed of five unrelated cards with the rank of 8 or lower, captures half the pot. A hand like 7♣6♥4♠3♦A♣ beats 7♦6♣5♥3♠A♦, but will lose to 7♠4♥3♥2♣A♠.

TIP

Determining the best low hand takes a bit of practice, but if you always begin with the highest of the low cards and continue in descending order, you can't go wrong.

The Lowdown on Betting

Without betting, Poker would just be a game of luck, and the best hand would always win. Betting is the key to Poker, and minimizing losses when holding a poor hand while maximizing wins with good hands is what Poker is all about.

Every betting interval requires a check or a bet from the first player to act. Each player to the left of the first player to act may either check or bet if no one else has bet. Whoever makes the first bet is said make the *opening bet.* If a bet has been made, other players may fold, call, or raise.

When a player *folds*, he goes out of the hand. He loses any chips he has contributed to that pot and has no further interest in the hand. After the final betting round, a showdown among the players still active in the hand determines the winner.

Here are some other key terms to describe the action that occurs during the betting phase:

>> **Ante:** A token sum of money contributed by each player before the cards are dealt. Antes are used in Seven-Card Stud, Seven-Stud/8, Razz, and many other games.

>> **Blind bet:** A forced bet by one or more players before the cards are dealt. This takes the place of an ante. The requirement to post a blind bet rotates around the table from hand to hand so each player pays his fair share. Blind bets are common in Texas Hold'em and Omaha. In most casino games, there are two blinds: a big blind and a small blind. These blinds are considered *live,* which means that players who post the blind have the opportunity to raise when the action gets back around to them.

>> **Call:** To equalize the amount wagered by putting the amount of money wagered into the pot.

>> **Check:** A *check* is a bet of zero dollars. By checking, a player retains the right to call any bet made by player who acts after he does, or even to raise. But if someone's already bet when it's your turn to act, you can no longer check, and must either fold, call, or raise.

>> **Checkraise:** To check and then raise if one of your opponents bets. This is generally done to trap players for a bet or two, when the checkraiser has a very powerful hand.

>> **Raise:** To increase the amount wagered by an amount equal to your opponent's bet — or by a greater amount, if the game is spread limit, pot limit, or no-limit.

Different types of games call for specific kinds of betting:

>> In a *fixed limit* game, no one may bet or raise more than a predetermined number of chips. This limit, however, usually varies with the round of the game. In Stud Poker, betting limits usually double when the fifth card is dealt. Thus, a $10–$20 game means that the first two rounds of betting are based on limits of $10, while the last three are in increments of $20. In Texas Hold'em, with four betting rounds, betting limits usually double on the third round.

>> *Spread limit* games are similar to fixed limit, but the bettors can wager any amount within the limits. A limit might be $2–$10 any time, which means that wagers can be made in any amount within those limits at any time, with the proviso that a raise must be at least the equal of the bet that preceded it.

>> In *pot limit,* bets or raises are limited only by the amount of money in the pot at the time the wager is made. A player who raises may count her call as part of the pot. If there is $10 in the pot and someone wagers $10, a raiser may call that bet, making the pot $30 and then raise the entire pot. When she is done, the pot will contain $60.

>> In *no limit,* a player may bet or raise any amount of chips she has in front of her at any time.

In most limit games, a bet and either three or four raises per betting round are permitted.

Comprehending the Rules of the Road

Call them rules, conventions, or Poker etiquette, some guidelines are common to all forms of Poker, especially Poker in card clubs or casinos. Although you may find some minor variations from one casino to another, many card casinos are working diligently toward a uniform set of guidelines.

Going all-in

If you don't have enough to cover the bets and raises, you are said to *go all-in* and are simply contesting that portion of the pot your money covers. Others who are active in the hand can still make wagers, but those bets constitute a side pot. At the hand's conclusion, the side pot is decided first, then the main pot. You aren't eligible to win the side pot because you invested no money in it, but you can win the main pot. You can buy more chips or put more money on the table between hands.

THE FORBIDDEN STRING-RAISE

In a western, someone's always saying: "Mighty big bet, cowboy. I'll just see your twenty," while reaching back into his stack for more chips, and with a long, lingering glance for effect, drawls "and raise you forty!" As dramatic as that move may seem, you won't see that in a real Poker game. Calling a bet, then reaching back for more chips and announcing a raise is called a *string raise.* It is not permitted. Rest assured someone will shout "String raise!" The dealer then informs the hopeful raiser that a string raise just occurred, and he'll have to take his raise back and simply call. Now, if someone shouts "String raise!" and another opponent says something like "That's okay. Let his raise stand," be assured that player's hand is in big trouble — real big trouble!

The string-raise rule prevents a player from reading the reactions of his opponents while he puts some chips in the pot, then deciding to raise if he thinks he's got the best of it.

You can't drive someone out of a pot just by betting more money than he has in front of him. The player with the limited chip supply goes all-in — by calling with the remainder of his chips. If the all-in player loses, he either buys more chips or leaves the game.

Knowing how to raise

If you want to raise, just say "Raise." Then you can go back to your stack and count out the proper amount of chips. If you want to let your action announce your intention, you usually must put the correct amount of chips into the pot, and do it all in one motion.

No splashing

Avoid *splashing* the pot: Don't toss chips into the center of the table where they mingle with the others. Instead, stack your chips neatly on the table about 18 inches in front of you. The dealer will pull them into the pot when the action has been completed on that round of betting.

If it's your first time in a public cardroom, tell the dealer so he can help you through the mechanics of the game. After a few sessions, you'll be familiar and comfortable with the majority of playing procedures. Soon you, too, will feel like a regular.

Protecting your hand; cards speak

REMEMBER

In a casino, unlike in many home games, you are always responsible for your hand. Toss it in the *muck* (the pile of discarded cards), and your hand is fouled and cannot win. The rule in all cardrooms is that cards speak — your hand is worth whatever value the cards have. Dealers, however, can make mistakes. If you think yours is the best hand, turn your cards face up and announce it. Place it halfway between your chips and the pot, and hold on to it while the dealer determines the outcome.

If you're not sure whether you have the best hand, turn all of your cards face up at the end of the hand and allow the dealer to read your hand. If you are in a Poker club or casino and there is a doubt or debate, even if the hand is over, casino security cameras can review the hands that were shown down to determine the winner.

Sticking to table stakes

Most games, including most casino games, are *table stakes.* You can't add chips or money to the amount in front of you during the play of the hand. If you run out of money during a hand, you can contest only that portion of the pot that your bets cover. You can't *go light* — that is, pull more money out of your wallet — as you might do in a home game. You can, of course, always add more money to your playing stake between hands.

Taking time out

Anytime you are unsure of anything, the best procedure to follow is to call "Time!" This freezes the action. Then get your questions resolved prior to acting. Poker etiquette suggests that you not abuse this privilege, particularly if you are in a game where you are charged a fee for sitting at the table. Players usually want a fast, efficiently run game with as few interruptions as possible.

Dealing and decks

Dealers — and decks — generally rotate every half-hour. In addition, players unhappy with their run of cards are prone to holler "Deck change!" Most cardrooms permit a change once a deck has been in play for an entire round.

Grasping the finer points: Etiquette

Poker rules and etiquette helps speed the game along and keep it orderly. These conventions are as much a part of the game as the cards themselves. In fact, when you play casino Poker for the first time, Poker etiquette may take more getting used to than the game itself.

REMEMBER

Keep in mind the following points of Poker protocol:

>> **Act in turn.** Each player is expected to act in turn as play proceeds clockwise around the table. If someone bets and you plan to discard your hand, wait until it's your turn to act before doing so. Not only is acting out of turn impolite, it can give a big advantage to one of your opponents. If he knows you'll fold your hand, it makes it easier for him to bluff and is unfair to the rest of the players. In Poker, as in most things, it's considered polite to wait your turn.

>> **Keep your cards in plain sight.** In order to maintain the integrity of the game, players must keep their cards on the table during the play of the hand. The best way to protect your hand is to keep it on the table and look at the cards by shielding them with your hands while lifting a corner of each card to peek at it. In a game like Texas Hold'em, where players have only two cards in front of them, it's customary to leave them on the table after looking and to place a chip on top of them. This alerts the dealer that your hand is still in play.

>> **Avoid discussing hands in play.** Discussing your hand with others, even if you have released it and are no longer contesting that pot, may provide information that would give another player an unfair advantage. If you want to discuss a hand with a neighbor, wait until the hand concludes.

>> **Practice toking.** We're not blowing smoke here, but *toking* (Poker parlance for *tipping*) the dealer is customary when you win a pot. In Poker casinos, tokes constitute a significant part of each dealer's income. The size of the pot and the game's betting limits generally determine the amount of the toke. If you're new to casino Poker, take your toking cue from the other players at the table. In games with betting limits of $10–$20 or higher, a dollar is a typical toke for all but the smallest pots. In smaller games, tokes of fifty cents are the rule.

Identifying What Your Opponents Will Be Like

The kinds of players sitting at your table in a Poker parlor will vary with the limits you play. If you play in low-limit games, you are not going to find either last year's World Series of Poker winner, the eight toughest card players in your hometown, or any legends of the game. Although there are many ways to classify players as you try to build a book on your opponents, the easiest way is to group your opponents into the following four types.

Casual recreational players

Casual recreational players love the game, but when push comes to shove, they're not that concerned about winning or losing. They play for the fun of it. It's simply a hobby, and no matter how much they lose, it is less expensive than keeping horses, restoring classic automobiles, or pursuing a hundred other hobbies that devour money. Naturally, you'd love to play exclusively with recreational players. If you can't beat a table full of these players, you just might want to find something else to do in your spare time. No one, however, will come right out and admit to being a casual recreational player. If someone does, watch out. He probably isn't, and you're forewarned: Take heed when he fires a raise at you.

Cardroom regulars

Regulars come in a wide variety. This includes retirees, homemakers, students, people with no fixed job hours, dealers who are playing before or after their shift, and almost anyone else you can imagine. Some regulars have independent sources of income and often play in big games. Take it for a fact that all the regulars you encounter have more playing experience than you do. Even if you are a stronger player but are just making the transition from home games to casino Poker, they will have the best of it for a while. After all, they are in playing shape. You, on the other hand, are in spring training and will need some time to adjust to this entirely new environment.

Regulars and casual recreational players constitute the majority of Poker devotees. Some are good. Most aren't. But they're in action on a regular basis.

Professionals

You find professionals and semi-professionals in most of the larger games. Generally speaking, you don't encounter these players at limits below $10–$20. While a pro would have an easier time of it at lower betting limits, she just can't earn a living in a $2–$4 game. In these lower limit games, you'll be competing with regulars and recreational players, not professionals. But when you graduate to the higher limits, you can expect to encounter some players who earn all or part of their living playing Poker.

Proposition players

Proposition players, or props, play on their own money but are paid a salary by the club to help start or prop up games. You'll typically find them late at night when the club is trying to keep games going, and early in the morning when it's trying to start up a new game.

A prop's life can be tough. Playing in short-handed games or games struggling to get off the ground isn't always a bed of roses. The minute a live player wants his seat, the prop is pulled from it — often when the game is just starting to bear fruit. Props typically play better than most regulars do, but not as well as top players do. Their defining characteristic is that they tend to be conservative.

Many cardroom newcomers panic at the thought of a prop in their game. Because the casino pays the prop, players often believe he has a big advantage. Not true. Props play their own money, and as long as they're reliable and maintain a playing bankroll, the card club cares not a whit whether they win or lose. We suspect that given a choice, any cardroom would prefer to employ a weak player as a prop, rather than a strong one, simply because the weaker player is a bigger draw. In fact, the ideal prop would be a poor player with a winning personality and an unlimited bankroll.

Playing in a Casino

Casino Poker differs from typical home games. Although kitchen-table Poker may be long on camaraderie and unusual variants of the game, there are many reasons to play in a public cardroom. The most important factor may be that there is always a game. In fact, you frequently have a choice of games, which are often available 24 hours a day, seven days a week.

Another major advantage, especially in the very large Poker clubs in urban locations, is the safety of public cardrooms. These venues offer professional dealers, floorpersons, and video security the equal of any Las Vegas casino to ensure that games are run squarely. Because people walk around cardrooms with large sums of money, there are more security guards than you'd find in most banks. Parking lots are brightly lit, well patrolled, and free of strong-arm crime. Because most large clubs offer check cashing, safe deposit boxes, and ATMs, there's no need to walk around with large sums of money in your pocket. You can also take advantage of the *players banks* available at many large clubs. Although you can't write checks against it, a players bank is like a conventional bank account except that it's in a casino. You can deposit money and withdraw cash when you need it.

In a public cardroom, there's never any pressure to stay. Nobody minds if you quit the game a winner. Someone else is usually waiting for your seat. You do, however, have to pay to play. It costs more to play in a casino than a home game where all you have to do is split the cost of food and drinks.

Casinos, however, offer a variety of games. If you don't feel like playing Texas Hold'em you can play Stud, Lowball, or Omaha High-Low Split. If weak players are at your table, you can punish them continuously. Weak players in home games eventually become ex-players if they can't win some of the time.

You'll find the pace of a casino game to be much faster than most home games. Dealers in a casino try to maintain a quick pace. If you are playing in a game with a time collection, you are paying the same fee per half-hour of play regardless of how many hands are dealt. Consequently, dealers act efficiently, and players are expected to make prompt decisions.

Things you've probably done in home games just won't happen in a card room. No one ever fishes through the discards. The dealer handles the deck. You play your cards without the help of a neighbor.

Entering a game: The how-to

When you enter a cardroom, you may see a white board full of players' initials. These initials are listed under games that are available. For example, if you walk into a large casino, you might find seven players ahead of you waiting for a $2–$4 Hold'em game. Just give your initials to the board attendant and indicate the games you want to be listed for. You might say: "My initials are ABC. Put me up for the $2–$4, $3–$6, and $5–$10 Hold'em, the $5–$10 Stud, and the $4–$8 Omaha High-Low Split games."

That's all there is to it. It's as easy as taking a number at Ben and Jerry's. Your initials will go up on the board for each game you request, and you'll be called as seats become available. If the board for a particular game is so long that the club can start another, the attendant will announce that game and call the players in the order they are listed. When you hear your initials, go to the table and grab a vacant seat. You're in the game.

Some cardrooms don't use a board. Just give your initials or first name to the attendant and tell him the games you want to play. In small cardrooms, where there are only one or two tables, ask the dealer if a seat is available or if there is a waiting list for the game.

Buying chips

When you first sit in the game, either the floorperson or dealer will ask you how much you want in chips. Each game has a minimum buy-in. Give the floorperson your money, and you'll get your chips. Large casinos have chip attendants. One of them will take your money, announce to the table that "Seat five (or whatever seat you occupy) is playing $200 behind." That means you bought in for $200, and the casino is in the process of fetching your chips. You can play that hand, even though your chips have not yet arrived. The dealer will either lend you some chips or keep count of how much you owe the pot. Your chips should arrive about the time that the first hand is played to its conclusion.

Shuffling and dealing

You may never have noticed, but the shuffle procedure in a casino is much more rigorous than it is in a game with amateur dealers. Home game players are usually unfamiliar with the mechanics of a good shuffle, and many lack the manual dexterity to perform one. Well-trained casino dealers assemble the deck so the cards face the players, frequently preceding that by scrambling the cards on the table. This is followed by a four-step procedure of shuffle, shuffle, riffle, and shuffle. Finally, the dealer cuts the deck and deals. The procedure is efficient, quick, and designed so no cards are flashed in the process.

Distinguishing Casino Poker from Home Games

If you've watched a few games in a card club while waiting for a seat, you'll notice that players don't play as many hands as they do in home games. Although there is seldom a spoken agreement to play every hand in a home game, because of the chummy atmosphere, many players simply play lots of hands. That's not the case in a casino. Players are more selective. Still, the biggest mistakes most players make are playing too many hands and calling on early betting rounds when they should have folded.

Tighter than home games

Low-limit cardroom games, while tighter than comparable home games, are still much too loose. In tight games, the players with the stronger hands tend to enter the pots, while in a looser game, more players enter more pots than they really should. If you simply play better starting cards than your opponents do in these low-limit games, you will usually be a *favorite* (favored to win money in the long run).

However, you won't be a favorite in any game right off the mark. Because it will take you some time to get familiar with cardroom play, give serious consideration to starting in very small-limit games. You'll probably be *paying for lessons* the first five or ten times you play in a public cardroom, and there is no reason to make these lessons any more expensive than they need be.

Players are more selective about the hands they play

If you come from a home game into a public cardroom, especially the fun-to-play, jam-it-up kind of home game, you quickly realize that you can't play every hand, or even many hands, for that matter! You need standards so you know what your minimum calling hands and raising hands should be. This is true for all forms of Poker.

When you set your standards before you sit down at the table, you give yourself more time to study your opponents and to determine what makes the current hand different from similar hands you've seen before.

REMEMBER

You don't have to play every hand you're dealt. Folding weak hands that will prove to be unprofitable in the long run is — like discretion — the better part of valor. Each form of Poker has its own set of good hands, and you'll find out what they are as you work your way through this book. For now, it's enough to remember that you should fold more hands than you play.

Games are faster

The first few times you play in a casino, the speed of the games might startle you. You may also think that the players are better than your home game cronies are. But after becoming familiar with the environment, you'll find that your skill level is right up there with your opponents' abilities. Most of them aren't students of the game. Recreational players want to have fun and that's it. Most of the regulars, who run the gamut of skill levels, don't bother to study the game. Though many of them have been playing in cardrooms for years, they simply repeat and reinforce the same errors they've been making for decades.

Don't worry too much about the skill level of your opponents when you first begin playing in a public cardroom. By studying and playing the game, you should soon catch the field — begin to play as well, or better, than your opponents. And through frequent play and study, you can improve at a much more rapid rate.

Chapter 2

Applying Essential Strategies

B asic strategic knowledge is critical for any Poker player. If you have no basis for making decisions about whether to call, fold, raise, or reraise, you may just as well play the lottery. Sure, you'll win occasionally because everyone gets lucky now and then. Without strategy and knowledge, you'll exercise no control over your destiny as a card player.

If you picked 100 Poker players at random and asked them about the objective of Poker, most would say something about winning the pot, but they couldn't be further from the truth.

REMEMBER

The goal of Poker — in addition to the enjoyment of playing the game — is winning money, not pots. If your goal were to win the most pots, that would be easy to do. Just play every hand and call every bet and raise until the bitter end. You'd win a lot of pots. In fact, you'd win every pot you possibly could. But you'd lose money. Plenty of it, and rapidly.

So the objective of Poker is to win money. And that means tempering enthusiasm with realism by being selective about the hands you play. There's no need to play every hand. The very best players play relatively few hands, but when they do enter a pot, they are usually aggressive and out to maximize the amount they win when the odds favor them.

This is the essence of Poker: Anyone can win in the short run, but in the long haul — when the cards even out — the better players win more money with their good hands, and lose less with weak hands.

REMEMBER

Because of the short-term luck involved, Poker is a game where even atrociously poor players can — and do — have winning nights. This isn't true in most other competitive endeavors. Most of us wouldn't have a prayer going one-on-one with an NBA basketball player, or attempting to hit a 95 mph big-league fastball. What's more, we realize it. Yet most of us think we are good Poker players.

If you took a poll at any Poker table, the majority of players would rate themselves significantly above average. But that's not the case. It can't be. In the long run, good players beat bad players — though the bad players will win just often enough to keep them coming back for more.

It's this subtle blend of skill and luck that balances the game. That balance also rewards good players who are realistic about how they assess their ability and that of their opponents. This chapter can help you develop those skills.

Knowing That Everyone Was a Beginner Once

In the beginning, everyone was a bad player — you, me, the guy winning all the money at your table tonight, as well as every player who has ever won the World Series of Poker. Once upon a time, Peyton Manning couldn't throw a football, Alex Rodriguez couldn't hit, and Michael Jordan was once cut from his high school basketball team. They were beginners too, and guess what: They were bad. Raw talent? Sure, they were blessed with an abundance of raw talent, but they all had to work long and hard to refine it.

So don't bemoan your current skill level as a Poker player. You can improve, and you will if you're willing to pay the price. Every good Poker player has been where you are now, and they've improved. To be sure, some progressed by leaps and bounds, while others have taken baby steps, one after the other, until they reached their goal.

Build a foundation first . . .

You can reach your Poker-playing goals. You probably have some innate potential as a Poker player, and if playing winning Poker is important, you need to build a foundation that will help you reach your potential as quickly as possible. Everyone who has progressed from neophyte to journeyman to expert to superstar shares one trait in common: They built a solid foundation, and that foundation allowed them to spread their wings and fly. And fly they can.

TIP

But in Poker, as in life itself, you can't fly until you've built a rock-solid foundation and mastered the fundamentals. If you're still grappling with fundamentals, you're not yet ready to fly. But once those fundamentals are imprinted on your Poker consciousness and you can execute them instinctively, then, and only then, can you think about digressing from these basics and improving. Book 2, Chapter 1 has more about building the groundwork when playing Poker.

. . . Then you can improvise

When you listen to great jazz musicians, you're hearing improvisation at its best. That improvisation, however, is based on a solid grounding of music theory. Charlie Parker, Miles Davis, the Modern Jazz Quartet, Sonny Rollins, Gerry Mulligan, Charles Mingus, Thelonius Monk: These jazz giants are masters of improvisation, but their innovation and creativity stood on a platform of musical theory, knowledge of time signatures, an understanding of harmony, skill in ensemble playing, and an ability to use rhythm to underpin melodic themes and harmony. Without possessing these basic skills, innovation would not have been possible.

The price wasn't cheap, either. It took lots of playing, lots of years, and more clubs, sessions, and after-hours joints than those musicians would want to count. But the product was sweet, free-flowing music: riffs that seem to possess a life of their own, springing unbounded from horns, keyboards, and strings, and filling the night with magic.

Poker is the same way. No matter which game you play, you have to know the basic rules before you can take risks (aka improvise). Your risks will be small at first, but as you succeed and build confidence, you'll find yourself taking bigger risks — and you'll see them pay off.

Keeping Track of Basic Poker Concepts

Your first efforts should center on grasping basic Poker concepts. Even when you understand them, this know-how must be continuously applied. The knowledge and abilities that compose basic Poker skills are not a pill to be swallowed once. They need to be continuously refined.

Andres Segovia, the greatest classical guitarist of his generation, did not spend the majority of his practice time learning new pieces or practicing his concert repertoire. He spent four to six hours per day playing scales and études. Segovia spent 75 percent of his practice time on basics, and did this every day. You'll have to take our word for it, but this analogy holds true for Poker, too.

The following sections give you some important information to help you with the basics. Book 2, Chapter 1 also provides some additional Poker basics.

Understanding blinds and antes

Every Poker game begins as a chase for the antes or blinds. An *ante* is a small portion of a bet contributed by each player to seed the pot at the beginning of each hand. A *blind* is a forced bet by one or more players before any cards are dealt. In Stud games, players usually ante; in Texas Hold'em and Omaha Hold'em, blind bets are used.

Regardless of whether a blind or an ante is employed, every game needs seed money to start the action. Without it, players could wait all day for unbeatable hands before entering the pot.

Playing for an empty pot would make for a slow and boring game. Blinds and antes serve the same purpose: to tempt and tantalize players, enticing them into the pot and creating action because there's a monetary target to shoot at.

Knowing your opponents

Suppose you're playing Texas Hold'em and have been dealt A♥K♥, and your opponents are Rick and Barbara, two players who are known for calling much too frequently.

"Fantastic," you say to yourself when you look at the flop and see J♥5♥9♣. "I have position, two overcards, and a nut-flush draw." You remember something about semi-bluffing and implied odds, and when your opponents check on the flop, you bet. They call. The turn brings 4♠, and it's checked to you. You bet, thinking they might fold and you can win it right here.

Maybe you even have the best hand and would win in a showdown right now. Perhaps a heart — or even an ace or king — will come on the river (at the last common card). But you are up against players who sleep very well each and every night of the week, secure in the knowledge that no one, but no one, ever steals a pot from them.

The river is no help; it's 4♣. Rick and Barbara check again. You still might have the best hand if you show it down. But you bet and you're called, and you lose to Rick, who holds a 6-5 of mixed suits.

"What went wrong?" you ask yourself. "I had the perfect opportunity to semi-bluff." Perfect, that is, only from the perspective of the cards on the table and those in your hand. But it was far from perfect if you stopped to consider your opponents. Your mistake involved considering only the cards while choosing a strategy. Semi-bluffing doesn't work with players who always call. You have to show them the best hand to take the money. Although there was nothing you could have done to win that pot, you certainly could have saved a bet on the river.

Nothing was wrong with the strategy itself. It might have worked if the cards were the same but your opponents were different. Knowing your opponents is as important to winning at Poker as understanding strategic concepts.

REMEMBER

Strategy is situationally dependent. Skilled players realize they need to be aware of the big picture while simultaneously paying attention to small details. Understanding strategic concepts is only part of the battle. How, and under what circumstances to apply them, are equally important. If you can do this, you'll find that you have become a better player and a more creative one, too.

Preparing to win

Success demands preparation. Knowledge, plus preparation and experience (and whatever innate talent one may have), equals know-how. That's what it takes to be a winning Poker player.

REMEMBER

The primary step in making behavioral changes and eliminating bad habits is to be responsible for you. Adopt the irrevocable assumption that you are personally responsible for what happens to you at the Poker table. If you put the blame on forces outside of yourself, you haven't committed yourself to making changes; you're denying the problem.

Keeping Some Poker Perspective

The information explosion is everywhere, and Poker is no different. More has been written about Poker in the past 20 years than had previously been written in the entire history of the game.

After you've made a commitment to reach for the stars, you have to decide where to begin. If you aspire to Poker excellence, the first — and probably the most important step — is to develop a perspective that enables you to put each piece of information into a hierarchical structure. After all, some things are more important than others, and you may as well concentrate your efforts where they'll do the most good. These sections can help you know what's important and what's not.

Knowing why some tactics are important in Poker and others aren't

Imagine that we could teach you a terrific tactical ploy that would require some real study and practice to perfect — but once learned, could be used to earn an extra bet from an opponent. What if we also guaranteed this ploy to be absolutely foolproof: It would work perfectly every time you used it. Have we piqued your interest?

But suppose that we also told you that this tactic works only in very special circumstances that occur about once a year. Do you still want to invest the time required to learn it? Probably not. Although your ability to execute this particularly slick maneuver might brand you as a tough player in the eyes of your opponents, the fact that you might use it only once a year renders it meaningless. In the course of a year's worth of playing, one extra bet doesn't amount to a hill of beans. It doesn't even amount to a can of beans.

Making frequent decisions

Tactical opportunities that occur all the time are important. Even when the amount of money attributed to a wrong decision is small, it will eventually add up to a tidy sum if that error is made frequently. Always defending your small blind in Hold'em, for example, is a good example. You have to decide whether to defend your small blind every round — and that's frequent. If you always defend it, you are investing part of a bet on those occasions when it is wrong to do so. At the end of a year, those mistakes add up.

Suppose that you're playing $10–$20 Texas Hold'em, with $5 and $10 blinds, and you decide to always defend your small blind, even when you're dealt hands like 7♥2♣. Just to keep this simple, we'll assume that your small blind is never raised. Based on the random distributions of cards, you're probably dealt a throwaway hand about one-third of the time. At the rate of 30 hands per hour, you'll be dealt the small blind three times every 60 minutes. If you always call, you'll wind up calling once each hour when you really shouldn't have. That's only $5 each hour, but after 1,000 hours of Poker, you've essentially given away $5,000. It adds up fast, doesn't it?

Avoiding costly decisions

Playing correctly requires a great deal of judgment — the kind that comes from experience, not books. No matter how skilled a player you eventually become, you'll never reach the point where you always make these decisions correctly. Don't worry; that's not important. Just err on the side of protecting yourself from catastrophic mistakes, and you'll be on the right track.

Decisions that cost a significant amount of money when they occur, even if they don't happen too often, are also important. If you can't decide whether to call or fold once all the cards are out and your opponent bets into a fairly large pot, that's an important decision. If you make a mistake by calling when you should have folded and your opponent wins the pot — that's an error, but not a critical one. It cost only one bet. But if you fold the winning hand, that's a critical error because the cost of that error was the entire pot.

Now we're certainly not advising you to call each and every time someone bets on the last card and you're unsure about whether you have the best hand, but deciding to call instead of fold doesn't have to be correct too often to render it the mistake of choice. If the cost of a mistaken fold is ten times the price of a mistaken call, you only have to be correct slightly more than 10 percent of the time to make calling worthwhile.

Making more decisions and taking subsequent actions

Choices can also be important because of their position on the decision tree. Those that are first in a long sequence of subsequent choices are always important because subsequent choices are usually predicated on your initial selection. Make an incorrect move up front and you run the risk of rendering each subsequent decision incorrect, regardless of whatever else you might do. That's why the choice of which hands you start with in Poker is generally a much more critical decision than how you play on future betting rounds. If you adopt an " . . . any cards can win" philosophy, you have set yourself up for a disaster that even the best players could not overcome on later rounds.

Poker's single most important decision

REMEMBER

Choosing the right game is the most important decision you'll encounter as a Poker player. Choose the wrong game and little else matters. Choose the right game and you might even make money even on nights when you're experiencing a below-average run of cards.

Starting with standards

After you choose the best game and select the best available seat at that table, what's important to winning play? Early decisions predicate subsequent choices, so deciding which hands to start with (your starting standards) is critically important.

It's human nature to seek the best bang for the buck, and Poker players are no different. There are hands where the return on your investment is positive, and others that will prove costly in the long run. In the heat of battle, you don't have the time to thoroughly assess your hand. You should have made these decisions long before you hit the table. That's why standards are critical. If you incorporate solid starting standards into your game, you are light-years ahead of any opponent who hasn't done this — never mind how long he's been playing or how much experience he may have in other phases of the game.

Starting standards also provide a basis for deviation, but only under the right conditions. Those conditions are impossible to recognize — and capitalize on — unless you've developed standards and integrated them so completely into your game that they are second nature to you. Only when that's accomplished can you hope to find those very few exceptions that allow you to profitably deviate from them.

Having hand selectivity

Hand selection is one of the most important keys to winning. Most people play too many hands. I'm not referring only to beginners. Some players have been at it for years, and the single most important flaw in their game is that they still play too many hands.

After all, the majority of Poker players are recreational players. They're not playing Poker to make their living; they play to enjoy themselves — and much as they'd have you believe their goal in playing is to win money, that's really secondary to their main objective: having fun. The difference between a player who has come out to have fun and another who is playing to win money is that the recreational player will look for reasons to play marginal hands and to continue playing them even when subsequent betting rounds are fraught with danger. The money player will look for reasons to release hands, avoid unnecessary danger, and dump speculative hands whenever the potential reward is overshadowed by the risks.

Being aggressive, but being selective

Winning Poker requires selectivity and aggression. Every top player knows that concept, and every credible Poker book emphasizes it. If you have any doubts, consider the need to be selective. Picture someone who calls every hand down to the bitter end unless she sees that she's beaten on board. Her opponents would soon discover that it never pays to bluff her. Of course, every time they had the smallest edge, they'd bet, knowing that she'll call with the worst of it. These value bets would soon relieve our heroine of her bankroll.

If selectivity is clearly correct, what about aggression? Consider the passive player. He seldom bets unless he has an unbeatable hand — and they don't come around all that often. More often than not, you'll find yourself in pots where you believe, but aren't absolutely certain, that you have the best hand. Even when you are 100 percent certain that yours is the best hand at the moment, you might recognize it as one that can be beaten if there are more cards to come. This occurs more often than you might realize, and you can't win at Poker by giving your opponent a free card. If they have to draw to beat you, make them pay the price.

GOOD GAMES NEED BAD PLAYERS

Would you rather be the best Poker player in the world at a table with the eight other players who are ranked second through ninth, or would you prefer being a good player at a table full of fish? Against a table full of weak players you'd win more money — much more, in fact, than the world's best player could ever win against tough competition!

Here's why. Most of the money you'll win at Poker comes not from the brilliance of your own play, but from the ineptitude of your opponents. Never mind that you might be the world's best Poker player. You're not all that much better than those immediately beneath you. And your opponents, all of whom are world-class players in their own right, will not present you with much of a target to shoot at. Bad players are another story entirely. They offer huge targets. They call with weak hands. They stay in hopes of catching a miracle card. They believe that Poker is like the lottery — all a matter of luck — and it's just a little while until everything evens out and they get theirs. And their bad play costs them money day after day.

The sad truth is that bad players simply don't realize the extent to which they bleed their money away. The gap between the good player and the fool is infinitely greater than the gap between the world's best player and any cluster of other world-beaters. It's not even close. That mythical journeyman professional Poker player — the kind you aspire to be — may be a mile away from the world's best, but 10 miles ahead of the fools.

TIP

GETTING THE BEST SEAT IN THE HOUSE

Selecting the best available seat depends on the skills that your opponents have. Think about their playing style and level of experience.

Here are the types of players you want on your left:

- Timid players, who are likely to release their hands if you bet or raise
- Players who will call whenever you bet but will raise infrequently
- Predictable opponents

Here are the types of players you want on your right:

- Very aggressive players, especially those who raise too frequently
- Skilled, tough opponents
- Unpredictable players

Being patient

Patience is certainly related to the "be selective" portion of the "be aggressive, but be selective" mantra. Few players dispute the need to be selective. Nevertheless, most aren't very selective about the hands they play. After all, Poker is fun, and most aficionados come to play, not fold.

When the cards aren't coming your way, it's very easy to talk yourself into taking a flyer on marginal hands. But there's usually a price to be paid for falling off the good-hands wagon.

Sometimes it all boils down to a simple choice. You can have a lot of fun, gamble it up, and pay the inevitable price for your pleasure, or you can apply the patience required to win consistently.

Focusing on position

In Poker, position means power. It is almost always advantageous to act after you've had the benefit of seeing what your opponents do. Their actions provide clues about the real or implied values of their hands. This is true in every Poker game, and is particularly important in fixed-position games, like Hold'em and Omaha. In these games, position is fixed for the entire hand, unlike Stud, where it can vary from one betting round to another.

Coping When All Goes Wrong

Unfortunately, no magic elixir eliminates the fluctuations everyone experiences at Poker. But it's little consolation when you've been buffeted by the ups and downs of fate to realize that you're not the only poor soul tossing about in the same boat. When all seems lost, you need to remember this: There is opportunity in adversity. In fact, losing provides the best opportunity to examine and refine your own game.

Face it. Most players don't spend much time in careful self-examination when they're winning. It's too much fun to stack the chips and revel in the money that's rolling in. But when they lose, they pore over each decision they made, wondering how they could have improved it. "What could I have done differently," they ask over and over. Losing turns them from expansive extroverts into brooding introverts whose thoughts bring them back to the same ground time and time again, in search of reasons and strategies that will prevent losses like these from ever happening again.

Change gears if you're on a losing streak

TIP

While no guarantees about future losses are available, we do recommend one course of action to any player mired in a losing streak: Just change gears. We all change gears during a Poker game, sometimes consciously, as a planned strategy, and sometimes we just wind up playing differently than we did when we first sat down.

When you're losing, consider gearing down. Way down. This is a time for lots of traction and not much speed; a time for playing only the best starting hands. Not marginal hands, not good — or even very good — starting hands, but only the best hands. That means you'll be throwing away hand after hand, and it takes discipline to do this, particularly when some of these hands would have won.

When losing, most players want to minimize fluctuations in their bankrolls and grind out some wins. Gearing down accomplishes this because you're not playing any of the "close call" hands you normally might. By playing hands that have a greater chance of winning, you're minimizing the fluctuations that occur with speculative hands. Of course, you're also cutting down your average hourly win rate, but it's a trade-off because you are less apt to find yourself on a roller coaster ride. You can still win as much; it will just take more hours at the table.

Narrowing the target

Gearing down also prevents your opponents from kicking you when you're down. When you're winning, your table image is quite different than when you're losing. Win, and you can sometimes bluff with impunity. It's a lot tougher when you're losing. After all, your opponents have watched you lose hand after hand. They believe you're going to keep losing. When you bet, they'll call — or even raise — with hands they might have thrown away if you had been winning steadily.

Chapter 3

Succeeding at Seven-Card Stud

S even-Card Stud is the most popular of all the stud games, and has been since it first appeared sometime around the Civil War. There are also six- and five-card variants, but they're not nearly as popular as the seven-card version. With three down cards and four exposed cards in each player's hand at the end of the hand, Seven-Card Stud combines some of the surprises of Draw Poker with a good deal of information that can be gleaned from four open cards.

Seven-Card Stud has five rounds of betting that can create some very large pots. Skilled Seven-Card Stud players need an alert mind and good powers of retention. A skillful player is able to relate each card in his hand, or visible in the hand of an opponent, to once-visible but now folded hands in order to estimate the likeli-hood of making his hand, as well as to estimate the likelihood that an opponent has made his.

In Seven-Card Stud almost every hand is possible. This is very different than a game like Texas Hold'em, in which a full house or four-of-a-kind isn't possible unless the board contains paired cards, and a flush is impossible unless the board contains three cards of the same suit.

With nearly endless possibilities, Seven-Card Stud is a bit like a jigsaw puzzle. You must combine knowledge of exposed and folded cards with previous betting patterns to discern the likelihood of any one of a variety of hands that your opponent might be holding.

What to Do If You've Never Played Seven-Card Stud Poker

REMEMBER

Seven-Card Stud requires patience. Because you're dealt three cards right off the bat — before the first round of betting — it's important that these cards are able to work together before you enter a pot. In fact, the most critically important decision you'll make in a Seven-Card Stud game is whether to enter the pot on *third street* — the first round of betting.

The next critical decision point is whether you should continue playing on the third round of betting, called *fifth street.* In fixed-limit betting games, such as $6–$12, fifth street is where the betting limits double. There's an old adage in Seven-Card Stud: If you call on fifth street, you've bought a through-ticket to the *river card* (the last card).

Figure 3-1 shows a typical hand of Seven-Card Stud after all the cards are dealt. The first three cards, beginning from the left, are considered to be on third street, the next single card is fourth street, and so on, until seventh street.

At the conclusion of the hand, when all the cards have been dealt, the results are as follows:

> **Player 1** now has a full house, aces full of 4s. He is likely to raise.
>
> **Player 2** has an ace-high diamond flush.
>
> **Player 3,** who began with a promising straight draw, has two pair — 9s and 8s.
>
> **Player 4** has a full house, queens full of jacks, but will lose to Player 1's bigger full house.
>
> **Player 5** has three 5s, the same hand she began with.
>
> **Player 6** has a king-high straight.

In Seven-Card Stud, each player makes the best five-card hand from his seven cards. The highest hand out of all the players wins. (In Figure 3-1, Player 1 takes the pot.)

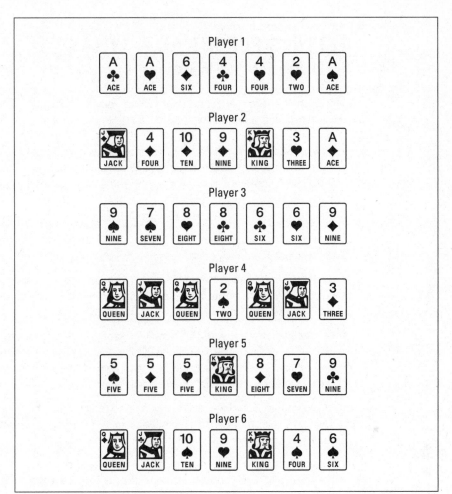

FIGURE 3-1:
A sample hand of
Seven–Card Stud.

© John Wiley & Sons, Inc.

Although most stud games don't result in this many big hands contesting a pot, you can see how the best hand changes from one betting round to another, and how a player can make the hand he is hoping for, yet not have any chance of winning.

TIP

Seven–Card Stud requires a great deal of patience and alertness. Most of the time, you should discard your hand on third street because your cards either don't offer much of an opportunity to win, or they may look promising but really aren't because the cards you need are dead. (For details about dead cards, see the section titled "Comprehending the Importance of Live Cards" in this chapter.)

GETTING PERSONAL — WHAT YOU NEED TO WIN

Being a winning Seven-Card Stud player requires more than technical Poker skills. It also takes strength of character, determination, and grit.

- **Be patient.** In Poker, money flows from the impatient to the patient. If you lack patience, you'll never become a good player, regardless of how much knowledge you acquire. Stud Poker is a waiting game — one that requires the patience of a saint.

- **Be observant.** If you don't pay close attention to visible cards, you'll have a hard time winning on a consistent basis. If you're not aware of the discards, it is too easy to lose money by drawing to hands you probably won't make.

- **Be determined — play only live hands.** This skill is closely related to the need to be observant. Don't throw money away on hands that are really much more of a long shot than they might appear.

- **Be studious.** Because you'll throw away most of your starting hands, there's plenty of down time that can be put to good use by observing your opponents. Learn the kinds of hands they play. Observe their mannerisms, too. See if you can pick up any telltale clues about what they might be holding.

- **Be aggressive.** Don't be afraid to raise or even reraise if you think you have the best hand. Don't be afraid to checkraise either. It can be a good way to trap opponents when you have a powerhouse hand.

- **Be judicious.** Don't feel like you must play every hand dealt to you — that's a sure-fire way to lose your hard-earned money. Remember the "F-word." We're not talking expletives here, either. In Poker the "F-word" is *fold*. Don't ever be afraid to toss your hand away and wait for a better opportunity.

Antes, the Deal, and the Betting Structure, Oh My

Before the cards are dealt, each player posts an ante, which is a fraction of a bet. Each Poker game begins as a chase for the antes, so this money seeds the pot.

Players are then dealt two cards face down, along with one face up. The lowest exposed card is required to make a small bet of a predetermined denomination. This bet (and the person who makes this bet) is called the *bring-in*. If two or more players have an exposed card of the same rank, the determining factor is the alphabetical order of suits: clubs, diamonds, hearts, and spades.

Betting

The player to the immediate left of the bring-in has three options. He may fold his hand, call the bring-in, or raise to a full bet. In a $20–$40 game, the antes are usually $3 and the bring-in is $5. The player to the bring-in's left can either fold, call the $5 bring-in bet, or raise to $20 — which constitutes a full bet.

If that player folds or calls the bring-in, the player to his immediate left has the same options. As soon as someone raises to a full bet, subsequent players must fold, call the full bet, or raise again.

Once betting has been equalized, a second card is dealt face-up, and another round of betting ensues. This time, however, it's in increments of full bets. The player with the highest ranking *board cards* (cards that are face up) acts first.

If there are two high cards of the same suit, the order of the suit determines who acts first. The highest suit is spades, followed by hearts, then diamonds, and finally, clubs.

The first player to act may either check (a check, in actuality, is a bet of nothing) or bet. If a player has a pair showing (called an *open pair*), whether that pair resides in her hand or that of an opponent, she has the option to make a big bet in most cases. For example, in a $20–$40 game, the betting is still in increments of $20 on fourth street, except when there is an open pair. Then it's the discretion of any bettor to open for either $20 or $40, with all bets and raises continuing in increments that are consistent with the bet. (If the first two cards dealt face up to Brenda in a $20–$40 Stud game were a pair of jacks, then she or anyone else involved in that hand can bet $40 instead of $20.) This rule allows someone with an open pair to protect her hand by making a larger wager.

Raising

Most casinos allow three or four raises per betting round, except when only two players contest the pot. In that case, there is no limit to the number of raises permitted.

In Stud, the order in which players act (called *position*) is determined by the cards showing on the board and can vary from round to round. With the exception of the first round of betting on third street, where the lowest ranked card is required to *bring it in*, the highest hand on board acts first and has the option of checking or betting.

The highest hand could range anywhere from four-of-a-kind, to trips (three-of-a-kind), to two pair, to a single pair, or even the highest card, if no exposed pair is present.

Double bets

Betting usually doubles on fifth street, except if there's a player on fourth street who holds a pair. When there is, anyone involved in the hand has the option of making a double bet, and those players still contesting the pot are dealt another exposed card. *Sixth street* is the same. The last card, called *seventh street* or *the river*, is dealt face down. At the river, active players have a hand made up of three closed and four exposed cards. The player who acted first on sixth street acts first on seventh street too.

Showdown

If more than one player is active after all the betting has been equalized, players turn their hands face up, making the best five-card hand from the seven cards they are holding, and the best hand wins in a showdown (see Figure 3-1).

Spread-limit games

Many low-stakes Seven-Card Stud games use spread limits rather than fixed limits. Many casinos will spread $1–$3 or $1–$4 Seven-Card Stud games. These games are usually played without an ante. The low card is required to bring it in for $1, and all bets and raises can be in increments from $1–$4 — with the provision that all raises be at least the amount of the previous bet. If someone bets $2 you can raise $2, $3, or $4 — but not $1. If the original bettor had wagered $4, you can fold, call his $4 bet, or raise to $8.

Identifying Winning Hands

Winning Seven-Card Stud generally takes a fairly big hand (usually two pair, with jacks or queens as the big pair). In fact, if all the players in a seven-player game stayed around for the showdown, the winning hand would be two pair or better more than 97 percent of the time. Even two pair is no guarantee of winning, however, because 69 percent of the time the winning hand would be three-of-a-kind or better, and 54 percent of the time the winning hand would be at least a straight.

A straight is the median winning hand: Half the time the winning hand is a straight or better, half the time a lesser hand will win the pot.

If you plan to call on third street, you need a hand that has the possibility of improving to a fairly big hand.

TIP

Because straights and flushes are generally not made until sixth or seventh street, you should raise if you have a big pair (10s or higher). In fact, if someone else has raised before it's your turn to act, go ahead and reraise — as long as your pair is bigger than his upcard. The goal of your raise is to cause drawing hands to fold so your big pair can win the pot — particularly if it improves to three-of-a-kind or two pair.

Big pairs play better against a few opponents, while straights and flushes are hands that you'd like to play against four opponents (or more). It's important to realize that straights and flushes start out as straight- and flush-draws. *Draws* are hands with no immediate value and won't grow into full-fledged straights and flushes very often. But these draws have the potential of growing into very big hands, and those holding them want a lot of customers around to pay them off whenever they are fortunate enough to complete their draw.

Comprehending the Importance of Live Cards

Stud Poker is a game of live cards. If the cards you need to improve your hand are visible in the hands of your opponents or have been discarded by other players who have folded, then the cards you need are said to be *dead*. But if those cards aren't visible, then your hand is *live*.

Many beginning Seven-Card Stud players are overjoyed to find a starting hand that contains three suited cards. But before you blithely call a bet on third street, look around and see how many cards of your suit are showing. If you don't see any at all, you're certainly entitled to jump for joy.

But if you see three or more of your suit cavorting in your opponents' hands, then folding your hand and patiently waiting for a better opportunity may be the only logical course of action.

Even when the next card you're dealt is the fourth of your suit and no other cards of your suit are exposed, the odds are still 1.12-to-1 against completing your flush. Of course, if you complete your flush, the pot will certainly return more than 1.12-to-1, so it pays to continue on with your draw. But remember: Even when you begin with four suited cards, you'll make a flush only 47 percent of the time.

CONSIDER THE ODDS

Here are some odds that will help you put the game of Seven-Card Stud in perspective.

- **424-to-1:** The odds against being dealt three-of-a-kind. (At an average of 30 hands per hour, you'll start with three-of-a-kind every 14 hours or so. That's why it hurts so much when you're dealt a hand like this and lose!)

- **5-to-1:** The odds against being dealt *any* pair on your first three cards.

- **18-to-1:** The odds against being dealt three suited cards.

- **3.5-to-1:** The odds against making a full house if your first four cards make two pair.

- **6-to-1:** The odds against making a straight if your first three cards are sequenced.

- **5-to-1:** The odds against making a flush if your first three cards are suited.

- **1.2-to-1:** The odds *in favor* of improving to at least two pair if you start with a straight flush draw like 10♦J♦Q♦.

- **1.4-to-1:** The odds against making two pair if you start with a pair in your first three cards. The odds are 4.1-to-1 against making three-of-a-kind or better.

- **1.1-to-1:** The odds against making a flush if you begin with three suited cards and catch a fourth card of your suit on the next round. But if you don't catch a fourth suited card on fourth street, the odds against making that flush jump all the way to 2-to-1!

- **4-to-1:** The odds against making a full house if you hold three-of-a-kind and three other cards on sixth street.

If you don't make your flush on fifth street, the odds against making it increase to 1.9-to-1 — which means you'll get lucky only 35 percent of the time. And if you miss your flush on sixth street, the odds against making your flush increase to 4.1-to-1. With only one more card to come, you can count on getting lucky about only 20 percent of the time.

This also holds true for straight draws. If your first four cards are 9-10-J-Q, there are four kings and an equal number of eights that will complete your straight. But if three kings and an eight have already been exposed, the odds against completing a straight are substantially higher and the deck is now stacked against you, and even the prettiest-looking hands have to be released.

The first three cards are critical

Starting standards are important in Seven-Card Stud, just as they are in any form of Poker. Those first three cards you've been dealt need to work together or contain a big pair to make it worthwhile for you to continue playing.

Position

Position (your place at the table and how it affects betting order) is important in every form of Poker, and betting last is a big advantage. But unlike games like Texas Hold'em and Omaha, where position is fixed for all betting rounds during the play of a hand, it can vary in stud. The lowest exposed card always acts first on the initial betting round, but the highest exposed hand acts first thereafter.

Because there's no guarantee that the highest exposed hand on fourth street will be the highest hand on the subsequent round, the pecking order can very from one betting round to another.

Subsequent betting rounds

If you choose to continue beyond third street, your next key decision point occurs on fifth street — when the betting limits typically double. Most Seven-Card Stud experts can tell you that a call on fifth street often commits you to see the hand through to its conclusion. If you're still active on fifth street, the pot is generally big enough that it pays to continue to the sometimes bitter end. In fact, even if you can only beat a bluff on the river, you should generally call if your opponent bets.

By learning to make good decisions on third and fifth street, you should be able to win regularly at most low-limit games.

Going Deeper into Seven-Card Stud

Seven-Card Stud is a game of contrasts. Start with a big pair, or a medium pair and a couple of high side cards, and you want to play against only a few opponents — which you can achieve by betting, raising, or reraising to chase out drawing hands.

If you begin with a flush or straight draw, you want plenty of opponents, and you'd like to make your hand as inexpensively as possibly. If you're fortunate enough to catch a scare card or two, your opponent will have to acknowledge the possibility that you've already made your hand or are likely to make it at the earliest opportunity. If that's the case, he may be wary of betting a big pair into what appears to be a powerhouse holding such as a straight or flush.

That's the nature of Seven-Card Stud. The pairs do their betting early, trying to make it expensive for speculative drawing hands, and those playing draws are betting and raising later — if they've gotten lucky enough to complete their hands.

Starting hands

Most of the time you'll throw your hand away on third street. Regardless of how eager you are to mix it up and win a pot or two, Seven-Card Stud is a game of patience. If you lack patience — or can't learn it — this game will frustrate you to no end.

Many players lose money because they think it's okay to play for another round or two and see what happens. Not only does this usually result in players bleeding their money away, the very fact that they entered a pot with less than a viable starting hand often causes them to become trapped and lose even more money.

Before making a commitment to play a hand, you need to be aware of the strength of your cards relative to those of your opponents, the exposed cards visible on the table, and the number of players to act after you do. After all, the more players who might act after you do, the more cautious you need to be.

Starting with three-of-a-kind

The best starting hand is *three-of-a-kind*, which is also called *trips*. But it's a rare bird, and you can expect to be dealt trips only once in 425 times. If you play fairly long sessions, statistics show that you'll be dealt trips every two days or so. Although it's possible for you to be dealt a lower set of trips than your opponent, the odds against this are very long. If you are dealt trips, you can assume that you are in the lead.

You might win even if you don't improve at all. Although you probably won't make a flush or a straight if you start with three-of-a-kind, the odds against improving are only about 1.5-to-1. When you do improve, it's probably going to be a full house or four-of-a-kind, and at that point you will be heavily favored to win the pot.

With trips, you will undoubtedly see the hand through to the river, unless it becomes obvious that you're beaten. That, however, is a rarity.

Because you'll be dealt trips once in a blue moon, it's frustrating to raise, knock out all your opponents, and win only the antes. Because you are undoubtedly in the lead whenever you are dealt trips, you can afford to call and give your opponents a ray of hope on the next betting round.

The downside, of course, is that one of your opponents will catch precisely the card he needs to stay in the hunt and beat you with a straight or flush if you're not lucky enough to improve. When you have trips, you're hoping that one of your opponents will raise before it's your turn to act. Then you can reraise, which should knock out most of the drawing hands.

Most of the time the pot is raised on third street, the player doing the raising either has a big pair or a more modest pair with a king or an ace for a side card. But your trips are far ahead of his hand. After all, he is raising to eliminate the drawing hands and hoping to make two pair in order to capture the pot. Little does he know that you're already ahead of him, never mind the fact that you also have ample opportunity to improve.

Your opponent will probably call your reraise, and call you all the way to the river especially if he makes two pair. Here's what usually happens. In the process of winning the pot, you earn three small bets on third street, another on fourth street, and double-sized bets on fifth, sixth, and seventh streets. If you're playing $10–$20, you'll show a profit of $100 plus the bring-in and the antes. If you've trapped an additional caller or two who wind up folding their hand on fifth street, your profit will exceed $150.

Big pairs

A *big pair* (10s or higher) is usually playable and generally warrants raising. Your goal in raising is to thin the field and make it too expensive for drawing hands to continue playing. A single high pair is favored against one opponent who has a straight or a flush draw. Against two or more draws, however, you are an underdog.

REMEMBER

It's always better to have a *buried pair* (both cards hidden) than to have one of the cards that comprise your pair hidden and the other exposed. There are a number of reasons for this. For one thing, it's deceptive. If your opponent can't see your pair — or even see part of it — it will be difficult for him to assess the strength of your hand.

If fourth street were to pair your exposed card and you come out swinging, your opponent would be apprehensive about your having three-of-a-kind. This might constrain his aggressiveness and limit the amount you can win. But if your pair is buried, and fourth street gives you trips, no one has a clue about the strength of your hand, and they won't until you've trapped them for a raise or two.

MASTER A WINNING STRATEGY

Become a winning Seven-Card Stud player by mastering these strategic elements:

- If you have a big card showing and no one has entered the pot on third street when it's your turn to act, you should raise and try to steal the antes.

- This game requires immense patience, especially on third street. If you don't have a big pair, big cards, or a draw with live cards, save your money.

- Drawing hands offer great promise. But to play them, your cards must be live. Draws are also more playable if your starting cards are higher in rank than any of your opponents' visible cards. This can enable you to win even if your draw fails but you are fortunate enough to pair your big cards.

- After all cards have been dealt and you have a single opponent who comes out betting, you should call with any hand strong enough to beat a bluff.

- Seven-Card Stud requires strong powers of observation. Not only must you be aware of whether the cards you need are live or not, you must also be aware of the cards most likely to improve your opponent's hand.

- Fifth street, when the betting limits double, is a major decision point. If you buy a card on fifth street, you've probably committed yourself to see the hand through to its conclusion.

Big pairs play best against one or two opponents and can sometimes win without improvement. But you're really hoping to make at least two pair. If you are up against one or two opponents, your two pair will probably be the winning hand.

WARNING

Having said that, a word of caution is in order. It's critically important not to take your pair against a bigger pair, unless you have live side cards that are bigger than your opponent's probable pair. For example, if you were dealt J♦A♥/J♠, and your opponent's door card is Q♠, her most likely hand is a pair of queens if she continues on in the hand. (The slash mark indicates that the two cards to the left of the slash were dealt to the player face-down. The card to the right of the slash was dealt face-up.)

As long as your ace is live, you can play against the opponent. For one thing, she might not have a pair of queens. She might have a pair of buried 9s, in which case you're already in the lead. Even if she does have queens, you could catch an ace or another jack, or even a king. An ace gives you two pair that's presumably bigger than your opponent's hand, while trip jacks puts you firmly in the lead.

Even catching a live king on fourth street can help you. It offers another way to make two pair that is bigger than your opponent. You may be behind at this point, but you still have a number of ways to win.

Small or medium pairs

Whether you have a pair of deuces or a bigger pair is not nearly as important as whether your side cards are higher in rank than your opponent's pair. If you hold big, live side cards along with a small pair, your chances of winning are really a function of pairing one of those side cards — and aces up beats queens up, regardless of the rank of your second pair.

Small or medium pairs usually find themselves swimming upstream and need to pair one of those big side cards to win. Although a single pair of aces or kings can win a hand of stud, particularly when it's heads-up, winning with a pair of deuces — or any other small pair, for that matter — is just this side of miraculous; it doesn't happen very often.

Playing a draw

If you've been dealt three cards of the same suit or three cards that are in sequence, the first order of business is to see if the cards you need are available. (Carefully check out your opponent's exposed cards to see if any of the cards you need are already out.) If the cards you need are not already taken, you can usually go ahead and take another card off the deck.

If you see that your opponents have more than two of your suit or three of the cards that can make a straight, you really shouldn't keep playing. If your cards are live and you can see another card inexpensively, however, go ahead and do so. You might get lucky and catch a fourth card of your suit, or you could pair one of your big cards and have a couple of ways to win. Your flush could get back on track if the fifth card is suited, or you could improve to three-of-a-kind or two big pair.

WARNING

Drawing hands can be seductive because they offer the promise of improving to very large hands. Skilled players are not easily seduced, however, and are armed with the discipline required to know when to release a drawing hand and wait for a better opportunity to invest their money.

Beyond third street

Fourth street is fairly routine. You're hoping your hand improves and that your opponents don't catch the cards you need or a card that appears to better their own hand.

When an opponent pairs his exposed third street card, he may well have made three-of-a-kind. When this happens, and you have not appreciably improved, it's usually a signal to release your hand.

Fifth street is the next major decision point. This is when betting limits typically double. If you pay for a card on fifth street, you'll generally see the hand through until the river, unless it becomes obvious that you are beaten on board. It's not uncommon for any number of players to call on third street and again on fourth. But when fifth street rolls around, there are usually only two or three players in the hand.

Often it's the classic confrontation of a big pair — or two pair — against a straight or flush draw. Regardless of what kind of confrontation seems to be brewing, unless you have a big hand or big draw, you'll probably throw away many of your once-promising hands on fifth street.

In fact, if you throw away too many hands on sixth street, you can be sure that you're making a mistake on both fifth and sixth street.

REMEMBER

If you are fortunate enough to make what you consider to be the best hand on sixth street, go ahead and bet — or raise if someone else has bet first. Remember, most players will see the hand through to the river once they call on fifth street. When you have a big hand, these later betting rounds are the time to bet or raise. After all, good hands don't come around all that often. When you have one, you want to make as much money as you can.

When all the cards have been dealt

If you've seen the hand through to the river, you should consider calling any bet as long as you have a hand that can beat a bluff (assuming you're *heads up* — playing against just one other player). Pots can get quite large in Seven-Card Stud. If your opponent was on a draw and missed, the only way for her to win the pot is to bluff and hope you throw away your hand. Your opponent doesn't need to succeed at this too often to make the strategy correct. After all, she is risking only one bet to try to capture an entire pot full of bets.

Most of the time you'll make a *crying call* (a call made by a person who is sure he will lose), and your opponent will show you a better hand. But every now and then, you'll catch her *speeding* (bluffing), and you'll win the pot. You don't have to snap off a bluff all that often for it to be the play of choice.

IN THIS CHAPTER

Understanding the basics

Taking a deeper look

Checking out starting hands

Getting to know the ins and outs of raising

Chapter 4

Tackling Texas Hold'em

Texas Hold'em is the most popular game played in casino Poker rooms. Although playing expertly requires a great deal of skill, Hold'em is easily learned and deceptively simple. It is a subtle and complex game, typically played with nine or ten players to a table, and is a faster, more action-filled game than Stud or most other games. Texas Hold'em is also the fastest growing Poker game in the world, and it's the game used to determine the world champion at the World Series of Poker.

In this chapter, we cover the basics of Hold'em. We get into a lot more details about the game in Book 3.

Understanding the Basic Rules

In Hold'em, two cards are dealt face-down to each player, and a round of betting takes place. On the first round, players may either call or raise the blind bet, or they must fold their hand. Most casinos allow a bet and three or four raises per betting round, with one exception: When only two players contest the pot there is no limit on the number of raises permitted.

When the first round of betting is complete, three communal cards, called the *flop*, are turned face-up in the center of the table. (See Book 3, Chapter 3 for more on playing the flop.) That's followed by another round of betting. On this and each succeeding round, players may check if no one has bet when it's their turn to act. If there is no bet, a player may check or bet. If there is a bet, players may fold, call, raise, or reraise.

A fourth communal card — called the *turn* — is then exposed (see Book 3, Chapter 4). Another round of betting takes place. Then the fifth and final community card — known as the *river* — is placed in the center of the table followed by the last round of betting (see Book 3, Chapter 5). The best five-card Poker hand using any combination of a player's two private cards and the five communal cards is the winner.

That's all there is to the play of the game. Yet within this simplicity lies an elegance and sophistication that makes Texas Hold'em the most popular form of Poker in the world.

Looking at Blind Bets

Before cards are dealt, the first two players to the left of the dealer position are required to post *blind bets*, which are used instead of antes to stimulate action. (Those two players post their bets before they see any cards and, thus, are "blind.")

In a $10–$20 Hold'em game, blinds are usually $5 and $10. Each blind is considered live. Because blinds represent a forced, first bet, the blind bettors can raise (but only on the first round) once the betting has gone around the table and it's their turn to act again. (For more on blinds, see Book 3, Chapter 1.)

Unlike Stud, where each player's exposed cards determines position, referred to as his *board*, the player with the dealer button (see the section "Position, position, and position," later in this chapter) acts last in every round of betting — with the exception of the first one.

Getting to Know Hold'em in General

While Hold'em is exciting, exhilarating, and enjoyable, you should know something before diving in and plunking your money down — even if Hold'em is the lowest-limit game in the house. This section offers a few of those somethings we wish we had known when first making the transition from Seven-Card Stud to Texas Hold'em.

Hold'em only looks like Stud; it plays differently

With a total of seven cards, some of which are turned face-up and others down, Hold'em bears a resemblance to Seven-Card Stud. But this furtive similarity is only a "tastes like chicken" analogy.

TIP

One major difference is that 71 percent of your hand is defined on the flop. As a result, your best values in Hold'em are found up front; you get to see 71 percent of your hand for a single round of betting.

WARNING

Staying for the turn and river demands that you either have a strong hand, a draw to a potentially winning hand, or good reason to believe that betting on a future round may cause your opponents to fold. Because there are only two additional cards dealt after the flop, along with the fact that the five communal cards play in everyone's hand, there are fewer draw-outs in Hold'em than Stud. (A *draw-out* happens when you draw cards that make your hand better than your opponent's.)

Also, because Hold'em uses exposed communal cards in the center of the table that combine with two hidden cards in each player's hand to form the best Poker hand, it's more difficult for an opponent to draw-out on you than in Stud Poker. For example, if you were dealt a pair of jacks and your opponent held a pair of 9s, the presence of a pair of 5s among the communal cards gives each of you two pair. But you still have the best hand. Unless one of those 5s helped an opponent complete a straight, the only player helped by that pair of 5s would be an opponent fortunate enough to have another 5 in his hand.

The first two cards are critical

REMEMBER

You'll frequently hear players say that any two cards can win. Although that's true as far as it goes, it doesn't go far enough. The whole truth is this: Although any two cards can win, they won't win enough to warrant playing them. Like all forms of Poker, you need *starting standards.* Players who lack starting standards take the worst of it far too often. See Book 2, Chapter 1 for more detail about starting standards.

Position, position, and position

There's an old real estate bromide that says the three most important features of any property are location, location, and location. In Hold'em, the important features are position, position, and position. Where your place is at the table (your *position*) is so important that some two-card holdings, which can't be played profitably from early position, are cards you might raise with when you're last to act.

In a typical nine-handed game, *early position* includes both blinds and the two players to their left. The fifth, sixth, and seventh players to act are in *middle position,* and the eighth and ninth players are in *late position.* (Find more details about position, including the hands you should play in a particular position, in Book 3, Chapter 2.)

Because house dealers deal casino games, a small disk — called a *puck,* a *buck,* or, most commonly, a *button* — is used as a marker to indicate the player in the dealer position. That player is always last to act. The button rotates clockwise around the table with each hand that's dealt. The expression "passing the buck" does not refer to dollar bills, but to Poker. And President Harry S. Truman, an avid Poker player himself, had a sign on his desk in the White House that read, "The buck stops here."

The flop should fit your hand

TIP

No matter how sweet your first two cards may appear, an unfavorable flop can render them nearly worthless. A key concept is that the flop must fit your hand. We call this concept "fit or fold." If the flop doesn't strengthen your hand or offer a draw to a very strong hand, you should usually release it. (Book 3, Chapter 4 goes into more detail about playing the flop.)

Suppose you called on the first round of betting with A♦ J♦, and the flop is Q♦ 5♦ 3♠. You don't have a strong hand at this point. What you do have, however, is a hand with extremely strong potential. If another diamond falls on the turn or the river, you'll make a flush. Not any flush, mind you, but the best possible flush, since your ace precludes any of your opponents from making a higher one.

Even if you don't make a flush but were to catch a jack or an ace instead, that may be enough to win the pot.

Beyond the flop

As a general rule, you shouldn't continue beyond the flop without a strong pair and a decent side-card (or *kicker*), or a straight or flush draw with at least two opponents to ensure that the pot is big enough to make it worthwhile.

Because of the communal cards, players frequently have the same hand, with the exception of their unpaired side card, or kicker. When that happens, it's the rank of each player's kicker that determines who wins the pot in question. That's why most Hold'em players love to be dealt A-K (or "Big Slick," as players call it). If the flop contains either an ace or a king, the player holding Big Slick will have the top pair with the best possible kicker.

Game texture — the relative aggressiveness or passivity exhibited by the players — is also important in determining whether to call that bet or raise. But a feeling for the game's texture and how it should influence your play can be obtained only from live game experience. In the absence of that experience, err on the side of caution. It costs less.

Success at Hold'em demands that you be patient, pay close attention to position, and take comfort in the knowledge that good hands are run down less often than the best Seven-Card Stud hands.

Considering Starting Card Combinations

Combinations of Poker hands number literally in the millions; in Hold'em, however, there are only 169 different two-card starting combinations. That number, of course, assumes that a hand like K♦ Q♦ is the equivalent of K♣ Q♣. If three diamonds were to appear on the flop, the K♦ Q♦ would be significantly more valuable than K♣ Q♣. But the future can neither be predicted nor controlled, and these two hands have identical value before the flop.

Each one of these 169 unique starting combinations fits into one of only five categories:

>> Pairs
>> Connecting cards
>> Gapped cards
>> Suited connectors
>> Suited gapped cards

That's it. Five categories. That's all you have to worry about.

If you are not dealt a pair, your cards will be either *suited* (of the same suit) or *unsuited.* They also can be *connected* (consecutive) or *gapped* (unconnected). Examples of connectors are K-Q, 8-7, and 4-3. Unconnected cards might be one-, two-, three-gapped, or more, and would include hands like K-J (one gap, with Q missing), 9-6 (two gap, missing 7-8), or 9-3 (five gap, missing 4-5-6-7-8).

Small gaps make more straights

Generally, the smaller the gap, the easier it is to make a straight. Suppose that you hold 10-6. Your only straight possibility is 9-8-7. But if you hold 10-9, you can make a straight with K-Q-J, Q-J-8, J-8-7, and 8-7-6.

Every rule has exceptions. A hand like A-K can make only one straight. It needs to marry a Q-J-10. An A-2 is in the same boat and needs to cozy up to a 5-4-3. Although connected, each of these holdings can make only one straight because they reside at the end of the spectrum.

Other exceptions include a K-Q, which can make a straight only two ways, by connecting with A-J-10 or J-10-9; and 3-2 is in a similar fix. The only other limited connectors are — yes, you guessed it — Q-J and 4-3. These two holdings can each make three straights. The Q-J needs A-K-10, K-10-9, or 10-9-8. It can't make that fourth straight because there is no room above an ace. The 4-3 is similarly constrained because there is no room below the ace. But any other connectors can make straights four ways, and that's a big advantage over one-, two-, or three-gapped cards.

Unless you are fortunate enough to wrap four cards around one of your four-gappers, there's no way these cards can make a straight. But don't worry about that. If you take our advice, you will seldom, if ever, play hands that are four-gapped or worse unless they are suited — and then only under very favorable circumstances.

Gapped cards

Gapped cards, in general, are not as valuable as connectors because of their difficulty in completing straights. But if you were to make a flush there's no need to be concerned about the gap. After all, a flush made with A♥6♥ is just as good as an A♥K♥ flush. But A-K is more valuable for other reasons. Suppose that flush never comes. You can make a straight with A-K; you can't with A-6 (unless four cards come on the board to help your straight).

You might also win if you catch either an ace or a king. If an ace flops, you'll have made a pair of aces with a 6 side-card, or kicker, and could easily lose to an opponent holding an ace with a bigger companion. But any pair you'd make with the A-K would be the top pair with the best possible kicker.

Acting last is a big advantage

Acting later in a hand is a big advantage, so you can afford to see the flop with weaker hands when you're in late position. If you're last to act, you've had the advantage of knowing how many opponents are still in the pot and seeing how each of them acted on the current round of betting. That's a big edge, because some starting hands play better against a large number of opponents, while others play better against a smaller field.

FIVE TIPS FOR WINNING HOLD'EM PLAY

If you play Hold'em correctly, you'll incorporate all these tips into your game:

- Play few hands from early position. You'll throw lots of hands away, but you'll be saving money.

- Position is critical in Hold'em. Certain hands that you would fold in early position can be raising hands in late position.

- Fit or fold: If the flop does not help your hand, you must consider folding, regardless of how sweet it may have looked before the flop.

- Many of your opponents will play A-K as strongly as a pair of aces or kings, but it is not. A-K is a powerful drawing hand, but it usually needs help on the flop to win the pot.

- Hold'em only looks like Seven-Card Stud. In reality, it's a very different game due to the use of community cards, the positional aspect of the game, and the fact that on the flop you will see 71 percent of your hand for a single round of betting.

In late position you'll also know which of your adversaries are representing strength by betting or raising. The later you act, the more information at your disposal. And Poker is a game of information — incomplete information, to be sure, but it's a game of information nevertheless.

Mastering the Art of Raising

Raising adds spice to the game of Poker and money to the pot. Raising is an act of aggression and causes everyone to sit up and take notice. When there's a raise or reraise, the level of excitement escalates. Sometimes you'll be raised, and sometimes you'll do the raising. Regardless of whether you're the raiser or raisee, it's time to sit up and take notice whenever a raise is made.

You've been raised

If the pot has been raised before it is your turn to act, you must tighten up significantly on the hands you play. Savvy players might raise with almost anything in late position if no one except the blinds are in the pot, but if a player raises from early position, give him credit for a good hand, and throw away all but the very strongest of hands.

REMEMBER

You need a stronger hand to call a raise than to initiate one. After all, if you raise, your opponents might fold, allowing you to win the blinds by default. If you call a raise, you have to give your opponent credit for a strong hand, and you should generally only call if you believe your hand to be even stronger.

When someone's raised after you've called

When an opponent raises after you've called, you are essentially committed to calling his raise, seeing the flop, and then deciding on the best course of action.

But when you call only to find yourself raised and raised again by a third opponent you should seriously consider throwing your hand away unless it is extremely strong.

Suppose that you called with a hand like 10♥ 9♥. Just because this hand may be playable in a tame game doesn't mean you must play it. In a game with frequent raising, it may not a playable hand because it is speculative and best played inexpensively from late position. The ideal way to play this hand is from late position, with a large number of opponents, in a pot that has not been raised. Now this hand is worth a shot. You can always throw it away whenever the flop is unfavorable.

Recognizing when to raise

Hold'em is a game that requires aggressive play as well as selectivity. You can't win in the long run by passively calling. You have to initiate your share of raises too; and here are some raising hands:

>> You can always raise with a pair of aces, kings, queens, jacks, and 10s. In fact, if someone has raised before it's your turn to act and you have a pair of aces, kings, and queens in your hand, go ahead and reraise. You probably have the best hand anyway. Reraising protects your hand by thinning the field, thus minimizing the chances of anyone getting lucky on the flop.

>> You can also raise if you're holding a suited ace with a king, queen, or jack, or a suited king with a queen. If your cards are unsuited, you can raise if you're holding an ace with a king or queen, or a king with a queen.

>> If you are in late position and no one has called the blinds, you can usually safely raise with any pair, an ace with any kicker, and a king with a queen, jack, 10, or 9. When you raise in this situation, you're really hoping that the blinds — which are, after all, random hands — will fold. But even if they play, your ace or king is likely to be the best hand if no one improves.

IN THIS CHAPTER

Getting acquainted with Omaha/8

Knowing when to hold and when to fold

Covering Omaha/8 in depth

Playing the turn

Playing the river

Chapter 5

Becoming an Expert at Omaha

O maha Hold'em, 8-or-Better High-Low Split Poker is quite a mouthful — so you can just call it Omaha/8 for short. "The game of the future," as many Poker pundits predict, is a variation of Texas Hold'em in which each player receives four cards dealt face-down. Like its cousin, Texas Hold'em (see Book 2, Chapter 4 for an introduction to Hold'em; see Book 3 for details and strategies on the game), five community cards — which every player can use — are dealt face-up in the center of the table. The best high hand and the best low hand split the pot.

As in most split-pot games, lots of chips may be on the table because some players are trying to make the best low hand, some the best high one, while others are trying to scoop the entire pot.

Omaha/8 also creates action because each player is dealt four cards rather than the two that Texas Hold'em players receive. Naturally, with four cards to choose from, many players don't have any trouble finding a hand they think is worth playing.

Although you may get confused at times trying to ferret out the best five-card Poker hand from among the five community cards in the center of the table and the four private cards in each player's hand, don't worry — if you can play Texas Hold'em, you can play Omaha/8.

Playing Omaha/8 for the First Time

Omaha/8 looks almost like Texas Hold'em (see Book 2, Chapter 4 and/or Book 3), but you can expect four major differences:

>> Omaha/8 is a high-low split game, which means more players in each pot, more chips in the center of the table, and more action.

>> Each player must make his best five-card Poker hand by using exactly two cards from his hand and three communal cards. In Texas Hold'em, you can form the best hand using two, one, or even none of your private cards. If you are playing Texas Hold'em and you hold the ace of spades when the board contains four additional spades, you have a flush. But in Omaha, you have nothing at all. That's because you must play two cards — no more, no less — to make a valid Omaha hand.

>> Because you have four cards to work with, you can form six different starting combinations. In other words, by receiving four private cards, you have six times as many potential starting hands as you do as you do in Texas Hold'em. As a result, the winning hands tend to be quite a bit bigger than they do in Texas Hold'em.

REMEMBER

>> Straights and flushes are common; and two pair, which is often a winning hand in Texas Hold'em, seldom wins in this game. Regardless of how powerful a high hand you make, whenever three unpaired communal cards with a rank of 8 or lower are on the board, someone probably made a low hand and that big pot you were hoping to win has effectively been chopped in half.

Blind bets

Before any cards are dealt, the first two players to the left of the dealer position are required to post blind bets, which are used instead of antes to stimulate action. (For a more thorough discussion of blind bets, see Book 2, Chapter 2.)

In a $6–$12 Omaha/8 game, blinds are usually $3 and $6. Each blind is considered *live.* Because blinds represent a forced first bet, the players forced to post those bets can raise (but only on the first round) after the betting has gone around the table and it's their turn to act again.

Unlike Stud Poker, where position is determined by the cards showing on the board, the player with the dealer button acts last in every round of betting — with the exception of the first one.

The deal and betting structure

Four cards are dealt face-down to each player, and a round of betting takes place. On the first round, players may either call or raise the blind bet or fold their hands. Most casinos allow a bet and three or four raises per betting round, with one exception. When only two players contest the pot, the number of possible raises is unlimited.

When the first round of betting is complete, three communal cards, called the *flop*, are simultaneously turned face-up in the center of the table. Another round of betting follows. On this and each succeeding round, players may check if no one has bet when it's that player's turn to act. If there is no bet, a player may check or bet. If there is a bet, players must either fold, call, raise, or reraise.

A fourth communal card — called the *turn* — is then exposed. Another round of betting takes place. Then the fifth and final community card — known as the *river* — is placed in the center of the table, followed by the final betting round.

REMEMBER

The best five-card high Poker hand and the best five-card low Poker hand split the pot — with these provisos:

>> A player must use exactly two cards — no more, no less (from among his four private cards) to construct a Poker hand.

>> To have a low hand, a player must combine any two unpaired cards with a rank of 8 or lower with three unpaired communal cards with a rank of 8 or lower.

A player can make a high and a low hand by using different cards from his hand to construct the two hands. For example, if your private cards are A♣ 2♦ 3♥ K♥ and the five communal cards are Q♥ 9♠ 7♥ 6♥ 4♠, you have a flush. The flush is made by mating your K♥ 3♥ with the communal Q♥ 7♥ 6♥. You'd have a low hand too, which would be created by combining your A♣ 2♦ with the board's 7♥ 6♥ 4♠.

You'd have a terrific two-way hand. Although it's possible for an opponent to have made a bigger flush if she held the A♥ and any other heart in her hand, no one could have a better low hand than you do. You could be tied for low by anyone who also has an ace and a 2. In that case, you'd simply split the low side of the pot. But take our word for it — this is a terrific holding, and one that doesn't come around all that often.

TIP

Beginning players often have difficulty in determining the best Omaha hand. Before you plunk your money down and get in a game, we recommend dealing out some hands and trying to identify the best high and best low hands.

A sample hand

Figure 5-1 shows a sample hand of Omaha, with all cards dealt.

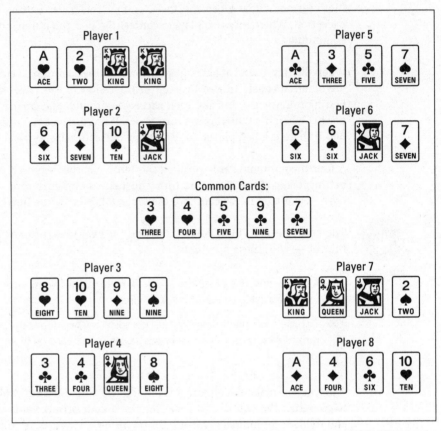

FIGURE 5-1:
A sample hand of
Omaha/8.

So, at the end, when all the common cards are dealt out, the hands are as follows in Table 5-1:

TABLE 5-1 **Possible Hands in Figure 5-1**

Player	Best High Hand	Best Low Hand
1	Pair of kings	5 low wheel (the best possible hand)
2	7-high straight	7-6 low
3	Three 9s	No low hand

Player	Best High Hand	Best Low Hand
4	Two pair — 3s and 4s	No low hand
5	Ace-high flush	7-5 low
6	7-high straight	7-6 low
7	No pair	No low hand
8	Pair of 4s	6-5 low

You can see that Player 1 will win the low and Player 5 will win the high. Player 8 has a good low, but may lose a lot of money.

Knowing When to Hold 'em and When to Fold 'em

Although Omaha looks confusing, you can take solace in the fact that even professional casino dealers sometimes have trouble determining the best hand. Having to look for high as well as low hands with so many card combinations probably leads to brain-lock on occasion. Don't worry. When you get used to the game, you'll be able to quickly spot potential draws and winning combinations.

With four cards in their hands, many players can always find something worth playing. These players are, of course, playing far too many weak hands that really don't warrant an investment and should be discarded rather than played. Even beginning Omaha/8 players can be considered a favorite in lower-limit games simply by playing better starting cards than their opponents play.

REMEMBER

Even experienced players often fail to realize that split-pot games are illusory in the sense that it appears as though one can play many more hands than they can in a game where only the high hand wins. But winning players are more selective than their opponents, and they enter pots only with hands that are superior to those that their opponents play most of the time.

Omaha/8 seems even more confusing when you have a two-way hand and must determine whether you have the best low hand as well as the best high one.

Although determining the best high and low hands (see Figure 5-1) requires concentration, Omaha/8's underlying precept is simple: The ideal hands are those that can capture the entire pot. That usually means beginning with low hands that also offer an opportunity to grow into a straight or flush. You can also start with big, high cards and hope for a flop containing nothing but high cards. When this happens, the pot will tend to be a bit smaller. But it won't be split either. Whenever the flop contains three big cards, all the one-way low draws have to fold. Their investment is *dead money* in the pot, and the pot will go to the winning high hand.

Position, position, and position

Position is fixed for the entire hand in Omaha/8, just as in Texas Hold'em. This means that if you're in late position and the pot hasn't been raised, you can see the flop with hands that are a bit weaker than you normally would consider playing because you have less chance of being raised. Position can give you an opportunity to get lucky with certain hands that can't profitably be played in a raised pot.

In a typical nine-handed game, early position includes both blinds and the two players to their left. The fifth, sixth, and seventh players to act are in middle position, and the eighth and ninth players are in late position.

The flop should fit your hand

Poker writer Shane Smith coined the phrase, "fit or fold." It's particularly true in Omaha/8. The flop must fit your hand by providing you with a good, strong hand or a draw to the best possible hand. If the flop doesn't meet those criteria, you likely should release your hand.

Going Deeper in Omaha/8

Nearly endless combinations are possible with four-card starting hands, but you need not be concerned with too many of them — most are easily recognizable as hands you'll release with neither remorse nor regret.

The best Omaha/8 starting combinations are coordinated, and they work together in some way. Many of your opponents will play hands in which only three of the four cards are coordinated, and others will play any four cards that look good.

Starting hands

The following sections offer examples of Omaha/8 starting hands; of course, these aren't the only possibilities. In the first example, a hand like A-2-3-5 is just about as good as A-2-3-4.

The very best

These hands are considered excellent:

>> A♣ 2♣ 3♦ 4♥: A suited ace with three low cards can make the nut low, as well as a straight, and the nut flush. By having sequenced low cards, you have protection against being counterfeited if one, or even two, of your low cards hit the board. You are said to be *counterfeited* if one of your low cards is duplicated on the board, thus weakening your hand considerably. For example, you hold A-2-7-9, and the board is 3-4-8. At this point, you have the best possible low hand (8-4-3-2-A). Suppose the turn card is a deuce. Now your low hand is 7-4-3-2-A, but it is no longer the nut low, and if an opponent holds A-5 in his hand, he will have an unbeatable low hand, as well as a 5-high straight (called a *wheel* or *bicycle* for a high hand, too).

>> A♣ K♦ 3♦ 4♣: A-K double-suited offers two flush combinations, two straight combinations, a draw to a very good low hand, and protection against making a low and having it counterfeited.

>> A♣ A♦ 2♦ 3♣: A pair of aces, two nut flush draws, a low hand with counterfeit protection, and a draw to the nut low are the features of this hand.

>> A♣ A♥ K♣ K♥: No low possibilities here, but a double-suited A-K is a very powerful hand, because you can make a straight, two flushes, and sets of aces or kings that can become a full house if the board pairs.

>> A♣ 2♣ 3♦ 9♥: Only three of the cards are coordinated, but with a large number of players in the pot, you have a draw to the nut low with counterfeit protection.

Very good hands

These hands are pretty good:

>> A♣ 2♣ 5♦ 5♥: Flush draw, nut low draw, straight draw are some of the possibilities. You might also flop a set to your pair of 5s. A-2 suited with any pair can be counterfeited for low and is not as strong as the very best hands, but it's a good hand nevertheless.

>> A♣ Q♣ J♦ 10♥: You'd like to see either all picture cards on the flop in hopes of making the best possible straight, or three clubs. If you flop a flush and two small cards are present, you must bet or raise at every opportunity to make it as costly as possible for low hands to draw against you. If a low hand is made, you've lost half your equity in this pot.

>> 2♣ 3♦ 4♥ 5♠: You're hoping an ace falls along with two other low cards. If it does, you've made the nut low and you probably have a straight draw, too.

» **A♥ 3♦ 5♠ 7♥:** Although this is good low draw along with nut flush possibilities, you won't make the best possible low hand unless the community cards include a 2. But you can easily make the second best low hand, which often spells trouble. Suppose that David holds A-3-x-x, Karen has 3-4-x-x, and Abby has A-2-x-x. Suppose that, at the end of the hand, the board is K-K-8-7-5. All three players made low hands, but Abby made the best possible low hand. David's hand is the second-best possible low hand, and if he were to bet and Abby were to raise, David would lose the low half of the pot.

Other playable hands that aren't ready for prime time

These hands aren't the best:

» **K♣ 2♦ 3♦ 4♥:** This hand offers a draw to a flush, though it's not the nut flush, and a draw to a low hand that won't be the best low unless an ace hits the board. Nevertheless, it's playable in late position, although this kind of hand often must be released if the flop doesn't fit it precisely.

» **K♣ K♦ 10♦ 10♠:** Here's a hand that can make a straight, albeit with great difficulty, and can make a flush, although it's not the best flush. The hand can improve to a set or a full house, too. It's playable, but it's the kind of hand that looks a lot stronger than it really is.

» **8♠ 9♥ 10♦ J♣:** This is a straight draw with no flush possibilities. If you make a 5-6-7-8-9 straight, any low hand will take half of this pot. If you make a big straight, you run the risk of losing the entire pot to a higher one. Midrange cards are dicey holdings in Omaha/8, and this is another of those hands that looks a lot better than it is.

» **K♣ Q♦ 2♦ 3♣:** This is a good-looking hand that can also lead to trouble. On the plus side, it's double-suited, providing two flush draws. And two straight draws are also possible, as well as a low hand. But the down side is that neither flush draw contains an ace, and you can't make the best possible low unless an ace appears among the communal cards. This hand and many others like it are what Poker players call trouble hands. They're seductive, and even when you catch what appears to be a good hand, it might be more trouble than it's worth. Hands like this are always treacherous and often can be disastrous.

» **5♣ 6♦ 7♦ 8♣:** Midrange cards spell trouble — even double-suited, as in this example. With midrange cards, you stand very little chance of scooping a pot. On the other hand, you can be scooped, particularly when you make a straight and your opponent makes a higher card straight.

Getting good at hand selection

Every form of Poker requires a blend of skills. But in Omaha/8, hand selection far outweighs other skills. Because any hand that is possible is also probable in Omaha/8, you need not be an expert at reading your opponents. Just reading the community cards to ascertain the best possible hand is usually enough. Bluffing, too, is not nearly as important in Omaha/8 as in other forms of Poker.

For example, if you're playing Texas Hold'em and all the cards are out, you may be successful if you try to bluff against one or two opponents. But not in Omaha/8. With four starting cards in their hands, each player has six starting combinations. Trying to bluff two players is like trying to run a bluff against a dozen starting hand combinations. The tactic's not going to work most of the time.

In fact, if you never bluffed at all in Omaha/8, you'd probably be better off.

REMEMBER

Because one does not need to bluff, or even possess the ability to read his opponents, the critical skill required to win at this game is hand selection.

Some players start with almost any four cards. If you can exert the discipline to wait for good starting cards — hands that are coordinated, with cards that support each other in some discernable way — you can have an edge over most of your opponents.

Acting last is a big advantage

You can afford to see the flop with weaker hands when you're in a late position. The later you act, the more information you can expect at your disposal, and Poker is a game of information — incomplete information, to be sure, but a game of information nevertheless.

Looking for a flop

Before you decide to call with the four cards you've been dealt, ask yourself what kind of flop would be ideal for your hand. And when you see the flop, determine which hand would be perfect for it. This kind of analysis will help you ascertain how well the flop fits your hand.

Here are eight convenient ways to characterize Omaha/8 flops:

>> **Paired:** When a pair flops, the best possible high hand is four-of-a-kind (which players refer to as *quads*), unless a straight flush possibly exists. Although flopping quads is a rarity, a full house is a distinct possibility.

>> **Flush or flush draw:** Three or two cards of the same suit.

>> **Straight or straight draw:** Three or two cards in sequence, or gapped closely enough so a straight is possible.

>> **High:** Three or two cards above an 8. If three cards higher in rank than an 8 flop, no low hand is possible.

>> **Low or low draw:** Three or two cards with the rank of 8 or lower.

These groupings are not mutually exclusive. Some of these attributes can appear in combination. For example, if the flop were A♣ 2♣ 2♦ it would be both *paired* as well as *low*, and contain a *flush draw* as well as a *straight draw*.

REMEMBER

It's important to recognize when a flop has multiple possibilities and to understand how your hand stacks up in the pecking order of possibilities.

Suppose you called on the first round of betting with A♦ 2♦ 3♣ K♠, and the flop is Q♦ 5♦ 4♠. You don't have a completed hand at this point. But you do have a draw to the best flush and the best low hand. In Poker parlance, you have a draw to the nut flush and the nut low. Any diamond gives you the best possible flush. Of course, if that card happens to be the 4♦, someone else could make a full house if that player holds a pair of queens or a pair of 5s in his hand, or he would make four-of-a-kind if he is holding a pair of 4s.

If any card with the rank of 8 or lower falls and it does not pair one of the low cards on the board, you have the best possible low hand. You also have a straight draw, and if a third diamond shows its face and doesn't pair the board, you also hold the nut flush.

If a 2 falls, then the 2 in your hand is said to be counterfeited because that 2 on the board belongs to everyone. Nevertheless, you still have the best possible low hand. That third low card in your hand provides insurance against being counterfeited.

The unpleasant experience of being quartered

When you win only one-fourth of a pot because you've split the low half of that pot with another opponent, both of you are said to have been *quartered*.

If only three players contest a hand, and two of them tie for low, each of the low hands loses money even though each wins one-fourth of the pot. Here's how to figure it: Suppose each of you put $40 dollars in the pot. If you are quartered for low, the high hand takes half of the $120 in the pot for his share. The remaining

$60 is then divided in half. Each of the low hands receives $30. Because each of you contributed $40, the return on your investment is only 75 cents on the dollar — if you keep winning pots like that, you'll go broke.

With four players in the pot, you can be quartered and break even. With five or more players, you come out a bit ahead if you're quartered. Nevertheless, being quartered is anything but a journey down the primrose path.

Worse than being quartered is playing hands that don't have much of a chance to make the best hand in one or both directions. If you play midrange cards, like 9-8-7-6, you may make a straight but wind up splitting the pot with a low hand. If you make the bottom end of a straight with Q-J-10, you don't have to worry about a low hand taking half the pot, but you do have to worry about losing the entire pot to a bigger straight.

REMEMBER

Playing low draws that don't contain an ace and a 2 is an invitation to make the second-best low hand, which is how many Omaha/8 players lose money. They play hands that look good, but aren't good enough to become the best hand in their direction.

Beyond the flop

As a general rule, you shouldn't continue beyond the flop without the best possible hand or a draw to the best possible high hand, low hand or both.

With six conceivable two-card combinations in each player's hand, a lot of hands are possible, so make certain you'll have the best hand if you catch the card you need.

Here's an example: Suppose the flop is K-8-7 of mixed suits, and you hold 2-3 among your four cards. If 4, 5, or a 6 hits the board, you'll make a low hand but so will your opponent who was drawing to an A-2. After you see the flop, here are some things to think about before deciding whether to keep playing:

>> **Draw quality:** If you make your hand, will it be the nuts? Suppose you have Q♠ J♠ among your starting cards and the flop contains two other spades. Although you have a flush draw, two higher flushes are possible. This is a dangerous hand. Drawing to the second or third best straight, drawing to the second or third best low hand, or thinking you have this pot won because you flopped the third best or second best set are common variations on this theme. Omaha/8 is a game of drawing to the nuts.

>> **Pot percentage:** How much of the pot are you hoping to win? Do you have a hand that might scoop the pot if you make it? Are you drawing for the top half

of the pot or drawing for low only? More than one player can have a draw to the best low hand, and unless you have at least four opponents, you can expect to lose money whenever you are quartered.

>> **Opponents:** Some hands play better against large fields; others play well short-handed. With a flush draw or a straight draw, you need five or six opponents to make the draw worthwhile if you figure to split the pot.

>> **Pot size:** Determine how much money you'll win if you scoop the pot, if you take half of it, or if you are quartered.

>> **Raised or not:** When the pot is raised before the flop in Omaha/8, the raiser usually has a superb low hand, such as A-2-3-4, or A-2-3-K, with the ace suited to another of his cards. If the flop contains all big cards, you probably have nothing more to fear from the raiser.

What to Do When You've Been Raised

TIP

If the pot has been raised before you act, tighten up on the hands you play. When you are raised before the flop, the raiser invariably has an outstanding low hand. If you have any low draw other than A–2 along with protection against being counterfeited, throw your hand away.

Since bluffing is infrequent in Omaha/8, if you are raised after the flop, the raiser usually has one of the following:

>> The best possible high hand

>> The nut low with a draw to a high hand

>> A big hand with a draw to a good low

As in all forms of Poker, you need a stronger hand to call a raise than to initiate one. Before you call a raise in Omaha/8, give your opponent credit for a strong hand — and quite possibly a strong hand in one direction and a draw to an equally strong hand in another. Call only if you believe your hand is stronger.

Flopping a Draw

Here's how to decide whether to continue with your draw if you flop a 4-flush or a 4-straight.

When you're facing three or more opponents, a draw is worthwhile if you think you'll win the entire pot by making your hand. If you have a draw to a high straight or flush and you are certain one of your opponents already has a low hand, half the pot will go to your opponent, so you'll need five or six opponents to make the draw profitable.

But if you have a draw and only two low cards are on the board, don't be afraid to bet, or even raise to make it expensive for opponents to draw for their half of the pot. If that low hand never materializes, their investment is dead money, and you'll claim it if you make your hand.

TIP

Table 5-2 shows how likely you are to make a low hand.

TABLE 5-2   **Likelihood of Making a Low Hand**

Number of Different Low Cards Dealt to You	Chances Before the Flop of Making a Low Hand	Chances of Making a Low Hand if Two New Low Cards Flop	Chances of Making a Low Hand if One New Low Card Flops
4	49%	70%	24%
3	40%	72%	26%
2	24%	59%	16%

Playing the Turn

If you survived the flop, keep playing if you have done any of the following:

>> Flopped the best high hand.

>> A draw to the best high hand.

>> Flopped the best low hand.

>> A draw to the best low hand.

>> Flopped a two-way hand. You may not have the best possible hand in each direction, but if you believe you can win in one direction and have a shot at the other, keep playing.

Should you play, or should you fold?

More often than not, the cards dealt on the turn won't clearly lead you to stay in or fold. When you're unsure of what to do, answer the following four questions to gauge whether it's a good idea to continue playing.

>> **How do my opponents play?** If your opponents are loose players, you can draw to the second best high hand; but if your opponents are tight players, you probably don't want to continue unless you have a draw to the best hand or have already made it.

>> **What in the world could my opponent be holding?** If the pot has been raised, you have to think about what kinds of hands your opponent would raise with, as well as the hands other players in the pot need to justify calling a raise.

>> **Where do I sit in relation to the other bettors?** If you think you might be raised if you call, you need a much stronger hand than you would if you have no reason to fear a raise.

>> **How much will it cost to see the hand through to its conclusion?** This is Poker's essential risk/reward issue. The amount of money you're likely to win if you make your hand should be higher than the odds against making your hand. In other words, if you think you'll win $30 on a $5 investment, it pays to stick around as long as the odds against making your hand are less than 6-to-1.

If you can win $30 for an investment of $5, the relationship between the cost of your investment and the size of the pot is 30-to-5, which reduces to 6-to-1.

If the odds against making your hand are only 3-to-1, then this represents a good bet. But if you were a 9-to-1 underdog, you're better off folding your hand.

Playing the turn at Omaha/8

If you survive the flop, here are some tips for playing the turn successfully:

>> Bet or raise aggressively if you've made the best possible hand on the turn.

>> If you have the nut low along with another low card to protect your hand from being counterfeited, bet and call all bets, but be wary of raising. You do not want to drive out other hands that would otherwise pay you off, and you want to avoid being drawn and quartered.

>> If you have the nut low hand along with a draw to a high hand, feel free to raise from late position. In this situation you want to get more money into the pot.

> You'll probably win the low end, and you want that additional money in the pot in case you win it all.

>> Call with a draw if the pot odds exceed the odds against making your hand and you know you'll have the best hand if you catch the card you need.

Playing the River

Because of all the straight, flush, and full house possibilities generated when each player's four-card private hands combine with five board cards, an Omaha/8 game is frequently decided on the last (or *river*) card. Omaha/8 is very different than Texas Hold'em in this regard. Texas Hold'em is a flop game, and the best hand on the flop is frequently the best hand on the river (see Book III, Chapter 5 for more details).

But that's not the case with Omaha. If there are five active players going into the river, you can be sure that at least three of them have one or more drawing combinations in their hands. Even the two players currently holding the best high and low hands also might have draws to better hands. With so many possibilities, you might imagine that almost any card will help someone.

Although the suspense can be frustrating, just imagine your joy when your draw comes in and you scoop a big pot. But the river can be treacherous, and here are some tips for navigating it safely.

When you make the best high hand

REMEMBER

If you have the best high hand after all the cards have been dealt, you can bet or raise without fear. You are assured of capturing at least half the pot, and may scoop it if there is no low.

This is the time to be aggressive. Get as much of your opponent's money in the pot as you can; at least half of it will come back to you.

When you have the best low hand

REMEMBER

Having the best low hand is not as simple as holding the best high hand. If you're absolutely sure you have the only nut low, you can bet or raise just as if you have the best high hand. But if one of your opponents has the same hand — and this is very common in Omaha/8 — you will be quartered. Making money when this happens is difficult. You need at least five players in the pot to show a profit, and it won't be much of a profit at that.

Suppose that five of you each has $20 in the pot. If you are quartered for low, you and the other low hand will each receive $25 — a scant $5 profit on your investment. The high hand will take $50, for a profit of $30.

If you have a two-way hand, you can be aggressive with it, particularly if you know you have the best hand in one direction. In the $20 per-player example, you would have won $100, for a net profit of $80, if you were able to scoop the pot.

That's why Omaha/8 and other split games are somewhat slippery slopes. Scooping the pot is not merely twice as good as winning one side of the confrontation — the win is usually much better than that.

Chapter 6

Trying Some Home Poker Games

Home Poker games have been around forever. A good home Poker game gives you something to look forward to with friends and colleagues. This chapter gives you advice on home games and how to set one up successfully.

Setting Up a Home Game

A successful ongoing home Poker game requires good planning and well-thought-out rules. The key to a good game, of course, is a friendly, fair game that people will want to keep coming back to on a regular basis.

This section shows you some key considerations for establishing a fair and fun game.

Rules

A good home game has rules established well before the game begins to avoid any controversy. Try to follow the rules that normally apply in card clubs and casinos so as to not confuse people who play in both.

Your rules should encompass answers to at least the following questions:

>> Is check-raising allowed?

>> How will antes be put up? By each player or only by the dealer?

>> What is the best low hand? (The great majority of card clubs say that A-2-3-4-5 is the best low, even though it's a straight.)

>> If you play a high-low game, how will the parties declare their hand? (Chips in the hand is the most common method.)

>> In a high-low game, if one person goes both ways, what happens if he ties one way?

>> Who splits the pot if a player going both ways wins only one way?

>> What constitutes a misdeal?

>> What happens if there is a misdeal?

>> If the pot is split between two players, who gets any odd chip?

Think about putting your rules on paper. Memories fade as to what was agreed upon, so it's helpful to bring out the rules in the event of any controversy.

Dealer's choice

Many home games involve a variety of Poker games, but dealer's choice is usually the deciding factor on the actual game to be played. That is, the dealer can choose the game she wishes to play for that hand or for a round.

The dealer may also designate any special rules such as:

>> Whether there will be a high-low split.

>> Whether the betting will increase in certain instances.

>> Whether there is a wild card.

>> Whether there is a bet after there is a "declare" of low or high in split games.

Of course, the dealer's decisions should be reasonable. You can't have a situation where the rules unduly favor the dealer.

Betting stakes

The betting stakes for a home game need to be agreed on clearly in advance. On the one hand, you want the stakes to be meaningful — enough to keep up people's interest and to allow bluffing and other strategies to potentially be effective. But on the other hand, you don't want the stakes to be so high that players can lose a very large sum in one night. Huge swings can ultimately kill a game because people will drop off for fear that they can't continue sustaining significant losses.

Some games allow an increase in the stakes in certain Poker games or in the last hour of the game.

REMEMBER

But remember, a home game is also often about camaraderie and friendship, so if you're going to err on betting stakes, err on the low side.

Wild cards

Most Poker purists play without wild cards, but some games do incorporate wild cards. A wild card is specified by the dealer and can be used to greatly improve a hand. So if you are playing with a wild card or cards, you have to expect the hands to be better than those in regular Poker. Gauge your betting accordingly.

The typical choices for wild cards are:

>> **Joker:** The joker can be used as any card or, alternatively, for only aces, straights, and flushes.

>> **Deuces:** Each 2 card is wild. So a hand consisting of 4-4-2-2-J is 4-4-4-4-J.

>> **One-eyed jacks:** The jack of spades and jack of hearts have only one eye each, and these jacks when played as wild cards can be any card you wish.

Our preference is to play without wild cards. Wild cards introduce a high element of luck. So if you are a great Poker player, you don't want to introduce a greater luck component in your game that your opponents can benefit from.

TIP

A TRICK TO MITIGATE LOSSES

Some home Poker players try to ease the pain of losing big by using the following strategy: Set aside a few dollars from each pot. At the end of the night, the big loser (or the two big losers) receive the set-aside amount. This is effectively a wealth transfer from the winners to the losers, but it lessens the loss.

Trying Some Home Poker Games

Time limit

Before the game starts, set a time when the game will end and stick to it. By setting the time limit, everyone is on notice and whining can be avoided by people who are losing and want to continue playing past a reasonable hour.

Near the end, it's often appropriate for the host of the game to announce that the time is drawing near and that three more hands or one more round will end the game. That warning enables players to plan their end strategy accordingly.

Food and drinks

The host for the game should arrange for appropriate food and drinks in advance. Here is our favorite Poker food:

>> Chips and dip

>> Pizza

>> Wings

>> Licorice

>> Cashews, peanuts, or other nuts

>> Beer and soda

Don't get any of that frou-frou stuff like salads and kale. If you do, you should suffer humiliating comments from your friends.

Reimbursing the host for all of the expenses in getting the food and drinks is also appropriate. This is best accomplished by taking a few dollars from each pot until the right amount is set aside.

Paying up

The rules should clearly set forth in advance as to how the losers will pay and the winners compensated. The key issues to address are:

>> Will payment be in cash or check or by electronic transfer (such as through PayPal)?

>> Will payment be at the end of the night or at the next game?

Selecting What You Want to Play: Your Game Options

Home games typically have more game options than card clubs or casinos. The type of games is limited only by the imagination of the players. This section describes a number of the most common home games.

Seven-Card Stud

Seven-Card Stud is very popular and can be played high-only or high-low. Two down cards and one up card is first dealt to each player. Four more cards are dealt, three up, and the last one down, with betting intervals following each card. From the seven cards played, the best five cards win. Head over Book 2, Chapter 3 for a detailed description of the game.

Texas Hold'em

In Hold'em, each player receives two cards face-down, and then a bet ensues. Then three common cards are dealt face-up, followed by a common fourth and a common fifth card, with betting intervals. The best five cards out of the two in your hand and the five on the board constitutes the hand. See Book 3 for details and great tips.

Omaha High

In Omaha High, each player gets four cards face-down, and then a bet occurs. Then three cards are dealt face-up all at once on the board as common cards, with a betting round. Then a fourth common card is dealt face-up with a bet, with a betting round, and a fifth common card is dealt face-up with a common card and with a betting round. A player must use two (and only two cards) from his hand, together with three of the common cards. Hands in Omaha tend to be higher than those in Seven Stud or Hold'em because of the greater number of cards dealt out and the greater number of possibilities. Check out Book 2, Chapter 5 for some terrific tips on Omaha.

Omaha High-Low, 8-or-Better

Omaha High-Low, 8-or-Better (Omaha/8) is played in the same way as Omaha (four cards in your hand, five common cards ultimately on the board), but there is a high hand and a low hand that splits the pot. A qualifying hand of 8 or better is needed for a hand to be in contention to win half of the pot. Check out Book 2, Chapter 5 for advice on playing this game.

Pineapple

Pineapple starts with three cards dealt face-down to each player, and then a betting round ensues. Then three common cards are dealt face-up followed by a betting round. Then each player must discard one of the cards in his hand. Then a fourth common card is dealt face-up followed by betting, followed by a fifth common card face-up and then betting. The best five cards from the two in your hand and five on the board are played. Pineapple can also be played high-low.

Five-Card Draw

In Five-Card Draw Poker, each player is dealt five cards face-down. After the deal, a betting round occurs. After the betting round, beginning with the player on the dealer's left, a player may discard one or more cards, and the dealer then deals her from the deck as many cards as she has discarded (the draw). A player doesn't have to draw and can stay pat. (For example, if you already have a straight, flush, or full house, you should stay pat and not draw any cards.)

After the draw, there is another betting round, followed by the show of hands. Some games limit the number of cards that can be drawn, some not.

In one variation of Five-Card Draw, a person is allowed to bet only if she has a pair of jacks or better.

Lowball

Lowball is like Five-Card Draw, but the lowest hand wins the pot. Ace always counts as a low card and A-2-3-4-5 is the best possible low. Straights and flushes don't count, although some players play that 6-4-3-2-A is the lowest hand.

Like Five-Card Draw, five cards are dealt face-down, followed by a betting round. Then a player may discard cards to improve his hand, followed by a final betting round.

The best hand is referred to by the highest card in your hand. If two players have the same card that is the highest card, then the next lowest card counts. For example,

    7-6-5-4-2 beats 8-6-4-3-2

    7-5-4-2-A beats 7-6-4-3-A

    6-5-3-2-A beats 6-5-4-2-A

No pair beats any pair. So even K-10-9-8-7 Beats 2-2-3-4-5.

Lowball is typically a game that should be played conservatively, waiting for pat hands or hands with one-card draws.

Five-Card Stud

In Five-Card Stud, each player gets one card down and one card up initially, followed by a bet. Then each player gets a second up card, followed by a bet. A third and fourth card face-up is given to each player, each followed by a bet.

The best high hand at the end wins. There are variations of the game where players are allowed to buy one or two replacement cards after all five cards are dealt. The game can also be played high-low, although in this variation, no minimum 8-low-or better is typically required.

A high pair in regular Five-Card Stud can often win the hand.

Baseball

Baseball is typically a version of Seven-Card Stud, where each player gets two cards down, four cards dealt face-up, and a final card face-down. But in Baseball, all 9s and 3s are wild. If a 4 is dealt face-up, it entitles the player to an extra down card.

Baseball is a game where big, big hands often come up. With eight wild cards, you can see four of a kind easily, with straight flushes and five of a kind happening not infrequently.

Black Mariah

Black Mariah (sometimes referred to as Chicago) is a Seven-Card Stud game, except that the high spade in the hole splits half the pot. Sometimes Q♠ counts as the highest spade.

If you have the highest spade in the hole in the first two cards you get, you can keep betting and raising at will.

Indian Poker

Indian Poker is a one-card game dealt face-down to each player. Each player, without looking at his card, simultaneously places it on his forehead so that other player can see all cards but his own. Then there is a single round of betting, and then a showdown.

Razz

Razz is Seven-Card Stud, played low. Each player starts with two cards down and one card up. Each player must ante initially, and the high card on the board is typically required to make a small bet. Subsequent players may then call or raise.

As long as he stays in, a player gets ultimately a total of three hole cards and four exposed up cards. The best hand is A-2-3-4-5. The key to this game is starting with three low cards and being able to read your opponents' hands and remember what cards have been already played and folded.

Crisscross (or Iron Cross)

Five cards are dealt to each player face-down. Then five cards are placed face-down on the board as common cards, in two intersecting rows forming a criss-cross arrangement. The common cards are revealed clockwise, with the center card last, and with betting after each exposed card.

Two cards from a player's hand and one row from the crisscross are used. The game can be played high-only or high-low.

Poker Etiquette in Home Games

Basic etiquette plays a vital role in society, and it even applies to Poker. Players who are rude and inconsiderate may soon find themselves excluded from games or the object of silent derision. We're not saying you need to stick a doily under your beer or soda bottle, but keep the following do's and don'ts in mind.

Do . . .

When playing at home, make sure you do the following:

>> **Be honest:** Don't try to short-change the pot or otherwise cheat.

>> **Play quickly:** No one likes a slow player.

>> **Be courteous and friendly:** No one likes a whiner.

>> **Be a good winner:** Gloating and making fun of other players is a definite no-no.

>> **Be a good loser:** We all lose. It happens. But show some class and don't show your temper, swear, or throw cards. Definitely don't insult the other players.

>> **Let the other players know if you plan to leave early:** It's courteous to let the other players know in advance if you plan to quit early.

>> **Bet in sequence:** Bet, call, or fold when it's your turn. Acting out of turn can adversely affect another player's hand.

Don't . . .

When playing Poker at home, make sure you avoid these goofs:

>> **Give a player advice in the middle of a hand even if he asks for it:** This is a no-win proposition: Either the player who asked will be upset at you if the advice is wrong or the person who loses against the player will be mad at you.

>> **Look at another player's hand, unless you have permission:** Some players strongly object to your looking at their hand.

>> **Play Poker with a guy named "Doyle," "Amarillo Slim," or "Harpo":** These guys are too good for your normal home game.

3

Staying North of the Border: Texas Hold'em

Contents at a Glance

Chapter 1

Just Tell Me How to Play: Texas Hold'em Basics

Thirty years ago, Texas Hold'em lived in relative Poker obscurity. When co-author Mark "The Red" Harlan was playing in casinos, it was fairly common for people to come up and ask him about the game.

A little more than a decade ago, the perfect Hold'em storm was created: Chris Moneymaker won the $10,000 Main Event of the World Series (pocketing more than $2 million off of a $40 entry fee), the World Poker Tour became the most successful program in the history of the Travel Channel, and online play became prevalent. Today people of all backgrounds play Hold'em around the kitchen table, in casinos, and online. It's the most popular variation of Poker around.

The first time you see Texas Hold'em played, it can feel a little bit like the inside joke that only *you* don't get. Don't sweat it, though. Hold'em is an easy game to understand.

What's not as obvious is how much money you should take to the table, as well as the social standards of playing. We cover it all in this chapter.

The Order of Play

When Hold'em is played in a professional cardroom (be it online or in a brick-and-mortar casino), a dealer button acts as the theoretical point that the cards are being dealt from (more on that in the following section). This button moves one position clockwise around the table at the conclusion of every hand.

The player in the position immediately to the left of the dealer (that is to say, clockwise) *posts* an automatic bet called the *small blind,* and the player immediately to *his* left (or two places to the left of the dealer) posts an automatic bet known as the *big blind.* These are forced bets that players *must* make in order to get dealt into the game. All other players get to see their hands "for free."

Players decide whether to play or *fold* (quit) in a clockwise position, starting with the player immediately to the left (clockwise) of the big blind. Any players who fold are no longer eligible for the pot and are skipped over in subsequent betting rounds for that specific hand.

In Hold'em, your position relative to the other players is critical. When you're in the beginning of the betting order, your cards *have* to be of higher quality than the cards you would normally play in later position — especially if lots of players are left in the hand — because you have no idea what evil may lurk beyond. (For more detail on playing by position, see Book 3, Chapter 2.)

Likewise, if you're riding at the back of the calling order, you can afford to play *looser* hands (those that aren't as high quality) and hope to catch cards to break people's dreams. In fact, *pot odds* (the amount you bet relative to the amount you would win) say that sometimes you *should* call, even when you have a lesser hand.

Understanding Who Deals: The Dealer Button

If you're used to playing Poker at your kitchen table, you're probably familiar with rotating the deal from player to player at the end of every hand.

In a professional cardroom, the house employee that deals the cards isn't actually involved in the hand. That casino employee (also, a little confusingly, called the *dealer*) merely acts as a sometimes-wise-cracking card-distribution and pot-collection/distribution mechanism. The house doesn't have a vested interest in the hand; instead, it makes its money through the *rake* (a percentage of every pot).

When cards are dealt, the house acts as though there is a virtual dealer at the table, using a small round white marker with a *D* on it (for *dealer*) to signify the chosen dealer of the moment. Cards are dealt around the table in an order as though they're coming from the dealer marker, and all betting action starts immediately clockwise from that position.

Moving the dealer button around the table ensures that all people get to play all positions throughout a long session of cards.

Dealing the Cards

The order in which Hold'em is dealt is very specific and, assuming you're playing with a table full of lucid, honest people, never changes.

The hole cards

Starting with the player clockwise from the dealer button, all players are dealt two *hole cards,* one at a time, in a clockwise fashion. You *are* allowed to look at your hole cards (in fact you should — unless your psychic powers are way, way up there, it would be hard to know exactly what kind of hand you had if you didn't). However, for the most part you should *not* show these cards to other players, even when folding — more on that in the "Following Poker Etiquette" section, later in this chapter.

REMEMBER

Be very careful to not expose your hole cards to other players as you peek at them. You're allowed to use both of your hands to look at your cards (although you're not allowed to take your cards off the edge of the table) and should do so to help keep them shielded from prying eyes. Always memorize your cards when you look at them, including the suit — this will keep you from having to refer to them again when something like a flush or straight draw hits the board (if you do, it'll be obvious that you're looking to see if you hit your straight or flush draw).

TIP

When you're dealt your hole cards, it's not a bad idea to wait and not look at either of them until it's your turn to act. This way you can watch other players around the table as they glimpse at their cards for possible hints as to what they may have (see Book 3, Chapter 6 for more on tells). This strategy also keeps you from being obvious about whether you're going to bet or fold well before it's your turn to act.

WARNING

If you *do* decide to wait to look at your hole cards, nearly every player at the table will be looking at you as you glimpse your cards. Have your best Poker face ready. (If you don't have the ability to generate a good Poker face, sneak a peek at each of your cards, one at a time as they are dealt.)

PROTECTING YOUR HAND

When playing in a casino environment, *protecting* your cards is essential. This means you should always have control of your hole cards either by keeping your hands on them (not a great choice, because forgetting and letting them go is too easy), or by placing something on top of your cards as they lie at rest on the table.

The protector you use can range from just an extra Poker chip in your stack, to your car keys, or maybe even your *Lord of the Rings* lucky charm.

If you don't protect your hand, and it's hit by cards being *mucked* (discarded) by other players, your hand is automatically folded. Another possibility is that the dealer assumes you have folded and just mucks the hand herself. (The underlying theory here is that you can't prove what hand you had out of the mess of cards sitting in front of you.)

Get in the habit of dropping a chip on top of your face-down cards at the table. When you fold, pass your hole cards face-down to the dealer, and leave whatever you're using as a "protector" in front of you.

The flop

After a round of betting for the hole cards (see "Betting" later in this chapter), a card is *burned* off the top of the deck (meaning discarded without being looked at — this is done in case the top card had somehow been exposed or marked), and three cards are dealt face-up to the center of the table. This is known as the *flop* and is the start of the *community cards* on the table — those cards that everyone may incorporate in his hand.

Everyone who has not folded now has a five-card hand — two hole cards combined with the three community cards. A round of betting takes place.

The turn

After the flop betting round, another card is burned from the deck and a fourth community card is exposed. This card is known as the *turn* (sometimes *fourth street*).

All players still in the hand now have six cards to choose from to make their best five-card Poker hands. There is another round of betting and one more card yet to be exposed.

The river

A card is burned and the most infamous of community cards, the *river* (sometimes called *fifth street*) is dealt. All remaining players have seven cards for selecting their best five-card Poker hand (their two hole cards combined with the five community cards). A round of betting takes place, and the best five-card hand at the table is the winner. (Book 3, Chapter 5 has more details about playing in the river.)

To determine their five-card hand, players may use zero, one, or both of their hole cards in combination with five, four, or three community cards, respectively.

REMEMBER

Because a player is required to use at least three community cards to make a hand, there can be no flushes if there are not three cards of the same suit (multiple suits with no flush possibilities based on the current exposed community cards is known as a *rainbow*). Nor can there be a straight if there aren't three cards from a five-card sequence (for example, 5-8-9).

In Figure 1-1, George is playing the board and has a king-high heart flush. John is using one hole card for an ace-high flush, but Ringo is the big winner using both hole cards for a straight flush.

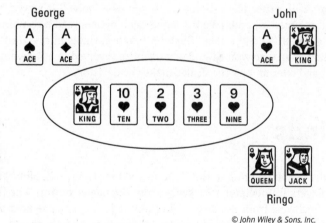

FIGURE 1-1:
Each player using a different number of hole cards to determine a hand.

© John Wiley & Sons, Inc.

The showdown

If everyone in a hand has folded, leaving a single player, that person wins the pot by default and is not required to show his hand to any player at the table in any way.

If more than one player at the table is still in a hand, and the final betting round has ended, the game has entered a phase known as the *showdown* (the part where people expose their cards to see who has won).

Anyone still in the hand may turn over his cards at this point, but people are usually reluctant to do so. If no one is making a motion to show his hand, the last person to raise (or the first person to bet if there were no raises on the river) in the final round of betting exposes his hand first — the theory being that this is the hand that everyone else called. (If no one bet on the river, the player closest to the dealer has to expose his hand first.)

Players are welcome, if not encouraged, to muck a losing hand without showing it. After a hand has been *mucked* (meaning turned face-down and pushed into the discards beyond the player's control), the hand is considered dead and no longer in competition for the pot.

After the first hand is exposed, remaining players expose their hands in a clockwise order. The dealer will muck losing hands one by one, leaving only the winning hand exposed for the awarding of the pot. When the dealer has determined a winner, she will push the pot in the direction of the player, and at that point, the winner is welcome to drag the pot in.

WARNING

Don't *ever* trust another player when he announces a hand at the end of a showdown and muck your hand based on that information. After you've mucked your hand, it is truly dead and you can never bring it back. If there is an error on a player's call, other players *may* lie to you as a "joke." It's even more likely that they'll misread a hand. (We bet we've seen people read a combined hand of four spades and three clubs as a "flush" a hundred times in my life.) If you have *any* question as to who won a hand when you're involved in a showdown, merely turn your hand over and let the dealer make the decision.

Posting Blinds

In order to start betting in Hold'em, forced bets (known as *blinds*) are made by the two players immediately clockwise from the dealer button. The person immediately clockwise from the dealer has the *small blind,* and the next player clockwise has the *big blind.* Making blind bets is known as *posting,* and this is done before any cards are dealt.

REMEMBER

The size of the bets is determined by the *limits* of the game that you're playing, and the small blind is nearly always half of the big blind (for more, see "Betting," later in this chapter). So a $2/$4 Limit Hold'em game has a small blind of $1 and a big blind of $2.

REMEMBER

Blinds are forced bets. The players in these positions *must* make these bets or they aren't dealt cards in the hand. These blinds, in turn, force betting action on the table after everyone has been dealt their hole cards.

Figure 1-2 shows a $2/$4 Limit Hold'em game. The hole cards have just been dealt, with Groucho as the dealer, Zeppo the small blind, and Chico the big blind. Harpo is the first to act and must now either call the $2 big blind bet, raise to $4, or fold (turn to "Limit Hold'em," later in this chapter, for a description on Limit betting). Checking is not an option for Harpo, because the big blind counts as a bet. Harpo's position of being first to act is known as being *under the gun*.

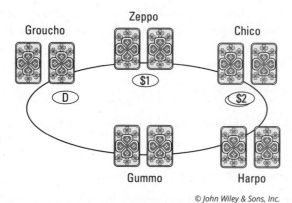

FIGURE 1-2:
Blinds are in place, and Harpo is the first to act.

© *John Wiley & Sons, Inc.*

FINE POINTS OF POSTING FIRST BLINDS

When you first sit down at a Hold'em table, the rules vary as to whether you have to post blinds (even if you're out of the normal blind positions for that hand) in order to be dealt a hand.

In Las Vegas, you're dealt a hand as soon as you sit down and have shown that you meet the table's minimum buy-in. You're not required to post a blind in order to get hole cards.

Conversely, in most California cardrooms, you're required to post a big blind in order to get your starting hand.

In cases where you're required to post a big blind before you're dealt cards, you're mildly better off just waiting until it would normally be your turn to get the big blind anyway, rather than jumping straight into the hand. Waiting like this keeps you from making an extra forced bet and gives an added bonus of being able to case the players at the table while you aren't actually playing. Dealers are used to this behavior and will probably ask you if you want to *sit out* (that is, wait until it's your turn to post the big blind).

How soon you post is a fine point, though, that doesn't really make *that* much difference. If you're itchin' to play, or if you've got a very limited amount of time to play, go ahead and jump in. The dealer will tell you whether you're required to post a big blind.

Betting: Just the Lowdown

A *bet* is when a player makes a wager on a Poker hand. In Hold'em, there are four betting *rounds* (times when players make betting action around the table). These rounds always come after players see the cards: after the hole cards are dealt, after the flop, after the turn, and after the river.

When it's a player's turn to *act* (meaning it's his turn to bet), the player has a few choices. If no bets have previously been made in the round, he may:

>> **Check:** That is, choose not to bet at the moment but still be in the hand.

>> **Bet:** Make a bet on the hand.

If someone has already made a bet when it's a player's turn to act in a round, the player may:

>> **Fold:** Muck his hand and lose any chance at winning the pot.

>> **Call:** Match the bet that has been made previously. He still has full rights to winning the pot.

>> **Raise:** Match the bet that was made previously and then add more (being careful not to *string raise* — see the "Poker Etiquette" section of this chapter for more). Everyone left at the table must call the size of this raise, or they can fold.

A betting round ends when all players have put the same amount of money into the pot (with the exception of all-in) and all players have had an opportunity to act.

The amount and the style in which you can bet in Hold'em are determined before the game has started. The betting types are known as Spread-Limit, Limit, Pot-Limit, and No-Limit.

Spread-Limit Hold'em

In *Spread-Limit* games, you're allowed to bet any amount, within a given range, during a betting round. So in a $1 to $5 game you're allowed to bet $1, $2, $3, $4, or $5.

About the only place you find Spread-Limit Hold'em is playing at other people's kitchen-table home games. Professional card houses dealing a Spread-Limit game are very rare, indeed, tending to happen only in places sitting in Poker backwaters.

Typically in Spread-Limit, your raise must be at least equal in size to the bet in front of you. If someone bets $3 in a $1 to $5 game, and you want to raise, you can raise by $3, $4, or $5 *only*. Don't be afraid to ask the dealer what the betting rules are if you come across a Spread-Limit game.

Usually, the minimum *buy-in* (the amount you need to start playing the game) in a Spread-Limit game is ten times the lowest betting amount — so $10 in a $1 to $5 game. There is no maximum.

Limit Hold'em

When you run into a Hold'em *ring game* (that is, a game where people are playing for money on the table, as opposed to a tournament with a prize structure) in a professional cardroom, the most common game you'll find (especially in the lower betting ranges) is the form known as *Limit*. In Limit, assuming you don't check, you must bet *exactly* the amounts prescribed by the game in each round — no more and no less.

Limit is always described by two numbers: The biggest is twice the size of the smallest — for example, $10/$20 (said, "ten-twenty" with the $ ignored). The smaller of the two numbers is the exact amount players must bet (or raise) after seeing their hole cards and the flop. This means the smaller number is also the size of the big blind (because that is the forced first bet in Hold'em) and the small blind is half that amount ($5 in a $10/$20 Limit game). The larger number is what must be bet (or raised) on the turn and the river.

In casinos and cardrooms, Limit games typically start at $2/$4 and run up into the hundreds of dollars. Limit typically has a minimum buy-in of ten times the smaller bet size. So a $2/$4 game requires a buy-in of at least $20. There is no maximum.

TIP

Limit tends to be the hardest variation of Poker to *bluff* (bet as though you have a good hand when you actually don't in an effort to get others to fold) because the bet sizes are regulated. (See Book 3, Chapter 7 for more on bluffing.)

Pot-Limit Hold'em

TECHNICAL
STUFF

Pot-Limit is the rarest form of Hold'em played today. We're listing it just to be complete, but don't sweat the details — you'll probably play a lot of Hold'em before you run across a Pot-Limit game.

Like Limit, Pot-Limit is always listed as two dollar figures, say $1/$2. You're typically allowed to buy in for a minimum of ten times the smaller dollar figure with no maximum.

In Pot-Limit, the amount you're allowed to bet is the same as it would be in Limit, but the amount you're allowed to raise is equal to the size of the pot. For example, say you're playing in a $1/$2 Pot-Limit game and you're under the gun. The blinds in front of you are $1 and $2. If you want to play in the hand, your minimum call is $2, just as if it had been a Limit game.

If you want to raise, the pot is calculated as though you already had called. You're allowed to raise anywhere between the amount of the bet to call and the size of the pot. In the $1/$2 game we've been talking about here, if you're under the gun, you could raise anything from $2 up to $5 (the pot being the two blinds [$1 + $2], plus the theoretical "call" you would have made of the big blind [$2]: $2 + $2 + $1 = $5). Additional raises are handled similarly

As you can see, it gets pricey fast (and with all this calculation, it's no wonder people never play it).

No-Limit Hold'em

It the olden days, say 30 years ago, *No-Limit* was a rarely played version of Hold'em — mostly, if not exclusively, attended by the extremely well heeled and the terminally vicious. Learning was an exercise in how far you were willing to drain your checking account.

Today, thanks to televised Poker broadcasting, running the gamut from the *World Poker Tour* to *Stars You Never Really Liked Play Poker!*, No-Limit is probably the best-known version of the game.

No-Limit Hold'em is a vicious and diabolical game, where the rules are only slightly more complicated than "you can bet any amount at any time."

REMEMBER

The most common way to see a ring game No-Limit table described is something like "$1/$2." When you do, these are the amounts of the blinds and the lower limits of the betting. The upper limit that can be bet on any given hand is however much any player has sitting on a table.

Buy-in is typically limited to a minimum of ten times the lower dollar figure and 100 times the upper dollar figure, so for a $1/$2 No-Limit game, your buy-in could be anything between $10 and $200. (The other way you'll sometimes see No-Limit described is by the maximum buy-in, say "$200." If you see a single number describing a No-Limit game, this is the maximum buy-in for that game — ask the dealer what the blinds are.)

As a general rule, you want to have something very close to the upper limit of the buy-in when you sit down at a table so you're not immediately intimidated (or just flat cleaned out) in a hand by someone with a considerably larger stack.

REMEMBER

When you sit at a No-Limit table, you're not allowed to remove chips from the table (that is to, say, pocket some of your winnings) until you leave the game altogether. When you *do* leave a game, you're typically not allowed to reenter for a specified time limit (usually 30 minutes or more).

WARNING

In case you haven't figured it out by now, No-Limit is an extremely dangerous form of the game. Just like doing trapeze without a net, the lack of limits on the betting doesn't make the tricks any more difficult — it just makes the penalties more severe. Starting out your Hold'em career with something like a No-Limit ring game is a very good way to watch your wallet walk south.

TIP

If you're interested in learning No-Limit, you should play Limit first until you're comfortable, and then move along to small buy-in tournaments.

Grasping the Importance of Your Bankroll

You have to pay to play, but all that play isn't going to last very long if you don't have enough supporting cash behind your game to survive the bad times.

REMEMBER

You don't *have* to play Poker to win. It's perfectly fine to just have your time at the table as a form of entertainment, but if you're playing to win, the total cash available to you (your *bankroll*) will make the difference between ongoing enjoyment of the game and sitting on the rail wondering what's on TV.

If you've never been exposed to the basic concept of necessary bankroll before, you're probably going to be shocked about the amount of money we're talking about here. So take a deep breath. Meditate. Go to your happy place. That's right, play with the cute puppy. Okay, now, read on. . . .

Recommended bankroll sizes

A bankroll is what will help you prosper when you're winning and stave off the poor times when you're losing. Because of the vagaries of luck, you need to have a thick cushion under you if you take a big fall.

Bankroll for Limit

If you begin as a Limit player, you should have a bankroll that is *at least* 300 times the maximum bet size. So for a $2/$4 game, you should have $1,200 earmarked for your Poker play.

That's not to say you should walk up to a $2/$4 table with $1,200 in your pocket (in fact, you definitely should *not* do that), but that amount should be the amount of cash that you think of being at your disposal against your Poker quests as a whole.

It's not unusual for a beginning player to lose as many as 50 big bets over the first several hours of Poker play. A bigger bankroll will let you ride over the top of this initial loss to watch things grow later on.

Bankroll for No-Limit

As you would guess, No-Limit, due to the brutal nature of the game, requires even more cushion. You should have an absolute minimum bankroll of ten maximum buy-ins for the game you're interested in playing. A $1/$2 No-Limit ring game will probably have a maximum buy-in of $200, so a minimum bankroll for this game would be $2,000 (and double that would actually be safer).

Bankroll for tournament play

Tournaments tend to have wilder swings — especially multi-table tournaments where you might have a dry streak that runs for weeks, only to hit a big one to win it all back.

REMEMBER

For single-table tournaments (like satellites for bigger tourneys), you should have 100 times the buy-in. If you play in $10 tournaments, that means $1,000.

REMEMBER

For multiple tables, you need even more. A bare minimum of 300 times the buy-in is more appropriate (and don't forget to count rebuys as part of the tournament fee). So if you're playing in $10 tournaments where you're rebuying twice, from your bankroll's point of view that's actually a $30 tournament. This means you need — yes, that's right — $9,000 to weather the storm. Told ya this would get your blood pressure up.

Moving up and moving down in limits

When you've got a nice cushy bankroll under you, you still have to be able to adjust to your wins and losses as you play merrily along.

Keeping records

REMEMBER

Assuming you want to be a winning player, to keep tabs on how you're doing overall, you *must* keep records of your play. You can be as sophisticated as you'd like (who was playing, time of day, what you ate), but really the most important thing is to track your wins and losses across each Poker session.

A simple spreadsheet or even just a small hard-bound notebook (spirals lose pages too easily) that you take with you will do the trick. Write down *every* session, no matter how big or how small the losses. And don't make an excuse to not record something, "I was really drunk at the time" doesn't matter to a diminishing stack of George Washingtons in your bank account.

How important is keeping records? If two players have exactly the same level of skill — one keeps records, and the other doesn't — the record keeper will win more money over time because he's more aware of how his game is affecting his bottom line and can adjust accordingly.

Going down

You need to be more leery of losing than winning, so it's the red ink in your ledger that you should be keeping an eye on. If you find that you've lost half your bankroll for the limit you assigned yourself, you need to move down one level in the limits that you play. So if your $2/$4 bankroll was $1,200 and you've seen it whittle down to $600, you need to move over to the $1/$2 table.

You also should examine your play in general for any *leaks* in your play — that is, mistakes that are costing you money.

Movin' on up

If you're in the envious position of having doubled your bankroll, you're now able to move up one limit at will. Yes, doubling your bankroll is a lot to win before moving, but it will prove, without a doubt, that you're not on a lucky streak and give you both the experience and confidence you need for the next level.

WARNING

Moving up one limit in Poker is *always* harder. If you assume that after you move up you'll automatically be as successful as you just were, you're opening yourself up for a (small) world of heartache.

Following Poker Etiquette

Poker etiquette goes beyond just being nice, being pleasant, saying "excuse me," and not chucking your chair at the dealer when he turns an unfriendly card. It's mostly rituals and customs for what happens around a card table. Repeatedly ignoring any of the rules listed in this section may get you removed from a professional Poker room.

Handling your cards

To play cards, you first have to know how to physically handle them.

>> **When you get your hole cards, don't take them beyond the edge of the table.** Look at them quickly, memorize them, and then protect them.

>> **If the cards you're playing with are cardboard-based (like the kind you messed around with when you were a kid), be careful not to bend or warp them.** If you notice a deck is being warped, notify your dealer. (All-plastic playing cards, such as Kem brand, can be bent considerably more without warping effects.)

>> **Keep your cards visible at all times.** This lets the other players and the dealer know that you still have a vested interest in the game.

>> **Don't rip your cards in half when you take the most unbelievable beat of your life from the guy who started dating your ex-girlfriend and who is now mocking you.** Well, maybe.

>> **Don't fold out of turn.** When you do fold, push them face-down to the dealer across the felt. After you've pushed your hand and let go of it, it's officially mucked and dead.

Handling your chips

You should know Poker chip basics as well.

>> **Keep in mind that only the chips on the table are eligible for that given hand.** You are not allowed to pull chips out of your pocket to play in a hand after cards have been dealt.

>> **In No-Limit, you're not allowed to take chips off the table until you've decided that you're going to leave the game.**

» **In tournament play, you must keep your keeps stacked and readily visible/countable to all players and tournament officials.** You also have to carry them in full sight of everyone when you move from table to table.

» **When you want to raise a player, say "raise" to the dealer and then place the bet on the table.** If you're playing No-Limit, you must move the total amount of the raise in one motion *or* you should call the exact amount you want to bet. (Putting money on the table as though it were a call and then saying "raise" to put more money out is strictly prohibited. Doing so is known as *string raise*.)

» **Place your bets out in front of you on the table, not mixed in with the rest of the pot (mixing with the rest of the pot is known as *splashing*).** Placing your bets in front of you lets the dealer make sure the pot has the correct bets and amounts from all the players in it.

» **Do not touch another player's chips.** Even if your halo is glowing that day.

» **Do not start moving a pot toward you until the dealer has declared your hand a winner and is moving the pot toward you.**

» **Do not bet out of turn.**

WHEN SHOULD YOU SHOW YOUR HAND?

In Hold'em, you only *have* to show your hand when you have a showdown winner. The rest of the time your exposure is at your option.

You *may* want to show a hand if you had a very strong hand or you were beaten by a lucky draw.

You *may* also want to show a hand if you pulled off a successful bluff to make your opponents slightly more incendiary.

Remember: When you show a hand, you're showing the tiniest bit of philosophy about you and your play — you're literally saying, "Yes, I play this kind of hand in this type of situation."

If you're comfortable with that, and *especially* if it's helping create a table image you want to convey (for example, "I only play the best hands — I *never* bluff"), then go for it.

Our advice is to *never* show a hand you don't have to. Keep your opponents guessing.

Don't ever show a hand to anyone at the table when the hand is still in play. Yes, this includes the girl with the low-cut blouse or the Benedict Cumberbatch look-alike who's sitting to your right and who isn't currently in the hand.

Playing in turn

Poker is played clockwise, with the first person to act being to the left of the dealer button (or to the left of the big blind pre-flop). The closest player to your right must act before you do, so you should be cuing off of her play. If you're sitting next to a player who tends to act out of turn, base your movement on the player to her right.

Playing in turn is especially important on the river. Be certain that all betting action has ceased and no one is still waiting to make a betting decision before you turn over your cards.

Tipping the dealer

In ring game play, tipping the dealer a buck when you win a hand is customary. Most dealers only make minimum wage and depend on your tips to make a living. Not to play the guilt card or anything. . . .

Keeping an eye on the game

When you play Poker, especially if you're in an unfamiliar environment, keep an eye on what's going on around you. You have two people you can turn to, your dealer and the floorperson.

Talking to your dealer

If you run across any problem at a table — be it the way a hand was declared or an incorrect deal — talk to the dealer immediately. The dealer is the boss of the table. You'll be amazed at how many know-it-alls on a table will try to straighten out problems or solve big messes. They don't have any authority in a Poker room, but the dealer does. Again, talk to the dealer.

Asking for a floorperson

In our experience, dealers are most likely to make mistakes in one of two ways:

>> By incorrectly paying a board that has been counterfeited

>> By getting too deeply involved in a conversation with someone else around the table

GLIMPSING SOMEONE ELSE'S CARDS

You'll be surprised how often you'll see someone else's cards when you're sitting at a table. It seems like nine times out of ten it's either someone who is drunk or someone who's otherwise out of it.

Here's how to approach this "problem" the same way. At the conclusion of the hand where it happens, say, "Excuse me, you need to protect your hand — I could see your cards there." Say it loud enough that most people at the table can hear it.

This strategy nearly always gets a "thanks" from the player you tell it to and should clear your conscience. If the player exposes his hand again, you've warned him; use this as another piece of information in your game.

If the dealer has made a mistake — for example, paid a hand off incorrectly, called a winning hand incorrectly, or allowed some type of action at the table that you think is clearly egregious — ask for the *floorperson.* The floorperson handles any problems at the table and is essentially the dealer's supervisor.

If you *do* need a floorperson, the demeanor of the table is likely going to be fairly aggravated and hot. Explain the situation with the floorperson and only speak when spoken to. Don't argue with other players, even if those players are talking directly to you.

Watching your manners

If you play Poker long enough, you *will* be beaten by the turn of an unlucky card. It's not a question of "if," it's a question of "when." If you can't deal with the pure concept of chance, you should seriously consider taking up an all-skill game like chess.

Nobody wants to hear someone whine about a beat he just took, and if you're new to the game, you can be certain someone else sitting at the table has just had exactly the same kind of horror unleashed upon her. Just suck it up and live with it.

WARNING

It's never okay to insult another player, throw cards at a dealer, or hurl your beer bottle through the mirror behind the bar. If the game is getting too tough or too intense, take a walk or call it a night. There's *always* another game somewhere.

REMEMBER

It's just a game, unless you're a professional. And if you're a professional, you should behave like one.

Chapter 2

Beginning with Two

Both the tease and the terror of Hold'em is the fact that you start with two hole cards. It's a lot like looking at the brochure for the house you'll ultimately own. Maybe the place that looks so great in the picture actually turns out to be on top of a toxic-waste dump. Or maybe that ratty little trap actually sits atop a gold mine.

Regardless of how you feel about the concept of judging a book by its cover, with starter cards in Hold'em, that's essentially what you have to do.

The start of a hand also determines your *position*, that is, your place on the table relative to the deal.

In this chapter, we take you on a stroll around the different positions at a table and talk about the relative strength of a hand according to where it sits.

Grasping the Importance of Position

Before we dive into talking about the hands you *should* be playing, it's worth understanding the general concept of position. Position will help decide if you should raise, call, or fold. Your position can leave you stumbling blindly through a hand or make you surprisingly educated about what's happening around the table.

The easiest way to think of a Poker table is by position relative to the dealer button and then group those seats into sets (see Figure 2-1). We use these groups throughout Book 3.

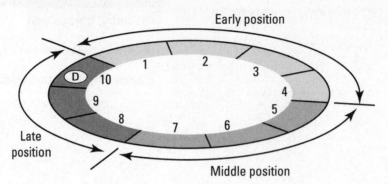

FIGURE 2-1:
Relative position of early-, middle-, and late-position seats.

© John Wiley & Sons, Inc.

Early position

Seats in the *early position* are the ones that are first, second, third, and fourth from the dealer button. The problem with these seats is that you have no idea what cards the people behind you have, and worse, there are a lot of people behind you. When you're forced to act in early position, you'll continually be acting early for every betting round. For this reason alone, you should act *only* when you have premium cards (and fold everything else). Jack-queen might look like a sweetheart here, but over the long run, it'll rip you to pieces when you play it from early position.

You may have noticed that early position has an interesting anomaly, and that is seats 1 and 2 from the dealer button are already covered by blinds. So in Seat 1 with the small blind, you may get a chance to see a hand for what is essentially half a bet (another small blind to see the big blind). In Seat 2 you might get to see the hand for "free," because if no one raised, you're already in.

When you're in the big blind, watch the betting round as it comes to you. If you try to fold when it's your turn, the dealer may push your cards back at you and say, "You can check for free," but all the people at the table will know you're now holding a hand that you have no interest in. Players can, and will, try to force you to fold based on this information.

In the blinds, you may be interested in playing hands because you already have a portion of a bet on the felt — and in some cases, that intuition is right. Never forget, however, that after the pre-flop betting round, the blinds are the first hands that will see action — and for this reason they're continually at more risk of being attacked than other hands at the table.

Unless you're playing No-Limit, where you have the ability of putting down a mercilessly large raise, raising from the blinds will almost never get other players in the game to fold. So although you'll essentially gain a round of betting by raising, you've also switched on a bright neon sign that blinks "Hey look! I've got a hand!" Although that may gain you one bet in the short run, it will lose you more in the long run. (Only the masochistic and the terminally dull will repeatedly call a player they *know* has a great hand throughout all the betting rounds.) With a big hand, you're better off not raising and slow-playing instead.

Middle position

The fifth, sixth, and seventh seats are known as *middle position,* and here things start to get interesting. You've already had a chance to see about half the table act (you can't be sure what the blinds are going to do unless you see a tell — see Book 3, Chapter 6) and in some cases if you place a bet, you'll be the first person to do so because everyone else has folded.

Because you're sitting farther back in the order, you can run a little wilder. Play cards that are a bit worse — then when you actually do manage to hit a hand, the people in front of you may try to bet and you can return with some neighborly favor like a raise.

This isn't like being in Candyland, though. You still have about half the table to act behind you, as well as those pesky blinds.

As you play from the middle, be sure to keep an eye on the actions of the people behind you, especially the people who are raising. Those people are indicating hands of strength and you don't want to go out blindly betting in following rounds only to get raised, yet again, by the guy who has already nailed you once pre-flop.

Late position

The eighth, ninth, and (if there is one) tenth seats (lots of online tables have only nine seats) are *late position.* These are the rumble seats on the Poker jalopy and are *way* fun. Because you've already seen all the action in front of you, you can make decisions like making calls purely on pot odds, raising with not-so-great hands when no one else has played, or folding marginal hands when it's clear there's going to be bloodshed in front of you.

Even if those bratty little people sitting in the blinds decide to raise you pre-flop (because they act after you), you'll be all over them like ugly on an ape after the flop because you get to act last *repeatedly.*

In a Poker game, money tends to flow around the table in a clockwise fashion. The reason for this is due almost exclusively to the concept of position, and especially late position. The last people to act bring in the most because people either fold to the late-position bets or call the late-position raises and lose.

"TAKE SEAT 4 ON TABLE 33"

If you're waiting for a seat in a professional cardroom (or if you've drawn a seat to play in a tournament) you'll be given a seat and table number.

Most tables are identified by number, either right next to the chip tray on the felt, or from signs hanging above them on the ceiling.

The seats are numbered clockwise from the dealer starting with 1 and going up to how-ever many, and the seats hold that number irrespective of the position of the dealer marker. If you ever have a question about the table you should be going to, ask your floorperson; if you ever have a question about sitting in the right seat, ask your dealer.

The only real difficulty of playing in late position is that everyone *knows* that it rocks. Just like Lovers' Lane, it has a reputation for being the spot where somewhat seedy things, such as *stealing the blinds* (raising from late position with garbage merely to try to gobble up blinds when no one else has bet) happens.

The Hands You Should Play, by Relative Position at a Table

Table 2–1 shows the starting hands you should play relative to your position around the table in Limit Hold'em.

TABLE 2-1   **Hands You Should Play by Relative Position**

	Early-Position Hole Cards	Middle-Position Hole Cards	Late-Position Hole Cards
Pairs	Aces through 9s	Aces through 7s	Aces through 5s
Suited cards	Ace with king through jack	Ace with king through 9	Any suited ace
	King with queen or jack	King with queen through 9	King with queen through 7
		Queen with jack through 9	Queen with jack through 8
		Jack with 10 or 9	Jack with 10 through 7
			10 with 9
			9 with 8
			8 with 7

	Early-Position Hole Cards	Middle-Position Hole Cards	Late-Position Hole Cards
Unsuited cards	Ace with king through jack	Ace with king through 10	Ace with king through 9
	King with queen or jack	King with queen through 10	King with queen through 9
		Queen with jack	Queen with 10 or 9
			Jack with 10

Although they're in early position, the small and large blinds do have a bit of play in them, exclusively because you were forced to play a bet when you were dealt the hand.

From the small blind, if you have *not* been raised, you can play:

>> Any set of suited connectors, even if they're gapped (for example, 7♥ 10♥)

>> Any set of connecting cards greater than 6 (for example, 6-7)

>> Any two cards if more than half the table is playing (good pot odds for you)

From the big blind you can call any single raise with anything in the preceding list.

If either blind is raised multiple times, call with any of the cards listed in the early position (refer to Table 2-1).

When playing either the small or large blinds, particularly if there are a lot of players in the hand, be ready to fold post-flop if your hand doesn't improve significantly.

Be aware of a few things relative to the table we've supplied:

>> **We advocate playing a tighter subset of hands than other professionals do.** It's easier to start with a tight game and then loosen a bit than it is to start loose and tighten it up. Early in your Poker career, your big goal will be to cut your losses to a minimum — and our recommendations will help.

>> **Many people recommend playing an Ace with a weak kicker out of a later position (known as a *dangling Ace*), but in our experience, especially with players just learning the game, these hands will lose you more over time than they win (usually from someone in the blinds having an Ace with a bigger kicker).** *Remember:* The more people who fold in front of you, the more implication there is that good cards are still left in the deck (or in the players' hands waiting to play).

» **Call any bet if there is a raise behind you, but be ready to let that hand go if you don't improve post-flop.** Your decision to play forward will be based partially on how you classify that player. (See Book 3, Chapter 6 for more on those tricks.)

» **If there is a raise in front of you, you should only call if you have hands that are the equivalent of sitting one positional group in front of where you are.** For example, from a late position, you should no longer call with a J-10, but can call a bet and a raise with Q-J. Again, be ready to let the hand go if it doesn't improve post-flop.

» **Be certain to vary your starting cards relative to the other players at the table if that makes sense.** (See Book 3, Chapter 6 for more on this.)

Considering the Players in a Hand

After you've figured out what hand to play and where, you're only beginning to get a true, deeper feel of the game. You have to keep track of a whole bunch of other things, too. We cover some of them in the following sections.

Keeping track of the number of players

The number of players in a hand is critical for your chances of success. Keeping track of the people in front of you is pretty easy because you're always hearing them yap it up about checking, betting, or raising.

The danger is it's sometimes easy to lose track of the players playing *behind* you because the pressure and excitement of your declaring your action has passed and you can easily drop into a low form of stupor waiting for your next turn to act.

You don't have to be a math wizard to know that the more people you see staying in a hand, the more likely you are to lose. Also, if people are staying in against multiple raises, either they're suicidal or, more likely, they have great hands.

Watching the types of players

The players in a hand make a huge difference as to whether you should be raising, checking, or folding. The madman who will play any two cards under the gun is to be treated in a very different way from the woman who will only play A-A in the same position.

If you have a choice at a Poker table, you always want the most aggressive player sitting to your right. Although it's true that if this person is a bit of a monster you'll see a whole lot of raising (much of it probably causing you to fold), it's *much* better to know that action is coming along than to have it happen behind you. Because when the Hell Raiser is behind you, you bet, and he raises, and then you may have to fold and just give a bet away.

Also, it's pointless to raise another player if he's continually going to call you when you don't think you have a better hand (or at least, are trying to convince him that you do). True, it sweetens the pot, but if it's not clear in your mind that you have a good shot at winning said pot, that extra money you're betting could just as easily walk away from you.

The harder a person is to bluff, the less you should try to bluff him. Keep an eye on those players and, when they are in, their position relative to you.

In general you want to get a good classification of the players sitting around a table. Just be careful that you don't become prejudicial about it.

For example, if you're playing and you notice that a person raises with pocket threes under-the-gun, that's a good indication that either she overvalues pocket pairs, or she doesn't fully understand the importance of position. As long as there aren't extenuating circumstances (like being a significant chip leader in a short-handed tournament), keep track of that in your mind — and your position of that person relative to your play. *Remember:* As the dealer button orbits the table, sometimes that person will be behind you in turn, and other times in front of you.

In Book 3, Chapter 6, we go into more detail on playing and classifying players, but here are some general things to watch for when it comes to the starting hole cards:

>> **Loose players:** These are players who either play too many hands or bet too much on the hands they do play.

>> **Tight players:** These players play only the very best starting hands — very possibly a smaller subset of the list I've described by position in Table 2-1.

>> **Aggressive players:** These are people who raise, raise, raise.

>> **Bluffers:** You should try to establish, very roughly, every player's likelihood to bluff at a table.

>> **Timid players:** These players are the ones who are likely to fold.

HOW GOOD *IS* THAT GUY'S STARTING HAND?

Imagine you're playing at a table and everyone has folded to a person just in front of you in middle position and that person raises. You look at your hand and you're holding an off-suit A-Q. A good hand and you can definitely call, but you may be able to get a better feel for what the other guy has by raising. If he's playing something close to the hands that we outline in this chapter, that hand could be anything ranging from A-A to J-Q off-suit (or even worse depending on his current mind-set and how much he values a hand like 4-4).

Now, it's true that your reraise helps indicate to the table that you have a very high-quality hand, but that's kind of the point. A lot of people behind you (maybe even all of them at a tight table) will fold. When the action comes back down on the original raising player, his action will tell you something.

If he does *not* reraise, that indicates he has a very good, but not great hand. If he comes right back at you with a raise, it may mean he has something very hot, or just doesn't want to be pushed around.

It's certainly not a foolproof method, but you'll be surprised how well it works — especially over time and at lower-limit tables.

Identifying Hands You Should and Shouldn't Play

We've already shown the hands you should play earlier in the chapter, and every-thing outside that list shouldn't be played. It's time to look at some more-specific examples.

Probable winners

There are a few big hands that when you have them, you have a very good chance to walk all the way through the hand with a winner. A-A, K-K, and Q-Q all fall in this category. But always be aware that the fewer players at the table, the more likely you are to win.

Big Slick (ace-king) is a great starting hand, more so if it's suited, but it is purely a drawing hand. As I cover in Book 3, Chapter 3, the flop determines the quality of that hand.

RIDING THE POCKET ROCKETS

On average, once every 220 hands you'll be dealt American Airlines — it is special enough of a hand to merit its own discussion.

If you're dealt A-A at a table and *everyone* calls all the way through, the odds are less than 50 percent that you'll win the hand. This is part of the reason it's important that you not only raise with this hand early to drop a few competitors out but also be aware that it's vulnerable. Yes, it's true that your raise will let people know you have a hot hand, but it may prevent a few less suckouts.

Pocket aces get beaten (*cracked*) all the time and are particularly vulnerable to people with smaller pairs catching trips as well as flushes in unmatching suits and lower straights.

The beauty of the hand is that it's the best possible starter. The bad thing is that it's not a very good drawing hand. There are only two more aces in the deck and for straights or flushes you have to have four community cards of that type.

Be happy when you have pocket rockets and don't be afraid to bet them. Just be aware that they're vulnerable and sometimes they *will* be beaten.

If you get in a hand that's starting to look bad, you can help dampen your losses by checking and calling. Or wet them down even more by getting out altogether.

Interesting side note: If you know, for certain, that your opponent has A-A, the best possible hand you can have in defense is a 6-7 in the suit that is *not* the same as either ace. Such a combination has flush possibilities, lots of straights, and caps any 2-3-4-5 community cards for the wheel play.

Quite possible losers

Small pairs are very dangerous. Especially on lower-limit tables, it's common to see people over-bet hands such as 5-5 and 6-6.

There also seems to be an infatuation with pocket Jacks and the *only* reason we can think of is that it has a lot of paint on it so it looks better than it is. In fact, if you're playing J-J against two other players with one having a king-X, the other having a queen-X (*X*s being any card less than jack), and the players play to the end, the pocket jacks have about a 50 percent chance of winning. And you're going to be running into hands that are *much* better than that.

Gapped connectors can also cause you problems, especially ones with triple gaps such as 6-10. The problem with this hand is the only way you're going to make it straighten out with both cards is to end up with a community play of 7-8-9. If someone is playing 10-jack here, you're dead meat.

Small suited connectors have similar problems. A little diamond mine like 2♦ 3♦ can be beaten by any two higher diamonds. Worse, you want to see the community cards come out with *exactly* three diamonds — because if there are four, anyone with another diamond beats you automatically. Gross.

Again, keep an eye on players at the table. If someone is playing extremely limited hands under the gun and you see him raise, you should be folding *any* hand that is not A-A, K-K, or A-K; because that's the only hand he would be playing out of that position.

Borderline hands

If you're playing any of the hands toward the bottom of Table 2-1, you're definitely down into borderline territory.

There's an interesting irony here because those hands are all much stronger against a fewer number of players, simply because they don't have to beat more people. But they pay better if you're up against multiple players.

The answer to this is conundrum is to go ahead and play them in both situations, but the flop is where the truth will start to be told. If you're up against multiple players, you must flop extremely well. If you're up against only one opponent, you may be able to bet in such a way that your opponent *thinks* you flopped well. (Read Book 3, Chapter 3 to find out about flop play and what it means.)

Using "Fold or Raise" to Make a Call

Before ending this chapter it's worth mentioning a general rule of Poker that you should incorporate deeply into your mind: It takes a better hand to call than it does to place an initial bet.

The easiest way to understand this rule is to look at an extreme example: Imagine playing at a table with ten players. Everyone is still in the hand, and with all five community cards face-up, nine players in front of you have called. You have the third highest pair with the board. What should you do?

Fold (of course). Someone has a better hand. In this situation there are just too many cards and too many players. The farther back you are in that ring, the better your hand needs to be because you're playing against *so many* players.

There's a good trick you can use with deciding to call — ask yourself if it's better to fold or raise in that position. If you don't feel good about raising ("There's no way this is a raise"), then it may well not even be a call. This isn't to say that you *have* to raise with your hand — you certainly can go ahead and call — but it sets a very good litmus test for you.

This theory applies across all forms of Hold'em, but it's a particularly good guideline in No-Limit. There, we take this theory one brutal step farther and instead of simply calling, we raise.

Chapter **3**

Flopping 'Til You're Dropping

O n the whole, the flop is the most critical part of a Hold'em hand. You go from having two hole cards to — *boom!* — having a full Poker hand. Love it or hate it, at least one of the cards you're staring at on the table will now be a part of your Poker hand.

The flop is also the place where you make your last "cheap" bet, because betting rounds on the turn and river will cost you double what they do here.

Fitting or Folding

When the flop hits the table, you have definition of your hand. Five-sevenths (or about 70 percent) of all the cards possible for the hand are now known.

A flop relative to your hand is a lot like the weather. When you wake up and look out the window, you don't have a guarantee of what the rest of the day is going to be like, but the general patterns give you a pretty good idea of what's up for the day.

The thing you need to be most concerned about is whether the flop *fits* your hand. In other words, does your hand improve with the flop you see? Likewise, you want to think about how that very same flop may or may not improve the other people's hands around the table.

Great flops

The flop fits your hand very well if any of the following are true (in descending order of greatness):

>> **You've flopped a straight flush.** It's always thrilling when it happens — and, if you're overtly emotional, it may give you a chance to see what your skeleton looks like when it jumps out of your body.

>> **You've flopped a full house.** Fun. Especially when it's something bizarre, like you hold 3-8 on the big blind (no one has raised, so you're playing for free) and the flop is 3-8-3.

>> **You've flopped the nut flush.**

>> **You've flopped the nut straight.**

>> **You've flopped quads.**

>> **You've flopped trips.**

>> **You've flopped two pair, with one of the pair being top of the board.** For example, you're holding A-3 and the board is A-10-3.

Good flops

The flop is definitely good for you in any of the following situations:

>> **You've flopped a flush or straight that is not the best possible for a given board.** You probably have a winner here, but you have to be just a tad leery of people holding cards over yours — this is particularly true for those players who are now holding a four-flush with a singleton that is above your best hole card.

>> **You've flopped two pair that do not include the bottom pair.**

>> **You've flopped top pair with the best kicker.** For example, you're holding A-K and the flop is A-8-4, or you're holding A-9 and the flop is 9-2-7.

>> **You hold a pocket pair that's higher than the board.** Say, you're holding 10-10 with a low-ball flop of 2-3-7. You still have a mild vulnerability here to trips and two pair (particularly from the blinds).

Very borderline flops

Then there are flops that make your hand better but leave you possibly exposed:

>> **You flop a pair that isn't the best possible.** Say you hold Q-J and the flop is K-Q-9, or you hold J-10 and the flop is A-Q-10.

>> **You flop a four-flush or a four-straight.** Odds are you won't make this hand on the next two cards, but you may be forced to play it for pot odds reasons.

>> **You flop top pair but have kicker trouble.** This situation is particularly a problem with aces, because the whole table likes to hold onto them. If you're playing a suited A-2 from late position with five people still in the hand and the flop is A-7-5 rainbow, we guarantee you that you have a loser. (Right this second — all it takes is an opponent who has an Ace and any card bigger than a 5.)

WARNING

From a bankroll perspective, you should think of the hands listed here as being some of the most dangerous hands at a Poker table. The problem is that they tease you along to play more (sometimes even jacking with your mind in such a way that you become more convinced that your opponents are bluffing), but they're rife with holes.

Downright dangerous flops

WARNING

Then there are those little places in Horrorville that occasionally crop up:

>> **You've hit the bottom end of a straight, but the flop is also flushing.** For example, you have 8♦ 9♦ and the flop is 10♠ J♠ Q♠.

>> **You hold a great pocket pair and bigger cards hit the board (especially when they're in quantity).** For example, you have Q-Q and the flop is A-A-K. If there is more than just a player or two in the pot, guess what? That's right, your great starter of pocket queens is now a loser.

>> **You have a flop that misses your hand, but still gives you over cards.** For example, you hold A-K in middle position and you see a Q-5-4 flop, with immediate action from the small or large blinds.

Just plain bad flops

Any flop that doesn't fit your hand at all (and you don't have a pocket pair) is bad — more so if you don't even hold an ace. The answer in this situation is almost always exactly what you'd guess: Fold.

In Hold'em, especially until you get a better feel for the game and your opponents, you want to start off with the fundamental concept that if the flop doesn't fit your hand, you should fold. Yes, you will occasionally be bluffed out, but caution and folding will save you money as you learn. Watching *other* people see if that guy who's betting is bluffing is less costly for you and will give you more objective feel for the other players at the table (because your money isn't at stake).

THE BEST OF BOTH WORLDS

You may get flops that play into your hand in multiple ways. For example, if you have A♣ 5♣ with a flop of J♣ 5♦ 3♣, you're now holding second pair (with best kicker) and the nut flush draw.

There are three obvious ways this hand can improve on the turn or river:

- If you draw a club, you have the nut flush.
- If you draw another 5, you have trips.
- If you draw an ace, you have a strong two pair.

(There's also the freak runner-runner of drawing a 4 and a 2 on the turn and river for making the wheel. But this possibility shouldn't be part of your decision making — it's not likely enough to happen, but it *is* part of the hand.)

Any time your hand works in multiple directions, it's far better than having only one path to victory, and you should be more eager to play it. This rule is especially true in No-Limit. You may have an instance where you know you have an identical hand with an opponent. Say you're holding A♦ K♦ and the board has Q♦ J♦ 10♠. From the play at the table, you're certain your opponent also has A-K. You should move as much money on the table as possible — not because you're trying to make your royal flush — but because any diamond turned will give you a flush and beat your opponent's Broadway straight.

In Poker slang, this situation, where you can draw cards at the mercy of your opponent with a currently identical hand, is called a *freeroll.* (Yes, it's the same term used to describe a tournament with no entry fee.)

Betting the Flop

Now that you have an idea of what category your flop falls into, we come down to the little details of betting. Unlike with your hole cards, where blinds force action at the table, checking all the way around the table after a flop *is* possible.

The way that players bet on the flop, and *especially* your position at the table, come into play here.

REMEMBER

When you're playing Hold'em, on the hole card and flop rounds, you bet one set amount. The amount you bet doubles on the turn and the river.

Because of this, you may want to make some bets now in an effort to not make more costly bets later. You may also want to wait and not represent a good hand just yet — this strategy may give you a chance to make more money later.

Sizing up the table for a bet

REMEMBER

The prime rule of anything economic — but *especially* Poker — is to maximize your wins and minimize your losses. With *all* betting actions at a Poker table, this concept should ride paramount in your mind.

Asking yourself a few questions helps. And don't sweat it: At first these questions may seem like a lot to consider, but after you've played some, they'll become second nature.

How many players do you want?

If you have a very good hand, you may well want as many players in the hand as you can keep. The amount you're betting will double on the next round, so anyone who is still in the hand at the end of this round will be forced to decide to play for double in the next. This is great if you're on top and sucks rocks if you're not.

If you make any fence sitters fold now, you definitely won't get their bets next round.

However, if you have a hand that can be beaten with a draw (or a wide number of draws), you may want to bet to get people out of the hand now — or at the very least make them pay to see cards.

Who is still left to act in the hand and how do they behave?

If you have some monster opponent at your table who *always* raises and *always* plays to the end, don't go out firing a bet if you lack confidence in your hand. You *know* that guy is going to raise, and there's no need to squander an extra bet.

Likewise, if you know that a player at the table only plays post-flop when she has a nut hand, go ahead and set a bet out right now. If she folds, you're done. If she calls, you know your hand has to get significantly better on the turn or she has you beat. It's still been a good bet on your part, though, because you found out the strength of her hand *now*, while the betting is half-priced.

TIP

Make sure to see Book 3, Chapter 6 for more information about getting an understanding of the players at a table.

Making the bet

If there has been heavy raising and reraising pre-flop, especially if any of it has come from behind you, you're better off checking around the table than letting that player bet again — regardless of what happened with your hand on the flop. Nine times out of ten the raiser will be on some kind of adrenaline rush anyway from looking at a nice pair of hole cards, and he'll go ahead and fire a bet right on out when given a chance.

By checking to him, you save yourself a raise, and even if you *want* to raise, the check-raise will almost certainly work here.

TIP

Assuming you don't have any maniacal super-aggressive beasts prowling at your table, if the flop has fit your hand, you should bet it. If you're playing the cards we recommend (and you should be, at least until you get supremely comfortable with the game), you're going to be folding the vast majority of hands. You'll be folding so much that when you *do* play a hand, you need a return on your betting investment.

REMEMBER

In general, it takes a better hand to call than it does to bet, so by betting, you're gleaning (somewhat imperfect) information about the hands around the table. You're also taking control of the game, which has some value.

If you get raised when you make a bet, consider both your opponent (for example, is she the kind of person who typically does this) and *especially* reexamine the flop (is there something in the flop you're missing?).

Straight draws and flush draws are the obvious threats, and they can easily sneak up on you. The other thing that will nail you is hidden trips. Someone (usually in late position) holds a smaller pair and may have managed to match the board.

If you have four cards to a straight or flush, from a purely mathematical point of view, the best thing to do is to check because the odds are that you will *not* be making your straight or flush. However, if you think that you have a pretty good chance of getting people to fold by betting, you should go ahead and bet the hand here.

If you're the last person to act and everyone has checked to you, you should bet if the flop fits your hand in any way. This bet implies to the table that you do, in fact, have a hand — and on extremely tight tables, it may win the pot for you outright.

From later position, check only if you have a true monster hand (which will guarantee a win on the next card at double the betting value) or the flop missed you entirely.

Calling a Bet

This is the edge of a more complicated territory.

If someone else has bet, you know a couple of things about his hand: He thought that his starting hole cards were good enough to play in the first place (or he was forced to play by being on the blinds), and now he's implying that the flop has somehow fit his hand.

REMEMBER

The most important thing to consider on a call is the character of the person who has placed the original bet. Is he aggressive? Timid? Hotheaded? Mad about losing the last hand? Drunk? Get a good feeling about this before you make a decision to call. (See Book 3, Chapter 6 for more about understanding your opponents.)

Hands that *somewhat* fit the flop can call. After all, this is still a cheap betting round and the turn may produce a card that fits your hand even better. Plus, your betting opponent *may* become less aggressive on the turn because he may not have that strong of a hand either and may have been just testing your mettle.

On the other hand, the turn card may come up anemic, making your not-so-great-fitting flop seem even worse — and making it easier to fold.

Hands that fit the flop well can call and can even consider raising, which we discuss in the following section.

REMEMBER

You do not have to have the winning hand of the moment to be correct in calling. In fact, you can *know* that you're an underdog — but as long as you have pot odds in your favor, you're still right in making a call.

TIP

If calling seems to be too hard of a decision, fall back on the old standby question: *With a bet in front of me, would I rather fold or raise with the hand I'm currently holding?* If you ask yourself this question and the answer is "raise," then you at least have a call. If the answer is "fold," then just give up the hand right now. The hand will only get more expensive and complicated from here, not cheaper.

WARNING

It is a supremely bad idea, especially in Limit, to decide on the flop that someone is bluffing and start calling them from now until the last bet on the river. If you think someone is bluffing, it's possible that

>> **You're wrong.** She actually *does* have a hand and you're watching your money walk away.

>> **She doesn't have a hand yet, but she'll end up making one.** This scenario is possible with a semi-bluff (see Book 3, Chapter 7) or if the player just gets lucky.

>> **She may have a hand that's better than yours — even if she *is* bluffing.**

Raising the Dough

TIP

The rough guidelines of raising are to (a) consider how you want the person you'll be raising to react to your bet, and (b) make the action that will most help you with these interests.

Ask yourself how likely a person is to fold to a raise, and then:

>> **If you want that person to fold and you don't believe she will, don't bother raising and just call.** You're not helping your situation.

>> **If you don't want the person to fold, but you believe she will, wait and just call the hand for now.** The river round will cost twice as much money and you'll make more that way.

>> **If you believe she may raise you back, and you don't want to call that raise, don't raise her right now.** The best way to stop a raising war is to not do it yourself.

>> **If you believe she may raise you back, and that's what you want, what are you waiting for?** Go go go. (Hey, are you *sure* you know what you're doing?)

>> **If you don't care whether the person raises or folds, you should raise.** You must have a pretty good hand, and if she folds, you know you win right now. If she doesn't fold, you'll probably just win even more money later.

>> **If you're not sure how she'll react, raise.** Then you'll find out — and you'll almost certainly control the hand on the turn.

REMEMBER

Bluffing is much more difficult in Limit than it is in No-Limit because the penalty for calling — at least in the short term — just isn't that severe. For now, you should hold back on your aspirations of getting people to back away from the pot with your 2-7 off-suit.

Check-Raising

If you check during your turn, then raise when someone behind you has bet, this is known as a *check-raise*. It is, very rightly, considered to be one of the most aggressive things you can do on a card table (but not as bad as, say, throwing your drink in someone's face).

TIP

You should check-raise on the flop in just a few, very specific circumstances:

>> **You have a very good hand, but the number of players currently playing is too big and needs to be reduced.**

>> **You're playing against someone whom you know you're beating and you're certain he'll call *and* be the first person to bet next round.** If he will *not* be the first to bet next round, you should simply call and raise on the turn — you get an extra bet out of him that way.

>> **You have the best hand, it's most likely going to remain the best, and you're playing at a table full of maniacs who will most likely cap all betting rounds, until . . . you pull down the largest pot of your life!** This is a level of thrill that is virtually unmatched in Poker.

>> **You think a check-raise will very likely work as a bluff now and get your timid competitor to fold before this same little stunt doubles in price next round.**

>> **You think you can get a "free card" by check-raising.** (See the "Getting a Free Card" section of this chapter for more.)

>> **You know that someone is playing for a draw, and you're beating him right this second, but you'll lose the hand if he's successful in getting the card he needs.** The reason to raise after checking is because you may be able to get him to fold right now — and even if you don't, you want to make him pay as dearly as possible to see each following card.

In any other situation, you're better off just calling and waiting for the next round. Check-raising always draws attention from even the sleepiest of players at the table, and it may well not be attention that you want.

REMEMBER

The best hand *does* win a pot, you don't have to bet it repeatedly to make it better, and on the flop round (which is only half-price), you very likely are losing extra money.

If you think of a bet-raise-and-call being worth 4 units from a total of two people after the final call (bet 1 + call 1 + raise 1 + call 1), that same play is worth 8 on the turn (bet 2 + call 2 + raise 2 + call 2). Even if your opponent folds on a check-raise on the turn, you've still made an extra 2 units from what you would have on a folded check-raise on the flop. (You would have called your opponent's single bet on the flop and then raised his 2-unit bet on the river — he put in 3, rather than 1.)

Check-raising definitely does have its place, but usually you'll find it later in the game.

No-Limit is a bit different. You want to *consider* using a very heavy check-raise on any opponent who's on a draw. The problem here, of course, is that you have to be dead certain that he *is* drawing (instead of just having you flat-out beaten), and there are many players who will semi-bluff back at you with an all-in.

Getting a Free Card

There is one big exception to the check-raising rule: If you think you can get a *free card* by doing it, it's worth trying. This exception is easiest to describe by example.

The free card setup

Typically, you want to try for a free card if you're trying to make a straight or flush draw.

Say you're playing J♦ 10♦ out of a late position, and there was one flat-caller pre-flop from a middle position — meaning, three people are still in: you, the flat-caller, and the big blind.

The flop is Q♦ 5♣ 2♦.

The big blind checked, the middle position bet, and the action is on you. You have a flush draw here, but most likely you don't have the best current hand (all it takes is one player with a card bigger than a jack). A call might barely give you pot odds.

But if you *raise* here, what's likely to happen?

>> Both players could fold and you win. That's pretty great.

>> One player could reraise you, in which case you know she has some form of a smokin'-good hand (either trips or an A-J in this situation). Assuming you don't have pot odds for drawing your flush, you could fold.

>> *Most likely,* one or both players will call. They perceive you as having a good hand (or maybe just trying to bluff), but the flop has slightly fit their hands as well. They call you, waiting to see the turn.

And here is where the beautiful part happens. On the turn, anyone still in the hand checks to you. If that player has made a hand, he's going to wait for you to bet so he can check-raise you. If he missed, or if he's still just in a so-so position, he's waiting for you to bet and then he'll make a decision on what to do. But because you're last to act, you don't *have* to bet. If you miss your card on the draw, you simply check and the dealer will summarily bang out the river card. If you made your hand, you just go ahead and bet.

What this effectively means is that you get a free river card. *And* you saw the turn for half-price, because your raise was less than a call on the turn would have been.

Defending against a free card

Now that you know the trick to get a free card, you can also defend against it. Any time on the flop that you see a raise behind you, with what appears to be a board draw — again, flushes and straights — you can either reraise before the turn if you have a very good hand, or simply call and then bet (instead of checking) when it's your action on the turn.

WARNING

Notice that we're talking about *draws* here, not made hands. Raising into a person with an all-club board showing is foolish at best, and suicidal at worst.

Chapter 4
Taking Your Turn

All in all, the turn isn't as pivotal a card as its name makes it seem. The flop holds the major moment of the hand, the river sets the stage for a victor, but the turn lies in the nether world. It's a nasty place of bad economics where the prices double and the number of cards is reduced.

Poker wags like to say that the "turn plays itself." That's a statement that's more true than it is false, but it doesn't mean it's not worth talking about.

Watching a Hand Fill Out

Of all the cards you receive in Hold'em, the turn is the least momentous. Only the clinically insane would have stayed through the flop for a double draw — meaning, drawing two cards to a straight or a flush — so it's unlikely that this is the point that your hand will suddenly be broken in *that* fashion.

However, bets double here and on the river, so if you make a mistake or a loose call here — as opposed to on the flop — it will cost you twice as much. And in the long run, the incorrect call on the turn is what will endanger your bankroll.

REMEMBER

In broad terms, on the turn your hand will either be improving or getting worse. This isn't *quite* as stupid as it sounds, because when you stop and think about it, if your hand is staying the same, it's potentially degrading relative to the field (if there are a lot of players in the hand, it *definitely* is degrading).

Odds are that your hand won't be improving on the turn because you have to either pair a card or improve a straight or flush. And in Hold'em, for any given hand, the odds are always against that improvement happening. Therefore, when you *do* improve, you're very likely gaining with respect to the rest of the table, and (assuming that card isn't helping your opponent even more) you may well be passing them.

That's great because these are exactly the kinds of problems you want to have in Poker. This particular one being the what-do-I-do-when-I'm-winning problem. Your big decision is whether you should check-raise or bet.

To check-raise or bet: That is the question

TIP

Here's a very good rule of thumb for check-raising on the turn: If you think your opponent behind you will initially bet *and* call your check-raise, you should check. If not, you should bet — and do it right now!

Looking at a hand that's good enough to check-raise, say Q-Q on a rainbow 2-4-9-Q board (the best possible current hand), if you check and your opponent checks, you've lost a bet.

If you check, your opponent bets, and you raise, your opponent may well pass — check-raises tend to do that to people. And it's true that you gained two units (remembering that the bet on the turn and the river is double what it is pre-flop and on the flop), but you've also given your opponent a chance to simply check. Your Q-Q may well have come with a pre-flop raise and a post-flop bet. For sure, people want to see another free card — and if you check, that's exactly what they'll get.

If you bet, people *could* call — in fact there is a whole classification of people who will call — but won't make a bet if you check to them (for example, someone holding a tail-wagging K-9).

Made flushes: The notable exception

A flush is a big powerful hand that, if you're lucky, has been made by the turn. (Dang. You are *so* lucky. It seems like you *always* do that.)

TIP

Treat these hands as described in the "To check-raise or bet: That is the question" section, but with one *big* exception: If you have a tiny flush that is potentially threatened by a larger four-flush held by someone to act behind you, you need to bet it *now*.

Consider, for example, that you're holding J♣ 10♣ in eighth position, but the other two people still in the game are behind you in the ninth and tenth seats. You're the first to act and the board shows 4♣ 7♣ Q♦ 2♣.

This is a great setup because you hold a club flush right now, and it's possible that either person behind you (one of whom opened the betting on the flop) hit a pair of queens. Unless the player drawing with a pair of queens has another pair to go with it (or holds the queen of clubs), he'll be drawing dead here. And even if he *does* have two pair, he still has to pair one of the board cards to make a full house on the river.

The lurking danger is a person holding something higher than your jack still being in the hand. The queen, king, and ace, to the best of your knowledge, are all still in play — and those are *precisely* the kinds of cards people hold and play (especially if someone paired a Q♣ in his hand with the one on the flop).

Betting your hand right now will force anyone on the draw to decide if the pot odds are such that a call is feasible. Your betting leaves lots of room for other players to make mistakes:

>> They may make a mistake calculating pot odds and fold when they should call (or do the equivalent of making a mistake by not knowing what pot odds are and simply making the wrong choice to begin with).

>> They may make a mistake calculating pot odds and call when they should fold. (Again, they may not know and may just make the wrong choice.)

>> They may try to bluff you by reraising right now with a hand that's drawing dead.

TIP

If you do get raised when you bet a made flush, you should call and check-call on the river. It's possible someone is trying to bluff you; if so, you'll beat that person on the river. It's also possible someone is holding a larger flush than yours (for example, K♣ Q♣), in which case you're just unlucky — but you need to minimize your losses by not firing the first bullet on the river.

And, of course, the smaller your flush is (like holding a suited 2-3 — shame on you!), the more dangerous the four-flush on the river is.

Watching for "hidden" improvements

On the turn, you need to keep your eyes open for opportunities that are making your hand better in ways that you didn't expect.

For example, if you were dealt 10♠ 10♣, a Q♣ 8♣ 3♥ flop isn't very exciting. As long as no one seems overly perky to see that queen hit, and there seem to be a lot of stragglers, you've got good reason to be here for the turn card.

But when the J♣ turn hits, things are both better and worse. You now have a fairly good flush draw. Because the jack and the queen are both exposed, the only clubs over your 10 are the king and the ace. You also have a gut shot straight draw of any 9 (with the 9♣ being your beyond-magical straight-flush draw — worth mentioning for novelty only, but not likely enough to change your mind in the overall scheme of things).

This means there are

>> Nine clubs left in the deck that will make your flush. This wins as long as there isn't one of the three bigger clubs sitting at the table.

>> Three more 9s left (we already counted the 9♣ above). This will be good enough to win as long as you're not fighting a flush already on the table, or a stray K-9 that is barking up a straight (except for the super-great 9♣ that's an automatic winner).

>> Two 10s left in the deck. This is probably good enough as long as someone isn't playing a 9-10 for a straight (fairly unlikely because that means all 10s from the deck would have to be in play, *and* that last 10 would have to be paired with a 9, *and* someone would have had to play it). Not impossible, just very unlikely.

Assuming your pair of 10s isn't any good right now (and it almost certainly is *not* if there are a lot of players — there's both a queen and a jack on the board), that means you have 14 outs in the 46 remaining cards (not all guaranteed winners — depending on the composition of other players' hands) on the draw.

This hand isn't good enough to bet straight-out, especially against a bunch of players — but if you're getting better than 3¼-to-1 pot odds on your call, you can stay in to see the river. Keep in mind that the odds are against you in this situation — this means you probably *will* lose the hand, but mathematically you'll win money in the long run if you call here.

If you see betting *and* raising in this situation before the action even gets to you, you should fold. It almost certainly means you're either drawing dead or you're under-drawing (meaning that the same card that helps you also helps someone else who will end up better — say someone holding a higher club).

Keeping Track of the Action

TIP

The most important job you have on the turn is to remember the betting action you see on this round and try the best you can to equate it with the actions you saw on the hole cards and the flop. You also need to etch all the betting plays you see here into your mind. The number-one most common place for players to set a trap is on the turn — because they just miss a hand on the flop and then make it on fourth street.

If you saw someone attacking a pot earlier, and then backing off on the turn, it's likely one of two things has happened: They've either hit a hand, or they've missed and they're trying to save some cash.

Determining a hit

Many people will anticipate a straight or a flush draw by betting — beginning players will oftentimes raise. When they hit a hand, they'll often back off, hoping to check-raise you.

Trapping opponents who flush

Consider a flop of 2♠ 5♠ 10♦ with a turn of Q♠. Big hands in early positions, like A♠ K♠, will have raised pre-flop and may have come out initiating betting on the flop (or maybe check-raising). These players are sitting on a spade four-flush with two dominant over-cards. That's enough to make the eyes of many players spin back in their heads and bet bet bet. When the other spade hits on the turn, they suddenly see the riches of the world on their doorstep and back off with the idea of check-raising you.

People in later positions like to play suited connectors, say 9♠ 10♠, and they too might get excited. Especially if they're catching top pair *and* a flush draw (also an example of a hidden improvement).

From a betting perspective, the event you're looking for is a ton of action, and then suddenly none. Again, it depends a *lot* on the players involved (see Book 3, Chapter 6 for more on reading other players), but all other things being equal, we'd say this person is setting a trap by checking in front of you.

To test the theory, your best bet is to check through on the turn and see what happens on the river. If your opponent comes out betting on the river first again, she probably has a hand and was trying to trap you. If she checks again, it means that she had something good (trip 5s, trip 10s, two pair?), but backed off when the spades hit the board because she thought she was bested.

Taking Your Turn

Of course, if *you* have the best hand (like the nut flush on the turn), then absolutely you should fire a bet off — especially if you're in the end of the betting order.

Putting you in a straightjacket

The other hand that gets made in the same fashion is a straight. Again, consider your opponents and their position around the table.

If someone very commonly plays connectors, or suited connectors, watch out for the player who limps in pre-flop, then gets excited by a set of cards like 5♥ 6♣ 10♠, but suddenly backs off on a 9♥ turn.

If you think about it, that kind of behavior doesn't make sense, because a 9 isn't a threatening card here. If someone had a hand they liked with a 4–5–10 board, how is a 9 going to make it any worse?

Easy. Either that person was bluffing, and has now backed off because he's afraid you're going to call again or, more likely with many opponents, because his 7–8 just went straight. Now, instead of bullying you with raises and hoping you might fold on semi-bluffs, he can back off because he has a made hand.

Comprehending the miss

Don't get so wrapped up in your inner psychic powers of analysis that the turban falls over your eyes and blinds you to the obvious signs that someone is afraid he's just been bested, or he's missing on a draw he was hoping for before.

Smelling someone's fear

For example, consider a flop of Q♠ 2♥ 4♥, and someone's betting strong. The A♠ hits on the turn and your adversary seems to back off. It's not because she just made a wheel, it's probably because she had paired the queens and is now afraid that the ace has counterfeited her in someone else's hand.

Although it's a fairly rare occurrence, another place you'll see people back off is when their trips have just been bested by a better set.

Here's an example that's easy to see: Nearly everyone who holds a suited K-Q pre-flop will bet it (some will bet it heavily). If a raising battle ensues, it's nearly always someone who is holding an ace with a big kicker (say a suited A-Q). Lesser pairs on the table will eventually back off — they just assume that there is a bigger pair over them.

A flop of A-K-K will bring heavy action from the player holding three kings, and the player with the aces will back off a tad (but almost certainly still stay in the hand, assuming that the other player is *maybe* holding a king), and only vaguely considering that his opponent really *does* hold the nightmarish trip Kings.

A turn of an ace will bring the player with the K-Q to a screeching stop. It's true, he now holds kings full of aces; but any opponent holding even a singelton ace now has aces full of kings. So when the man with the cowboys quits betting, he isn't trapping, he's trying to figure out how he got so unlucky.

Gazing at the unfortunate

Big bets pre-flop and on the flop but then backed off on the turn could also mean your opponent has been anticipating a straight or flush and has missed — or he was trying to bluff that he had hit early, and he's afraid that the bluff isn't working because it was *you* who had actually hit the hand when you called.

These types of boards will have slightly different looks. What you're looking for are single-suited flops, say 2♥ 4♥ J♥ followed by an 8♣.

The siblings to the flush-not-making-it board are the ones where the flops that had hinted and teased at a straight are now walking away from making those wanting hands successful. Q♥ J♦ 3♣ followed by a lame 4♣, would be one example.

TIP

In the cases of straights and flushes that are not coming to fruition, if you have a hand (even a medium-strength one), you need to fire bullets. When someone folds, you automatically win — everyone else should *always* pay to see cards they're drawing for.

Chapter 5

Dipping in the River

The river is where your Poker hand, both literally and figuratively, all goes down. Good luck! We hope you win.

Final Betting

From a pure theory point of view, the river card is very different from all the others in that your hand is determined. The card distribution is over and now it's just a matter of figuring out who has the best hand.

Well, almost. There is this little final betting detail left.

Fifth street is probably most akin to pre-flop action, in that it's the place where occasionally you'll see the bets really stack up. The variations mean that the river can take on a few different betting personalities, ranging from a nice quiet beer float trip to a life-threatening white-knuckle shoot through Class IV rapids.

All-checking, no dancing

Usually rivers are checked all the way around for one of three reasons:

>> The board is threatening (for example, five hearts or a full house is showing).

>> Extreme betting early on has caused people to back off (especially if the draws people were shooting for didn't come through).

>> Players' hole cards just missed the community cards entirely. (This is especially common when it's only the blinds that were left in the hand.)

TIP

If you're in a later betting position and everyone is checking, this can be a very good time to pick up a pot. In fact, your ability to pick up the stray pot in these situations may very well make the difference between being a winning and losing player. If you consider the action you've seen in the hand up until now and take into account the types of opponents that are still in the hand (as you've decided, using the super-clever Book 3, Chapter 6), you can then decide whether to check or bet in the following circumstances:

>> If there was heavy action and raising surrounding a flop with two of the same suit (say, J♣ 8♣ 3♥), but things have since cooled off, you may well be looking at a broken flush. Fire a bet out if you have a pair that matches the middle rank of the community cards or higher.

>> If the only people in the hand are the blinds, make a bet if you have any pair.

>> If someone has been betting heavily up to this point but suddenly backs away from betting on the river, they probably will *not* check-raise you (this is much more of an expert play), and instead have been bluffing by over-betting. Make a bet if you have middle pair or better; or you believe there is a better than 50/50 chance your opponent will fold.

>> If all else fails, or if you get flustered, or if you're just filled with doubt, check. It doesn't cost you anything.

Walking through the firestorm

Sometimes the river is the place where people sort of go insane and just start hurling bets at each other. You only want to get mixed up in this madness if you either have the nut (*maybe* second nut) hand, or the player you're up against is known to be looser than a broken jar of pennies in the bed of a pickup truck on a gravel road.

WARNING

The most important thing you can do in this situation is make sure you're reading the board correctly. Make sure you're not getting caught up in a situation where your good hand is blinding you to bigger possibilities. Because pots can grind up so high over the course of a hand, one mistake here can wipe out an entire week's (or more) worth of Poker winnings. Here are but a few examples that I've seen people self-destruct on:

>> **You've hit the nut flush on a board of 10♠ 10♣ 9♦ 6♠ 2♠ with A♠ 9♠.** Started off pretty good with two pair, and then you runner-runnered into the nut flush. Don't get so wrapped up with your flush that you ignore the full house possibilities here. A common starting hand, especially from late position, is 9-10. Likewise, anyone tripping his pocket 2s, 6s, or 9s is sitting full. For sure you should call any bets, but don't raise and reraise. If people seem really eager to move any money into the pot, just call.

>> **You trip on the board, holding a singleton.** For example, the board is Q♦ K♦ K♥ 7♠ 6♥ and you're holding K♣ J♣. Yes, you've got trip kings, but anyone who's tripped up with a pair (Q-Q, 7-7, 6-6), now has a full house.

>> **You play into a gapped straight like so: You hold Q-9 and the board shows K-J-10-2-4.** The good news is you're holding a king-high straight. The bad news is A-Q is a bigger straight than yours. Good slow-players love these kinds of set-ups. For some reason, the gapped straights are easier to be fooled by than holding 6-7 with a board of 10-9-8 because it's so obvious there's another possibility (J-Q) on top.

Yes, you might look at these hands right now and say, "Yeah, yeah, whatever," quickly blowing off the advice we're giving. Unfortunately in the passion of betting — especially big betting — when you have a hand that's made, it becomes remarkably easy to overlook another (better) hand. And if you *do* overlook another hand, you will not only pay, but pay *dearly.*

The telltale sign on No-Limit games on the river is if someone raises you the minimal amount, instead of pushing all-in, and (especially) if she does it *again* when reraised. What's happening here is the other player *knows* she has the nut hand and she's trying to maximize her return on the hand — she's afraid that if she pushes all-in, she'll lose equity in the hand by your folding.

Betting in moderation

REMEMBER

The most common thing to see on the river is a bet, maybe two, with people deciding if they're going to call. If a bet has been made in front of a player deciding to act, unless he's one of the world's great actors, what he's always doing is looking at the board and answering the following questions, probably in order:

>> What was the betting pattern of the person who placed the initial bet throughout the hand?

>> How does the pattern apply to the position of that player relative to the dealer (the cards the bettor would have started with) and the cards I see on the board?

>> What kind of player am I up against? Loose, tight, aggressive?

>> Can the hand I'm holding right now beat the hand I *think* this person has?

TIP

These are the steps you should be going through as well, but the reason we talk about watching someone *else* do them is it can give you a very good feel for the strength of *her* hand as she makes the decision. For some reason, even very top players will drop their emotionless facade on fifth street, sometimes even if there are players still to act behind them. And if you're acting even later than the person considering, you have the ability to make an even better read on the overall power of your hand.

REMEMBER

As a general rule, it takes a better hand to call than it does to make a bet. The more people calling, the better your hand has to be to win.

Deciding if you're being bluffed

A savvy player, especially if he's aggressive, or if he senses weakness in an opponent, will do exactly one thing when the river has determined he has a crappy hand: Bet. That is the *only* possible way to save the money that he's already put in the pot.

You now know this. The catch, of course, is that the person betting will *also* bet when he has a hand. So how do you know which is which? Again, the most important thing is to consider the player and ask yourself the following questions:

>> Is this person prone to bluffing?

>> How long has it been since this guy bluffed and does it seem like it's time again?

>> Is there something very clearly wrong on the board or the cards that would hint at a bluff (like two cards to a flush or a straight that never materialized, or possibly a low-ball board such that someone holding two large pocket cards would never have paired)?

REMEMBER

Even if you've determined that you believe your opponent *is* bluffing, you still have to be able to beat his "non"-hand. Any reasonable pair should be plenty.

TIP

The generally accepted rule is that you should look at the pot odds of your call. If there's $36 in the pot, and it costs you $6 to call, you can ask yourself if you think there's better than a one-in-six chance that you're being bluffed, and if so, call. And whatever you do, make sure to keep track of whether you were right or wrong against that player. Because even when you guess wrong, there may well be something in what happened that will keep you from making that mistake again.

Showing a Hand . . . or Not?

After the betting round of the river — even if there's no betting and all everyone has done is the boring action of "check" — there's still the *showdown*. It's that heart dropping moment when people expose their cards.

It's not unusual, especially in games where tensions are running high, for players to be overly reticent to show a hand — even when it's nothing more than a showdown. People are *so* protective of their hands that they don't even show them when they're supposed to. It's also not usual when this happens for dealers to say something smarmy like, "First hand over wins."

There is, however, a progression that is followed if the whole table suddenly gets deadlocked with the heavy task of just turning their friggin' cards over.

1. **Technically, the person who made the last raise (or initial bet, if there were no raises) is the person being called, so he exposes his hand first.**

2. **The dealer displays this hand to the center of the table and calls out what it is — for example, "Two-pair, 3s and 2s."**

   At least the dealer is *supposed* to do this — he doesn't always.

3. **In a clockwise fashion, every player either shows or mucks his hand.**

   Any hand that is mucked, without being shown, is officially dead and no longer eligible to win the pot.

   • If the newly exposed hand is beaten, the dealer turns it face down and mucks it, moving to the next hand.

- If the hand exposed beats the first hand shown, the newly exposed hand is moved to the center of the table and declared — for example, "Three 3s." The original hand that was shown is then turned facedown and mucked.

4. **The process continues until one hand is left face up on the table (or multiples if there is a tie), the dealer pushes the pot to the winning player, and the hand is mucked.**

If there are any side pots, a winner is determined for those first, working all the way back to the winner of the main pot.

During the showdown, you'll want to keep in mind the following:

>> **Unlike the rest of a Poker game, you do *not* have to expose your cards in order (unless no one else is showing, in which case you *must* when it's your turn).** If you think you have a winner, you can turn it over immediately.

>> **Be sure to keep your cards in front of you.** Don't send them sailing out into the middle of the table (it's also bad form to chuck them in your opponent's face). You need to be able to easily prove the hand is yours.

>> **You must expose *both* of your cards.**

>> **Even if you're heads-up and the other player immediately mucks her hand but has gone all the way to the showdown on the river, you still *must* expose your hand.**

>> **You *might* have the rights to see another player's hand if he's made it all the way to the showdown.** At some card houses, you must have a hand all the way to the showdown yourself to be able to ask and see it; at others, you merely have to have been dealt a hand. Ask your dealer what the house policy is. Strangely, asking to see the other player's hand is always considered to be a mildly socially unacceptable thing to do in a professional cardroom.

>> **The most important rule: Never believe a player has the hand he orally declares until you see it with your own eyes.** Every day someone, somewhere, misreads his hand. And this is cutting your opponent slack, assuming you're not dealing with someone who has sinister intent.

>> **After you muck your hand, the hand is dead.** Be *certain* you have a loser before you throw it away, or just let the dealer handle it for you.

>> **Do not begin to scoop the pot toward yourself.** Let the dealer make the first motion.

If you have a hand that has been declared a winner and you ask to see an opponent's hand that is headed for the muck, you're technically at a minor amount of risk. Because you've requested to see it, and you have a hand that has been declared a "winner," the hand you're asking to see is still considered to be live.

If the hand that was going to be mucked beats yours, you lose the pot. Dealers will yap on and on about how dangerous and foolhardy this move is, and we're sure it *can* happen, but we've never seen a winner come back out of the muck.

TIP

If you make it to the river and no one calls your final bet, don't show your hand unless:

>> You're convinced it will change (or enforce) an impression that you want to give other players about yourself, whatever that may be (you play tight, you play loose, you were bluffing, you weren't bluffing, and so on).

>> There is a potential prize associated with it, such as a high hand.

Watching for Mistakes

REMEMBER

Because the river is the place where the payouts happen, and it's the final stop of the (potentially crazy) train ride that this hand has represented, you need to really keep your eyes peeled for any last-minute weirdness that can happen. Although it's true that professional cardrooms are required by gaming laws to keep things on the up-and-up, mistakes can (and surprisingly often do) happen. Of all the people in a cardroom, *you* are the only person who has your best interests at heart.

In all the cases mentioned in this section, if you see something amiss, call the dealer's attention to it. If the dealer is of no help, ask for the floorperson. You don't need to be an ass about it — be friendly, but firm, and point out the discrepancy you see.

Things to watch for include

>> **Dealers who are raking too much:** Rakes in most establishments are posted on the tables themselves and capped at some amount. If you see a dealer taking more than the permissible rake, call him on it.

>> **Not being paid for your winning hand:** If you have the winning hand, be sure you're being paid for it. The most common thing dealers overlook is a counterfeit of this type: You hold A-Q, your opponent holds 8-8, and the board is K-K-9-9-3. You win with two pair, kings, and 9s with an ace kicker; your opponent has kings and 9s with an 8 kicker. (Another is when you hit a straight flush and your opponent holds the ace-high flush. Something like 4♠ 4♦ versus A♦ K♦ with a board of J♦ 8♦ 6♦ 5♦ 7♦.)

>> **Other players stacking your chips:** In a professional cardroom, don't let other players help you stack your chips. You'd be surprised how dexterous some people can be with their palming of a chip.

>> **Exposing your hand before betting action is done:** Be sure that all betting action is completed before you expose your hand. If you're uncertain of the state of the action, ask your dealer.

>> **Other players trying to get cards back from the muck:** Make sure players aren't trying to retrieve cards from the muck.

>> **Errors in huge tournaments:** Extremely large tournaments, such as the main event of the WSOP, tend to be more error prone. This is partially because everyone — all the participants, including the dealers at the table — is nervous. It is also due to the fact that, because large tourneys have to bring in an unusual force of dealers from elsewhere, large tourneys commonly use dealers who are off their normal work schedule (or from different cardrooms entirely). Communications with the dealers tend to be "less than ideal."

>> **When you win an all-in, you in fact win it all:** In No-Limit, be certain you have *all* chips of another player when you bust them out (including any house chip they were using to protect their cards). Ensure too that you have any paper currency that was part of the betting.

>> **When you lose an all-in, you pay the proper amount:** Also in No-Limit, if you lose an all-in and you have more than your opponent, be sure you're paying an amount equal to his stack (and not just pushing all of yours over with no leftovers for you).

>> **Flaws on the cards:** If you see flaws on the cards — nicks, folds, bends, or creases that make them stand out — point them out to the dealer. It's not very likely that people at your table are intentionally marring the cards, but Aces do get an unusual amount of wear and warp because of their importance relative to hole cards.

Chapter 6

Playing the Players

I f you ask us to give you the single most important factor in learning and playing Poker, it has to be gaining the best possible understanding of the people you're playing against.

If there's one chapter in Book 3 you absolutely need to read and fully digest, it's this one. Think of this entire chapter as being covered with a huge Remember icon.

A common assumption made by people who are just learning Hold'em is that it requires some high degree of mathematical skill. The implication is that if you're not a math genius, you don't really stand a chance at the tables. This misconception is further reinforced by TV shows giving you running percentages on hands as they're dealt and played (which also ignore little details like the fact that the players have no idea what their opponents are holding, but you do — making the numbers nonsensical in a way).

Although the math part does have a bearing on your play, it is *heavily* overshadowed by knowing the traits of people you're playing against.

If you can identify the traits of your opponents, and interpret the way those traits are presented at the table, you've found the master key to the game. Make no mistake about it, understanding your opponents at the table is *the* most important aspect of Poker.

Classifying Players

When you play against people at a Poker table, to the best of your ability you want to try to classify their play. Beginning and intermediate players tend to think of players by general categories of classification; we talk about those in this section and that's certainly a great place to start. Eventually, though, you'll want to classify each and every player individually. The more you can say about an individual player whom you're competing against, the more likely you are to beat her in the long run.

Aggressive versus passive players

In broad terms, many players tend to be either aggressive or passive in their play. Figuring out where your opponents are on the passive–aggressive spectrum can help you not only win more when *you* have a good hand, but also lose less when *he* does.

All aggression, all the time

Aggressive players are the easiest to pick out at a table. And by this, we don't necessarily mean they're the ones who are most likely to throw an empty beer bottle across the room when bad beat. Aggression can certainly be well defined, but you'll *feel* aggression as much as you actually see it, and the symptoms are fairly blatant.

Aggressive players tend to

>> **Raise and reraise fairly often when they're involved in the betting action.** Raising is what makes the aggressive players easily identifiable because dealers will *always* announce "raise," and all eyes on the table immediately turn there.

>> **Play from their position more heavily.** An aggressive player in late position will raise even more often than her usual trigger-happy self, based solely on her position (see Book 3, Chapter 2 for more on the importance of position).

>> **Start the betting rounds.** When given a choice between check and bet, an aggressive player usually bets.

>> **Check-raise.** Check-raising is the second most aggressive act you can do at a Poker table (the most aggressive act is reraising). And check-raising is sneakier because the original check implied that the player didn't have a Poker hand — the raise indicates very clearly that the person does.

>> **Be not at all intimidated by anyone at the table.** Aggressive players by their very nature are also more self-assured.

>> **Be less likely to fold a hand after they're playing.**

>> **Be more experienced Poker players.** As a rough rule, people become more aggressive the more comfortable they get with the game. This is especially true of people who have read a lot of Poker theory books (they repeatedly hammer home the importance of aggression at a table).

Those wimpy passive players

Passive players are a bit harder to spot at a table, mostly because their lack of aggression makes them easy to overlook. These are the players who

>> **Call rather than raise.** The passive player believes she has a hand — she just isn't interested in pushing it forward.

>> **Check instead of starting the betting.**

>> **Have a greater tendency to fold the hands they're playing.**

>> **May seem intimidated by one or more players at the table — or maybe even playing the game itself.**

>> **Typically have less Poker experience.** For a passive player, just the act of sitting at a table and betting is scary enough. He doesn't want the added tension of raising. His inexperience also means he hasn't had any exposure to advanced Poker texts that recommend raising.

Deciding tight versus loose

In addition to aggressiveness, you should try to make some sort of determination of how loose your opponent's play is.

Hearing the tight squeak

A player is considered to be *tight* if he plays an extremely limited set of starting hands. The starting set of hands we outline in Book 3, Chapter 2 would be just a tad on the tight side. And although you can't see a player's starting hand very often, you do see how often he decides to play a hand — and this in itself is a clue.

The starting set of hands described in Book 3, Chapter 2 will have you playing somewhere between 15 and 20 percent of all hands (including when you have the blinds and get to play for free or at a greatly reduced rate). If you see a player playing 1-in-5 hands or fewer (especially over a long period of time or several sessions), you're looking at a tight player.

Watching the loose rattle

Conversely, *loose* players will play a wide variety of starting hands, and as result, you'll see them in the pot more often. Any player playing something like a third of her hands, or more, over a long session would definitely be considered a loose player.

Combining your evaluations

The implication is that there are four different types of players, but that's true only from the very widest of standpoints. Again, as you gain Poker experience, you'll probably find yourself fine-tuning your evaluations to each individual, but the following is a good set of evaluations to begin with — along with some advice on how to combat them effectively.

Battling aggressive/tight players

Playing against an aggressive/tight player is fairly simple. Because he's tight, he'll play only the highest quality hands. When he does, your response is fairly straightforward: Fold unless you have a hand that is extremely good.

Tight players tend not to bluff much, so don't be afraid to throw away the occasional hand that's only okay by your estimation. And if you're going to start aiming your hole cards at the trash can, the earlier you can throw it away, the better — their raising and reraising will gnaw on your stack in a big way.

Playing a bit looser against a tight player will get you more small pots (especially if you're raising, where he tends to fold quickly early on). But when you do play loosely against him, you need to be very quick to drop a hand when you see aggression coming back at you.

Keep in mind that if a player *thinks* you're bullying him on the table, he *will* change his style of play — probably by loosening up a little and getting even more aggressive.

Playing against aggressive/loose players

Aggressive/loose players may seem a bit scary when you first come across them, but you'll quickly learn to think of them as one of the biggest assets to you at a Poker table. The aggressive play will bring money out on the table; the loose play will mean that it just keeps on coming.

An aggressive/loose player will have an interesting side effect of making the other players on the table loose and aggressive as well. And although you may be tempted to jump on the bandwagon yourself, your wallet will like it better if you instead opt for tighter and more passive play. Because your opponent is loose, if you play tight, you're more likely to win on any given hand (because you have a better set of starting cards). Over time, you'll take down more pots and find your stack ratcheting right on up.

TIP

Don't complain on the odd times you get a bad beat. Just think of it as the tax of doing business with one of your best customers.

Skewering passive/loose players

On the surface you may think that a passive/loose player is a rarity, but actually it's probably the most common category that beginning Poker players fall into. These people are the ones who play too many hands and then have no idea how to bet as the hand progresses.

If the player seems passive enough to fold merely by someone else being aggressive, that's what you should do every time you enter a pot. Her continual folding will float your bankroll pretty quickly.

Be careful, though — some beginning players *never* fold, which means bluffing against them serves no purpose. Against these players you should instead tighten your play (so you're only playing higher-quality hands) and fire away unmercifully when you're holding the good stuff.

Dealing with passive/tight players

Passive/tight players are an interesting anomaly because they will tend to stay in the hand when they have a winner, but not bet it. These types of players won't pad your bank account very much, but they're also easy to play against — just check through whenever they're in a hand.

Because he's playing tight, he may well have a winner over your hand, making betting mildly suicidal. However, you *should* bet if he's the passive kind of player who tends to fold.

Watching for the "unusual" play

WARNING

There is one thing you need to watch for: any unusual play from a player you believe you have classified correctly. Here are some examples:

>> **If you see a raise from a normally passive player who *never* raises, that means she has a hand.** Unless you have something *really* good relative to the board you're seeing, you should fold.

> » **If a typically aggressive player who is normally Mr. Bet-Bet-Bet suddenly checks, he's either playing for a draw or (probably more likely) trying to trap you.** Only bet against a player like this if you're willing to call a reraise.

> » **If an extremely aggressive player ever check-calls you, it almost certainly means she has a trapping hand.** If it happens to you, you definitely should *not* bet the next time you see action.

In No-Limit be especially careful of a player who flat-call the blinds from early position, when the typical action you've been seeing from her is raising pre-flop. This is a classic trick of someone holding a very large pocket pair (A-A or K-K). Don't fall for it.

TIP

As you're classifying players, try as best you can to get a read on how their play changes according to position as well. As you can see from the list of starting cards in Book 3, Chapter 2, even a basic Poker strategy encourages you to play tighter in early position and looser in the back. Keep your eyes out for people who violate this guideline in either way — either looser in front (especially those who play Aces with no kickers from early positions) or tighter in the back.

Looking for Tells

A *tell* is a hint that a player gives you as to what the strength of his hand may be — either through the way he bets or the way he physically behaves around the table. Successfully interpreting the tells of your opponents will make a huge difference in any given session you have at a Poker table.

Watching the right place at the right time

It *almost* goes without saying that in order to watch for tells in the first place, you need to be watching people. This tends to be easiest to do when you're not playing in a hand, but rather just sitting back and taking it all in. Although the other players not in the hand are watching television or reading the sports pages, you should be keeping an eye on your opponents. See how they face each other and how they react as they win or lose, bet or fold.

REMEMBER

You'll likely pick up more watching the table when you're not involved in the hand because you don't have that evil mix of paranoia combined with overconfidence or underconfidence that's present when it's *your* money on the line.

Also, you need to get out of the habit of immediately looking at your cards as soon as they're dealt, as well as the community cards as they're exposed. Instead you should watch the players around the table and see how *they* react as they see the cards for the first time. (By waiting until it's your turn to look at your hole cards, you also avoid creating a tell on yourself — see Book 3, Chapter 7 for more.)

Who's acting and who isn't?

Of course people *know* you're looking for a tell and will intentionally try to throw you off. What you need to figure out, then, is who is actually inadvertently showing a tell and who is merely trying to make your Poker experience even more confusing. (As you read through this section, remember that all these things apply to you as well — read Book 3, Chapter 7 for more on not exposing your own tells.)

The number-one rule of tells

REMEMBER

Because people associate bluffing with lying, they tend to interpret that as meaning you should act in the *opposite* manner to what people would expect. And this is the biggest tell of all, especially in beginning-to-intermediate play: *Players will most often intentionally act as though their hands are the opposite of what they are.*

A player who is bluffing will bet in a very aggressive fashion and stare you right in the eyes. A player with a strong hand will casually lay a bet and look away.

A whole lotta shakin' goin' on

WARNING

Another thing to keep a close eye out for is someone who is physically shaking as she goes to place a bet. I've seen many beginning players assume that this means a player is bluffing, and nothing could be further from the truth. A shaking player *always* is holding a good starting hand or has made a big hand on the board — it's nearly impossible to fake the nervous rattle of someone with a great hand. When you see it, it's the real thing, and you're in trouble. Fold and ask questions later.

Watching other people's hands

There is so much surveillance and counter-surveillance in the world of tells — especially if you're playing against more experienced players — that we find it difficult to get a truly accurate read on the players involved. Did we really just catch something, or are they faking it? Hmm.

There does, however, seem to be one fairly reliable version of a tell and that is how people use their hands at the table. I don't mean *hand* as in the two cards they're holding, but rather *hands* as in that part of the human body that is attached to a wrist.

Shaking hands typically indicate a crushing hand, but you can pick up a surprisingly larger amount of information from watching people's hands:

>> **Many people will hold their cards in a certain way (for them) if they're planning on folding a hand.** This gives you a chance to look behind you on any given betting action to see how many callers you might get.

>> **People thinking of betting will often fondle their chips before it's their turn to bet.** Many intermediate players do this to make you think they're either going to bet or call in an effort to get you to *not* bet because they would actually fold otherwise — yet another version of acting in a way that's opposite of how they're actually thinking.

>> **People who suddenly hit big hands, especially on the flop, will often flinch with their hands.**

>> **People who recheck their hole cards after an all-suited flop (for example, all spades) were not holding two spades to begin with or they wouldn't be rechecking.**

>> **People who check their hole cards twice pre-flop (or give their hole cards an exceedingly long stare) often have a very big pair.** For some reason, people with large pocket pairs need to look at them again.

>> **One signal for checking is to tap the table when it's your turn to bet; some people, as hard as this is to believe, will tap it one way for a true check (say with just an index finger), but do another (say, rap the table with a fist) if they intend on check-raising.**

>> **In No-Limit, players who are becoming short stacked will often count out their stack relative to the size of the blinds.** What they're doing is figuring out how many big blinds their stack represents, and on a surprising number of occasions, you'll find these people pushing all-in soon afterward. Anytime you see someone counting out a stack in such a fashion, you should be leery of the all-in play behind you when you're first to act. Be sure to play tighter in these situations so you won't be afraid to call the raise.

Listening to what people say

You can find out quite a bit just by listening to people talking at the table.

When people say the obvious

The most obvious tell of all is the player who announces his hand every time the cards are exposed. He says things like, "Now I've got two pair," "I'm sittin' on a big flush draw," and so on. Many players either ignore the chatterbox or don't believe him.

When you run across a player who's decided to become the MC of the Poker table, your task becomes pretty easy: Hand him the microphone and listen to what he says. On those rare times when you *do* see his cards, see how they line up with what the player is saying. It's very possible that you're hearing nothing more than some player spewing static that he somehow finds "funny," but you'll find a surprising number of times when it's actually a tell (whether it's lying [which you then mentally reverse] or telling the truth).

Also when players show a big hand at a table to prove they weren't bluffing, it's fairly common for others to chime in about what they were playing. And while this isn't 100 percent foolproof, the things the other players say tend to be more accurate than not (because those people don't really gain anything by lying about the hands that they folded). Keep track of what those players said they had, what their relative position around the table was, and try to remember the way they acted as they went through the betting phases.

Listening to those who already know

TIP

Also keep an eye on how players who are very well acquainted with each other react *to* each other. For example, if you visit Las Vegas in the off-season, it's common to sit at a table with four or five retirees who know each other. These people play often enough, and know each other well enough, that it's not unusual for them to know (and often openly announce) the tells of all their pals.

In these cases, if you see one player always backing away from another in a given set of circumstances, you should start doing it too. There's no need to play against Lonnie for 20 years just to find out that he always snorts when he has Big Slick — especially when Big Sal has already done the investigation (and reporting) for you.

Keeping track of the mundane

Keeping track of mundane conversations that have nothing to do with the card game you're playing is a good idea. The way people behave when they're responding and reacting to the world around them can be revealing.

For example, someone takes a sip of coffee and says, "This is the best cup of coffee I've ever tasted!" If it is a great cup of coffee, then you know what the person sounds like when she's telling the truth. You can watch her body posture and any other little detail that seems relevant. Likewise, if the coffee is actually closer to sludge, you've just seen how she reacts when she's lying.

Involuntary reactions

Many people have involuntary reactions to their play. We mention hand shaking earlier in this chapter, but there are also things such as sweating (people with big hands pre-flop tend to sweat) and racing heart rates. Phil "The Unabomber" Laak plays with a hooded sweatshirt, sometimes drawing it all the way up. Phil Hellmuth plays in a track suit with the collar turned up. Both of them do this expressly so you can't see their veins pounding in their necks.

When you watch for involuntary reactions from your opponents, don't forget to factor in the raw importance of the event you're seeing. Anyone making the final table of a major tournament will, by default, be wound up tighter than usual.

In general, though, the more keyed up a person is, the more likely he is to have a big hand.

Failing all else . . .

You can sit and analyze and analyze your opponents and the situations you're in, and if you're not careful, you will *over*analyze them. If you find that you're driving yourself bonkers and you're not able to get a proper read, you do have a couple more options.

Look at the hand positionally

If you find yourself getting overly confused with the situation, forget trying to read your opponent for a tell. Instead consider her betting pattern on this particular hand and how it could relate to starting hands of different types. Consider nuances such as trips, flushes, and straight draws. Don't forget to factor in her actions on the hand pre-flop and be certain to consider the player's position at the table.

Trust your gut

The reason you're able to live, breathe, eat, drink, and play Poker is because your ancestors made it through some pretty dark times. They did this by fleeing from the big scary things that could eat them and pounding on the little annoying things that were threatening but beatable. These epic battles, fought over eons, ended up putting you at a card table. And you still hold all these fight-or-flight impulses. You should listen to them.

When all else fails, trust your instincts. If it just really *feels* like you're being trapped, you probably are. Fold.

If there's just something basically wrong with that lady's last big bet — it just doesn't feel right somehow — call it. This isn't math and it isn't science — it's instinct. Use it and you'll be right more than you're wrong.

Just fold already

Okay, what started all this was that you were confused by the tells you were seeing. Then you looked at the hand positionally and couldn't come up with any hints as to what that psycho on the other side of the table might have. Then you wanted to try your gut feeling, but the hot dog you had for lunch is burning a little too much to get the right kind of read.

In cases like this, especially as you're starting out, you should just fold. Sure, you'll lose some equity and occasionally be bluffed out of a hand. But one bad fold costs you a *lot* less than a string of bad calls (which is what happens if you're chasing an opponent who's actually trapping you).

REMEMBER

You can always fold now and just play the next hand. The cards *will* be different there, and you'll have a whole new set of possibilities. Don't let your impatience with a hand — or especially your current stack size — affect the quality of plays you're making at a table. If you think the quality of your play is suffering, take a break and evaluate your situation. Figure out if you should buy in for more or just call it quits for the day.

Zeroing In on Specifics

To *really* figure out a table, you should turn your beady little eyeballs into laser beams and heavily home in on the table around you. Here are a couple tricks you can use for help.

Figuring out the table in order

After a couple hours of play you should be able to mentally walk around the table and talk about every player you're playing against. You don't need to go into excruciating detail, but you should be able to lay down generalities. A sample might look like this:

Seat 1: Aggressive player who raises pre-flop only in later positions with no previous callers.

Seat 2: Passive/tight player. Only calls when he thinks he has the best hand.

Seat 3: Dangerous player. Varies betting sizes and styles. Hard to figure out.

Seat 4: Was playing well early, but got a bad beat and is now tilting.

Seat 5: Beautiful genius. (Oh, that's right, this seat is you.)

Seat 6: Inexperienced player. Tends to fold when raised.

Seat 7: Only calls with good hands. Only raises with the nuts.

Seat 8: Very loose player. Calls nearly every hand pre-flop. Almost never sees a turn card.

Seat 9: Uncertain. Player is either having a bad run of cards or is playing far too tight.

Seat 10: Aggressive. Likes to take control of the betting action every round.

As you go through this mental list in your head, as much as you can, make note of how the players interact with each other. For example, the player who was bad beat in Seat 4 almost certainly holds a grudge against the player who beat her. You want to make sure you're not interpreting something as a tell that is actually some other type of interaction. That doesn't mean that you can't exploit these types of situations to your benefit (you can and should), but make sure you're correct about the underlying reason behind the actions you're seeing.

Looking at individuals

By far the best way to figure out people at a table is to study them individually. If you pick one person and watch him *every* hand, through all of his moves — check, bet, call, fold, raise, win, lose, and ordering something to eat — you'll discover a tremendous amount.

Players expect to be watched when they're involved in a hand or farther down the line in the betting order. They aren't expecting it so much when their play is less consequential, and because of this you're more likely to see their true and/or real reactions to situations. You can use these real responses as a baseline to the other behavior you see at the table in a hand.

Whenever you're having trouble figuring out an individual player — especially if you seem to be getting conflicting signals in recurring situations (like the way she behaves heads-up) — drop everything else and just spend time studying her.

When you do, don't be belligerent about it, like giving her a continual icy stare-down. Instead, just make her a constant part of your attention for a few orbits of the dealer button — you might even try striking up a conversation. Your chances of figuring her out will rise substantially.

TIP

After your next Poker session, come back and read this chapter again. It will give you deeper insight into the play you've just experienced and give one more rein-forcement of the most valuable thing you can learn about playing Poker.

Chapter 7

Bluffing: When Everything Isn't What It Appears to Be

When people first become acquainted with Poker, they run quickly into the concept of *bluffing* — intentionally misrepresenting your hand in such a way that the other players are misled as to what you have (usually to make the other players fold).

Aside from luck of the draw, bluffing is *the* element that elevates Poker from nearly all the other games of pure skill, such as chess.

In our opinion, writing about bluffing is similar to writing about painting. Really the best way to learn to bluff is to go out and practice, but it's a heck of a lot easier to practice if you have a rough idea of the underlying concepts. In this chapter, we walk you through the hows, whens, and whys of bluffing.

Bluffing Basics

The most important thing in playing a Poker hand is understanding the players at the table. Bluffs depend almost entirely on how other players will react to the information you're going to pretend to convey at the table.

TIP

Before you head any farther, make sure you have a basic understanding of Book 3, Chapter 6 and what it means to play the other players at the table — those concepts are the keys you need to understanding bluffs and making them work.

Your turn not to tell

In order for any bluff to work, you first have to turn off all the other tells you normally broadcast in a game. For example, if you always riffle your Poker chips on the table whenever you have a marginal hand, people are going to be one heck of a lot less likely to believe your big bet represents a good hand if you're shuffling your chips like a bored roulette dealer before you make it.

Of course, one of the problems of becoming overly stoic at the table is that all your small, and otherwise usually not noticeable, tells become much more pronounced. "Gee, I never noticed that you rub your fingertips together for one second whenever you have a bad hand, but now that you don't shuffle those chips anymore, it's a whole lot more obvious."

TIP

The best way to get a feel for the way you broadcast at a table is to either videotape yourself playing cards with your friends in a home game, or better yet, designate one of your pals as your Poker watchdog and have him give you a rundown on the way you act and play. The only problem with assigning a watchdog is you essentially eliminate playing that person for money for the rest of your life — so if you do choose someone, it's probably better to pick the girl who beats you all the time rather than the guy who helps subsidize your rent every month.

If you can't shut off your emotional broadcasting system as you play, you should at least be aware of what your tells *are* so you can mimic them in situations when you want to bluff.

REMEMBER

When you first start playing Poker, at least up through intermediate play, players will indicate the opposite of what they are. It's as though bluffing equates with "lying," so people will act the opposite — if their hands are weak they'll act strong, if their hands are strong they'll act weak. Don't fall into this same trap yourself. If you're not highly skilled, you're better off conveying no expression than trying to misdirect someone with an "act."

Don't bluff people worse than you

Okay, okay, the title isn't strictly true, but we've put it up there in headline bold to make a point and have you think about it. Bluffing people worse than you are, especially if they're *considerably* worse than you are, doesn't always work the way you want it to.

You're more likely to run across these types of people early in your Poker career. For *some* reason, they don't seem to end up playing the game for years on end. In the following sections, we tell you why *not* to bluff them.

Some people might call anyway

The killing phrase you want to listen for at a Poker table is, "I just called to keep you honest." If you ever hear someone say that at a table, and you're convinced it's not a bigger part of some general Poker ruse, that's a player you don't want to bluff. Essentially what he's saying is, "You know what? I'm a bonehead. I'm so stupid I'll actually call you with a hand that can't beat what you're representing, and yes, I *do* believe you have it. I'm just going to give my money away to you." And instead, he beats you.

If you run across a player like that, you *can* beat him, sure. But the way to do it is to bet when you have a good hand, not a bad one.

Some people don't understand what "lucky" means

Many beginning players don't have a basic understanding of the mathematics behind Poker, and may call simply because they don't understand what's at stake.

For example, let's say the board shows a rainbow K-K-8-2 and the only hands you've shown all night have had kings in them. You're sitting with A-Q in a No-Limit game and decide to push all-in to feign a set of kings. To your dismay, your opponent says, "I know you have three kings, but I've got pocket rockets here, and I'm going to call and hope for that ace."

You've gone from having a person not understand what it means to draw to only two outs to a much larger problem of drawing dead for all the marbles.

Assuming the river card wasn't an ace, if you had waited to make this all-in bluff, you would have fared much better.

Now it's true that you may not have any idea just *how* far gone some of your "lesser" opponents may be, but if you're patient and let the game ride for a while, you'll get some idea.

TIP

For opponents who seem too dull (or just too weird) to successfully bluff, you're better off not relying on bluffing and instead taking advantage of other types of errors they may make — like playing too many hands or misjudging the relative strength of their hands to the rest of the table.

Making your bluff count

You only want to bluff where it matters, not where it doesn't.

To look at an extreme example, if you're sitting in the small blind with 4-2 off-suit in a No-Limit ring game and bet all-in to gobble up the big blind, what have you proven?

If that player passes, you've won a single bet on the table by risking your entire stack. That's the upside.

The downside is that you've mildly aggravated the player with the big blind and, worse, you've drawn the attention of the table to you. Everyone saw the play; everyone has marked you as a potential bluffer. Slow-players love to eat players alive who do that kind of stuff.

And if the player *does* call (slightly more likely than usual because everyone else at the table has folded), you're going to be behind in the race.

TIP

You're better off bluffing in situations in which

>> There are more chips in the pot (you actually get something if you're right).

>> The bluff could make a difference in your tournament position/standing.

>> You have a reason to establish a stronger table image.

When to Bluff

One of the key elements to bluffing is knowing when to do it. If a bluff is well timed, it will mean more to your stack and it's more likely to succeed.

Bluffing based on your image of "predictability"

There are two polar-opposite philosophies about how opposing players should view you as a player at the card table. One is to have people think of you as an unknown-and-hard-to-classify player; the other is to be thought of as being *very* predictable. Both have their advantages and disadvantages.

Playing the part of the wild man

The advantage of being an unpredictable player at a table is that no one is sure what you have and what it means. Is he bluffing? Is he just over-betting? Does he have something but wants us to think he's bluffing?

There is certainly a kind of satisfaction in being thought of as the loose cannon at the Poker table that can be had in few other ways (aside from doing something like standing up in the middle of a restaurant and starting to sing). The problem, however, is it will cause people to just stick closer to their pure game.

From a pure bluffing point of view, you're better off conveying a sense of predictability.

Playing the role of the predictable player

If you have a very predictable presence at the table — meaning players are always fairly certain they *think* they know what you have — a bluff is much easier to pull off.

To illustrate: If the only hands you've ever shown are very strong opening hands (like those we talk about in Book 3, Chapter 2), people will start making predictions on what your hand is, based on the boards that they're seeing. Say a flop were to show a rainbow Q-J-10, someone bet in an early position, and you raised from a middle position (Book 3, Chapter 2 also has more on the importance of position), you'd probably get players spinning into this type of thinking: "Let's see, she called pre-flop and now I'm looking at that board. . . . She's been playing only tight hands and very conservatively. . . . She's got something like a Broadway straight or trip Queens." Even though you may only have 7-7 for a pair lower than the board.

In fact, if someone *does* raise here, you're almost certainly behind and you need to see a 7 on the turn. Continuing to bet the hand to anyone calling the flop-raise on the turn and the river is probably suicidal because if he's good enough to call you early on, he'll be good enough to check-call you throughout the entirety of the hand.

Looking at your hand from the outside

When you bluff, try to get inside your opponent's head, or at least take an objective view of the board. This can be harder than it sounds because everyone has a natural bias toward his own play — people tend to think of themselves as better players than they actually are and their opponents as worse than they actually are.

TIP

Boards that hint at the dangerous cards a player *could be holding* make the best bluffing opportunities. Here are some examples of "more bluffable" boards:

>> **Flush draws:** A board with four clubs looks ominous. (More so if you don't actually hold any clubs in your hand, eh?) If you're up against only one other opponent, the chances are he doesn't have a club either. (If you're up against two opponents, odds are that one of them *does*.) You may want to take advantage of it.

>> **Straight draws:** Any board showing a straight draw can be scary. Something like 6-7-8-9 is even scarier if people see you betting from a later position. If they know Poker theory (or at least have been paying attention), they'll assume that you had a lower-quality hand and are overlapping the cards they are seeing.

>> **Hidden trips:** Boards like 2-4-7 only get heavily bet one of two ways: Either someone has a big over pair, like pocket Kings, or someone has hit trips on the board. This bluff is harder to pull off against beginning players than it is against intermediates.

>> **Overt trips:** A-A-2 is the type of board that's just screaming for someone to have tripped up (especially because people love to tag along into the game with aces). Yet, half the aces in the deck are gone, so acting as though you have one can potentially be a safer bet than it first appears.

REMEMBER

You can never bluff a person who already has the best hand, or worse, holds the hand you're acting like *you* have. And you *will* run across these players sooner or later. Accept that as a risk, understand it will happen, and move on with your plans.

Bluffing in the right game

Some games are easier to bluff than others. In general Limit tends to be a much more difficult game to bluff. It's certainly not impossible, but the amount that a person can bet at any one time (and, therefore, lose at any one time) is limited. Typically, bluffing in Limit works best either in games with extremely advanced players or in games with beginners who don't fall into the "I never fold" category.

No-Limit is a much easier game to bluff because the stakes are higher, so the penalty of a bad call is more crushing. Obviously, it makes the bluffing risk that much higher, but that is both the beauty and horror of No-Limit.

Who to Bluff

Bluffing isn't something you do in a vacuum; you need to have a target. And the bigger and rounder you can paint that target, the easier it is to hit.

Preying on weak personalities

If the concept of picking on people when they're down just generally turns your stomach, Poker may be a bad game for you. If you're not willing to just keep beating on an opponent — even when he's down — you better believe that that opponent is more than willing to come back and pound more than a little on you after he gets some footing.

TIP

BLUFFING HANDS IN THE MIDDLE GROUND

Nearly all your successful bluffs will happen in the area we call "the middle ground." You can think of hands as being divided into three large categories:

- Good hands
- Bad hands
- In-between hands

When your opponent has a good hand, for the most part you're not going to be able to bluff her unless she thinks you have a *great* hand. So bluffing against a good hand is either rare, impractical, or foolish.

When your opponent has a bad hand, all you're really going to do is make her fold faster. Although it's true that semi-bluffs (discussed later in this chapter) work against these hands, for the most part if you're even a *little* aggressive in your play, you'll win these.

The in-between hands, however, are the middle ground where it all happens. You want to be aware of, and probing for, the hands that your opponent has that she just isn't *that* committed to. *Those* are the hands you can bluff against *no matter what you have*, because, quite simply, your opponent would rather let them go than fight with 'em.

Think about how *you* feel about an in-between hand. Now fight that insecurity in your opponent.

Knowing weakness when you see it

Bluffing will always work the best on opponents who are willing to drop a hand or those who can somehow be convinced that it's just easier to let this hand go for now and fight for a better one later.

The thing you want to look for in opponents are those who only play with the absolute best of hands, or better still, those who only call raises when they feel that they have something very close to the best hand possible on the table. These are the people you need to turn your bluffing attention to because they will fold more than they should.

Playing against those who show no weakness

You'll run across people (especially early in your Poker career) who simply refuse to fold a hand. The underlying theory is that they figure you're a pathological liar and try to bluff every hand. (Actually, it's more likely that they just don't want to be embarrassed by having been bluffed.)

If you run across these overly macho types, your best bet is to not bluff at all (it's not going to work because they won't fold) and instead only play hands of the highest quality. Unless you run into that awkward situation where your good hand is beaten by their great hand, you'll actually win money more quickly off these folks than you do off the ones you bluff.

Taking advantage of other situations

Bluffing may work to your advantage for other reasons. Those reasons run the gamut, but here are a few:

>> **Some people, whether they win or lose, will set a definite limit of how far down they'll allow their chip stack to fall.** If you run across people with this proclivity, you can nearly always bluff them when they're getting close to whatever line they draw because they don't want to cross a mental boundary.

>> **It's easier to bluff people who are preoccupied.** If your opponent is taking a phone call from a nagging boyfriend (my editor made me change the gender), playing at another table simultaneously online, watching the grill at your Poker game, or getting paged for dinner in the casino restaurant, it's *much* easier to convince her to let go of a hand with a big bet or raise.

>> **Chip leaders in tournaments can bully the smaller stacks.** This is especially true when you get near the bubble that determines who will end up in the money and who won't.

> » **Bluffing is cheaper on the hole cards and flop than it is in on the turn and river.** It's essentially half-price to bluff early on and may gain you an early pot win, or as you can see in Book 3, Chapter 3, a free card.
>
> » **Bluffing is easier with fewer players.** As a rule, you want to be up against, at most, two other players when you bluff — and being up against only one other player is a considerably more favorable situation for you. **_Remember:_** When you're bluffing, you're trying to get people with intermediate hands to drop — if you try to push enough of them at one time, one of them will not be pushed.

The Semi-Bluff

A *semi-bluff* is where you bet a hand a little bit stronger than you should or make a bet implying a hand is a bit better than it is. Usually the hope and prayer behind a semi-bluff is that if someone calls you, you have a decent chance of outdrawing your opponent.

Think of a semi-bluff like having a pit bull puppy with a deeper-than-normal bark. It sounds evil enough that most people will stay away. And for those who venture into the yard? Well, maybe it'll grow big enough that by the time your opponent opens the door to your house, the dog can tear his leg off.

When to semi-bluff

The rules for semi-bluffing are nearly identical to those of regular bluffing. The biggest difference is you're going to be playing more heavily with the concept of drawing with a semi-bluff (whereas a full-on bluff tends to deal more with the community cards that are already dealt).

Here's an example: Imagine you have K♥ 10♥ and the flop is Q♦ Q♥ 9♥. You're sitting in later position, and someone bets in front of you. A raise here is a semi-bluff. You don't really have a hand yet to speak of — just a straight draw, a flush draw, and a straight-flush draw. The hidden beauty of a raise, however, is that it may make people think you have trip queens this instant and are trying to do something like drive the flush draws away.

Here's another example: Say you have A♠ 3♠ playing from a late position and the flop is a rainbow 9♠ 5♥ 3♣. That's a truly anemic and shaky flop — so much so that there's a pretty good chance no one's going to touch it with his hole cards. A raise post-flop isn't *that* bad of play in and of itself, but considering that you can catch an ace, or have a freak shot at two running spades for a flush, a raise here falls into the category of semi-bluff. (If you got a caller here and then saw another spade on the turn, it's probably worth following it with yet another semi-bluff. Your opponent almost certainly would put you on trips at that point because he wouldn't think you'd be crazy enough to play for a running spade flush.)

Obviously, people who are more likely to fold to a flat-out bluff are also more likely to pass on a semi-bluff.

Why semi-bluff?

There are a couple of reasons to consider a semi-bluff:

>> **When someone folds, you get their money 100 percent of the time.** There are no bad beats, no lucky draws — you just flat-out win. The more often you can make this happen at a Poker table, the better your game will do in the long run. Semi-bluffing gives you chance at making that happen.

TIP

>> **Semi-bluffing is also a nice toe into the water of the bluffing pool.** It's not a full-on bluff, so you may not be as uncomfortable about doing it (either consciously or unconsciously) because you feel you can actually make things better with a draw. This comfort, in turn, may make the play seem more "natural" to other players at the table and make them more likely to pass. Getting this kind of emotional support and security over your bluffing habits will do nothing but help your game.

>> **Semi-bluffing is harder for opponents to read and figure out, even after they see your cards.** Unless you're playing in a home game, and *especially* if the people around the table are a little fatigued and the game has essentially dropped into autopilot, what happened is often not totally clear. You may get a mild taint as being either insane or just a bad player if people can't put rhyme or reason to it. But it's not as if a reputation like that is going to bother your game.

Getting Caught — Now What?

First of all, understand that you *will* get caught bluffing. It's all a part of the game. When you do, don't freak out or let it rattle you. Instead, it's time, once again, to step outside yourself and try to see the hand through your opponent's eyes. This turns out to be considerably less difficult than evaluating your pre-bluff strategy because oftentimes your opponent will start crowing at you at length about how he just *knew* that you weren't telling the truth and that you never *were* a good bluffer and a whole bunch of other gibberish you'd rather not hear (but absolutely should listen to).

The immediate thing that your bluff tells other players is that, yes, you do in fact have the ability to bluff built into your character. This knowledge may cause a few players to immediately, completely reevaluate your play on the chance they thought you weren't capable of it.

You'll almost certainly be thought of as a looser player, no matter how tight or loose they thought you were before. This means you'll be more even more likely to be called, so tighten up on the hands you play a bit, but don't be afraid to go ahead and bet aggressively. Because players are more likely to call, you may well be able to recoup what you've lost in just a few large bets.

It may also indicate to other players that you're unable to read a tell on another player at the table if she happened to have a monster hand and you sort of missed that in your frenzy of trying to bluff against her. This, in turn, may cause the other players to be not quite as guarded toward you in their plays (because, after all, you're an idiot if you couldn't see *that* one coming) and you may find you're suddenly able to pick up *much* more information about other players (especially when playing only one other player heads–up in a pot).

4

Going Online to Play: Internet Poker

Contents at a Glance

Chapter 1

Creating a Winning Combination: Poker, the Internet, and You

The Internet revolutionized the game of Poker. All of a sudden, if you knew the basics of the game (or were willing to learn), had a decent Internet connection, and were willing to download some software, you could play a couple of hands whenever the urge struck. And if you were really confident and had a few bucks to spare, you could play for money.

However, the days of playing online for money (in most states) are over, but that doesn't mean you can't go online and play Poker anytime, night or day. You just have to be prepared for the differences between brick-and-mortar games and online games.

Book 4 concentrates on the specific nuances of Internet Poker. If you're not generally familiar with Poker as a game, have never played for hard currency, or don't have a good handle on crazy Poker lingo, you need to get a good primer and brush-up. Head to Book 2 for information about the basics of the game and an introduction to various Poker games like Omaha and Seven-Card Stud. Book 3 covers Texas Hold'em, one of the most popular forms of Poker today, in depth.

In this chapter, we explain why you can no longer play online Poker for money. Then we talk about the differences between online play and brick-and-mortar play. Finally, we give you some tips about creating your online persona.

Answering the Big Question: Why Can't I Play Online Poker for Money?

Between 2000 and 2011, online Poker practically took over the Internet. If a person was into Poker and had a bit of money to spare, he likely had at least one account at an online Poker site. True fans had accounts at several sites. Money was changing hands faster than a magician's assistant disappears from the magic box. People were winning and losing pots (and their bankrolls) in every amount imaginable.

The Unlawful Internet Gambling Enforcement Act (UIGEA) was passed in October 2006. The act "prohibits gambling businesses from knowingly accepting payments in connection with the participation of another person in a bet or wager that involves the use of the Internet and that is unlawful under any federal or state law."

Some big companies (Party Poker and Paradise Poker) decided they didn't want to run afoul of the law and, at great financial cost, stopped accepting US players. US players who had accounts with those companies suffered great financial loss. However, at least three other big companies (Poker Stars, Full Tilt, Absolute Poker) remained open to US players in clear violation of the new law. With diminished competition, these companies drew more traffic and more revenue . . . until April 15, 2011, when the FBI shut them down and seized their bank accounts.

As of 2016, Delaware, New Jersey, and Nevada are the only states that have licensed online gambling. These states allow residents to play online Poker for money as long as the player is within the state's borders. That's why when you visit some Poker sites, you'll see a message telling you that you can play for real money only if you're in one of those three states; otherwise, you gamble with play money at these sites.

Many other sites operate illegally and accept US players. Some of these sites are scams and won't pay out winnings. Others are "legit" illegal sites that have developed good reputations. (But if you're a player with a complaint, what can you do? Sue?) New sites pop up and disappear all the time. The software is never as sophisticated as it was for the premier sites back in the day, and traffic is always lighter (which means you may have to wait for the game you prefer).

The majority of US online play today is illegal and unregulated. It's very sad for Poker.

WARNING

If you're tempted to deposit your hard-earned cash with an online Poker site that seems reputable, we have one word for you: *Don't!* Do not. Forget about it. Send your money to your friendly authors instead. There's no guarantee you'll be able to withdraw the deposited money or your winnings at a later date. Better to lose your money the old-fashioned way — by losing to a more skilled player in person — than to lose it to faceless scammers looking to make a fast and easy buck.

However, you can still play Poker on the Internet. You can find plenty of sites that let you sit down at a virtual table and play with other like-minded folks. You just won't finish richer than you started.

Recognizing that Internet Poker Is Still Poker

Even if you've "mastered" brick-and-mortar play, you can't simply walk in and take all the virtual candy from the online brats. You'll likely come screen to screen with some pretty savvy players. But coming out on top of your favorite game is certainly possible, and to do that you need to know your Poker theory.

REMEMBER

The most important thing to understand about Internet Poker is that you're still playing Poker.

With very few exceptions, nearly all the Poker theory you already know and have gleaned over your life applies in the virtual world. You must deal with nuances and fine points, yes (we cover those in detail in Book 4, Chapter 2), but Poker is Poker, no matter the form or forum.

TIP

If you're looking for general Poker theory, head to Book 2. If you aren't familiar with the nuances of Poker itself, you should read and study up on general theory first before you play online.

In any betting situation, the key to winning is being more informed than your opponent. If you fail to read up on Poker theory, the players who aren't so cavalier *will* beat you in the long run.

Stepping Out of the Casino Mentality

Although they both offer run-of-the-mill Poker, the online Poker environment is far different from the brick-and-mortar world. You need to give up what you know and love about playing in the casino and hunker down by yourself, in the corner, with your computer. Besides your physical surroundings, you experience other differences too . . . like when you want to play, you have to first download a Poker site's software. Next you have to realize that looking for tells is a bit different because your opponent may be sitting somewhere across the planet rather than across the table in front of you.

You also have many more paths you can take in the online world compared to brick-and-mortar casinos. You can play in tournaments or ring games. You can play Hold'em, Omaha, or Stud (and even wild card games). You can play at tables with as many as nine other players or head's up against a sole contender. What separates the Internet world is that you can play all these types of games at any time, not just when management gives you the go-ahead in a brick-and-mortar casino.

Looking for tells online

The most obvious difference between the physical and the online world is that you don't have another player glaring at you from across the table. The lack of player presence directs your focus to the game, whereas before you may have split your time between looking at your opponent and the cards in play.

But being alone doesn't mean that you play in a world devoid of tells and clues about another player's bluff (or worse, when he tries to sucker you in with a killer hand). It just means that the clues you want to keep track of and watch for are different.

Experiencing Poker in the pure

Experience shows that, in many ways, Internet Poker is a purer form of the game. The decisions you make tend to be more positional than in the brick-and-mortar world. Where you sit in relation to betting around the table and the number of chips you have relative to the other players (especially in tournament play) hold bigger roles.

In the online world, you see bigger betting (pushing all-in, for example), largely because you come across more novice players who don't have anything but time to lose. You also see less folding than in the brick-and-mortar world. We delve into these nuances, and more, in Book 4, Chapter 2.

Crafting Your Identity

Before you begin playing in the virtual realm, you need to make a few of the following decisions about your online persona.

What's your name?

The site asks you for a user identification name (*user ID*). This is the moniker that the site uses to identify you at the table. Unless you tell them, the other players at any table can never know your "for real" human name; nor can you know theirs.

WARNING

After you pick a user ID, you're stuck with it for the life of that site; so make sure you pick something you like. Being called "Spice Girls" may have been cool in 1997, but it isn't so great now (although, personally, we'd *kill* to have that one).

Expect obscene and semi-obscene user IDs to provoke a reaction from your Poker site's Thought Police; you can avoid the hassle by not goading them in the first place. Keep it clean.

What's your sign?

Some sites give you the opportunity to pick a small thumbnail-sized icon to represent your presence at the virtual table. Again, choose something you can be happy with for a l-o-n-g time because some sites only let you change your icon once. Others never do.

TIP

Regardless of your gender, you may be tempted to choose a picture of some super-hunky dude or ultra-busty chick as your icon. We encourage you to think twice about this tactic, unless you really like the idea of talking about that image *every* time you sit down at a table.

REMEMBER

People don't have a whole lot to focus on when they sit at an online table; you may find that some become obsessed with what little eye candy they do see. We've met several players from the virtual world who turned their chat off because they just couldn't take bantering about their picture any more.

Chapter 2

Putting Internet Poker's Nuances to Work in Your Play

The online Poker world is truly its own environment with a unique set of paradigms, customs, and standards. In this chapter, we talk about the fundamental differences between online and live players, take a tour of the cyber version of the table, and raise your hip Poker vocab with some Internetese (spoken with a distinctive Poker accent, of course).

Comparing the Real-World Game to the Online Version

A few characteristics of the computer Poker realm can be pretty jarring when you first run across them. The most obvious examples: the speed of play, the type of opponent you encounter, and the way your focus changes when you don't have a real-world Poker-playing environment around you.

Considering the differences in speed

In a real-life cardroom, the physical manipulation of the cards (the dealing and folding of hands) and the general orchestration of the game (players placing blinds, taking seats, not paying attention to the game, flirting with cocktail waitresses, and so on) take more time than in the online world, which features automatic dealing, immediately placed blinds, and a lack of drinks spilling on the felt. Shuffling, dealing, and repeatedly asking slowpokes to hand in their cards at the end of a hand burn time on the clock. In the online world, these delays don't exist.

How fast is online play? A typical brick-and-mortar cardroom, with an efficient dealer and a full table, churns about 30 hands per hour (add two or three more hands per hour if the dealers use automatic shufflers); the online equivalent plays about 60 hands per hour, increasing to 65 or more at turbo tables (see the section "Going for super-speedy online play" later in this chapter for more). After you gain experience and make it to a head's-up match against only one other player, you can expect that number to jump to as high as a whopping 150 hands per hour!

The speed of the Internet creates a different feel. The first time you play online, the action and the decisions can feel a little bit blurry. What's funny, though, is that in a short time you adjust to the new speed and you start to want to go faster.

Beating the online timer

In the online world, you're under a time clock for every betting decision you have to make, which is somewhat similar to the shot clock in basketball. The timing method varies from site to site, and it depends on whether you play in *ring games* (cash games where you can come and go) or tournaments. Some sites use a set number of seconds per betting decision (usually between 15 and 30); others have a set number of seconds of total delay you're allowed at that table during a single session (usually 60). Reading a site's documentation or experimenting on a play money table can familiarize you with an online site's timing custom.

Until you get used to it, beating the timer can be psychologically troubling. In fact, you may overreact by trying to decide too quickly. Don't be afraid to take all the time you need to act. Thirty seconds is longer than you think.

TIP

Play with your computer's volume turned on. All Poker sites beep when your turn to act comes, especially if you start to run short on time. The alarm becomes especially useful when you want to work within other applications on your computer, play on another table simultaneously, or turn away from your machine for a few moments. (Don't get us wrong, we think playing distracted, especially by playing another table, is a bad, bad thing. See Book 4, Chapter 3 for how shameful we think it all is.)

WARNING

If your time limit expires and you haven't yet made a betting decision, nearly all sites fold your hand.

Going for super-speedy online play

As if the online game doesn't move fast enough already, some sites provide even faster play. Like crazed mechanics in a pit crew, they shave the individual timing intervals down and use a few other tricks and gimmicks to jack up the need for speed. These tables always have augmented names like "Turbo," "Speed Play," or "Make That a Triple Espresso." If you're new to the online environment, we don't recommend playing on these tweaked tables. Wait until you're comfortable with online play first.

Adjusting to a variety of opponents

In the real world, you know several things about your opponents immediately. Some traits are (usually) obvious, such as their sex and general age range. A few characteristics you may automatically take for granted without even thinking about them, like what time zone they play in. Others are subtle, like the ticks and tells some people exhibit while they play. But the online world is a different beast.

Analyzing your opponent

You play people not only in different time zones, but also very possibly in other countries. The Internet provides you someone to play against in another place. He may be in the middle of his day, or it may be smack dab in the middle of his night. A tired player is always easier to beat than an alert player.

Any tidbit of information can be valuable to you as the game progresses. For example, someone playing from the city hosting that day's Super Bowl team may be watching the game while he plays on the laptop in front of the tube. Look for any edge you can find, based on even the smallest of information threads because some edge is better than none; and in the online world, advantages are harder to glean than in the brick-and-mortar environment. You lose a lot by not having your opponent sitting at the table across from you.

Not everyone you run across in the virtual cardroom speaks English as a first language; a few may not speak English at all. Don't worry; their money is good (and never forget, so is yours), but you may not always get a snappy conversation.

TIP

On nearly all sites you can hover your cursor over an opponent's nameplate and find out his hometown, country of origin, or both. Do so.

STICKS AND STONES MAY BREAK MY BONES, BUT INTERNET SLURS CAN'T HURT ME

Unfortunately, because they feel empowered in the somewhat anonymous online environment, more rude opponents unleash their ugly behavior than in a brick-and-mortar establishment, especially in the emotional aftermath of losing a big hand.

You should shrug off their vile comments or turn off the chat feature of your table if their slings and arrows upset you. We suggest ignoring the behavior and looking closely for patterns and tells that your opponent may unintentionally display.

Watch for them to go on *tilt,* which means they may become more aggressive and stay in more pots because of their frustration.

Betting more aggressively

We find that online players bet more aggressively than their offline counterparts — especially in the smaller pot-limit and no-limit games where a player can risk her chip stack at any point to gain advantage in a hand. A generalization no doubt, but one that seems to hold true. For more on different game types offered online (limit versus no-limit, ring games versus tourneys), see Book 4, Chapter 4.

A few sites offer a *bet the pot* button as one of their options in the betting round. In the real world, this action involves the player estimating the current pot, counting out chips to match that pot, placing that amount in front of her (possibly in multiple steps for large bets), and then making the verbal bet; an arduous process that often weeds out players trying to buy a pot (if for no other reason than the player's opponents can sit and watch her very closely for tells as she goes through the motions). The wonderful world of computers makes this process automatic because it does the counting and places the bet in one step. And automatic means easy. And easy means more people use it more often than in the real world.

You may also find that your online competitors are more willing to push all-in compared to their felt-scraping equivalents. It becomes much easier on the mind when you don't have to physically see the stack of chips, feel the stares upon you, and wrestle with the enormity of the decision at the table environment. All it takes is a simple flick of the no-limit button control for betting, and whoomp, there it is.

REMEMBER

Players betting all-in more often means that you see more variance in the game than you're probably used to in the real world. You're more likely to double your chip stack and more likely to go bust because the frequency of big betting is higher. This doesn't mean that you should alter your play or strategy, but you do have to prepare yourself, or the frequency may shock you.

Keeping your focus on the game

What you experience when you play online differs profoundly from the environment during a real-world game. In the real world, your senses experience an overload: The sights of the people and events around you, the sounds of hundreds of clay Poker chips clacking together, the inevitable flickers of 20 televisions broadcasting a dozen different sports channels, the smells of a million cigars past, and the tactile nature of the cards and the table all add to your sensory perception of the game.

In the virtual world, your senses are strictly confined. The noises you hear from the computer are unnecessary artifacts, or mimics, of the real world: noises like card shuffling, chips banging together, and sound effects for checking and folding. But the site adds them artificially; they don't have to be there for the game to run properly.

Motion and visual information is extremely limited. The deprivation of typical sights, sounds, and observations causes you to focus much more intently on the few things you do see: the size of a person's bet, the amount of time he takes to make this bet, and (to a much lesser extent) the conversation he has at the table through the chat system (more about this in the section "Speaking the Poker Dialect of Internetese" later in this chapter).

The more you force yourself to focus on these factors, the better you can exploit them to your advantage. (Of course, we don't think that the online world is necessarily all focus — you are, after all, sitting in front of a computer. We talk about avoiding your in-home distractions in Book 4, Chapter 3.)

Getting a Feel for the Virtual Game

Many websites model their online Poker tables after real-world equivalents, and you may find them comfortably familiar if you've spent some hours in brick-and-mortar cardrooms. Still, you should pay attention to the details, particularly if home games, not casino play, make up your past experience.

Figure 2-1 shows a fairly typical representation of a classic Internet Poker table. Most sites on the Net make their tables look something like this.

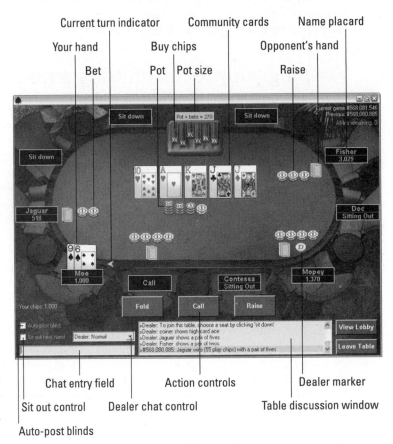

FIGURE 2-1:
A typical fixed-limit Hold'em Internet Poker table.

The classic table closely mimics the real-world equivalent, and first-time users shouldn't have much trouble navigating and understanding the setup.

Unfortunately, mimicking the real world isn't always the best way to design the layout of a graphical computer program, nor is it necessarily the easiest to quickly understand visually or use with a mouse. These limitations have brought about a newer, *modern* table (see Figure 2-2).

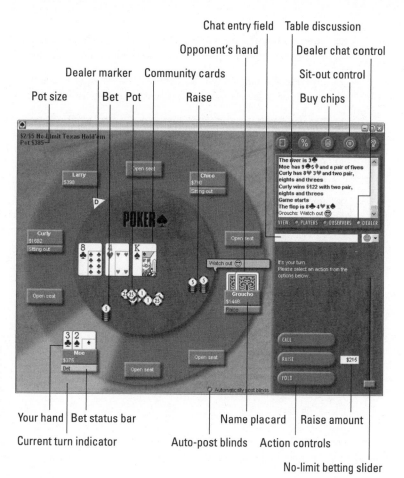

Chat entry field **Table discussion**

Opponent's hand **Dealer chat control**

Dealer marker **Community cards** **Sit-out control**

Pot size **Bet Pot** **Raise** **Buy chips**

FIGURE 2-2:
A modern no-limit
Hold'em Internet
Poker table. Note
the added space
for user controls
in the modern
table over the
classic (refer to
Figure 2-1).

Your hand | **Bet status bar** **Name placard** | **Raise amount**

Current turn indicator **Auto-post blinds** **Action controls**

No-limit betting slider

© John Wiley & Sons, Inc.

Laying it all on the table

Some features of the online table mirror the details of the brick-and-mortar Poker
world, and others are unique to the Net. We cover them all in this section to get
you up to speed and ready to hit the virtual felt with confidence.

The following list highlights the important terms you need to know to get started
(and you can check out Figures 2-1 and 2-2 for visual images of the following
features):

>> **Name placard:** Shows the screen name of each player, how much money the
player has, and each player's current status (playing or sitting out). If no player
occupies the seat, the site marks it as open, and you merely click on the name
placard to sit down.

- >> **Individual bet:** Shown in front of a player's seating position. You can hover your cursor over the chip stack to see the amount of the bet.

- >> **Individual raise:** Shown as a separate stack from the original bet. You can hover over the raise with your cursor to see the total amount.

- >> **Pot:** Shown in the middle of the table. You can see the size of the pot by hovering your cursor over the chips in the middle.

- >> **Action controls:** You place a check, bet, raise, or fold by using the action buttons. The buttons display the action for fast and easy use.

- >> **Betting slider:** You can move this control to bet a variable amount during no-limit play (see Figure 2-3). You can also type the amount you want to raise in the corresponding text box.

FIGURE 2-3:
A no-limit slider, which allows you to make a bet or raise above the minimum amount, from a classic Internet table.

© John Wiley & Sons, Inc.

- >> **Community cards:** Hold'em and Omaha flops, turns, and rivers are shown in the middle of the table.

- >> **Your hand:** The site always shows your hand face-up in front of your name placard while you're still in the pot. After you fold, your hand disappears from the table.

- >> **Your opponent's hand:** Shown face down until the showdown, at which point the site turns the other player's cards face up if he beats you. If you beat your opponent's hand, he typically has the option of showing you what he had or mucking without a display.

- >> **Table discussion window:** Shows all the dealer chat (like what's happening in the hand) interspersed with all the player chat.

- >> **Dealer chat control:** Adjusts the chattiness of the dealer. You can typically set the chat on three levels:

  - • **Succinct:** Essentially, who wins and loses the hand

  - • **Normal:** Information about the cards shown on the table, along with the results of the hand

  - • **Verbose:** Tells you about everything you can see

On the classic table, you adjust verbosity with a pull-down menu; on the modern table, you adjust it by clicking on the little light menu and cycling through your choices (red for succinct, yellow for normal, and green for verbose).

>> **Chat entry field:** Where you type comments to other players that show up in the table discussion window. The modern design allows you to add smiley faces (*emoticons*).

>> **Chip addition:** You click on the adding chips control button on the modern table. On the classic table, you click on the chip rack.

>> **Dealer marker:** Shows the last person to act and moves clockwise around the table at the end of every hand to signify the dealer position.

In the online world, just as in a brick-and-mortar casino, the house doesn't participate in the game; it just provides a place for you to play and takes a piece of the action in the form of the rake.

>> **Sit out control:** Any time you don't want to be dealt a hand, but you also don't want to leave your seat, you use this button. Sitting out is the polite thing to do if you need to take a break from the game because it keeps players from waiting for you to act when you participate in other activities.

REMEMBER

After you sit out (either by clicking the control or by timing out), you have to click the "I'm back" button that appears. If you sit out during a tournament, the site continues to post your blinds on your turn.

>> **Current turn indicator:** Shows you who acts next. On the classic table, you may have trouble seeing this control, although you always get sound indicating your turn to act. On the modern table, the indicator is a light beam that sweeps from player to player.

Acing the action controls

Action controls are unique to the online world, with no brick-and-mortar equivalent. You click on these buttons to make your betting decisions (check, bet, raise, or fold) associated with a hand.

Present action buttons

When the betting action comes to you, the screen presents you with a set of *present action buttons* to choose from. Clicking one indicates your betting decision at that point in the hand. If no betting action has come in front of you, you can check, bet, or fold (nearly all sites remind you that you can check for free instead of folding here), just as in a brick-and-mortar game.

If a player bets in front of you, you can call, raise (if further raises are allowed, meaning that the betting limit hasn't been reached), or fold. You can see examples of present action buttons in Figures 2-1 and 2-2.

No-limit and pot-limit games also tend to have both a slider for easy betting use (see Figure 2-3) and a text entry box for manual betting for the particularly meticulous when you want to bet any amount over the minimum. You can see a no-limit slider on the modern table in Figure 2-2, and Figure 2-3 shows one from a classic table. (Due to table layout styles, the classic slider is horizontal, and the modern slider is vertical.)

After you make a present action choice, the site relays your decision to the other players at the table and the betting action passes to the next player clockwise from your position, just as in the real world.

Future action buttons

Before your turn to act arrives, if you already know what you want to do based on a strategic choice or an obvious decision (and assuming the betting situation doesn't change), you have the option of indicating your choice in advance. To do so, you use *future action buttons* (see Figure 2-4). Using these buttons may go against your instincts at first (because on a real-world table, the rules state that you can't act out of turn), but after a little experience they become second nature and certainly help to speed the game along.

FIGURE 2-4:
You use future action buttons to make your betting decisions instantaneous when your turn arrives.

© John Wiley & Sons, Inc.

When you make a decision with a future action button, nothing happens from the table's perspective until the action comes to you. The site automatically acts out your request, and you don't have a chance to interact with present action buttons. The betting action moves along to the next person clockwise.

REMEMBER

If you choose a future action that isn't compatible with a subsequent play in front of you — say you choose to check but a bet comes in front of you — the site erases your future action and presents you with a set of present action buttons.

If you make a future action selection and someone increases the bet in front of you (by placing a bet when everyone else checks or by making a raise on a bet that a player previously made), the site resets your choice as though you never made a selection. Now you need to make another choice. This feature keeps you from making involuntary raises or calls if your eyes wander off the screen.

REMEMBER

Unlike the present action buttons, you don't *have* to make a future action button selection. If you don't select a future action button, the present action buttons simply replace them when the action comes to you.

If no players have raised, your future action choices are check, call, raise, or fold. You also have the interesting option of "check/fold," which means you check if everyone else checks in front of you; but if someone bets, you fold. Check/fold keeps you from having to select the present folding action if you wanted to check a weak hand.

Figure 2-4 shows future action choices that you find on the fixed-limit version of any online game (a dollar amount of the bet normally shows up on the bet button as well). Notice the gap in the future action bar — this feature prevents you from trying to hit the check button and accidentally raising if the betting status changes in front of you (and therefore changing your future action button choices).

If a bet gets placed in front of you, your future action choices change to call, raise, or fold. Checking goes away, of course, because you can't check when you face a bet (see Figure 2-5).

FIGURE 2-5:
Your future action buttons change if another player places a bet.

Again, the dollar amount typically shows up on both the call and the raise buttons. You can compare the future action buttons in Figure 2-5 to the ones in Figure 2-4 to see how the design avoids button overlap. (For more on button overlapping, refer to the following sidebar and check out Figures 2-6 and 2-7 for examples.)

WARNING

If you want to play no-limit, be very cautious about playing the *Check/Call Any* future action button. If a player bets a large amount in front of you, you may end up making a heftier call than you had originally planned.

THE DREADED OVERLAPPING ACTION BUTTONS

WARNING

Some sites have been a bit sloppy in the way they place their action buttons on the screen, and occasionally you find future action buttons that the site, on your turn, replaces with present action buttons that have a different intent in the same exact area of the screen. You can start to click on one item and then have the buttons switch out from under you, causing you to accidentally click on something else.

For example, before the action comes to you at the table, you may want to choose to check in turn with a future action button. Unfortunately, when your turn comes, clicking on that same exact screen location causes you to choose to call, thereby putting your money in the pot when you didn't intend to (and also possibly causing you to put your fist through your computer screen when you didn't intend to). A slow movement on your part to click that check button may cause you to bet.

For this reason, you should always play for several minutes with play money on any site you're not familiar with before you play with hard currency to check for overlapping issues. If they arise, get out of dodge and choose another saloon.

Another way to dodge this overlapping button problem is to never use future action buttons, if you can't get away from your trusted dive.

FIGURE 2-6:
If your site has overlapping action buttons, you may intend to click Check in Turn and instead click on Call when the site changes the buttons.

© John Wiley & Sons, Inc.

FIGURE 2-7:
Here we see the new buttons that pop up after a site changes its action bar. This makes it quite easy to accidentally click on the wrong action button.

© John Wiley & Sons, Inc.

Other action preferences

Some Poker sites offer unique selections, usually in the form of preferences, to help speed up play.

AUTO POST

The most common selection is *Auto Post* if you play Hold'em or Omaha or *Auto Ante* if you play Seven-Card Stud. Choosing this feature automatically makes those pesky blind or ante housekeeping bets for you and moves the game along. Your opponents can get *very* cranky if you don't auto-post because you slow the general action of the game; for this reason alone you should check it. (In tournaments, the sites make this choice for you automatically.) If you choose to sit out and you enable the Auto Post feature, the action automatically skips you without posting your blinds (except in tournament situations, where you have to post).

TIP

If you're playing Hold'em and you want to leave the table before you're in the big blind, you should uncheck the Auto Post button. That way, when you need to post the big blind, the site prompts you to place the blind manually instead of automatically dealing you in the hand. At that point you can walk away cleanly without playing yet another lap of a dealer marker (an *orbit*) around the table.

AUTO MUCK

You also have the option of choosing *Auto Muck.* Auto muck automatically throws away (or *mucks*) any hand that doesn't win a given pot, speeding up the play.

WARNING

With auto muck on, you typically can't show any losing or winning hand that goes uncalled. If you want to show any of your hands at some point during your session, turn auto muck off.

Playing Your First Hand

Enough with the gabbing already, start playing some cards!

Selecting your table and seat

The entry point for all Poker sites is the home screen (many call this the *lobby* — see Figure 2-8), which gives you a selection of tables, games, and limits.

© John Wiley & Sons, Inc.

FIGURE 2-8:
The Internet
Poker home
screen presents
you with all your
gaming options.

You can observe any table, so poke around a bit and watch a few games being played at various stakes. When you take your first tour, refrain from conversation, especially with people at the money tables. Just observe. You only see the action buttons if you actually play, but everything else, like the chips, the cards, and all the player chat, you see in plain sight. Your objective here is to get a feel for the way the online world looks and how it behaves. Just take it all in.

TIP

Even if you're an experienced online player, you should practice with free chips for a bit on an unfamiliar site. It doesn't cost anything to practice, and you get a chance to understand the idiosyncrasies of any given site's interface. Any site offering games for hard currency also offers games with free chips. To start your practice, head to the site's home screen.

Instead of standing and shivering on the diving board after you finally decide to jump in, make sure to select a table that has several players and an open seat for you. An open seat and willing enemies ensures you some playing action.

Click on the seat that looks coziest at the table of your choice and settle in. (This isn't a big decision; all Poker seats in the online world are the same.) When you sit at the low-limit free tables, expect the play to be very loose (with nonsensical, overly aggressive, or atypical betting occurring with players who play every hand). Don't sweat it; you don't play these tables to make money, you play them to discover the online world.

Getting a feel for how everything works

Playing online is nearly automatic. Just sit back, relax (but pay attention), and play the deserving hands the best you can. Don't worry about getting a handle on everything all at once; let the game proceed at its own (what may at first appear to be frenetic) pace.

It sounds dumb, but the best thing you can do for yourself, especially at first, is to focus on the game with as few other distractions from the real world as possible. Turn off your television, put down that chainsaw, have your roommate put the muffler back on his low rider, and listen to the sounds of the game. Beeps, blats, and flashing icons remind you when you need to act.

Become familiar with the pacing. Keep an eye on the conversations and dealer chat in any text window giving you info, like when you have the option to bet and when another player makes a raise. These nuances can serve as the clues and hints to help you along in your game. The site can't tell you how to play better, but it does tell you what to do and when.

Take your time to explore the interface. Every site has small differences and features, such as the location of control buttons it uses, the way its chat mechanism works, and the controls you use to go to the site's home screen while you sit at a table. Play several orbits of the dealer marker (one lap is called an *orbit*). Poke, pry, and prod until you feel like you have a really good feel for what's going on. Play money tables really give you a good outlet for this kind of exploration.

If something bugs you about the interaction of your particular site, see if you can find a way to override it, and if you can't, play somewhere else. Testing a site is just like test-driving a new car. If something bothers you a little bit now, you may be insanely chewing on your keyboard in two months. Life's too short, and your computer is a bit too valuable, for that kind of aggravation.

Speaking the Poker Dialect of Internetese

If you use online instant messaging (*IM*) or send texts on your cellphone, you're familiar with some of the shorthand abbreviations prevalent in the Internet world (for example, LOL means "laugh out loud"). Internet Poker has been around long enough to develop its own extensions to the messaging lingo. Although you certainly aren't required to speak this language, it does make the game more enjoyable and at the very least lets you know what people have to say about the Poker prowess of the table (including what they say about you).

With the exception of referring to a card with capital letters (AKQJT), the custom with abbreviations leans toward using lower case because UPPER CASE MAKES IT SEEM LIKE YOU'RE YELLING. See Table 2-1 for a list of some of the common Poker phrasing that shows up on the Internet.

TABLE 2-1 ## Common Internet Poker Chat Abbreviations

Abbreviation	Meaning
86	To remove or ban
Ac	Ace of clubs (or Ac)
Ad	Ace of diamonds (or Ad)
Ah	Ace of hearts
As	Ace of spades
bb	Big blind
bl	Better luck
brb	Be right back
C	Clubs
D	Diamonds
gc	Good call (rarely good catch)
gg	Good game
g1	Good one
gl	Good luck
H	Hearts
h/l	High-low
J	Jack
JK	Jack king
j/k	Just kidding
K	King or okay, depending on context
L8(r)	Late(r)
lol	Laugh out loud

Abbreviation	Meaning
M8	Mate
n1	Nice one
N	Nice or no, depending on context
nc	Nice catch (usually referring to a lucky turn or river draw)
Ne1	Anyone
nh	Nice hand
nhs	Nice hands (usually used when a great hand beats a good hand)
nl	No limit
o	Off-suit, written as 78o
ott	Over the top
pl	Pot limit
pls	Please
Q	Queen
qed	Math geek speak for so it is proven
rofl	Rolling on the floor laughing
ru	Are you
S	Spades
sb	Small blind
sob	I think you're a particularly nice person; we should have dinner
str8	Straight
T	Thank you or 10, depending on context
tx	Thanks
ty	Thank you
u2	You too
X	Any non-specific card
Y	Yes
y?	Why?

(continued)

TABLE 2-1 *(continued)*

Abbreviation	Meaning
yw	You're welcome
:)	Smiley face
: (	Frowny face

From a general decorum and demeanor point of view, the online Poker world is pretty similar to its brick-and-mortar equivalent. You play with good guys and loud mouths, goofs and silent mummies. Most people play online to kick back and unwind from their otherwise glamorous lives. The anonymity of the Net does produce a slight bit more aggression than you may otherwise find in the physical world, so when you sit down, don't wear your heart on your sleeve.

If you're playing at a table and an opponent takes an inordinately long time to make a betting decision, it does no good to comment on the fact. They have all the alerts and controls you do, and the triple beep of the site's "time's up!" alert does a better job than any nagging you can throw in a chat window. The vast majority of the time a delay like this happens, your opponent has connection trouble, so the last thing he needs or wants is aggravation from another player.

If a player's repeated delays bother you (even if he can't control it), pick up and move to another table. That lowers your blood pressure and keeps you on the karmic good side of the Internet Poker world.

Your general rule of conduct is simple: be congenial, be polite, or be quiet. The guy who just beat your pocket aces with 2-9 off-suit may also drive a Gremlin and listen to *The Archie's Greatest Hits* 20 times a day, but you still shouldn't launch into a tirade. The percentages are on your side in situations such as this one, but percentages aren't certainties; play enough hands and the player with exactly one out (the only card that can help) will beat you eventually.

Chapter 3

Adapting to the World of Internet Poker

On your first pass, the online Poker world may seem to be nothing more than a dim shadow of the real-world brick-and-mortar equivalent. If you can't see the face of your opponent sitting across the table from you, what's the point?

After you dig under the surface a bit, however, you discover that online Poker is profoundly different in some very interesting ways. Psychologically, you experience a very different game: You see *far* more hands than in the brick-and-mortar world, you play with fake money, and because everything happens on a computer, you encounter a whole new set of ways for things to go wrong.

In this chapter, we cover some of the fundamental underpinnings of online Poker — characteristics that make it truly different from the brick-and-mortar world — and we look at ways to understand and deal with them.

Grappling with the Ramifications of Speed

From a psychological point of view, the biggest differences between online play and the brick-and-mortar world include the radical increase in the speed of play.

In the online world, you have a chance to play between two and three times as many hands per hour as you get in the normal brick-and-mortar environment. Online Poker rooms do everything in their power to accelerate play, resulting in some interesting (and sometimes odd) ramifications in the way a player perceives the game.

Coming to grips with quick-hitting bad draws

Probably the biggest psychological hardship for any Poker player is the *bad beat,* a situation where you have a better hand than another player during the first couple betting rounds, but your opponent draws a long-shot card and beats you toward the end of the hand. A lesser hand outdrawing you is a hard thing to take under any circumstance.

As you play online, it may seem like you see more bad beats than you do in the real world, and guess what? You do. Because you see two or three times as many hands, you also see two to three times as many bad beats. You see all types of hands more often. You need to keep a realistic perspective because if you focus solely on the bad beats, you slowly drive yourself crazy. But if you can balance the bad-beat blues with the realization of how many more winning hands you see and have, you can hang on to your sanity.

TIP

If you ever encounter a streak of bad beats (and if you play long enough, a streak *will* come), our advice is to keep your wits about you and don't let the statistical weirdness of the past affect your play in the present. Take time off because you need to adjust and recoup. And make certain that you just ran into bad luck and didn't expose some fundamental flaw in your Poker strategy. Think back to what you thought before your plays, the time you took betting, and your betting strategy to search for a pattern.

Celebrating the micro-second win

Along with moving past the increase in bad beats of the Net (see the previous section for advice), you have to psychologically adjust to the wins also coming far more quickly. If you catch a really big hand or have a very unusual sequence of cards hit the board, baddabing, baddaboom: The screen displays the hands still in play, the site pays out the pot, and the play continues with new cards. You may have played your entire life waiting for a royal flush and then, when it *finally* hits your Seven-Card Stud hand in the online world, the site treats it with exactly the same dignity and respect as a king-high hand full of junk. Be warned: Online Poker is a place where you have to provide your own celebrations. Best get the party poppers out before you log on.

DEALING WITH BAD BEAT WHINERS

You can't find an Internet Poker room where players don't type a phrase like, "This never happens in the real world!" every second. The fact of the matter is, yes, bad beats *do* happen in the real world. When the randomness comes out of a computer rather than a dealer's ring-laden hand, the whole process just seems more suspicious.

And the online world seems to have a disproportionate number of people who complain, and then *keep* complaining, about their bad beats. Part of it, no doubt, is due to the anonymity of the Internet; people can whine without really losing face. Some of it probably has to do with the number of bad beats that any given person sees. And a few whiners may be people who don't have much raw playing experience, so they taste the bitter end of the bargain for the first time.

In any event, it pays to be psychologically braced for opponents who take a bad beat and suddenly lose it.

As a player you have a couple of choices. One is to ignore your table's version of Mount Vesuvius and wait for the eruption to cease. If you need help focusing, always remember that you can turn off player or observer chat.

If the whiners get threatening or abusive, you can also report them to your site's support personnel for corrective action. Nobody needs to hear that kind of stuff, so you do all players a favor.

The one thing you shouldn't do is engage the hothead in baiting conversation, no matter how tempting it may be. If the site does decide to levy ramifications on the jerk, you don't want to be associated as an instigator or accomplice.

Dodging (and Dealing with) Online Pitfalls

Problems unique to the online Poker world have nothing to do with the game of Poker itself and everything to do with the fact that you play on a computer. Here are a few steps you can take to avoid trouble, along with what to do when you find yourself stuck.

Staying sane in a world of distraction

In the brick-and-mortar world, your distractions consist of a few nattering players, televisions silently showing the latest sports analysis, and a cocktail waitress who's always elsewhere no matter how badly you need her.

Thanks to the wonders of modern computing, your online environment can be about 1,000 times worse. If you let your eyes and mind wander, you may realize that you're playing under an animated billboard with the computer stereo blasting and an Internet mailman knocking on your door every 10 seconds with new email. And that only covers the happenings on your computer. (It gets more complicated if you've got kids, pets, or angry spouses who think you play too much Internet Poker.)

Tie your hands to your sides or wear blinkers like a racehorse if you have to, but when you play, stay focused. Ask yourself the same question you should ask when contemplating whether to play multiple tables (as discussed in the following section): "If my opponent doesn't have the same distractions as me, does she have an edge?"

Steering clear of multiple-table play

You can't play multiple tables simultaneously in the brick-and-mortar world, due to both physical and rule restrictions.

In the online world, however, you can play at multiple tables (playing different game types and limits) simultaneously. Some sites restrict the number of tables you can play; others make the sky the limit.

When you first start playing online, especially on the Hold'em tables, you may find the speed a little disconcerting. Just the thought of playing two tables at once may seem a little overwhelming. It doesn't take long, however, to get into the swing of the action. After you play only one table for some time, you start to picture yourself playing on another table simultaneously. In fact, your inner action monkey may start to crave it.

TIP

Think of this situation exactly like you think of repeatedly hitting your hand with a hammer: Just because you can do something doesn't mean you should.

The problem with playing more than one table at a time, as if we even need to state it, is splitting your attention between multiple games. You have more opponents to keep track of and more hand and chip stack information to be aware of. You take on a lot of responsibility, and it gives your opponents (who may not be playing multiple tables; use the site's player-finding feature to get a report) an immediate advantage over you.

Avoiding a wrong click

If you run multiple applications on your computer, you naturally click on a window in the background to bring it forward. But if you click on an actionable area and make a betting decision, the program passes, processes, and acts on the click in the application window.

For example, you decide to work on a spreadsheet of your Poker history in the foreground and play at a table in the background. You receive an alert from the game indicating your turn to act, and you click on the Poker window to bring it forward. If you happen to accidentally click the *Raise* button when you just want to bring the table to the front of the screen, guess what? Yep, you raise the hand accidentally.

TIP

To avoid mis-clicking, you should call the application forward by clicking on the icon on your toolbar or grab the Poker window by the top of its windowpane. (If you accidentally click the close box of your Poker table, don't worry. All sites ask you if you're sure you want to leave the table.)

Be aware that some sites force your game table to the foreground when your turn arrives. If you want to work on a spreadsheet during your game (which you shouldn't because you should focus on the game), you may easily make a click that gives you more than you bargained for if the table pops to the forefront when you're not expecting it.

Coping with disconnection

No matter how bulletproof your computer is or how reliable your Internet service provider may be, sooner or later you find yourself disconnected from an online Poker game. If this happens, nearly all sites fold your hand.

Getting disconnected is only a big deal during tournaments because the site slowly but surely blinds your chips off. You have to get back on if you want to save your stack. In a ring game, the site simply changes your status to *sitting out*, and eventually you lose your seat. The site re-credits the chips you had at the table to your account.

Getting disconnected is a jarring experience, but after it happens, you need to put it behind you. Focus harder than you normally do on the game and calm down. You already had to deal with the inconvenience the disconnection handed you — you don't need to make it worse by playing it over and over in your head.

Resuscitating your game (and computer)

The first hint you get that you're disconnected is the normal flow of the game suddenly stops. No bets. No cards being dealt. No chat from players. Nothing.

One of two things may be wrong: Your computer or the site dropped its Internet connection.

To find out which is the case, quickly launch a new browser window and do a search for something (anything) you've never searched for before (just look across your room and type in the name of the first object you see if you have trouble thinking of something). If you can bring up information from your search, the problem belongs with your Poker site, in which case you should just sit tight and wait. If the Poker application quits while you wait (sites often reset if they have a wide outage), re-launch it.

If your web search doesn't go through, the connectivity problem is on your side. Perform the following tasks in order:

1. **Quit your Poker application.**

2. **Quit your Internet connection and restart.**

3. **After you reconnect, launch your Poker application. If you can't, try to avoid chewing on your arm (which doesn't help you get your slowly blinding chip stack back).**

4. **Log in to your Poker site.**

5. **Perform the *find a player* search on yourself and go to your table if the site doesn't immediately direct you there.**

Practicing Poker Patience Online

You need to be patient when playing online, just as patient as you are when playing in a brick-and-mortar environment. Remember you're going to catch long streaks of dead cards. You take your share of bad beats. Rough spots happen to every player, so the better you can ride through them, the higher you can rise above the other guy in the long run. Here are some things you can do to remain calm and learn from each online experience.

Taking a break from play

Many players find it just a little too easy to play like a demon online.

Win or lose a tournament? Doesn't matter. Click, click, and you enter into a new one. Just lost your 50th hand in a row? You can shake it off. Keep playin'. Or don't.

You should take stock of what happens as you play. Are you winning or losing? Do certain opponents always beat you? Can you find a consistency in the way you lose or win? Are you beginning to show repeatable, predictable behavior?

TIP

If you experience some bad luck in play, stop for a moment, take a deep breath, and answer the previous questions. What you find may give you deeper insight into your game.

Keeping a Poker journal

An excellent way to stay on top of your game and analyze the happenings in your Poker world is to keep a Poker journal. Obviously you want to add information that makes the most sense to you, but we suggest tracking the following:

>> The number of players in your session

>> Unusual plays you make that work and those that don't

>> Mistakes you make, and how you can try to avoid them in the future

>> The time of day you play

>> The stakes and game you play

>> Your wins and losses

You can set your journal up in any format you like. Microsoft Excel is good for laying out spreadsheet information, of course — and it's free if you already have it on your computer. If you want something that's more in-depth or has already been created for you, try www.Pokercharts.com or www.Pokertracker.com. However, these sites charge for access after the free 30-day trial.

Chapter 4

Exploring Your Online Game Options

The online Poker world is a wild and wooly place. Large sites can have more than 10,000 people playing at any one time. (Can you imagine walking into a brick-and-mortar room of that size? You could *never* find a cocktail waitress.) Because of the high-traffic of online play, you can find almost any kind of game you want at nearly any table or stake size: Hold'em, Omaha, or Seven-Card Stud; and tournaments or ring games. We explore the staggering array of options in this chapter.

Melding in Ring Games

Ring games (the fancy term for a Poker game where you can buy in and cash out as you please) are the most popular games on the Internet. Even though you don't play with real money, you can still find games that allow you to bet as if you were using good ole greenbacks. Betting typically comes in three forms: *no-limit*, where you can bet any amount at any time; *pot-limit*, where you can bet any amount up to the size of the current pot at any time; and *fixed-limit* (sometimes referred to solely as *limit*), where you bet in specific, predetermined amounts.

TIP

With the no-limit and pot-limit games, if you're unclear about the buy-in and limits from looking at the home page, go to any table and try to sit in an open seat — the site gives you very explicit details of limits and buy-ins from the chip purchase dialog (and you can always cancel if the requirements are too rich for your blood).

Hankering for Hold'em

Texas Hold'em overtook Five-Card Draw as the serious Poker player's game of choice in the middle of the 20th century. The takeover was so complete that the player who wins the $10,000 buy-in no-limit Hold'em event at the World Series of Poker in Las Vegas automatically attains "World Poker Champion" status. No questions asked.

Hold'em has such a stranglehold on the brick-and-mortar world that you can barely tell other variations of Poker even exist. And the online world is no different. Hold'em easily outstrips all other games that you can play online.

The game dynamic in any environment is simple. All players are dealt two hole cards and take a round of betting. Three community cards are dealt face up (the *flop*), followed by another round of betting. A fourth community card is dealt (the *turn;* more rarely called *fourth street*), and the remaining players bet again. A final community card is dealt (known as the *river, fifth street,* or when Lady Luck flips you the bird, your favorite string of expletives), and the final round of betting ensues. The player with the best five-card hand takes the pot — you can use zero, one, or both of your hole cards to make your hand. (For more on the intricacies of Hold'em, check out Book 3.)

AN EXAMPLE HOLD'EM HAND

You receive A♥ 10♥ as your hole cards. The round of betting ensues.

The flop appears on the center of the table A♦ 2♦ J♣. You go through the second round of betting. (You have a pair of aces and bet on it.)

The turn is the K♦. You bet with your pair of aces and straight draw.

The river is the Q♦. You decide to keep betting your hand.

The good news is that you have an A-10 straight (known in Poker slang as *Broadway*); the bad news is that any player still in who holds even one diamond beats you with a flush.

Hold'em is extremely well suited for computer play, adding to its popularity and domination of the Internet. Dealing happens automatically with no delay for shuffling, and because your visual focus falls almost exclusively on the community section at the center of the table, even the little chicklet versions of the playing cards aren't too troubling.

In sheer number of players, Hold'em games outnumber all other forms of Internet Poker combined roughly 6 to 1. That doesn't mean you can't play other games, but it does mean that you find the most competition, the largest spread of limits, the widest tournament variety, and the greatest selection in table size if you play Hold'em.

REMEMBER

The overall skill level of an Internet Hold'em player is widely variable, but roughly speaking the situation is exactly what you may expect: The higher the table limit, the better the competition.

Sampling Omaha

The playing mechanics of Omaha are identical to those of Texas Hold'em (see the previous section for Hold'em info), with two big exceptions: You receive four hole cards rather than two, and when determining your best five-card hand you must use exactly two of your hole cards combined with exactly three of the five community cards.

Until you warm up to this dynamic (especially if you've resided under the polluting influence of Hold'em for years on end), playing Omaha can be mind-bending. When you first start playing the game (or if you're tired), you can easily misread a hand. Some Poker sites have coaching text that tells you the best value your hand can represent at any given moment ("You have two pair, aces and eights," for example). If you play on a site that evaluates your hand on the fly, keep an eye on what the computer knows you have versus what you think you have or have a chance of making.

Omaha just squeaks over Seven-Card Stud as being the second most popular card game on the Net, but Hold'em is so overwhelming in popularity that many sites may have only a table or two where you can play Omaha (especially in the wee hours of the morning when the Poker crowd thins out).

You can play Omaha in two versions: standard Omaha (sometimes referred to as Omaha High) and Omaha High/Low, which is a split-pot game where both the high and low hands reap equal shares of the pot. You generally play Omaha, in all forms, with pot-limit or fixed-limit betting. No-limit is an Omaha rarity. (For more on the ins and outs of Omaha, flip to Book 2, Chapter 4.)

Omaha High

In the standard version of Omaha, the best (highest) hand takes the entire pot. Sites offer Omaha almost exclusively as a pot-limit game, and to us it seems to be the hardest game to beat on the Internet.

REMEMBER

As a gross generalization (but still an essentially true generalization), Omaha players tend to be very skilled and very dedicated. Compared to Hold'em, experts haven't written nearly as much about Omaha. As a result you tend to see more experienced players in the game, while the truly bad players stay away.

Pot-limit Omaha is the most popular game in Europe, and it also enjoys extreme popularity in the southern United States. The pot-limit version is a gambler's game in a big way — you see a huge variance in the hands compared to Hold'em, and it seems as though pretty much any hand has a shot pre-flop. The skill in this game, for sure, is knowing when to run away and knowing when to stand and fire.

TIP

If you decide to start playing Omaha online and you haven't played it before, you need to read some of the rare theory books to have a fighting chance. Head to Book 2, Chapter 2 and nail down basic strategy there.

DECISION TIME: OMAHA HIGH

You receive A♥ K♦ 10♠ 10♥ as your hole cards. You bet during the first round.

The flop comes 7♠ 7♣ J♦. At this point you have two pair: sevens and tens, with a jack kicker. (Remember, you must use exactly two of your hole cards.) You decide to check and call a bet.

The turn is the J♥. You still have two pair: tens and jacks with a seven kicker. You're worried about another player having trips or a J-7 making a full house. You call a moderate bet.

The river is the 10♦. You now have a full house: tens full of jacks. Anyone who holds J-7, J-10, 7-7, or J-J as hole cards beats you, but you have a pretty good hand. Decision time!

Omaha High/Low

Easy now Tex: You can't automatically count on your three Cowboys taking down this pot. In the High/Low version of Omaha, the high hand splits the pot with the low hand if, and only if, the low hand contains no pairs and no cards higher than an 8 (with aces counting as 1). Straights and flushes don't matter for the low hand. If no low hand is possible, the high hand scoops the entire pot. In High/Low, you can use different cards for your high hand and for your low hand. In both cases, you must use exactly two cards from your hand and three cards from the board to determine your high and low hands. You find roughly the same number of players in both the pot-limit and fixed-limit forms of this game, based on nothing more than personal preference.

Omaha High/Low, certainly at the low limits, is a great game to cut your teeth on, especially if you need a break from Hold'em. The split pots mean that you can enjoy the fun of seeing the site rake chips to your side of the table about twice as often. (The increased action can, however, be a little psychologically dangerous because you can get used to the new scooping rhythm of Omaha and end up staying in too many pots when you go back to Hold'em.)

WARNING

If you see a game labeled solely as Omaha, always expect it to be Omaha High. Make sure before you evaluate betting on a possible low hand that you're playing at a High/Low table. If you don't and you're playing Omaha High, you end up betting on a losing hand.

AN OMAHA HIGH/LOW WINNER — SQUARED

You receive A♠ 3♣ J♠ J♦ for your hole cards, a good starting hand with both high and low possibilities.

The flop comes over 4♠ 7♦ J♣. You now have three jacks for the best high hand currently possible. Your A-3 gives you a shot at the second lowest possible hand if another card 8 or less that doesn't pair the A, 3, 4, or 7 shows up on the board.

The turn is the 2♠. You now have the lowest possible hand at the moment (A 2 3 4 7), the highest possible hand, and a shot at the nut flush draw. Not a bad situation.

The river is the 3♠. An odd draw. You no longer have the nut low hand (A-5 beats you with a *wheel,* ace through five). You now have an ace-high flush, and only someone holding the 5♠ 6♠ can beat you with a straight-flush. If no player has a wheel or the straight-flush, you play your A-3 for your low hand and the A-J for the high hand, taking the whole pot.

Serving up Seven-Card Stud

Seven-Card Stud is probably the best-known Poker game to people who have wandered no farther than their kitchen table to play cards. Every player is dealt two hole cards and an up card, which is followed by a round of betting. The remaining players get another up card (referred to as *fourth street*), followed by a round of betting. Another up card is dealt (*fifth street*), and everyone bets. Yet another up card is dealt (*sixth street*), and everyone bets again. Players who haven't folded by this point receive a final card face down (a third hole card — referred to as either *seventh street* or, as with the last card in Hold'em, the *river*), and the final betting round follows. To recap: All players still in on the river have three cards down and four cards up. The best five-card hand takes the pot.

Like Omaha (see the previous section), you can play Seven-Card Stud in two forms: standard and high/low (head to Book 2, Chapter 3 for more on Seven-Card Stud). And, again as with Omaha, you can expect to find significantly fewer active games to join on the Internet compared to the number of Hold'em games because it simply isn't as popular with today's Poker generation.

Aesthetically, Stud often doesn't translate as well to the computer screen as Omaha and Hold'em do, primarily because you have to look at many more cards spread around the screen instead of seeing them grouped in one community playing area. Sites that use smaller card images can really make you squint.

SLOW AND STEADY SEVEN-CARD STUD

In a brick-and-mortar environment, Seven-Card Stud is the slowest game in the house; the physical mechanics of pushing a ton of cards around on the table and the perpetual delay of slowpokes who wait to toss in their antes at the start of each hand can slow play to a snail's pace.

Online, however, the feeling is a bit more disconcerting and herky-jerky. With Stud, some of the action comes faster (like the general dealing mechanics), but other actions (like players evaluating their hands) are nearly the same. Because of this, to us at least, Stud never feels quite right.

Obviously this is a matter of personal preference. If you're a big fan of Stud in the brick-and-mortar world, you should give it a whirl in cyberspace and see what you think. People who play Stud exclusively in the brick-and-mortar world usually love it online, but players who simply want to play a variety of games on their computer may not be as thrilled.

TIP

If you play online Stud, be sure to put your screen in a glare-free spot — you don't want to experience the aftertaste of not seeing an opponent's four aces showing because of a bad reflection.

You play online Stud almost exclusively with fixed-limit betting, in both tournament and ring-game situations. To be honest, we aren't sure exactly why, but it may have something to do with the game's history. Stud is an older, slower game, played before the new fangled "big betting" methods of pot-limit and no-limit.

Standard Seven-Card Stud

As with Omaha, if you ever see a listing that labels the game "Seven-Card Stud," the highest hand wins the entire pot.

In general, standard Stud games are very accessible, playable, and winnable — especially at the lower limits. The general level of play doesn't seem as good as it does in Hold'em and Omaha, possibly because not as many people play, or possibly because Stud scholars haven't written as much on the game, allowing for fewer Stud scholars to develop. For information on general strategies for playing this game, check out Book 2, Chapter 3.

TIP

As a general rule, if you can't beat what you see face up from the other players' hands, get out while you can. If you can't quickly improve your medium pair, and an opponent has two queens showing, you may be throwing money away trying to catch cards on a dead hand.

Exploring Your Online Game Options

STRAIGHT FROM A STUD'S MOUTH

An example from a standard Seven-Card Stud game:

You receive 8♥ 8♦ as your hole cards and the 7♠ face up. (Online, your hole cards are shifted down slightly in the card lineup.) You go through a round of betting with your pair of eights.

Fourth street is the 6♣. You bet.

Fifth street is the 10♣. You bet. You still have a pair of eights with an inside straight draw.

Sixth street, your last up card, is the K♦. Your hand hasn't changed much with the king.

Seventh street, your third hole card, is the 6♥. You bet with your two pair, sixes and eights.

Seven-Card Stud High/Low

As you may have gathered from the name, in High/Low the high hand splits the pot with the low hand, if, and only if, the low hand doesn't include a card higher than an 8 (the *qualifier*). Straights and flushes don't count against the low. (You can have an ace through five straight for the high *and* the low, however.)

Seven–Card Stud High/Low is beatable, but it takes more time to master than its standard (high only) cousin. As with Omaha High, this game tends to breed specialists, and you have *very* little written theory at your disposal. You should play low limits until you get comfortable with the different pacing and have a good feel for the kind of behavior you see from better players.

GETTING QUARTERED

Imagine this situation: You're playing a High/Low game with two other players, and you're dealt the best possible low hand, A 2 3 4 5 (the hand known as the *wheel*), so you know you're guaranteed at least half the pot. You should raise without abandon at every possible opportunity here, right?

Not necessarily.

You encounter a problem if one of your opponents also has a wheel and a third player has a better high hand than your five-high straight. Your opponent with the high hand takes half the pot. You split the other half between you and the other player holding a wheel. Although you contributed one third of the pot with your bets, you only get one-quarter of the pot back when you tie for the low; therefore, you lose the difference between the quarter of the pot you won and the third of the pot you contributed (namely $1/12$ th of the total amount of the pot). Unfortunately, you've been *quartered*. (Of course, this scenario is exacerbated if you have to split with even more players.)

Getting quartered is rare in Stud High/Low, where everyone plays their own unique hand, but the situation is surprisingly common in Omaha, where players share community cards.

If you suspect you may be in a situation where you're donating money, even if you have a wheel, you should merely call all bets. Don't raise and don't make the first betting action (allowing for someone else to raise you). You may hear the expression "Don't raise a naked low" in Omaha High/Low, which is exactly the situation we're referring to: a case where you have a low hand that may be duplicated, giving you no shot at winning the high hand.

YOU SEVEN-CARD STUD . . .

You receive Q♥ 2♠ as your hole cards and the 8♠ as your first up card. You go through the betting round with your queen high and two cards toward a low hand.

Fourth street is the 3♠. You have a three-card flush draw and three cards toward a low hand.

Fifth street is the Q♠, giving you a pair of queens with a flush draw for high hand and three cards toward a low hand. You stay in through the betting round.

Sixth street brings the 4♠. You now have a queen-high spade flush for your high hand. You also have a pretty good low drawing hand — you need one more card under an 8 that doesn't pair up. You keep on through the betting round.

Your third hole card is the 5♠. Your high hand is a Q 8 5 4 3 spade flush. You also qualify for a low hand with 2 3 4 5 8 (remembering that the flush doesn't matter). Unless another player has a monster hand, you should rake in at least half the pot. Well done!

Playing Crazy Pineapple, Five-Card Stud, and more

Hold'em, Omaha, and Seven-Card Stud are the staples of online play. But other games come and go occasionally as sites experiment with what customers want to play. Each of the following games is, or has been, available online. Have a look on any given Poker site in the lobby under something akin to the "Other Games" tab to find these little creatures.

You can't really find much written theory on any of the following games, but you always play them for low stakes, due to a general lack of popularity. You also don't swim into waters with many sharks, which is a nice break from the normal Hold'em, Stud, and Omaha minefield.

Pineapple and Crazy Pineapple

Crazy Pineapple is a variant of Hold'em with one big exception: You get three hole cards rather than the usual two. You bet and see the three community cards, bet again, and then discard your least-helpful hole card before you see the fourth community card. From there, play continues like regular Hold'em. In the less-common *Pineapple,* you receive three hole cards and discard one before the flop.

Winning in both forms of Pineapple takes experience because you regularly face stronger hands compared to Hold'em. You may be amazed at how often you find yourself holding the second-best hand. The good news for a beginner, however, is that you don't come across many Pineapple players, and because of that, all the games you find are low stakes and fixed-limit ring play only.

TIP

Watch a bit of the action first instead of playing right away. And after you get started, always keep an eye out for specialists who lurk, waiting to pounce on your stack.

Five-Card Draw

Yep, we're talking the *Five-Card Draw* of the Old West. All players are dealt five cards and then bet. Players discard (you can throw out none, some, or all your cards) and receive replacements from the dealer, and then you make the final round of bets. Lay your cards on the table and become the toast of the saloon (or the target of a few six-guns).

Five-Card Draw works surprisingly well online because you focus only on your cards until the showdown, and all you have to do is click on the cards you want to discard. The pacing online is near perfect, very close to any home game. Even if you haven't played before, it takes only an hour or so to warm up to the betting and game dynamics, as well as the caliber of hand you need to win any given pot.

Unlike the rest of the online Poker world, every Five-Card Draw table we've played on has been congenial (if opponents chat between play), and most games have been outright fun. As with Pineapple, you can't find much Five-Card Draw action, and you can expect low fixed-limit ring games.

TIP

If you need a break from the tedium of the larger Internet games, the western movie's game of choice can be an excellent decision. If you want a Poker game on the Internet that you can just dive right into, Five-Card Draw is it (because of the congenial atmosphere, and general pacing of the game).

Five-Card Stud

In *Five-Card Stud,* all players are dealt a hole card and an up card. After a betting round, you receive three more up cards with betting rounds following each. The remaining players have a total of five cards. Best hand wins.

Five-Card Stud has the same game-dynamic problems as Seven-Card Stud (see the "Serving up Seven-Card Stud" section earlier in this chapter), although we like it even less. Having images of cards (often small ones) spread about the screen just doesn't feel right. You can easily overlook someone else's hand, especially if a lot of players are in the pot. And overlooking another player's hand can be financially deadly.

In Five-Card Stud, you can't expect a whole lot of mystery to come with any hands, because 80 percent of what you have is face-up. No mystery leads to no thrill. We know there must be a reason why people want to play this game; we just don't know what it is.

Wild card games

You break out the kitchen table games, like *Baseball, Follow the Queen,* and *Spit in the Ocean,* when you play with your Poker buddies. These games often require less skill and more luck, and because anyone can get lucky, these games allow more people to play more hands, and you tend to see more betting going on than in the Stud games online. Sitting down at the kitchen table and playing a game like Spit in the Ocean gives you a chance to have more fun playing and spend less time thinking about strategy.

Brick-and-mortar cardrooms have never provided wild card games, partially because players take too long evaluating the hands. You also run into discrepancies in the ways different players interpret the rules. You can, however, find online Poker sites with these games offered. Online sites spell out the rules precisely and never misevaluate hands, making the Internet the best wild card game destination outside of your kitchen.

Player's choice (mixed games)

If playing only one type of game puts you in a funk, or if you want to get a feel for your overall Poker prowess, player's choice may be for you. In this world the game changes, typically after every orbit of the dealer marker (after the deal makes its way around the table). You can play a round of Hold'em, followed by a round of Seven-Card Stud, a round of Omaha, and so on.

You get variety without changing tables, and you get to exercise different parts of your Poker brain. And player's choice isn't some online whim: You can play a mixed game at the World Series of Poker. *H.O.R.S.E.,* which stands for Hold'em, Omaha, Razz (Seven-Card Stud, low hand wins), Seven-Card Stud, and Seven-Card Stud High/Low (E for eight-or-better), combines all the major Poker games.

WARNING

The shift in rhythm can get to you, particularly if you're tired, and you always have to avoid misreading your Omaha hand after you play rounds of Hold'em.

Taking On Tournaments

One way in which the online world truly trumps the brick-and-mortar world is through tournaments. The concept of a Poker tournament is very simple. Everyone *buys in* to the tournament for a set amount and receives a fairly huge stack of chips. Play commences, with players busting out one by one, until only the victor remains.

Whatever interpersonal elements you lose by not having the other players seated across from you like in a real-world tournament are replaced with other perks in virtual-world tourneys. You don't have to deal with prolonged seating delays, poorly organized tournament directors controlling the show, and the endless movement involved in setting up and tearing down tables as a tournament progresses.

Online tournaments give you a chance to play considerably more hands than what you get in ring games, an opportunity to be king of the mountain, and quick-and-easy chances to hone your tournament skills. When you play online, you have the opportunity to play literally any time, in table sizes as small as head's up (against one other player) to huge affairs with several thousand players.

DECIDING WHAT TO PLAY

Now that you have a feel for all the different online Poker opportunities available to you, the big question is: What do you want to play?

Your decision is obviously a matter of personal taste, but we recommend taking the following approach:

- Play several hands with free chips to get comfortable with the user interface of your Poker site and the general playing dynamic.

- After you get a good feel for the game, switch over to hard currency in a low-limit ring game. Play a bit. Win a bit.

- Move up in stakes in your ring game play until you reach about half the limit size you want to eventually play.

- At this point you have a choice. You can continue to move up in your ring game stakes, or you can play in (or move entirely over to) tournaments. Again, start at a low entry fee tournament and work your way up.

WARNING

After you register for a tournament, you will play in it unless you hit the "un-register" button. After the tournament starts, you don't get a chance to un-register. If you're unavailable to play, the site automatically makes your blind bets and folds your hand in turn (known as being *blinded-off*), and you eventually lose all your chips.

Hold'em tournaments tend to be no-limit affairs (although you can find fixed-limit games). Omaha tourneys, in all variations, use pot-limit betting. And Seven-Card Stud tourneys are fixed-limit.

Sitting down for single-table tournaments

On-demand single-table tournaments run rampant in the online world, and in the online world only. You register for the tournament, and after enough people register based on the table format, you play. On-demand, single-table tournaments are very common; the players at your table make up the entirety of the tournament.

Full single-table tournaments

If you look at the numbers of people playing full single-table tournaments online on a daily basis, you see why full table is the most popular form in the single-table tournament world. The tournament starts when your table seats fill up (with either nine or ten players, depending on the site) and ends with only one player remaining.

Single-table tournament experience proves valuable, even if your interest lies in larger tournament types. If your luck and skill bring you to the end of a large tournament, you end up playing a single-table tournament (known as the *final table*).

The huge successes of online Poker players in the brick-and-mortar tournament world (such as Chris Moneymaker winning the main event at the World Series in 2003 and Greg Raymer in 2004) may be due to the online players' single-table tournament experience. Experience can be the best teacher, and before the Internet, final-table experience was very difficult to obtain without becoming a leather-bottomed casino regular.

If you have any interest in the tournament world, single-table events are a good place to start. The tournaments are relatively short (typically an hour if you make it to the very finish), and you get plenty of Poker practice for your buck.

TURBO TOURNAMENTS: PLAYING AT BREAKNECK SPEED

At the request of players, some sites have sped up their game play by reducing the amount of time it gives players to act (say, reducing your action time on any given decision from 15 to 7 seconds) and by having the tournament blinds increase at a faster rate. You see these tables or tournaments listed under headings such as "Turbo."

Although you do see a few multi-table tournaments run in turbo format, the vast majority are on-demand single tables.

The caliber of play is nearly identical to turbo's slower siblings. We've never had any problem playing at these tables, although some people may find the speed difference disconcerting. If you play turbos and you start wigging out, consider dropping back down to regular speed play. The difference in speed isn't worth the difference in mind-set.

Turbos are definitely not the place to start your online career, but you may want to try them out after you broaden your online experience. We talk more about the concept of speed in online Poker in Book 4, Chapter 2.

Short-handed tournaments

In short-handed tournaments, you play at a single table of five or six players (depending on the site).

Oddly, we find that these tournaments play radically different from the full-size single-table version. The players you oppose here tend to specialize in this form, making the games extremely difficult to win.

You gain valuable experience by playing short handed at some point in your online Poker career, but you should think of short-handed tourneys as one of the very last stones you turn over.

Head's-up tournaments

Head's-up tournaments are easily the most brutal and cutthroat form of Poker, which may be why you almost exclusively find them in the online world. You find yourself versus just one other player, and the winner takes all. Until you get used to playing head's up, the dynamic can be a little intimidating and disconcerting due to the game speed and the fact that you put your entire focus on one other person. Unless you have the skill to dominate brick-and-mortar tournaments, gaining head's-up experience means playing online.

The advantage of these tournaments is their speed — you usually finish in less than 30 minutes, and because you only face one other player, your winning percentage is higher.

Head's-up is definitely worth trying, but not as your first online tournament. But as you gain experience and skill and get serious about online tournaments, you need to master head's-up Poker. Good head's-up play literally means the difference between finishing first and finishing second in a tournament — often double the difference in cash.

Mixing in multi-table tournaments

Multi-table tournaments take any and all comers, literally attracting thousands of players. As people get knocked out one by one, the site continually rebalances individual table populations to keep them full. For example, say you're playing in a tournament with 100 players. After ten players bust out, the site chooses a table at random, breaks it up, and sends each of its players to fill the empty seats at other tables.

TIP

Be sure you budget enough time to play. You can approximate by checking out how long other tournaments have lasted; just look through the lobby under the tournament tab for completed tournaments of roughly the same size and compare the start time to the end time. To win the tournament you have to play until the end.

Multi-table tournaments usually have breaks — something like five minutes of every hour. You stay in the game as long as you have chips, so even if you get disconnected or miss a few hands to talk to your mom on the phone, you still have your seat in the tourney. The site blinds you off and folds your hands in turn until you come back.

REMEMBER

THE TABLE-BALANCING ACT OF MULTI-TABLE TOURNEYS

Multi-table tournaments have an interesting dynamic in that, due to table balancing, you essentially play at a full table for several hands (sometimes hours) on end, with at most one or two empty seats at any time. Toward the end of the tournament, you start playing at tables with a few seats open; and then half the seats empty (when barely two tables remain); and then a single full table that withers down to the eventual winner.

At times it can feel extremely disconcerting to get moved to a new table due to table balancing — roughly approximating what it feels like to travel by transporter beam. After you land at your new table, make sure to take stock of the differences in chip stacks to get a feel for whom the strong and the vulnerable players are.

5

More Than Just an Old Folks' Game: Bridge

Contents at a Glance

Chapter 1

Going to Bridge Boot Camp

You can't go wrong by learning to play Bridge. You can play Bridge all over the world, and wherever you go, you can make new friends automatically by starting up a game of Bridge. Bridge can be more than a game — it can be a common bond.

In this chapter, you discover some basic concepts that you need to have under your belt to get started playing Bridge. Consider this chapter your first step into the game. If you read this whole chapter, you'll graduate from Bridge Boot Camp. Sorry — you don't get a diploma. But you do get the thrill of knowing what you need to know to start playing Bridge.

Starting a Game with the Right Stuff

Before you can begin to play Bridge, you need to outfit yourself with some basic supplies. Actually, you may already have some of these items around the house, just begging for you to use them in your Bridge game. What do you need? Here's your bottom-line list:

>> Four warm bodies, including yours. Just find three friends who are interested in playing. Don't worry that no one knows what they're doing. Everyone begins knowing nothing; some of us even end up that way.

>> A table — a square one is best. In a pinch, you can play on a blanket, on a bed, indoors, outdoors, or even on a computer if you can't find a game.

>> One deck of playing cards (remove the jokers).

>> A pencil and a piece of paper to keep score on. You can use any old piece of paper — a legal pad, the back of a grocery list, or even an ancient piece of papyrus will do.

TIP

Here are a few hints on how you can make getting started with the game a little easier:

>> Watch a real Bridge game to observe the mechanics of the game.

>> Follow the sample hands in this book by laying out the cards to correspond with the cards in the figures. Doing so gives you a feel for the cards and makes the explanations easier to follow.

Ranking the Cards

A deck has 52 cards divided into four suits: spades (♠), hearts (♥), diamonds (♦), and clubs (♣).

REMEMBER

Each suit has 13 cards: the AKQJ10 (which are called the *honor cards*) and the 98765432 (the *spot cards*).

The 13 cards in a suit all have a rank — that is, they have a pecking order. The ace is the highest-ranking card, followed by the king, the queen, the jack, and the 10, on down to the lowly 2 (also called the *deuce*).

REMEMBER

The more high-ranking cards you have in your hand, the better. The more honor cards you have, the stronger your hand. You can never have too many honor cards.

Knowing Your Directions

In Bridge, the players are nameless souls — they are known by directions. When you sit down at a table with three pals to play Bridge, imagine that the table is a compass. You're sitting at due South, your partner sits across from you in the North seat, and your opponents sit East and West.

REMEMBER

In this book, you're South for every hand, and your partner is North. Just as in the opera, where the tenor always gets the girl, in a Bridge diagram, you're represented as South — you are called the *declarer*, and you always get to play the hand. Your partner, North, is always the *dummy* (no slur intended!). Don't worry about what these terms mean just yet — the idea is that you play every hand from the South position. Keep in mind that in real life, South doesn't play every hand — just in this book, every newspaper column, and most Bridge books!

Figure 1-1 diagrams the playing table. Get acquainted with this diagram: You see some form of it throughout this book, not to mention in newspaper columns and magazines.

FIGURE 1-1:
You're South, your partner is North, and your opponents are East and West.

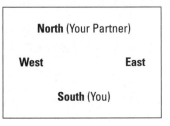

North (Your Partner)

West   **East**

South (You)

© John Wiley & Sons, Inc.

Playing the Game in Four Acts

First and foremost, Bridge is a partnership game; you swim together and you sink together. Your opponents are in the same boat. In Bridge, you don't score points individually — you score points as a team. (We cover scoring in Book 5, Chapter 6, and we suggest you ignore keeping score until you have a handle on the ins and outs of the game.)

Each hand of Bridge is divided into four acts, which occur in the same order:

Act 1.   Dealing

Act 2.   Bidding

Act 3.   Playing

Act 4.   Scoring

Act 1: Dealing

The game starts with each player seated facing his or her partner. The cards are shuffled and placed on the table face down. Each player selects a card, and whoever picks the highest card deals the first hand. The four cards on the table are returned to the deck, the deck is reshuffled, and the player to the dealer's right cuts the cards and returns them to the dealer. (After each hand, the deal rotates to the left so one person doesn't get stuck doing all the dealing.)

The cards are dealt one at a time, starting with the player to the dealer's left and moving in a clockwise rotation until each player has 13 cards.

TIP

Wait until the dealer distributes all the cards before you pick up your hand. That's Bridge etiquette lesson number one. When each player has 13 cards, pick up and sort your hand using the following tips:

>> You can sort the cards in any number of ways, but we recommend sorting your cards into the four suits.

>> Alternate your black suits (clubs and spades) with your red suits (diamonds and hearts) so you don't confuse a black spade for a black club or a red diamond for a red heart. It's a bit disconcerting to think you're playing a heart, only to see a diamond come floating out of your hand.

>> Hold your cards back, way back, so only you can see them. Think vertically. Winning at Bridge is difficult when your opponents can see your hand.

Act 2: Bidding for tricks

Bidding in Bridge can be compared to an auction. The auctioneer tells you what the minimum bid is, and the first bid starts from that point or higher. Each successive bid must be higher than the last, until someone bids so high that everyone else wants out. When you want out of the bidding in Bridge, you say "Pass." After three consecutive players say "Pass," the bidding is over. However, if you pass and someone else makes a bid, just as at an auction, you can reenter the bidding. If nobody makes an opening bid and all four players pass consecutively, the bidding is over, the hand is reshuffled and redealt, and a new auction begins.

In real-life auctions, people often bid for silly things, such as John F. Kennedy's golf clubs or Andy Warhol's cookie jars. In Bridge, you bid for something really valuable — tricks. The whole game revolves around *tricks*.

Some of you may remember the card game of War from when you were a kid. (If you don't, head back to Book 1, Chapter 9.) In War, two players divide the deck between them. Each player takes a turn placing a card face up on the table. The player with the higher card takes the *trick*.

In Bridge, four people each place a card face up on the table, and the highest card in the suit that has been led takes the trick. The player who takes the trick collects the four cards, puts them face down in a neat pile, and leads to the next trick. Because each player has 13 cards, 13 tricks are fought over and won or lost on each hand.

REMEMBER

Think of bidding as an estimation of how many of those 13 tricks your side (or their side) thinks it can take. The bidding starts with the dealer and moves to his left in a clockwise rotation. Each player gets a chance to bid, and a player can either bid or pass when his turn rolls around. The least you can bid is for seven tricks, and the maximum you can bid is for all 13. The bidding goes around and around the table, with each player either bidding or passing until three players in a row say "Pass." (See Book 5, Chapter 5 for bidding basics.)

The last bid (the one followed by three passes) is called the *final contract*. No, that's not something the mafia puts out on you. It's simply the number of tricks that the bidding team must take to score points.

Act 3: Playing the hand

After the bidding for tricks is over, the play begins. Either your team or the other team makes the final bid. Because you are the star of this book, assume that your team makes the final bid for nine tricks. Therefore, your goal is to win at least nine of the 13 possible tricks.

If you take nine (or more) tricks, your team scores points. If you take fewer than nine tricks, you're penalized, and your opponents score points. In the following sections, we describe a few important aspects of playing a hand of Bridge.

The opening lead and the dummy

After the bidding determines who the declarer is (the one who plays the hand), that person's partner becomes the dummy. The players to the declarer's left and right are considered the *defenders.* The West player (assuming that you're South) *leads,* or puts down the first card face up in the middle of the table. That first card is called the *opening lead,* and it can be any card of West's choosing.

When the opening lead lands on the table, the game really begins to roll. The next person to play is the dummy — but instead of playing a card, the dummy puts her 13 cards face up on the table in four neat vertical columns starting with the highest card, one column for each suit, and then bows out of the action entirely. After she puts down her cards (also called the *dummy*), she says and does nothing, leaving the other three people to play the rest of the hand. The dummy always puts down the dummy. What a game!

Because the dummy is no longer involved in the action, each time it's the dummy's turn to play, you, the declarer, must physically take a card from the dummy and put it in the middle of the table. In addition, you must play a card from your own hand when it's your turn.

The fact that the declarer gets stuck with playing both hands while the dummy is off munching on snacks may seem a bit unfair. But you do have an advantage over the defenders: You get to see your partner's cards before you play, which allows you to plan a strategy of how to win those nine tricks (or however many tricks you need to make the final contract).

Following suit

The opening lead determines which suit the other three players must play. Each of the players must *follow suit,* meaning that they must play a card in the suit that was led if they have one. For example, pretend that the opening lead from West is a heart. Down comes the dummy, and you (and everyone else at the table) can see the dummy's hearts as well as your own hearts. Because you must play the same suit that is led if you have a card in that suit, you have to play a heart, any heart you want, from the dummy. You place the heart of your choice face up on the table and wait for your right-hand opponent (East, assuming that the dummy is North) to play a heart. After she plays a heart, you play a heart from your hand. Voilà: Four hearts now sit on the table. The first trick of the game! Whoever has played the highest heart takes the trick. One trick down and only 12 to go — you're on a roll!

What if a player doesn't have a card in the suit that has been led? Then, and only then, can a player choose a card, any card, from another suit and play it. This move is called a *discard*. When you discard, you're literally throwing away a card from another suit. A discard can never win a trick.

In general, you discard worthless cards that can't take tricks, saving good-looking cards that may take tricks later. Sometimes, however, the bidding designates a *trump suit* (think wild cards). In that case, when a suit is led and you don't have it, you can either discard from another suit or take the trick by playing a card from the trump suit. For more info, see "Understanding Notrump and Trump Play" later in this chapter.

WARNING

If you can follow suit, you must. If you have a card in the suit that's been led but you play a card in another suit by mistake, you *revoke*. Not good. If you're detected, penalties may be involved. Don't worry, though — everybody revokes once in a while.

Playing defense

Approximately 25 percent of the time, you'll be the declarer; 25 percent of the time, you'll be the dummy; and the remaining 50 percent of the time, you'll be on defense! You need to have a good idea of which card to lead to the first trick and how to continue after you see the dummy. You want to be able to take all the tricks your side has coming, trying to defeat the contract. For example, if your opponents bid for nine tricks, you need at least five tricks to defeat the contract. Think of taking five tricks as your goal. Remember, defenders can't see each other's hands, so they have to use signals (legal ones) to tell their partner what they have. They do this by making informative leads and discards that announce to the partner (and the declarer) what they have in the suit they are playing.

Winning and stacking tricks

The player who plays the highest card in the suit that has been led wins the trick. That player sweeps up the four cards and puts them in a neat stack, face-down, a little off to the side. The declarer "keeps house" for his team by stacking tricks into piles so everyone can see how many tricks that team has won. The defender (your opponent) who wins the first trick does the same for his or her side.

REMEMBER

The player who takes the first trick *leads first,* or plays the first card, to the second trick. That person can lead any card in any suit desired, and the other three players must follow suit if they can.

The play continues until all 13 tricks have been played. After you play to the last trick, each team counts up the number of tricks it has won.

Act 4: Scoring, and then continuing

After the smoke clears and the tricks are counted, you know soon enough whether the declarer's team made its contract (that is, took at least the number of tricks they have contracted for). The score is then registered — see Book 5, Chapter 6 for more about scoring.

After the hand has been scored, the deal moves one player to the left. So if South dealt the first hand, West is now the dealer. Then North deals the next hand, then East, and then the deal reverts back to South.

Understanding Notrump and Trump Play

Have you ever played a card game that has wild cards? When you play with wild cards, playing a wild card automatically wins the trick for you. Sometimes wild cards can be jokers, deuces, or aces. It doesn't matter what the card is; if you have one, you know that you have a sure winner. In Bridge, you have wild cards, too, called *trump cards.* However, in Bridge, the trump cards are *really* wild, because they change from hand to hand, depending on the bidding.

The bidding determines whether a hand will be played with trump cards or in a *notrump contract* (a hand with no trump cards). If the final bid happens to end in some suit as opposed to notrump, that suit becomes the trump suit for the hand. For example, suppose that the final bid is 4♠. This bid determines that spades are trump (or wild) for the entire hand.

More contracts are played at notrump than in any of the four suits. When the final bid ends in notrump, the highest card played in the suit that has been led wins the trick.

Chapter 2

Counting and Taking Sure Tricks

I f you're sitting at a Blackjack table in Las Vegas and someone catches you counting cards, you're a goner. However, if you're at a Bridge table and you don't count cards, you're also a goner, but in a different way.

When you play a Bridge hand, you need to count several things; most importantly, you need to count your tricks. The game of Bridge revolves around tricks. You bid for tricks, you take as many tricks as you can in the play of the hand, and your opponents try to take as many tricks as they can on defense. Tricks, tricks, tricks.

In this chapter, we show you how to spot a sure trick in its natural habitat — in your hand or in the dummy. We also show you how to take those sure tricks to your best advantage. (See Book 5, Chapter 1 for an introduction to tricks and the dummy.)

REMEMBER

Before the play of the hand begins, the bidding determines the final contract. However, we have purposely omitted the bidding process in this discussion. For the purpose of this chapter, just pretend the bidding is over and the dummy has come down. We want you to concentrate on how to count and take tricks to your best advantage. After you discover the trick-taking capabilities of honor cards and long suits, the bidding makes much more sense. (We introduce bidding in Book 5, Chapter 5.)

Counting Sure Tricks after the Dummy Comes Down

The old phrase "You need to know where you are to know where you're going" comes to mind when you're playing Bridge. After you know your *final contract* (how many tricks you need to take), you then need to figure out how to win all the tricks necessary to make your contract.

Depending on which cards you and your partner hold, your side may hold some definite winners, called *sure tricks* — tricks you can take at any time right from the get-go. You should be very happy to see sure tricks either in your hand or in the dummy. You can never have too many sure tricks.

Sure tricks depend on whether your team has the ace in a particular suit. Because you get to see the dummy after the opening lead, you can see quite clearly whether any aces are lurking in the dummy. If you notice an ace, the highest ranking card in the suit, why not get greedy and look for a king, the second-highest ranking card in the same suit? Two sure tricks are better than one!

REMEMBER

Counting sure tricks boils down to the following points:

>> If you or the dummy has the ace in a suit (but no king), count one sure trick.

>> If you have both the ace and the king in the same suit (between the two hands), count two sure tricks.

>> If you have the ace, king, and queen in the same suit (between the two hands), count three sure tricks. Happiness!

In Figure 2-1, your final contract is for nine tricks. After you settle on the final contract, the play begins. West makes the opening lead and decides to lead the ♠Q. Down comes the dummy, and you swing into action, but first you need to do a little planning. You need to count your sure tricks. What follows in this section is a sample hand and diagrams where we demonstrate how to count sure tricks.

Eyeballing your sure tricks in each suit

You count your sure tricks one suit at a time. After you know how many tricks you have, you can make further plans about how to win additional tricks. We walk you through each suit in the following sections, showing you how to count sure tricks.

North (Dummy)
- ♠ 7 6 5
- ♥ J 10 9
- ♦ A 2
- ♣ J 10 9 6 5

FIGURE 2-1:
Looking for nine
sure tricks is
your goal.

South (You)
- ♠ A K 8
- ♥ A K Q
- ♦ K Q J 5
- ♣ 4 3 2

© John Wiley & Sons, Inc.

Recognizing the two highest spades

When the dummy comes down, you can see that your partner has three small spades (♠7, ♠6, and ♠5) and you have the ♠A and ♠K, as you see in Figure 2-2.

Because the ♠A and the ♠K are the two highest spades in the suit, you can count two sure spade tricks. (If you or the dummy also held the ♠Q, you could count three sure spade tricks.)

TIP

When you have sure tricks in a suit, you don't have to play them right away. You can take sure tricks at any point during the play of the hand.

MIND YOUR MANNERS: BEING A DUMMY WITH CLASS

The dummy doesn't do much to help you count and take sure tricks except lay down her cards. After her cards are on the table, the dummy shouldn't contribute anything else to the hand — except good dummy etiquette.

As the play progresses, the dummy isn't supposed to make faces, utter strange noises, or make disjointed body movements, such as jerks or twitches. Sometimes such restraint takes superhuman willpower, particularly when her partner, the declarer, screws up big time. Good dummies learn to control themselves. If you end up as the dummy and get fidgety or anxious, you can always leave the table to calm down.

North (Dummy)

♠ 7 6 5

FIGURE 2-2:
Digging up sure
spade tricks.

South (You)

♠ A K 8

© John Wiley & Sons, Inc.

Counting up equally divided hearts

Figure 2-3 shows the hearts that you hold in this hand. Notice that you and the dummy have the six highest hearts in the deck: the ♥AKQJ109 (the highest five of these are known as *honor cards*).

North (Dummy)

♥ J 10 9

FIGURE 2-3:
Your hearts are
heavy with honor
cards.

South (You)

♥ A K Q

© John Wiley & Sons, Inc.

Your wonderful array of hearts is worth only three sure tricks because both hands have the same number of cards. When you play a heart from one hand, you must play a heart from the other hand. As a result, after you play the ♥AKQ, the dummy won't have any more hearts left and neither will you. You wind up with only three heart tricks because the suit is *equally divided* (you have the same number of cards in both hands).

REMEMBER

When you have an equal number of cards in a suit on each side, you can never take more tricks than the number of cards in each hand. For example, if you both hold four hearts, it doesn't matter how many high hearts you have between your hand and the dummy; you can never take more than four heart tricks. Take a look at Figure 2-4 to see how the tragic story of an equally divided suit unfolds.

North (Dummy)
♥ K

FIGURE 2-4:
An honor collision causes some honor cards to become worthless.

South (You)
♥ A

© John Wiley & Sons, Inc.

In Figure 2-4, you have only one heart in each hand: the ♥A and the ♥K. All you can take is one lousy heart trick. If you lead the ♥A, you have to play the ♥K from the dummy. If the dummy leads the ♥K first, you have to "overtake" it with your ♥A. This is the only time you can have the ace and king of the same suit between your hand and dummy and take only one trick. It's too sad for words.

Attacking unequally divided diamonds

In Figure 2-5, you can see that South holds four diamonds (♦K, ♦Q, ♦J, and ♦5), while North holds only two (♦A and ♦2). When one partner holds more cards in a suit, the suit is *unequally divided*.

North (Dummy)
♦ A 2

FIGURE 2-5:
An unequally divided suit can be a gem.

South (You)
♦ K Q J 5

© John Wiley & Sons, Inc.

Strong unequally divided suits offer oodles of tricks, provided that you play the suit correctly. For example, take a look at how things play out with the cards in Figure 2-5. Suppose you begin by leading the ♦5 from your hand and play the ♦A from the dummy, which is one trick. Now the lead is in the dummy because the dummy has taken the trick. Continue by playing ♦2 and then play the ♦K from your hand. Now that the lead is back in your hand, play the ♦Q and then the ♦J. Don't look now, but you've just won tricks with each of your honor cards — four in all. Notice if you had played the king first and then the ♦5 over to dummy's ace, dummy would have no more diamonds and there you'd be with the good queen and jack of diamonds in your hand, perhaps marooned forever!

Lean a little closer to hear a five-star tip: If you want to live a long and happy life with unequally divided suits that contain a number of *equal* honors (also called *touching* honors, such as a king and queen or queen and jack), play the high honor cards from the short side first. What does *short side* mean? In an unequally divided suit, the hand with fewer cards is called the short side. In Figure 2-5, the dummy has two diamonds to your four diamonds, making the dummy hand the short side. When you play the high honor from the short side first, you end up by playing the high honors from the *long side,* the hand that starts with more cards in the suit, last. (In this example, South has the longer diamonds.) This technique allows you to take the maximum number of tricks possible. And now you know why you started by leading the ♦5 over to the ♦A. You wanted to play the high honor from the short side first. You are getting to be a player!

Finding no sure tricks in a suit with no aces: The clubs

When the dummy comes down, you may see that neither you nor the dummy has the ace in a particular suit, such as the club suit in Figure 2-6. You have ♣4, ♣3, and ♣2; the dummy has ♣J, ♣10, ♣9, ♣6, and ♣5.

North (Dummy)
♣ J 10 9 6 5

FIGURE 2-6:
You can't count sure tricks in a suit where your team doesn't have the ace.

South (You)
♣ 4 3 2

© *John Wiley & Sons, Inc.*

Not all that pretty, is it? The opponents have the ♣A, ♣K, and ♣Q. You have no sure tricks in clubs because you don't have the ♣A. If neither your hand nor the dummy has the ace in a particular suit, you can't count any sure tricks in that suit.

Adding up your sure tricks

After you assess how many sure tricks you have in each suit, you can do some reckoning. You need to add up all your sure tricks and see if you have enough to make your final contract.

Just to get some practice at adding up tricks, go ahead and add up your sure tricks from the hand shown in Figure 2-1. Remember to look at what's in the dummy's hand as well as your own cards. The total number of tricks is what's important, and you have the following:

>> **Spades:** Two sure tricks: ♠A and ♠K.

>> **Hearts:** Three sure tricks: ♥AKQ.

>> **Diamonds:** Four sure tricks: ♦AKQJ.

>> **Clubs:** No sure tricks because you have no ace. Bad break, buddy.

You're in luck — you have the nine tricks that you need to make your final contract. Now all you have to do is take them. You can do it.

More often than not, you won't have enough sure tricks to make your contract. You can see what will become of you in Book V, Chapter 3, which deals with various techniques of notrump play designed to teach you how to develop extra tricks when you don't have all the top cards in a suit.

Taking Sure Tricks

Having sure tricks is only half the battle; taking those sure tricks is the other half. In the following sections, we show you how to do it.

Starting with the strongest suit

When you have enough sure tricks between the two hands to make your contract, you *don't* have to take the tricks in any particular order. However, a reliable guideline to get you off on the right foot is to start by first playing winning cards in your strongest suit (the suit that offers you the most tricks). In the case of the hand shown in Figure 2-1, start by playing diamonds.

Recall that West's opening lead was the ♠Q. Suppose you take the trick with the ♠A, and now the lead is in your hand. You then take your four diamond tricks (♦AKQJ), and then you can take three more heart tricks by playing the ♥AKQ. Finally, you take your ninth trick with the ♠K. Your opponents take the last four tricks. No big deal — you've taken nine tricks and made your contract.

Taking sure tricks in unequally divided suits

The cards in Figure 2-7 show another example of the advantage of starting with the short-side honor cards.

North (Dummy)
♠ Q J 4 3

```
    N
 W     E
    S
```

FIGURE 2-7:
Serving up sure
tricks, starting
with the short-
side honor cards.

South (You)
♠ A K 2

© John Wiley & Sons, Inc.

In the example shown in Figure 2-7, you decide to play spades, an unequally divided suit. You also (smartly) decide to first play the high honors from the short side (your hand is the short side because you have three cards to dummy's four cards). Play the ♠A and then the ♠K. You remain with the ♠2, and the dummy has two winning tricks, the ♠Q and ♠J. Lead your ♠2 and take the trick with the dummy's ♠J. The lead is now in the dummy, and you can take a fourth spade trick with the ♠Q. You have just added four tricks to your trick pile. They can't stop you now!

Chapter 3

Using Winning Trick Techniques at Notrump Play

Winning at Bridge is a breeze if you always have enough sure tricks to make your contract. The sad news is that you seldom have enough. You must come up with other ways of taking tricks, ways that may mean temporarily giving up the lead to your opponents. In this chapter, we show you clever techniques to win those extra tricks that you may need to make your contract in notrump play. Specifically, we explain how to establish tricks with lower honor cards and take tricks with small cards.

Throughout this chapter, you may notice that many figures show cards in only one suit. Sometimes we want you to focus on one suit at a time, so in the following figures, you see suits that are ideal for creating extra tricks. Don't forget: We always put you in the hot seat by making you South, where the action is! (Your partner is North, and your opponents are West and East. See Book 5, Chapter 1 for more details about positions in Bridge.)

Establishing Tricks with Lower Honor Cards

When you don't have the ace in a suit, you're in bad shape as far as sure tricks are concerned (see Book 5, Chapter 2 for more about sure tricks). Not to worry. Your new friend, *establishing tricks,* can see you through the tough times and help you win extra tricks you may need to make your contract. Check out the following sections for surefire techniques on establishing tricks.

Establishing tricks is about sacrificing one of your honor cards to drive out one of your opponents' higher honor cards. You can then swoop in with your remaining honor cards and take a bundle of tricks.

REMEMBER

In case you're wondering, your opponents don't just sit around and admire your dazzling technique of establishing tricks. No, they're busy trying to establish tricks of their own. In Bridge, turnabout is fair play. Whatever you can do, your opponents can also do. Many a hand turns into a race for tricks. To win the race, you must establish your tricks earlier rather than later. Remembering this rule will keep you focused and help you edge out your opponents.

Driving the opponents' ace out of its hole

The all-powerful ace wins a trick for you every time. But no matter how hard you pray for aces, sometimes you just don't get any, and you can't count any sure tricks in a suit with no aces. Sometimes you get tons of honor cards but no ace, and you still can't count even one sure trick in that suit. Ah, the inhumanity!

Cheer up — you can still create winning tricks in such a suit. When you have a number of equal honors in a suit but not the ace, you can *attack* that suit early and *drive out the ace* from your opponent's hand. Here's what you do:

1. **Lead the highest honor card in the suit in which you're missing the ace.**

To get rid of the ace when you have a number of equal honors, lead the highest honor. So if you have the KQJ6, lead the king to drive out the ace. If they don't take the trick with the ace, play the queen. One way or another you must take two tricks with the KQJ. If you lead a low card, like the 6, 7, or 8, your opponents won't have to play the ace to take the trick. They can simply take the trick with a lower card, such as the 9 or 10, and they still have the ace! Not good.

REMEMBER

When you have equal honors in your hand (where they can't be seen), such as the KQJ, and want to lead one, use the higher or highest equal to do your dirty work. It is more deceptive. Trust us.

If the equal honors are in the dummy where everyone can see them, you have the option of which one to play. It doesn't matter, but to be uniform in this book, we have you play the lower or lowest equal.

2. **Continue playing the suit until your opponents play the ace and take the trick.**

3. **After that ace is out of the way, you can count your remaining equal honor cards as sure tricks.**

Driving out the ace is a great way of setting up extra tricks. The cards in Figure 3-1 provide an example of a suit you can attack to drive out the ace.

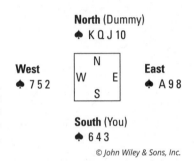

North (Dummy)
♠ K Q J 10

West
♠ 7 5 2

East
♠ A 9 8

South (You)
♠ 6 4 3

© John Wiley & Sons, Inc.

FIGURE 3-1:
You can drive out an ace to create winning tricks.

In Figure 3-1, you can't count a single sure spade trick because your opponent (East) has the ♠A. Yet the four spades in the dummy — ♠KQJ10 — are extremely powerful. (Any suit that contains four honor cards is considered powerful.)

Suppose that the lead is in your hand from the preceding trick, and you lead a low spade (the lowest spade you have — in this case, the ♠3). West, seeing the dummy has very strong spades, plays her lowest card, the ♠2; you play the ♠10 from the dummy; and East decides to win the trick with the ♠A. You may have lost the lead, but you have also driven out the ♠A. The dummy remains with the ♠KQJ, all winning tricks. You have *established* three sure spade tricks where none existed.

TIP

Suits with three or more equal honor cards in one hand are ideal for suit establishment. When you see the KQJ or the QJ10 in either your hand or the dummy, sure tricks in those suits can eventually be developed if you attack them early!

Surrendering the lead twice to the ace and the king

When you're missing just the ace, you can establish the suit easily by just leading one equal honor after another until an opponent takes the ace. However, if you're missing both the ace and the king, you will have to give up the lead twice to take later tricks.

REMEMBER

Bridge is a game of giving up the lead to get tricks back. Don't fear giving up the lead. Your high honor cards in the other suits protect you by allowing you to eventually regain the lead and pursue your goal of establishing tricks.

Figure 3-2 shows a suit where you have to swallow your pride twice before you can establish your lower honor cards.

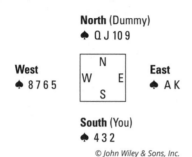

FIGURE 3-2:
Flushing out the ace and the king.

Notice that the dummy in Figure 3-2 has a sequence of cards headed by three *equal* honors — the ♠QJ10. The ♠9, though not considered an honor card, is equal to the ♠QJ10 and has the same value. When you have a sequence of equals, all the cards have equal power to take tricks — or to drive out opposing honor cards. For example, you can use the ♠9 or the ♠Q to drive out your opponent's ♠K or ♠A.

In Figure 3-2, your opponents hold the ♠AK. To compensate, you have the ♠QJ109, four equals headed by three honors — a very good sign. You lead a low spade, the ♠2; West plays the ♠5; you play the ♠9 from the dummy; and East takes the trick with the ♠K. You've driven out one spade honor. One more to go. Your spades still aren't established, but you're halfway home! The next time you have the lead, lead a low spade, the ♠3, and then play the ♠10 from the dummy, driving out the ♠A. Guess what? You started with zero sure spade tricks, but now you have two: the ♠Q and ♠J.

Playing the high honors from the short side first

REMEMBER

Never forget this simple and ever-so-important rule: When attacking an unequally divided suit, where either your hand or the dummy holds more cards than the other in that suit, play the high equal honors from the shorter side first (see Figure 3-3). Doing so enables you to end up with the lead on the long side (the dummy), where the remainder of the winning spades are. If you remember to play your equal honors from the short side first, your partner will kneel down and declare you Ruler of the Universe.

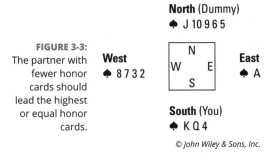

North (Dummy)
♠ J 10 9 6 5

West
♠ 8 7 3 2

East
♠ A

South (You)
♠ K Q 4

FIGURE 3-3:
The partner with fewer honor cards should lead the highest or equal honor cards.

Liberation time! As you see in Figure 3-3, the short hand (your hand) has two equal honor cards, the ♠KQ. Start by playing the ♠K, the higher honor on the short side, and a low spade from the dummy, the ♠5. As it happens, East must take the trick with the ♠A because she doesn't have any other spades.

You've established your spades because the ♠A is gone, but you still need to remember the five-star tip of playing the high remaining equal honor from the short side next. When you or dummy next regains the lead in another suit, play the ♠Q, which takes the trick, and then lead the ♠4. The dummy remains with the ♠J109, all winning tricks. You have established four spade tricks by playing the high card from the short side twice.

Using length to your advantage with no high honor in sight

In this section, you hit the jackpot — we show you how to establish tricks in a suit where you have the J1098 but you're missing the ace, king, and queen!

If you don't have any of the three top dogs but you have four or more cards in the suit, you can still scrape a trick or two out of the suit. When you have *length* (usually four or more cards of the same suit), you know that even after your opponents win tricks with the ace, king, and queen, you still hold smaller cards in that suit, which become — voilà! — winners.

REMEMBER

Perhaps you're wondering why you'd ever want to squeeze some juice out of a suit in which you lack the ace, king, and queen. The answer: You may need tricks from an anemic suit like this to make your contract. Sometimes you just get the raw end of the deal, and you need to pick up tricks wherever you can eek them out.

When you look at the dummy and see a suit such as the one in Figure 3-4, try not to shriek in horror.

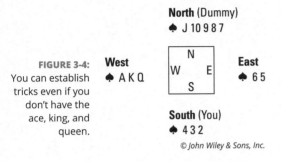

FIGURE 3-4:
You can establish tricks even if you don't have the ace, king, and queen.

North (Dummy)
♠ J 10 9 8 7

West
♠ A K Q

East
♠ 6 5

South (You)
♠ 4 3 2

© John Wiley & Sons, Inc.

True, the spades in Figure 3-4 don't look like the most appetizing suit you'll ever have to deal with, but don't judge a book by its cover. You can get some tricks out of this suit because you have the advantage of length: You have a total of eight spades between the two hands. The strength you get from numbers helps you after you drive out the ace, king, and queen.

Suppose you need to develop two tricks from this hopeless-looking, forsaken suit. You start with a low spade, the ♠2, which is taken by West's ♠Q (the dummy and East each play their lowest spade, the ♠7 and ♠5, respectively). After you regain the lead in some other suit, lead another low spade, the ♠3, which is taken by West's ♠K (the dummy plays the ♠8, and East plays her last spade, the ♠6). After you gain the lead again in another suit, lead your last spade, the ♠4, which loses to West's ♠A (the dummy plays the ♠9). You have lost the lead again, but you have accomplished your ultimate goal: The dummy now holds two winning spades — the ♠J10. Nobody at the table holds any more spades; if the dummy can win a trick in another suit, you can go right ahead and cash those two spade tricks. You had to work, but you did it!

TIP

Sometimes a friendly opponent (in this case West) will help you out by taking spades tricks early, leaving you with good spades in the dummy without your having to do any work!

Practicing establishment

Practice makes perfect, they say, so we want you to practice making your contract by establishing tricks. In this section, you hold the entire hand shown in Figure 3-5. Your final contract is for 12 tricks. West leads the ♠J. Now you need to do your thing and establish some tricks.

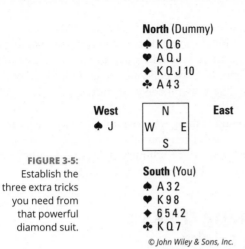

North (Dummy)
- ♠ K Q 6
- ♥ A Q J
- ♦ K Q J 10
- ♣ A 4 3

West
- ♠ J

```
    N
  W   E
    S
```

East

FIGURE 3-5:
Establish the three extra tricks you need from that powerful diamond suit.

South (You)
- ♠ A 3 2
- ♥ K 9 8
- ♦ 6 5 4 2
- ♣ K Q 7

© John Wiley & Sons, Inc.

Before you even think of playing a card from the dummy, count your sure tricks (see Book 5, Chapter 2 if you need some help counting sure tricks):

>> **Spades:** You have three sure tricks — ♠AKQ.

>> **Hearts:** You have another three sure tricks — ♥AKQ. (Don't count the ♥J; you have three hearts in each hand, so you can't take more than three tricks.)

>> **Diamonds:** No ace = no sure tricks. Sad.

>> **Clubs:** You have three sure tricks — ♣AKQ.

You have nine sure tricks, but you need 12 tricks to make your contract. You must establish three more tricks. Look no further than the dummy's magnificent diamond suit. If you drive out the ♦A, you can establish three diamond tricks and have 12 just like that. Piece of cake.

TIP

When you need to establish extra tricks, pick the suit you plan to work with and start establishing immediately. *Do not* take your sure tricks in other suits until you establish your extra needed tricks. Then take all your tricks in one giant cascade. Please reread this tip!

First you need to deal with West's opening lead, the ♠J. You have a choice: You can win the trick in either your hand with the ♠A or in the dummy with the ♠Q. In general, with equal length on both sides, you want to leave a high spade in each hand. Leaving the king in the dummy and the ace in your hand gives you an easier time going back and forth if necessary. However, on this hand it really doesn't matter where you win the trick; you have three spade tricks regardless. But to keep in practice, say you take it with the queen.

Remember, your objective is to establish tricks in your target suit: diamonds. Following your game plan, you lead the ♦K from the dummy. West takes the trick with the ♦A and then leads the ♠10. Presto — your three remaining diamonds in the dummy, ♦QJ10, have just become three sure tricks because you successfully drove out the ace. Your sure-trick count has just ballooned to 12. Don't look now, but you have the rest of the tricks and have just made your contract.

Next comes the best part: the mop-up, taking your winning tricks. You capture West's return of the ♠10 with the ♠K. Then you take your three established diamonds, your three winning hearts, your three winning clubs, and finally your ♠A. You now have 12 tricks, three in each suit. Ah, the thrill of victory.

Steering clear of taking tricks before establishing tricks

Establishing extra needed tricks is all about giving up the lead. Sometimes you need to drive out an ace, a king, or an ace *and* a king. Giving up the lead to establish tricks can be painful for a beginner, but you must steel yourself to do it.

WARNING

You may hate to give up the lead for fear that something terrible may happen. Something terrible is going to happen — if you're afraid to give up the lead to establish a suit. Most of the time, beginners fail to make their contracts because they don't establish extra tricks soon enough. Very often, beginners fall into the trap of taking their sure tricks before establishing tricks.

We know you'd never commit such a grievous error as taking sure tricks before you establish other needed tricks. But just for the fun of it, take a look at Figure 3-6 to see what happens when you make this mistake. This isn't going to be pretty, so clear out the children.

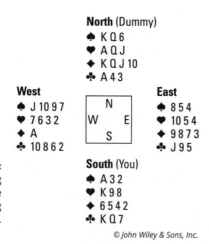

North (Dummy)
♠ K Q 6
♥ A Q J
♦ K Q J 10
♣ A 4 3

West
♠ J 10 9 7
♥ 7 6 3 2
♦ A
♣ 10 8 6 2

East
♠ 8 5 4
♥ 10 5 4
♦ 9 8 7 3
♣ J 9 5

South (You)
♠ A 3 2
♥ K 9 8
♦ 6 5 4 2
♣ K Q 7

FIGURE 3-6: Beware of taking sure tricks before establishing needed tricks.

© John Wiley & Sons, Inc.

In this hand (showing all the cards from the hand in Figure 3-5), the opening lead is the ♠J, and you need to take 12 tricks. Suppose you take the first three spade tricks with the ♠AKQ, and then the next three heart tricks with the ♥AKQ, and finally the next three club tricks with the ♣AKQ. Figure 3-7 shows what's left after you take the first nine tricks. (Remember: You need to take 12 tricks.)

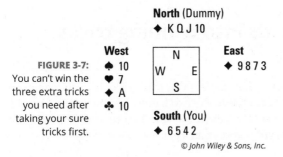

North (Dummy)
♦ K Q J 10

West
♠ 10
♥ 7
♦ A
♣ 10

East
♦ 9 8 7 3

South (You)
♦ 6 5 4 2

© John Wiley & Sons, Inc.

FIGURE 3-7: You can't win the three extra tricks you need after taking your sure tricks first.

You lead a low diamond. But guess what — West takes the trick with the ♦A. The hairs standing up on the back of your neck may tell you what I'm going to say next: West has all the rest of the tricks! West remains with a winning spade, a winning heart, and a winning club. Nobody else at the table has any of those suits, so all the other players are forced to discard. West's three cards are all winning tricks, and those great diamonds in the dummy are nothing but dead weight, totally worthless.

A word to the wise: Nothing good can happen to you if you take sure tricks before establishing extra needed tricks.

REMEMBER

Taking Tricks with Small Cards

Grab a man off the street, and he can take tricks with aces and kings. But can that same man take tricks with 2s and 3s? Probably not, but you can!

Only very rarely do you get a hand dripping with all the honor cards you need to make your contract. Therefore, you must know how to take tricks with the smaller cards. *Small cards* are cards that are lower than honor cards. They are also called *low cards* or *spot cards*. You seldom have enough firepower (aces and kings) to make your contract without these little fellows.

REMEMBER

Small cards frequently take tricks when attached to *long suits* (four or more cards in the suit). Eventually, after all the high honors in a suit have been played, the little guys start making appearances. They may be bit actors when the play begins, but before the final curtain is drawn, they're out there taking the final bows — and taking tricks.

In the following sections, we give you the scoop on using small cards to your great advantage.

Turning small cards into winning tricks: The joy of length

Deuces (and other small cards for that matter) can take tricks for you when you have seven cards or more in a suit between the two hands. You may then have the length to outlast all your opponents' cards in the suit. Figure 3-8 shows a hand where this incredible feat of staying power takes place.

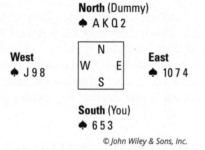

North (Dummy)
♠ A K Q 2

West
♠ J 9 8

East
♠ 10 7 4

South (You)
♠ 6 5 3

© John Wiley & Sons, Inc.

FIGURE 3-8:
Small cards
attached to
honor cards can
become winners.

You choose to attack spades in the hand in Figure 3-8. Because the ♠AKQ in the dummy are all equals, the suit can be started from either your hand or the dummy. Pretend that the lead is in your hand. You begin by leading a low spade, the ♠3, to the ♠Q in the dummy, and both opponents follow suit. With the lead in the dummy, continue by leading the ♠K and then the ♠A from the dummy. The opponents both started with three spades, meaning that neither opponent has any more spades. That tiny ♠2 in the dummy is a winning trick. It has the power of an ace! The frog has turned into a prince.

REMEMBER

Whenever you have four cards in a suit in one hand and three in the other, good things can happen. If your opponents' six cards are divided three in each hand and you lead the suit three times, leaving each opponent *without* any cards in that suit, you're destined to take a trick with any small card attached to the four-card suit.

WARNING

Don't expect that fourth card to turn into a trick every time, though. Your opponents' six cards may not be divided 3-3 after all. They may be divided a more likely 4-2, as you see in Figure 3-9.

FIGURE 3-9:
You may not be
able to use small
cards to your
advantage
when your
opponents' cards
are split 4-2.

North (Dummy)
♠ A K Q 2

West
♠ 10 9

```
  N
W   E
  S
```

East
♠ J 8 7 6

South (You)
♠ 5 4 3

© John Wiley & Sons, Inc.

When you play the ♠AKQ as you do in Figure 3-9, East turns up with four spades, so your ♠2 won't be a trick. After you play the ♠AKQ, East remains with the ♠J, a higher spade than your ♠2. Live with it.

REMEMBER

Bridge is a game of strategy and luck. When it comes to taking tricks with small cards, you just have to hope that the cards your opponents hold divide evenly (3-3 instead of 4-2, for example).

TIP

SUBTRACTING YOUR WAY TO SUCCESS

Happiness is having small cards that turn into winning tricks. Misery is having small cards that are winning tricks and not knowing it. Total misery is thinking your small cards are winning tricks only to find out they aren't.

To know when your small cards are winners, you must become familiar with the dreaded *c* word, *counting*. If you count the cards in the suit you're playing, you can tell whether your little guys have a chance. You have to do a little simple subtraction as well, but we can assure you it's well worth the effort.

A neat way of counting the suit you're attacking is with the *subtraction-by-two method*. Follow these steps for successful counting every time:

1. Count how many cards you and the dummy have in the suit.

2. Subtract the number of cards you and dummy have from 13 (the number of cards in a suit) to get the total number of cards your opponents have in that suit.

3. Each time you lead the suit and both opponents follow suit, subtract two from the number of cards your opponents have left.

4. When your opponents have no cards left, all your remaining small cards are winning tricks.

With this method, the numbers get smaller and become easier to work with. Some people think doing stuff like this is fun — with any luck, you're one of these people.

Turning low cards into winners by driving out high honors

Sometimes you have to drive out an opponent's high honor card (could be an ace, a king, or a queen) before you can turn your frogs into princes (or turn your deuces into tricks). Figure 3-10 shows you how (with a little luck) you can turn a deuce into a winner.

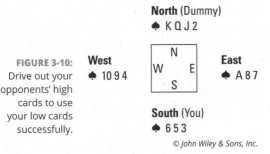

North (Dummy)
♠ K Q J 2

West
♠ 10 9 4

N
W　E
S

East
♠ A 8 7

South (You)
♠ 6 5 3

© John Wiley & Sons, Inc.

With the cards shown in Figure 3-10, your plan is to develop (or establish) as many spade tricks as possible, keeping a wary eye on turning that ♠2 in the dummy into a winner. Suppose you begin by leading a low spade, the ♠3, and West follows with a low spade, the ♠4. You play the ♠J from the dummy, which loses to East's ♠A. At this point, you note the following points:

>> The ♠KQ in the dummy are now both winning tricks because your opponents' ♠A is gone.

>> Your opponents started with six spades. By counting cards, you know that your opponents now have only four spades left. Four is your new key number.

After regaining the lead by winning a trick in another suit, lead another low spade, the ♠5, to the ♠Q in the dummy (with both opponents following suit). Your opponents now have two spades left between them. When you continue with the ♠K, both opponents follow suit again. They now have zero spades left — triumph! The ♠2 in the dummy is now a sure trick. Deuces love to take tricks — doing so makes them feel wanted.

REMEMBER

Make sure you count the cards in the suit you're attacking. You're in a pretty sad state if you have to leave a low card in your hand or the dummy untouched because you don't know (or aren't sure) whether it's a winner.

Losing a trick early by making a ducking play

Suits that have seven or eight cards between your hand and the dummy, including the ace and the king, lend themselves to taking extra tricks with lower cards, even though you have to lose a trick in the suit. Why do you have to lose a trick in the suit? Because the opponents have the queen, the jack, and the 10 between them. After you play the ace and the king, the opponent with the queen is looking at a winning trick.

TIP

When you know you have to lose at least one trick in a suit that includes the ace and king, face the inevitable and lose that trick early by playing low cards from both your hand and the dummy. Taking this dive early on is called *ducking a trick*. It only hurts for a little while.

Ducking a trick is a necessary evil when playing Bridge. A ducking play in a suit that has an inevitable loser allows you to keep your controlling cards (the ace and the king) so you can use them in a late rush of tricks.

When you duck a trick and then play the ace and king, you wind up in the hand where the small cards are — just where you want to be. In the following sections, we present two situations in which you can duck a trick successfully.

When you have seven cards between the two hands

The cards in Figure 3-11 show how successful ducking a trick can be. You have seven cards between the two hands with ♠AK in the dummy — a perfect setup for ducking a trick. You can only hope that your opponents' six cards are divided 3-3 so they'll run out of spades before you do. To find out, you have to play the suit *three* times.

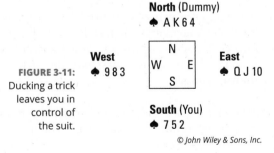

FIGURE 3-11:
Ducking a trick leaves you in control of the suit.

North (Dummy)
♠ A K 6 4

West
♠ 9 8 3

N
W   E
S

East
♠ Q J 10

South (You)
♠ 7 5 2

© John Wiley & Sons, Inc.

You know you have to lose at least one spade trick because your opponents hold ♠QJ10 between them. Because you have to lose at least one spade trick, your best bet is to lose the trick right away, keeping control (the high cards) of the suit for later.

TIP

Play a low spade from both hands! No, you aren't giving out presents; actually, you're making a very clever ducking play by letting your opponents have a trick they're entitled to anyway.

After you concede the trick with the ♠2 from your hand and the ♠4 from the dummy, you can come roaring back with your big guns, the ♠K and the ♠A, when you regain the lead. Notice that because your opponents' spades are divided 3-3, that little ♠6 in the dummy takes a third trick in the suit — neither opponent has any more spades.

When you have eight cards between the two hands

If the dummy has a five-card suit headed by the ace and the king facing three small cards, you can usually take two extra tricks with a ducking play. See Figure 3-12, where you make a ducking play, and then watch the tricks come rolling in.

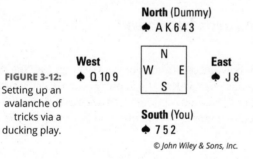

North (Dummy)
♠ A K 6 4 3

West
♠ Q 10 9

East
♠ J 8

South (You)
♠ 7 5 2

FIGURE 3-12: Setting up an avalanche of tricks via a ducking play.

© John Wiley & Sons, Inc.

In Figure 3-12, the opponents have five spades between the two hands, including the ♠QJ1098. You have to lose a spade trick no matter what, so lose it right away by making one of your patented ducking plays. Lead the ♠2. West plays the ♠9, you play the ♠3 from the dummy, and East plays the ♠8. West wins the trick. Not to worry — you'll soon show them who's boss!

The next time either you or the dummy regains the lead, play the ♠K and ♠A, removing all of your opponents' remaining spades. The lead is in the dummy, and the dummy remains with ♠64, both winning tricks.

TIP

When you have five cards in one hand and three in the other, including the ace and the king, you have a chance to take four tricks by playing a low card from both hands at your first opportunity. This ducking play allows you to save the highest cards in the suit, intending to come swooping in later to take the remaining tricks.

Finding heaven with seven small cards

Having any seven cards between the two hands may mean an extra trick for you — if your opponents' cards are divided 3-3. The hand in Figure 3-13 shows you how any small card(s) can morph into a winner when your opponents' cards are split evenly. You have seven cards between your hand and the dummy, the signal that something good may happen for your small cards. Of course, you'd be a little happier if you had some higher cards in the suit (such as an honor or two), but beggars can't be choosers.

FIGURE 3-13:
You hold no honor cards, but you have length in one hand to help you win tricks.

North (Dummy)
♠ 9 4

```
      N
  W       E
      S
```

West
♠ A Q J

East
♠ K 10 8

South (You)
♠ 7 6 5 3 2

© John Wiley & Sons, Inc.

Remember Cinderella and how her stepsisters dressed her up to look ugly even though she was beautiful? Well, those five tiny spades in the South hand are like Cinderella — you just have to cast off the rags to see the beauty underneath.

Suppose you lead the ♠2, and West takes the trick with the ♠J. Later, you lead the ♠3, and West takes that trick with the ♠Q. You've played spades twice, and because you've been counting those spades, you know that your opponents have two spades left.

After you regain the lead, you again lead a *rag* (low card) — in this case, the ♠5. Crash, bang! West plays the ♠A, and East plays the ♠K. Now they have no more spades, and the two remaining spades in your hand, the ♠7 and ♠6, are winning tricks. You conceded three spade tricks (tricks they had coming anyway) but established two tricks of your own by sheer persistence.

Avoiding the tragedy of blocking a suit

Even when length is on your side, you need to play the high honor cards from the short side first. Doing so ensures that the lead ends up in the hand with the length — and therefore the winning tricks. If you don't play the high honor(s) from the short side first, you run the risk of blocking a suit. You *block* a suit when you have winning cards stranded in one hand and no way to enter that hand in order to play those winning cards. It hurts to even talk about it.

Figure 3-14 shows you a suit that's blocked from the very start. It's a Bridge tragedy: seeing the dummy come down with a strong suit, only to realize that it's blocked and you can't use it. You have five spade tricks but may be able to take only two. After you play ♠AK, you're fresh out of spades, and the dummy remains with the ♠QJ10. Without an entry to the dummy, the ♠QJ10 are stranded never to be used. Yes, it's very sad.

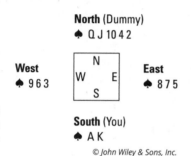

North (Dummy)
♠ Q J 10 4 2

West
♠ 9 6 3

East
♠ 8 7 5

South (You)
♠ A K

© John Wiley & Sons, Inc.

FIGURE 3-14:
Some suits are born blocked.

If you don't have an *entry* (a winning card) in another suit to get the lead over to the dummy (called a dummy entry), dummy's three winning spades will die on the vine. A side-suit ace is a certain dummy entry, and a side-suit king or queen may turn out to be a dummy entry.

The more poignant tragedy is when you accidentally block a suit by failing to play the high card(s) from the short side first. Then you wind up in the wrong hand, instead of winding up in the long hand where the winning tricks are. Instead, you wind up in the short hand that has no more cards in the suit. The long hand may not have a side-suit entry to enter the hand with the winning tricks. It hurts.

IN THIS CHAPTER

Discovering the pros and cons of
playing in a trump suit

Disarming your opponents by drawing
trumps

Searching for eight-card or longer
trump fits

Keeping track of losers and extra
winners

Chapter 4

Introducing Trump Suits

The previous chapters focus on notrump play because the basics of taking tricks are easier to understand without the complicating factor of trump suits. But this chapter introduces you to an exciting new aspect of the game. Trump suits are an unavoidable (and intriguing) part of Bridge.

In this chapter, you discover how to use the trump suit to your best advantage. We show you how to knock the wind out of your opponents' sails by preventing them from taking scads of tricks in their strong suits. We also show you the proper sequence of plays, which allows you to take your winning tricks safely. In short, this chapter gives you your first taste of the wonderful powers of the trump suit.

Understanding the Basics of Trump Suits

In Bridge, the bidding often designates a suit as the *trump suit*. If the final contract has a suit associated with it — 4♠, 3♥, 2♦, or even 1♣, for example — that suit becomes the trump suit for the entire hand. (See Book 5, Chapter 5 for a primer on bidding.)

REMEMBER

Often, in Bridge books such as this one, a single card like the four of spades is written ♠4 because it saves space. Similarly, a bid made by any player, such as four spades, is written 4♠ (notice the difference). A final contract is written the same way as a bid, so a contract of three diamonds usually appears as 3♦.

When a suit becomes the trump suit, any card in that trump suit potentially has special powers; any card in the trump suit can win a trick over any card of another suit. For example, suppose that spades is the trump suit and West leads with the ♥A. You can still win the trick with the ♠2 if you have no hearts in your hand.

Because trump suits have so much power, naturally everyone at the table wants to have a say in determining the trump suit. Because Bridge is a partnership game, your partnership determines which suit is the best trump suit for your side or whether there shouldn't be a trump suit at all.

In the following sections, we show you the glory (and potential danger) of trump suits.

Finding out when trumping saves the day

You can easily see the advantage of playing with a trump suit. When the bidding designates a trump suit, you may well be in a position to neutralize your opponents' long, strong suits quite easily. After either you or your partner is *void* (has no cards left) in the suit that your opponents lead, you can play any of your cards in the trump suit and take the trick. This little maneuver is called *trumping* your opponents' trick (which your opponents really hate). Your lowly deuce of trumps beats even an ace in another suit.

In contrast, if you play a hand at a *notrump contract,* the highest card played in the suit led always takes the trick (see Book 5, Chapters 3 for more information on playing at notrump). If an opponent with the lead has a suit headed by all winning cards, that opponent can wind up killing you by playing all those winning cards — be it four, five, six, or seven — taking one trick after another as you watch helplessly. Such is the beauty and the horror of playing a hand at notrump. You see the beauty when your side is peeling off the tricks; you experience the horror when your opponents start peeling them off one by one — sometimes slowly, to torture you.

The hand in Figure 4-1 shows you the power of playing in a trump suit.

On this hand, suppose that you need nine tricks to make your contract of 3NT (*NT* stands for *notrump*). Between your hand and the dummy, you can count 11 sure tricks: five spades (after the ♠AK are played and both opponents follow, the opponents have no more spades, so ♠QJ2 are all sure tricks), three diamonds, and three clubs. (Book 5, Chapter 2 has details on how to count sure tricks.)

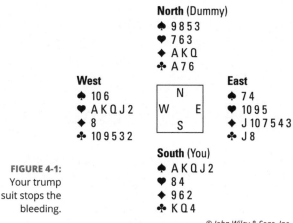

North (Dummy)
♠ 9 8 5 3
♥ 7 6 3
♦ A K Q
♣ A 7 6

West
♠ 10 6
♥ A K Q J 2
♦ 8
♣ 10 9 5 3 2

East
♠ 7 4
♥ 10 9 5
♦ J 10 7 5 4 3
♣ J 8

N
W　E
S

South (You)
♠ A K Q J 2
♥ 8 4
♦ 9 6 2
♣ K Q 4

FIGURE 4-1:
Your trump
suit stops the
bleeding.

If you play the hand shown in Figure 4-1 in notrump, all your sure tricks won't help you if your opponents have the lead and can race off winning tricks in a suit where you're weak in both hands, such as hearts. Playing in notrump, West can use the opening lead to win the first five heart tricks by leading the ♥AKQJ2, in that order. To put it mildly, this start isn't healthy. You need to take nine tricks, meaning you can afford to lose only four, and you've already lost the first five.

On this hand, you and your partner need to communicate accurately during the bidding to discover which suit (hearts, in this case) is woefully weak in both hands. When you both are weak in the same suit, you need to end the bidding in a trump suit so you can stop the bleeding by eventually trumping if the opponents stubbornly persist in leading your weak suit.

In Figure 4-1, assume that during the bidding, spades becomes the trump suit and you need ten tricks to fulfill your contract. When West begins with ♥AKQ, you can trump the third heart with your ♠2 and take the trick. (You must follow suit if you can, so you can't trump either of your opponents' first two hearts.) Instead of losing five heart tricks, you lose only two.

Seeing how their trumps can ruin your whole day

WARNING

Bear in mind that your opponents, the defenders, can also use their trump cards effectively; if they hold no cards in the suit (called a *void*) that you or the dummy leads, they can trump one of your tricks. Misery.

After you have the lead, you want to prevent your opponents from trumping your winning tricks. You don't want your opponents to exercise the same strategy on you that you used on them! You need to get rid of their trumps before they can hurt you. This move is called *drawing trumps,* which we show you how to do in the following section.

Eliminating Your Opponents' Trump Cards

If you can trump your opponents' winning tricks when you don't have any cards in the suit that they're leading, it follows that your opponents can turn the tables and do the same to you. Instead of allowing your opponents to trump your sure tricks, play your higher trumps early on in the hand. Because your opponents must follow suit, you can remove their lower trumps *before* you take your sure tricks. If you can extract their trumps, you effectively remove their fangs. This extraction is called *drawing* or *pulling trumps.* Drawing trumps allows you to take your winning tricks in peace without fear of your opponents trumping them.

The dangers of taking sure tricks before drawing trumps

Send the children out of the room and see what happens if you try to take sure tricks *before* you draw trumps. For example, in Figure 4-1 (where spades are trump), after you trump the third round of hearts, if you lead the ♦2, West has to follow suit by playing the only diamond in his hand, the ♦8. You then play the ♦Q from the dummy, East plays a low (meaning lowest) diamond, the ♦3, and you take the trick. However, if you follow up by playing the ♦A, West has no more diamonds and can trump the ace with the ♠6 because the bidding has designated spades as the trump suit for this hand.

The same misfortune befalls you if, instead of playing diamonds, you try to take three club tricks. East can trump the third round of clubs with the lowly ♠4. Imagine your discomfort when you see your opponents trump your sure tricks. They, on the other hand, are thrilled over this turn of events.

REMEMBER

You should usually try to draw trumps as soon as possible. Get your opponents' pesky trump cards out of your hair. Then you can sit back and watch as your winning tricks come home safely to your trick pile.

The joys of drawing trumps first

To see how drawing trumps can work to your advantage, take a look at Figure 4-2, which shows only spades (the trump suit) from the hand in Figure 4-1. Remember, your goal is ten tricks.

TIP

Drawing trumps is just like playing any suit — you have to count the cards in the suit to know if you have successfully drawn all your opponents' trump cards. For more about counting cards, see Book 5, Chapter 3.

In the hand shown in Figure 4-2, you and your partner start life with nine spades between you, leaving only four spades that your opponents can possibly hold. Suppose that you play the ♠A — both opponents must follow suit and play one of their spades. You win the trick, and you know that your opponents have only two spades left. Suppose that you continue with the ♠K, and both opponents follow. Now they have no spades left (no more trump cards). You have drawn trumps. See? That wasn't so bad.

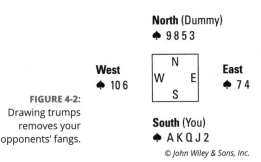

North (Dummy)
♠ 9 8 5 3

West
♠ 10 6

East
♠ 7 4

South (You)
♠ A K Q J 2

© John Wiley & Sons, Inc.

FIGURE 4-2:
Drawing trumps removes your opponents' fangs.

Refer to Figure 4-1 (where West begins with the ♥AKQ, and you trump the third heart with your ♠2). After you trump the third heart, you draw trumps by playing the ♠AK. You can then safely take your ♣AKQ and your ♦AKQ — you wind up losing only two heart tricks. You needed to take 10 tricks to fulfill your contract, and you in fact finished up with 11 tricks. Pretty good! Drawing trumps helped you make your contract.

Noticing How Trump Suits Can Be Divided

If you have eight or more cards in a suit between your hand and the dummy, particularly in a *major suit* (either hearts or spades), you try to make that suit your trump suit.

An *eight-card fit* (eight cards in a single suit between your hand and the dummy) gives you a safety net because you have many more trumps than your opponents: Your trumps outnumber theirs eight to five. Having more trumps than your opponents is always to your advantage. You may be able to survive a seven-card trump fit, but having an eight- or nine-card trump fit relieves tension. The more trumps you have, the more tricks you can generate and the less chance your opponents have of taking tricks with their trumps. You can never have too many trumps! The fewer trumps your opponents have, the easier it is for you to get rid of them.

In the following sections, we show you a variety of trump fits.

Scoring big with the 4-4 trump fit

TIP

During the bidding, you may discover that you have an eight-card fit divided 4-4 between the two hands. Try to make such a fit your trump suit. A 4-4 trump fit almost always produces at least one more trick in the play of the hand than it does at notrump.

At a notrump contract, the 4-4 spade fit in Figure 4-3 takes four tricks. At notrump, when you and your partner have four cards apiece in the same suit, four tricks is your max.

© John Wiley & Sons, Inc.

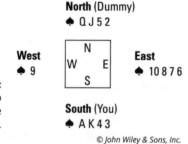

FIGURE 4-3:
In this 4-4 trump fit, you can take five tricks.

However, when spades is your trump suit, you can do better. In Figure 4-3, suppose that your opponents lead a suit that you don't have, which allows you to trump their lead with the ♠3. By drawing trumps now, you can take four more spade tricks by playing the ♠A and the ♠K from your hand (high honors from the short side first) and then playing the ♠4 over to the ♠J and ♠Q from the dummy. You wind up taking a total of five spade tricks — the card you trumped plus four more high spades. (Flip to "Eliminating Your Opponents' Trump Cards" earlier in this chapter for more on drawing trumps.)

REMEMBER

A 4-4 trump fit is primo. You can get more for your money from this trump combination. Every so often you can take six (or more) trump tricks when you have a 4-4 trump fit, so keep your eyes open for one. They are magic.

Being aware of other eight-card trump fits

Eight-card trump fits can come in different guises. Consider the eight-card trump fits in Figure 4-4. The figure shows examples of a 5-3, a 6-2, and a 7-1 fit. Good bidding uncovers eight-card (or longer) fits, which makes for safe trump suits. There is joy in numbers.

FIGURE 4-4:
Some of the many faces of an eight-card trump fit.

♠ Q 4 2	♠ J 4	♠ 6
North (Dummy)	**North** (Dummy)	**North** (Dummy)
♠ K J 7 5 3	♠ Q 10 7 5 3 2	♠ A J 9 7 4 3 2
1 **South** (You)	2 **South** (You)	3 **South** (You)

Counting Losers and Extra Winners

When playing a hand at a trump contract, instead of counting sure tricks (discussed in Book 5, Chapter 2), a better strategy is to count how many losers you have. If you have too many losers to make your contract, you need to look in the dummy for extra winners (tricks) that you can use to dispose of some of your losers.

REMEMBER

You may find this approach a rather negative way of playing a hand. But counting losers can have a very positive impact on your play at a trump contract. Your loser count tells you how many extra winners you need, if any. Extra winners are an indispensable security blanket to make your contract — extra winners help you get rid of losers.

In the following sections, we define losers and extra winners and show you how to identify them. We also explain when to draw trumps before taking extra winners and when to take extra winners before drawing trumps.

Defining losers and extra winners

When playing a hand at a notrump contract, you count your sure tricks (as we describe in Book 5, Chapter 2); however, when you play a hand at a trump contract, you count losers and extra winners. *Losers* are tricks you know you have to lose. For example, if neither you nor your partner holds the ace in a suit, you know you have to lose at least one trick in that suit unless, of course, one of you is *void* (has no cards) in the suit. Extra winners may allow you to get rid of some of your losers. An *extra winner* is a winning trick in the dummy (North) on which you can discard a loser from your own hand (South).

Get ready for some good news: When counting losers, you have to count only the losers in the *long hand*, the hand that has more trumps. The declarer usually is the long trump hand, but not always.

TIP

For the time being, just accept that you don't have to count losers in the dummy. Counting losers in one hand is bad enough; counting losers in the dummy is not only unnecessary but also confusing and downright depressing.

Recognizing immediate and eventual losers

Losers come in two forms: *immediate* and *eventual*. Immediate losers are losers that your opponents can take when they have the lead. These losers have a special warning signal attached to them that reads, "Danger — Unexploded Bomb!" Immediate losers spell bad news.

Of course, eventual losers aren't exactly a welcome occurrence, either. Your opponents can't take your eventual losers right away because those losers are temporarily *protected* by a winning card in the suit that you or your partner holds. In other words, with eventual losers, your opponents can't take their tricks right off the bat, which buys you time to get rid of those eventual losers. One of the best ways to get rid of eventual losers is to discard them on extra winners.

You help yourself by knowing which of your losers are eventual and which are immediate. Your game plan depends on your immediate loser count. See "Drawing trumps before taking extra winners" and "Taking extra winners before drawing trumps" later in this chapter for more about how to proceed after counting your immediate losers.

Because identifying eventual and immediate losers is so important, take a look at the spades in Figures 4-5, 4-6, and 4-7 to spot some losers. Assume in these figures that spades is a *side suit* (any suit that is not the trump suit) and hearts is your trump suit.

Figure 4-5 shows a suit with two eventual losers. In the hand in this figure, as long as you have the ♠A protecting your two other spades, your two spade losers are eventual. However, after your opponents lead a spade (which forces out your ace), your two remaining spades become immediate losers because they have no winning trick protecting them. Ouch.

In Figure 4-6, you have one eventual spade loser. With the spades in Figure 4-6, the dummy's ♠AK protect two of your three spades — but your third spade is on its own as a loser after the ♠A and ♠K have been played.

North (Dummy)

♠ 6 4 3

```
    N
  W   E
    S
```

FIGURE 4-5:
An ace protects
eventual losers —
temporarily!

South (You)

♠ A 9 2

© John Wiley & Sons, Inc.

North (Dummy)

♠ A K 8

```
    N
  W   E
    S
```

FIGURE 4-6:
The ace and king
protect only two
of your spades.

South (You)

♠ 7 5 3

© John Wiley & Sons, Inc.

In Figure 4-7, you have two immediate spade losers. Notice that you count two, not three, spade losers — you count losers only in the long trump hand (which presumably is your South hand). You don't have to count losers in the dummy. Actually, when you are playing a 4-4 trump fit, no long hand exists, so assume the hand with the longer side suit (five or more cards) is the long hand. When neither hand has a long side suit, the hand with the stronger trumps is considered the long hand.

North (Dummy)

♠ 9 4 3

```
    N
  W   E
    S
```

FIGURE 4-7:
You have a pair of
immediate losers
in your own
hand.

South (You)

♠ 8 2

© John Wiley & Sons, Inc.

Identifying extra winners

Enough with losers already — counting them is sort of a downer. You can get rid of some of your losers by using extra winners. Extra winners come into play only after you (South) are void in the suit being played. Therefore, extra winners can exist only in a suit that's unevenly divided between the two hands and are usually in the dummy. The stronger the extra winner suit (that is, the more high cards it has), the better.

Figure 4-8 shows you two extra winners in their natural habitat. The cards in this figure fill the bill for extra winners because spades is an unevenly divided suit, and the greater length is in the dummy. After you lead the ♠3 and play the ♠Q from the dummy, you're void in spades. Now you can discard two losers from your hand when you lead the ♠A and the ♠K from the dummy. Therefore, you can count two extra winners in spades.

North (Dummy)
♠ A K Q

FIGURE 4-8:
You find two extra winners in the dummy.

South (You)
♠ 3

© John Wiley & Sons, Inc.

By contrast, the cards in Figure 4-9 look hopeful, but unfortunately, they can't offer you any extra winners. They don't fit the mold for extra winners because you have the same number of spades in each hand. No matter how strong a suit is, if you have the same number of cards in each hand, you can't squeeze any extra winners out of the suit. You just have to follow suit each time. True, the ♠AKQ aren't chopped liver; although this hand has no spade losers, it gives you no extra winners, either. Sorry!

North (Dummy)
♠ A K Q

FIGURE 4-9:
You won't find any extra winners in this suit, no matter how hard you squint.

South (You)
♠ 8 6 4

© John Wiley & Sons, Inc.

The cards in Figure 4-10 contain no extra winners, either. The dummy's ♠AK take care of your two losing spades, but you have nothing "extra" over there — no ♠Q, for example — on which you can discard one of your losers. In Figure 4-10, your ♠A and ♠K do an excellent job of covering your two spade losers, but no more. You can't squeeze blood out of a turnip.

North (Dummy)
♠ A K 7 6

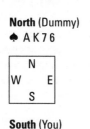

South (You)
♠ 4 2

© John Wiley & Sons, Inc.

FIGURE 4-10: This hand has losers but no extra winners.

Drawing trumps before taking extra winners

After counting your immediate losers (see "Recognizing immediate and eventual losers" earlier in this chapter), if you still have enough tricks to make your contract, go ahead and draw trumps before taking extra winners. That way, you can make sure your opponents don't swoop down on you with a trump card and spoil your party. Figure 4-11 illustrates this point by showing you a hand where spades is your trump suit. You need to take ten tricks to make your contract. West leads the ♥A.

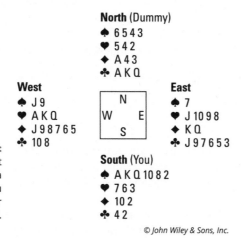

North (Dummy)
♠ 6 5 4 3
♥ 5 4 2
♦ A 4 3
♣ A K Q

West
♠ J 9
♥ A K Q
♦ J 9 8 7 6 5
♣ 10 8

East
♠ 7
♥ J 10 9 8
♦ K Q
♣ J 9 7 6 5 3

South (You)
♠ A K Q 10 8 2
♥ 7 6 3
♦ 10 2
♣ 4 2

FIGURE 4-11: Be sure to count losers and extra winners so you have a plan for the hand.

© John Wiley & Sons, Inc.

Before playing a card from the dummy, count your losers one suit at a time, starting with the trump suit, the most important suit. You can't make a plan for the hand until your opponents make the opening lead because you can't see the dummy until the opening lead is made. But as soon as the dummy comes down, try to curb your understandable eagerness to play a card from the dummy and first do a little loser and/or extra winner counting in each suit instead:

>> **Spades:** In your trump suit (spades), you're well heeled. You have ten spades between the two hands, including the ♠AKQ. Because your opponents have only three spades, you should have no trouble removing their spades. A suit with no losers is called a *solid suit.* You have a solid spade suit — you can never have too many solid suits.

>> **Hearts:** In hearts, however, you have trouble — big trouble. In this case, your own hand has three heart losers. But before you count three losers, check to see whether the dummy has any high cards in hearts to neutralize any of your losers. In this case, your partner doesn't come through for you at all, having only three baby hearts. You have three heart losers, and they're immediate losers.

>> **Diamonds:** In diamonds, you have two losers, but this time your partner does go to bat for you with the ♦A as a winner. The ♦A negates one of your diamond losers, but you still have to count one eventual diamond loser.

>> **Clubs:** In clubs, you have two losers, but in this suit your partner really does come through. Not only does your partner take care of your two losers with the ♣AK, but your partner also has an extra winner, the ♣Q. Count one extra winner in clubs.

Your mental score card for this hand reads as follows:

>> **Spades:** A solid suit, no losers

>> **Hearts:** Three losers (the three cards in your hand)

>> **Diamonds:** One loser, because your partner covers one of your losers with the ace

>> **Clubs:** One extra winner

Next, you determine how many losers you can lose and still make your contract. In this case, you need to take ten tricks, which means that you can afford to lose three tricks. (Remember, each hand has 13 tricks up for grabs.)

If you have more losers than you can afford, you need to figure out how to get rid of those pesky deadbeats. One way to get rid of losers is by using extra winners — and you just happen to have an extra winner in clubs.

Follow the play: West starts out by leading the ♥AKQ, taking the first three tricks. You can do absolutely nothing about losing these heart tricks — which is why you call them *immediate* losers (tricks that your opponents can take whenever they want). Immediate losers are the pits, especially if they lead that suit.

After taking the first three heart tricks, West decides to shift to a low diamond, which establishes an immediate winner for your opponents in diamonds and an immediate loser for you in diamonds when the ♦A is played from dummy. You may be strongly tempted to get rid of that loser immediately on the dummy's clubs — just looking at it may be making you nervous. Don't do it. Draw trumps first. If you play the ♣AKQ from the dummy before you draw trumps, West will trump the third club, and down you go in a contract you should make.

You need to draw trumps first and *then* play the ♣AKQ. West won't be able to trump any of your good tricks, nor will East — they won't have any trumps left. You wind up losing only three heart tricks — and making your contract!

The most favorable sequence of plays, after losing the first three heart tricks and winning the ♦A, is as follows:

1. Play the ♠AK, removing all your opponents' trumps.

2. Play the ♣AKQ and throw that diamond loser away.

3. Sit back and take the rest of the tricks now that you have only trumps left.

REMEMBER

Any time you can draw trump before taking your extra winners, do it.

Taking extra winners before drawing trumps

Sometimes your trump suit has an immediate loser. When you have more immediate losers in a side suit than your contract can afford but you also have an extra winner, you must use that extra winner immediately before you give up the lead in the trump suit (or in any other suit, for that matter). If you don't, your opponents will mow you down by taking their tricks while you still hold too many immediate losers. Of course, if you can draw trumps without giving up the lead, do that first and then take your extra winner as in Figure 4-11.

Figure 4-12 shows you the importance of taking your extra winners before drawing trumps. In this hand, your losers are immediate — if your opponents get the lead, you can pack up and go home.

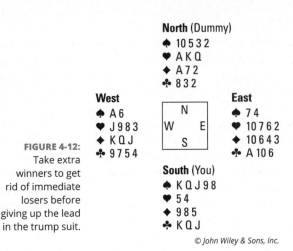

North (Dummy)
- ♠ 10 5 3 2
- ♥ A K Q
- ♦ A 7 2
- ♣ 8 3 2

West
- ♠ A 6
- ♥ J 9 8 3
- ♦ K Q J
- ♣ 9 7 5 4

N
W E
S

East
- ♠ 7 4
- ♥ 10 7 6 2
- ♦ 10 6 4 3
- ♣ A 10 6

South (You)
- ♠ K Q J 9 8
- ♥ 5 4
- ♦ 9 8 5
- ♣ K Q J

FIGURE 4-12:
Take extra winners to get rid of immediate losers before giving up the lead in the trump suit.

© *John Wiley & Sons, Inc.*

In the hand in Figure 4-12, your contract is for ten tricks, with spades as the trump suit. West leads the ♦K, trying to establish diamond tricks after the ♦A is played. After dummy's ♦A has been played, West's ♦Q and ♦J are promoted to sure winners on subsequent tricks.

After you count your losers, you tally up the following losers and extra winners:

>> **Spades:** One immediate loser — the ♠A

>> **Hearts:** One extra winner — the ♥Q

>> **Diamonds:** Two losers, which are immediate after you play the ♦A

>> **Clubs:** One immediate loser — the ♣A

You win the opening lead with the ♦A. Suppose you lead a low spade from dummy at trick two and play the ♠K from your hand, intending to draw trumps — *usually* a good idea. (See "Eliminating Your Opponents' Trump Cards" earlier in this chapter for more information on drawing trumps.)

However, West wins the trick with the ♠A and takes the ♦QJ, and East still gets a trick with the ♣A. You lose four tricks. What happened? You went down in your contract while your extra winner, the ♥Q, was still sitting over there in the dummy, gathering dust. You never got to use your extra winner in hearts because you drew trumps too quickly. When you led a spade at the second trick, you had four losers, all immediate. And sure enough, your opponents took all four of them.

If you want to make your contract, you need to play that extra heart winner *before* you draw trumps. You can't afford to give up the lead just yet. The winning play goes something like this:

1. **You take the ♦A at trick one, followed by the ♥AKQ at tricks two, three, and four.**

2. **On the third heart, you discard one of your diamond losers.**

   This play reduces your immediate loser count from an unwieldy four to a workable three.

3. **Now you can afford to lead a trump and give up the lead.**

   After all, you do want to draw trumps sooner or later.

If you play the hand properly, you wind up losing one spade, one club, and one diamond — and you make your contract of ten tricks. Congratulations.

REMEMBER

You may think that playing the ♥AKQ before you draw trumps is dangerous, but you have no choice. You have to get rid of one of your immediate diamond losers before giving up the lead if you want to make your contract. Otherwise, you're giving up the ship without a fight.

IN THIS CHAPTER

Breaking down how important bidding is to the game

Examining the progression of the bidding

Checking out a bid's structure and rank

Finding out who plays and who watches

Determining how strong your hand is

Chapter 5

Starting with Bidding Basics

B idding for the proper number of tricks is an important part of the game of Bridge. Some would say it's what the game is all about! Successful bidding can either make or break your chances of fulfilling your contract.

In this chapter, you discover some of the fundamentals of bidding. You find out how the bidding progresses around the table, the proper way to make a legal bid, and how to assess the strength of your hand (so you can make good decisions about how many tricks you and your partner can reasonably expect to take). You certainly shouldn't pass on this chapter.

Understanding the Importance of Bidding

Bidding determines the *final contract* for a hand. The pressure is on the partnership that gets (or *buys*) the final contract — that side has to win the number of tricks it contracts for. If the partnership fails to win that number of tricks, penalty points are scored by the opponents. If the partnership takes at least the number of tricks it has contracted for, it then scores points. (We talk about scoring in Book 5, Chapter 6.)

REMEMBER

In addition to determining how many tricks a partnership needs to fulfill the contract, the bidding also determines the following:

>> **The declarer and the dummy for the hand:** For the partnership that buys the final contract, the bidding determines who plays the hand for the partnership (the *declarer*) and who gets to watch (the *dummy*). See "Settling Who Plays the Hand" later in this chapter for details.

>> **The number of tricks the partnership needs to make the final contract:** Each bid is like a stepping stone to the number of tricks that a partnership thinks it can take. The goal of the partnership that buys the final contract is to take at least the number of tricks contracted for.

>> **The trump suit (if the hand has one):** Depending on the cards held by the partnership that winds up playing the hand, there may be a trump suit (or the bidding may end in a notrump contract). See Book 5, Chapter 3 to find out more about playing at notrump.

REMEMBER

Proper bidding also allows the partners to exchange information about the strength (the number of high-card points) and distribution of their cards. (See "Valuing the Strength of Your Hand" later in this chapter.) Through bidding, you and your partner can tell each other which long suits you have and perhaps in which suits you have honor cards (aces, kings, queens, jacks, and tens).

Based on the information exchanged during the bidding, the partnership has to decide how many tricks it thinks it can take. The partnership with the greater combined high-card strength usually winds up playing the hand. The declarer (the one who plays the hand) tries to take the number of tricks (or more) that his side has contracted for. The opponents, on the other hand, do their darndest to prevent the declarer from winning those tricks.

Partnerships exchange vital information about the makeup of their hands through a *bidding system*. Because you can't tell your partner what you have in plain English, you have to use a legal Bridge bidding system. Think of it as a foreign language in which every bid you make carries some message. Although you can't say to your partner, "Hey, partner, I have seven strong hearts but only one ace and one king," an accurate bidding system can come close to describing such a hand.

WARNING

The bidding (or *auction*) consists of only the permitted bids; you don't get to describe your hand by using facial expressions, kicking your partner under the table, or punching him in the nose. Your partner must also understand the conventional significance of your bids to make sense of what you're trying to communicate about your hand and to know how to respond properly.

Of course, everyone at the table hears your bid and everyone else's bid at the table. No secrets are allowed. Your opponents are privy to the same information your bid tells your partner. Similarly, by listening to your opponents' bidding, you get a feel for the cards that your opponents have (their strength and distribution). You can then use this information to your advantage when the play of the hand begins.

REMEMBER

Bridge authorities agree that bidding is the most important aspect of the game. Using a simple system and making clear bids is the key to getting to the proper contract and racking up the points. Bidding incorrectly (giving your partner a bum steer) leads to lousy contracts, which, in turn, lets your opponents rack up the points when you fail to make your contract. Of course, you have to know how to take the tricks you contracted for, or else even the most beautiful contracts in the world lead nowhere.

Surveying the Stages of Bidding

The bidding begins after the cards have been shuffled and dealt. The players pick up their hands and assess their strength (see "Valuing the Strength of Your Hand" later in this chapter for details). In the following sections, we explain the different elements of the bidding process one step at a time. Concentrate on the mechanics of the process.

Opening the bidding

The player who deals the cards has the first opportunity to either make a bid or pass. The dealer looks at her hand; if she has sufficient strength, she makes a bid that begins to describe the strength (honor cards) and distribution (how the cards are divided). If she doesn't have enough strength to make the first bid, called the *opening bid*, she can say *pass* (not considered a bid).

Being second in line

After the dealer bids or passes, the bidding continues in a clockwise rotation. The next player can take one of two actions (for now):

>> Make a bid higher than the dealer's bid (assuming that the dealer makes an opening bid)

>> Pass

He can't make a bid unless he bids higher than the dealer's bid. See "Bidding suits in the proper order" later in this chapter for more information on determining whether one bid is higher than another bid. If you've ever attended an auction, you can see why bidding is sometimes referred to as an auction — each bid must outrank the previous one.

Responding to the opening bid

After the second player bids or passes, the bidding follows a clockwise rotation to the next player at the table, the dealer's partner. After someone opens the bidding with something other than *pass* (it's not necessarily the dealer), the partner of the opening bidder is called the *responder*.

If the dealer opens the bidding, the responder has a chance to make a bid, called a *response.* This bid begins to describe the strength and distribution of the responding hand. The partnership is looking for some suit in which they have eight or more cards together, called an *eight-card fit.* It may take a few bids to uncover an eight-card fit. Sometimes it doesn't exist, which is a bummer. The responder also has the option to pass her partner's opening bid, which communicates more information (albeit of a rather depressing nature) about the strength of her hand.

Buying the contract

The bidding continues clockwise around the table, with each player either making a bid higher than the last bid or passing. After a bid has been made, three successive passes ends the bidding. The partnership that makes the last bid has *bought the contract* and plays the hand, trying to take at least the number of tricks that corresponds to the final bid.

TIP

During the bidding, think of yourself as being in an "up-only" elevator that doesn't stop until three of its passengers say "Stop!" (or, in this case, "Pass") consecutively. Furthermore, this elevator has no down button! The only way you can stop from driving the elevator up is by saying "Pass" when it's your turn to bid.

Passing a hand out

Note one special case that comes up once in a while during bidding. Sometimes no one wants to make an opening bid, as you can see in the following bidding sequence.

West	North (Your Partner)	East	South (You)
Pass	Pass	Pass	Pass

The hand has been *passed out.* Nobody wants to get on the elevator, not even on the lowly first floor! No player has a hand strong enough to open the bidding. When a hand is passed out, the cards are reshuffled and the same person deals again.

Looking At the Structure and the Rank of a Bid

Bridge bids have a legal ranking structure all their own. Remember that each new bid any player makes must outrank the previous one.

During the bidding, players call out their bids to communicate information about their hands. Each bid you make is supposed to begin painting a picture of your strength and distribution to help the partnership arrive at the best final contract. Of course, your partner is doing the same with the same goal in mind. Bridge is a partnership game.

In the following sections, you get acquainted with the look and feel of the bids you use to describe your hand to your partner.

Knowing what elements make a proper bid

A bid consists of two elements:

>> **The suit:** During the bidding you actually deal with five suits: spades, hearts, diamonds, clubs, and notrump. (Note this expanded meaning of a suit.)

>> **The number of tricks you're bidding for in that suit:** You start with an automatic, unspoken six tricks, called a *book,* and build from there. For example a bid of one spade means you are contracting for 6 + 1 = 7 tricks.

When you make a bid, you don't say, "I want to bid three in the spade suit." Instead you simplify it: You say "three spades," "four notrump," "two diamonds," and so on. When you see bids referred to in books (including the bids in this book), the bids are abbreviated to card number and suit symbol. For example, the written equivalent of the preceding bids looks like this: 3♠ (three spades), 4NT (four notrump), and 2♦ (two diamonds).

REMEMBER

Each Bridge hand consists of exactly 13 tricks, and the minimum opening bid must be for at least 7 of those 13 tricks. Because each bid has an automatic six tricks built into it, a 1♥ bid actually says that if the bidding ends in 1♥ you have to take seven tricks with hearts trump, not just one trick. In other words, your Bridge elevator starts on the *seventh* floor.

The numbers associated with a bid correspond to bidding levels. Bids of 1♠, 1♥, 1♦, and 1♣ are called *one-level bids.* A bid that starts with a 3 is a *three-level bid.* The highest level is the seven level. (Doing a little math tells you that 7NT, 7♠, 7♥, 7♦, and 7♣ are the highest bids because 7 + 6 = 13.)

Bidding suits in the proper order

During the bidding, players can't make a bid unless their bid is higher than the previous bid. In Bridge, two factors determine whether your bid is legal:

>> Which suit you're bidding

>> How many tricks you're bidding for in that suit

REMEMBER

During the play of a hand, the rank of the suits has no significance. The rank of the suits matters only during the bidding and the scoring. The suits are ranked in the following order:

>> **Notrump (NT):** Notrump isn't really a suit in the strictest sense of the word, but notrump is considered a suit! In fact, notrump is the highest suit you can bid. Notrump is the king of the hill when it comes to bidding — you can score the most points with notrump bids.

>> **Spades (♠):** Spades is the highest-ranking suit (just below notrump).

>> **Hearts (♥):** Hearts rank below spades; hearts and spades are referred to as the *major suits* because they're worth more in the scoring (discussed in Book 5, Chapter 6).

>> **Diamonds (♦):** Diamonds don't carry as much weight; they outrank only clubs.

>> **Clubs (♣):** Clubs are the lowest suit on the totem pole. Diamonds and clubs are called the *minor suits.*

TIP

To remember the rank of the suits (excluding notrump), look at the first letter of each suit. The *S* in *spades* is higher (later) in the alphabet than the *H* in *hearts*, which is higher than the *D* in *diamonds*, which is higher than the *C* in *clubs*.

To see how the rank of the suits comes into play during the bidding, consider the following example. Assume that you are seated in the South position:

South (You)	West	North (Your Partner)	East
1♥	?		

Suppose that you open the bidding with 1♥. Because the bidding goes clockwise, West has the next chance to bid. West doesn't have to bid if he doesn't want to; however, the most likely reason for not bidding is that West simply doesn't have a strong enough hand. West can say "Pass" (which is not considered a bid).

However, if West wants to join in the fun, he must make some bid that is *higher ranking* than 1♥. For example, West can bid 1♠ or 1NT because both of these bids are higher ranking than a 1♥ bid. However, he can't bid 1♣ or 1♦ because these suits are lower than the current heart bid.

On the other hand, if West wants to bid diamonds (a lower-ranking suit than hearts), West must bid at least 2♦ for his bid to be legal. That is, only by upping the *level* of the bid (from 1 to 2) can West make a legal bid in diamonds.

Making the final bid

When three consecutive passes follow a bid, the last bid is the *final contract.* The following issues are resolved when the bidding is over:

>> **Whether the hand will be played in notrump or in a trump suit:** If the final bid is in notrump, the hand will have no wild cards, or *trump cards* (see Book 5, Chapter 3 for more information on playing at notrump). If clubs, diamonds, spades, or hearts is named in the final bid, that suit is designated as the trump suit for the hand. For example, if the final bid is 4♥, the trump suit is hearts for that hand.

>> **How many tricks need to be won:** By automatically adding six to the number of the final bid, you know how many tricks you need to take. For example, if the final contract is the popular 3NT, the partnership needs to win nine tricks to make the contract (6 + 3 = 9).

Putting it all together in a sample bidding sequence

In the following example, you can see the bids each player makes during a sample bidding sequence. You don't see the cards on which each player bases his or her bid — they aren't important for now. Just follow the bidding around the table, noting how each bid is higher than the one before it. Assume that you're in the South position.

South (You)	West	North (Your Partner)	East
1♥	Pass	2♣	2♦
3♣	3♦	4♥	Pass
Pass	Pass		

After your opening 1♥ bid, West passes and your partner (North) bids 2♣. East joins in with a bid of 2♦, a bid that is higher than 2♣. When it's your turn to bid again, you show support for your partner's clubs by bidding 3♣. Then West comes to life and supports East's diamonds by bidding 3♦. Your partner (don't forget your partner) chimes in with 4♥, a bid that silences everybody. Both East and West decide to pass, just as they would at an auction when the bidding gets too rich for their blood.

It has been a somewhat lively auction, and your side has *bought the contract* with your partner's 4♥ bid, which means you need to take ten tricks to make your contract. (Remember, a book — six tricks — is automatically added to the bid.) If you don't make your contract, the opponents score penalty points and you get zilch. The final contract of 4♥ also designates hearts as the trump suit.

REMEMBER

Keep in mind the following points about the bidding sequence:

>> Each bid made is higher ranking than the previous bid.

>> A player can pass on the first round and bid later (as West did), or a player can bid on the first round and pass later (as East did).

>> After a bid has been made and three players in a row pass, the bidding is over.

Settling Who Plays the Hand

If your partnership buys the final contract, the bidding determines who plays the hand (the *declarer*) and who kicks back and watches the action (the *dummy*). For example, if the final contract ends in some number of hearts, whoever bid hearts *first* becomes the declarer, and his partner is the dummy.

Take a look at this sample bidding sequence:

South (You)	West	North (Your Partner)	East
1♥	Pass	2♣	2♦
3♣	3♦	4♥	Pass
Pass	Pass		

The contract ends in 4♥, which is the final bid because it's followed by three passes. Both you and your partner bid hearts during the bidding. However, you bid hearts first, which makes *you* the declarer.

The player to the left of the declarer (in this case, West) makes the opening lead, and the partner of the declarer (North) is the dummy. After the opening lead, the dummy puts down her cards face-up in four vertical columns, one for each suit: the trump suit, hearts, to her right and bows out of the action.

Valuing the Strength of Your Hand

During the bidding, try to work out the strength and distribution of your partner's hand, at the same time trying to tell your partner the strength and distribution of your hand. The point of this communication is to determine the best trump suit, including notrump, and then finally to decide how many tricks to contract for. Consider two elements when valuing the strength of your hand:

>> Your high-card points (see the following section for a definition)

>> The distribution of your cards (how your cards are divided in the various suits)

In the following sections, we give you an idea of what you need in terms of strength (high-card points) and distribution (the number of cards you have in each suit) to enter the bidding.

Adding up your high-card points

REMEMBER

Your honor cards (the ace, king, queen, jack, and ten in each suit) contribute to the strength of your hand. When you pick up your hand, assign the following points to each of your honor cards:

>> **Aces:** For every ace, count 4 points (A = 4 points).

>> **Kings:** For every king, count 3 points (K = 3 points).

>> **Queens:** For every queen, count 2 points (Q = 2 points).

>> **Jacks:** For every jack, count 1 point (J = 1 point).

TIP

The 10 is also considered an honor card, but, alas, it doesn't count when adding your points initially. Patience.

These points are called *high-card points* (HCP). Most players use this barometer to measure the *initial* strength of their hand.

Each suit contains 10 HCP, totaling 40 HCP in the deck. When you know from the bidding the total number of HCP your partnership has, you'll have an easier time deciding how many tricks to contract for.

Looking for an eight-card trump fit

Why should you care about the *distribution* of the cards (that is, how many cards you or your partner has in any one suit)? For you and your partner to land in a safe trump-suit contract, you want to have at least eight cards in the same suit between the two hands, called an *eight-card trump fit*. Bidding, to a great extent, is geared toward locating such a fit, preferably in a major suit.

Chapter 6

Wrapping Up with Scorekeeping

Can you imagine playing a game without knowing how to keep score? It's unthinkable. You wouldn't know who was winning, how many points you needed to win, or when to stop playing.

Bridge is no different. The bidding is intertwined with scoring. You can't bid effectively, play, or defend intelligently unless you know how to keep score.

Over the years, Bridge scoring has undergone some minor revisions, and what we present here is a current method of scoring, called *Chicago* (also known as *four-deal Bridge*). This form of scoring is exactly the way duplicate-Bridge tournaments are scored the world over. In this chapter you discover what you need to know about this important aspect of the game.

Understanding How Bidding and Scoring Are Intertwined

During the bidding, you hope to end up in a reasonable contract that you can make. If you make your contract, you score points; if you don't make your contract, they make points. Final contracts come wrapped in three packages: *game, partscore,* and *slam.* In this section I explain the basic aspects of scoring and then tell you how to score up the result of each hand depending on the final contract and how many tricks were taken by the side that bought the contract.

Tallying up your trick score

REMEMBER

You earn a certain number of points for each trick you take beyond the sixth one. The first six tricks, which are unspoken during the bidding, do not count in the scoring of any contract.

>> When a *major suit* (hearts or spades) winds up as the trump suit, each trick taken after the first six is worth 30 points.

>> When a *minor suit* (clubs or diamonds) winds up as the trump suit, each trick taken after the first six is worth 20 points.

>> The first trick in notrump after the first six is worth 40 points, but each subsequent trick is worth 30 points.

Table 6-1 saves you time figuring out scores for each contract. Because the first six tricks don't count, the tricks taken in Table 6-1 start with seven tricks.

TABLE 6-1   **Charting Your Score**

Tricks Taken	7	8	9	10	11	12	13
Notrump	40	70	100	130	160	190	220
Spades	30	60	90	120	150	180	210
Hearts	30	60	90	120	150	180	210
Diamonds	20	40	60	80	100	120	140
Clubs	20	40	60	80	100	120	140

As an example, say your final contract was 2♥ and you took nine tricks; you made an *overtrick* (one trick more than you contracted for). Start on the left where you see *Hearts* and follow the row across until you come to the 9 column. You can see that you made 90 points.

REMEMBER

Your goal on every hand is to make your contract; making overtricks is icing on the cake. They count, of course, but do not entitle you to any bonus points (see the following section). If you don't make your contract, you don't have to worry about this table, because you don't score any points — your opponents do! (See "Not

Making the Contract: Handling Penalties" later in this chapter for more information about how to score when you don't make your contract.)

Adding up game-contract bonus points

REMEMBER

Bridge has five special contracts called *game contracts:* 3NT, 4♥, 4♠, 5♣, and 5♦. They all give you a trick score of at least 100 points. If you arrive at any of these game contracts and make them, bonus points await. Lots of them.

By far the most common game contract is 3NT. Because six assumed tricks are always added to any bid, you need to take nine tricks to make this contract. The other game contracts require 10 or 11 tricks: 4♥ and 4♠ require 10 tricks, and 5♣ and 5♦ need 11 tricks.

After making your game contract and seeing your trick score (refer to Table 6-1), here come the bonus points!

If you bid and make a game contract, you get either 300 or 500 bonus points. Why two different bonuses? The amount of the game bonus depends on whether you are *not vulnerable* or *vulnerable.* There is no mystery to being vulnerable. It means you score a bigger bonus for bidding and making a game contract, but you also incur a greater penalty if you don't make the game or slam contract that you bid for.

In the later section "Keeping Track of the Score in Four-Deal Chicago," we further explain the terms and how you know whether your side is vulnerable or not. Fortunately, vulnerability is preordained when playing Chicago. In other words, everyone knows before the hand is dealt who is vulnerable and who is not, which makes the scoring easier.

REMEMBER

The formula for scoring up any game contract is the trick score + 300 for bidding and making a not-vulnerable game or the trick score + 500 for bidding and making a vulnerable game.

Say you bid and make 3NT, not vulnerable. Your trick score is 100 points + 300 bonus points = 400 points. If you were vulnerable, your trick score would still be 100 points, but you'd add 500 bonus points, making 600 points total.

If you bid and make 4♥ or 4♠, not vulnerable, your trick score is 120 points + 300 bonus points = 420 points. Vulnerable, your trick score would be 120 points + 500 bonus points = 620 points.

If you bid and make 5♣ or 5♦, not vulnerable, your trick score is 100 points + 300 bonus points = 400 points. Vulnerable, your trick score would be 100 points + 500 bonus points = 600 points.

Wrapping Up with Scorekeeping

Earning points for a partscore contract

Any final contract lower than a game contract is called a *partscore contract.* When you and your partner feel that the combined strength of the two hands doesn't warrant bidding game, just settle for a partscore contract. After all, making a partscore contract is better than going down in a game contract!

Scoring up a partscore contract that has been made is rather simple. You simply add 50 bonus points to your trick score (which you can find in Table 6-1). For example, say your contract is 2♥ and you make it by taking your needed eight tricks. Table 6-1 shows that 60 is your trick score. To this amount you add the automatic 50 bonus points, both vulnerable and not vulnerable, for making any partscore contract, and voilà, your total score on this hand is 110 points.

Scoring up a small slam

Sometimes you have enough strength between the two hands and are courageous enough to bid a *small slam,* meaning you have to take 12 of the 13 possible tricks to make your contract. This contract is exciting and perilous because if you come up short, penalties are involved: Your opponents get penalty points while you get nada. But we don't focus on the negative here (we save that for a later section "Not Making Your Contract: Handling Penalties"). Suppose you take those 12 tricks and you do make your contract.

REMEMBER

When you bid and make a small slam, you earn a bonus of 500 or 750 on top of your game bonus. Follow this formula:

>> **Not vulnerable:** Trick score + 300 (game bonus) + 500 (small-slam bonus)

>> **Vulnerable:** Trick score + 500 (game bonus) + 750 (small-slam bonus)

Say you bid and make 6♠, not vulnerable. Hooray for your side! Your trick score is 180 points. (Refer to Table 6-1.) You get to tack on your game bonus of 300 points, plus your not-vulnerable small-slam bonus of 500 points. It all comes to 980 points!

Had you been vulnerable, your trick score would still be 180, your game bonus would be 500, and your small-slam bonus would be 750. If you add it all up, it comes to a four-digit number: 1,430!

Cashing in on a grand slam

The granddaddy of all slams is the *grand slam.* You have to bid all the way up to the seven level, the very top of the elevator, which means contracting for and taking all 13 tricks! If you do it, your score is enormous, but if you take fewer tricks, you get nothing and the opponents get penalty points. It's unbearable.

REMEMBER

Scoring up a grand slam is similar to scoring up a small slam, only with larger slam bonuses and more tension. The formula remains the same: Trick score + game bonus + grand-slam bonus. As usual, vulnerability enters into the bonus points. It works like this:

>> **Not-vulnerable grand slam:** 1,000 bonus points

>> **Vulnerable grand slam:** 1,500 bonus points

Surprise: The grand-slam bonuses are double their small-slam counterparts.

Pretend your contract is 7NT, not vulnerable, meaning you have to take all 13 tricks, and you do! Your trick score is 220 (refer to Table 6-1), which you add to a 300 game bonus and a 1,000 grand-slam bonus. Add it all up and it comes to 1,520. Not bad.

More good news. If you make a vulnerable 7NT grand slam (you're going to like this), you get a trick score of 220 + the game bonus of 500 + the grand-slam bonus of 1,500! The grand total this time is 2,220 points! You could play for a week and not score that many points.

Incidentally, after you bid and make a grand slam and you want to see happiness, glance at your partner's face. If you want to see abject misery, glance at your opponents' faces!

Keeping Track of the Score in Four-Deal Chicago

You and your partner are about to give it a go against a congenial twosome (you hope). The game can last as long as all four players want to continue playing.

In any home game, including Chicago, of course, you may agree to play the whole session with the same partner, which is called a *set game*. Not all Bridge games are set games because some people like to rotate partners. In any case, the scoring is the same.

Setting up the score sheet and Bridge wheel

In this section we introduce you to the easiest and most popular form of Bridge scoring. But first, someone has to step up to the plate and be the official score-keeper for your game, and you have been elected!

Dig up a sheet of paper to be your score sheet. Take a look at Figure 6-1 to see what your score sheet looks like, and be sure to include a *We* and a *They*. From now on, any plus score your team makes goes under *We*, and any plus score your opponents make goes under *They*.

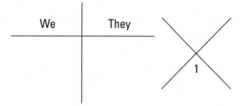

FIGURE 6-1:
Draw a few lines on your score sheet to start the scoring process.

© *John Wiley & Sons, Inc.*

You're almost ready. Now all you have to do is draw a *wheel,* which is the indicator of whose turn it is to deal the cards. Most people wouldn't know it was a wheel unless you told them! Check out Figure 6-1 again to see that all you have to do is draw a large X and call it a wheel. Think of this diagram as four open triangles, each representing a hand you are about to play.

You start by writing a *1* in the triangle directly in front of you. This mark indicates that you are the dealer on the first hand. In fact, you will be the dealer on the first hand of each new wheel. The deal and follow-up deals always rotate to the left in a clockwise manner.

REMEMBER

When playing Chicago, as well as when playing in a Bridge tournament, the vulnerability is arbitrarily assigned to you in advance. Yes, in advance!

>> **On deal 1:** Neither side is vulnerable.

>> **On deal 2:** The dealer's side only is vulnerable (your opponents).

>> **On deal 3:** The dealer's side only is vulnerable (you and your partner).

>> **On deal 4:** Both sides are vulnerable.

TIP

Keep in mind that the bonuses are different for making not-vulnerable game contracts and slams than they are for making vulnerable game and slam contracts. However, the 50-point bonus for making any partscore contract remains constant irrespective of vulnerability. Flip to the earlier section "Understanding How Bidding and Scoring Are Intertwined" for details on the various bonuses.

Scoring a Chicago wheel

Fun and games are over. Now it's time to experience playing and scoring your first Chicago wheel! Can you stand all this excitement?

On the very first hand, you're the dealer, and your side winds up playing a contract of 2♥. By sheer brilliance, you fulfill your contract and take exactly eight tricks. Your trick score is 30 × 2 = 60 + an automatic 50 for bidding and making a partscore contract (review the first half of this chapter for basic and partscore scoring). Drum roll, if you please: Chalk up 110 points and enter them so your score sheet looks like the one in Figure 6-2.

We	They
110	

1

FIGURE 6-2:
Enter your trick score on the first deal.

© John Wiley & Sons, Inc.

Now you're on to the second hand, in which the dealer's side is vulnerable. The person to your left (an opponent) deals the second hand. Before the cards are dealt, put a 2 in the triangle to your left, just as in Figure 6-3.

We	They
110	600

2
1

FIGURE 6-3:
On the second deal, they hit you with a vulnerable game!

© John Wiley & Sons, Inc.

Wrapping Up with Scorekeeping

This time, your opponents get most of the high cards and wind up in 3NT, vulnerable, and make it. They get a 100-point trick score + 500 bonus points for bidding a vulnerable game. Enter 600 points under *They*, as in Figure 6-3. Oh well, life goes on. In fact it goes on to hand 3, as shown scored up in Figure 6-4.

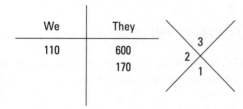

FIGURE 6-4:
Make a partscore
with an overtrick
on the third deal.

On hand 3, the dealer's side (your team) is vulnerable. With both sides bidding, the opponents eventually outbid you buying the contract at 3♠. They need nine tricks but actually take ten! They make an *overtrick* (an extra trick). Their trick score is 4 × 30 = 120 + 50 (the partscore bonus) = 170. Enter it on the *They* side, as in Figure 6-4.

Hand 4 is the last hand of the wheel. This time both sides are vulnerable, and your side is behind! You have 110 points on your side and they have 770 on theirs. Not to worry; we're rooting for you to win. On this last hand, your side bids 6♠, which is a small slam. You make it — with an overtrick! Remember the formula: the trick score (7 × 30 = 210) + the game bonus (500, because you were vulnerable) + the small-slam bonus (750; again, because you were vulnerable), and in one fell swoop you have just made 1,460 points. Enter them on the *We* side as in Figure 6-5.

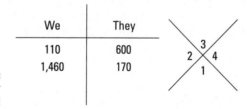

FIGURE 6-5:
Slamming your
way to victory!

After entering the 1,460 points on your side, the first wheel is history. Add up the scores under *We* (1,570) and under *They* (770) and calculate the difference, in this case 800. After you have that total, draw a double line under all scores and put 800 directly under the double line on the *We* side of the ledger (see Figure 6-6). This score represents your carryover (running total) going into the next wheel. Further scores go under the double line on either the *We* or the *They* side, and the process is repeated every four deals until quitting time.

	We	They	
	110	600	
	1,460	170	
	1,570	770	1
	800		
	(carryover)		

FIGURE 6-6: Carry over the difference, ready for the next wheel.

TIP

The carryover method of scoring is far easier than waiting until the session is over and then adding up all the scores, needing a calculator to see who has actually won! Most Bridge players like to know how they are doing as the play progresses by simply looking at the latest running total.

Not Making the Contract: Handling Penalties

In some wheels, neither side can make a contract even if their lives depend on it. When you don't make your contract, you're penalized when reckoning time comes at the end of the hand. Welcome to the sad world of *going set*, *going down*, or *failing*. All these terms mean the same ugly thing: You didn't take enough tricks to make your contract. When you come up short, the missing tricks are called *undertricks*, and in this section we tell you the sad truth about the points they'll cost you.

TIP

Don't despair when you don't make your contract. The fact is that about one-third of all contracts bite the dust. You may not have done anything wrong. You may have run into a ghastly suit division in the opponents' hands, making the contract impossible to realize. In fact, sometimes you get an advantage by bidding more than you think you can make because your loss is less than the number of points they could have made in the contract they were in. This move is called making a *sacrifice* bid — a big part of the game.

When you don't make your contract, opponents score penalty points on the *They* side of the score sheet.

>> **Not vulnerable:** 50 points per undertrick

>> **Vulnerable:** 100 points per undertrick

As an example, say your contract is 4♠ and you need ten tricks to make it. Alas, you wind up with only nine. The normal way to describe this scenario is 4♠ *down one*. Because you've gone down in a contract, your opponents get the penalty points. If you aren't vulnerable, they get 50 points; if you are vulnerable, they score 100 points.

Wrapping Up with Scorekeeping

6
Trying to Beat the House: Casino Gambling

Contents at a Glance

Chapter 1

Casino Gambling 101: The Inside Scoop

When you step into a modern megacasino, prepare to be dazzled. Blinking lights and ringing bells signal jackpots. Glittering chandeliers and rich furnishings and fabrics often mimic the sequined gowns and dapper dress of the folks at the high-roller tables. Clinking ice chills your drinks, and courteous staff appear to serve your every whim. When you see and hear these characteristics, you know you've walked into a fantasy world where every hand you play can be a winner, and every pull on the slot machine may make all your dreams come true.

Lucky gamblers make fortunes every day, but the reality is that most money ends up on the *other* side of the table. And the casino, or the *house*, is willing to pour millions of its profits into making sure you walk inside, stay inside, and — most important — gamble inside.

Always remember that, in addition to wanting your business, casinos provide a service to you, so you have every right to shop around for the establishment that best serves your needs. To assist you in your shopping, some casinos have websites where you can take a 360-degree virtual tour without ever leaving your house. We hope this chapter accomplishes a similar goal.

In this chapter we explain and prepare you for what to expect when you step foot into a casino and give you not only a glimpse of the razzle-dazzle designed to distract you but also the blueprint of the typical casino. We explain why this goes here, that goes there, and with whom you interact. Finally, we introduce you to who's watching you while you wander onward with your hand on your wallet and mind in the painted clouds on the starlit ceiling.

(Casino) Knowledge Is Power

The shrewdly packaged allure of the casino starts the minute you pull up to the glittering facade. From neon signs to valets to the smooth hum of the sliding-glass doors, the modern casino entrance is designed to attract you. Every possible consideration is given to design, color, and lighting.

The scheme doesn't end at the front steps, however. As you proceed through the casino's front door, every square inch of floor space entices you into moving forward. Like a siren call, the sounds of winning jackpots beckon you onward, as do the color schemes, floral arrangements, glittering lights, slot machines, and table games. If you aren't prepared, you may become disoriented inside a casino. The master plan behind the traffic flow is to bring you (and your wallet) into close proximity with the slot machines or table games at every opportunity. The pulsating pace of the gambling world is seductive and makes it hard for you to leave a winner.

Feeling overwhelmed — and not a little manipulated? It can be deflating to discover that the sounds, sights, and even smells are devised to lull you into a mesmerized state where you continue emptying your wallet into the casino coffers. But a casino visit doesn't have to be a Svengali-like experience.

REMEMBER

Don't let the harsh realities of the casino world turn you off. Embrace them, because knowledge is power. And by understanding the psychology of casino design and getting to know the employees who perform their duties within the casino, you put yourself in a better position not only to enjoy the casino as an entertaining leisure activity but also to maintain the level-headedness and critical thinking required to succeed at your gambling ventures.

Your mission is to educate yourself *before* you enter these temples of chance. If you build your understanding of the components of a casino and the people who make it run, you're more likely to make rational decisions when it comes to the games you choose to play — and less likely to part with the contents of your pocketbook because of some subliminal pull.

Entering the Casino: What You're Up Against

The first secret to gambling success is to understand the inner workings of the casino world before you're seduced by the flash and dazzle. Casinos are sophisticated and highly successful enterprises — and they don't get that way by giving away money. Your best bet, then, is to be aware of basic casino operations so you can manipulate the experience to your advantage.

Marketing their way to your wallet

They see you coming from miles away. They know exactly who you are, how much money you make, what you like and dislike, and whether you're married, single, or divorced. Who are these omniscient watchers who track your secrets? The IRS? CIA? Political campaign organizers?

None of the above. I'm talking about the marketing gurus at modern casinos. They're constantly studying reams of data on millions of gamblers to develop profiles of guests who most willingly spend their discretionary income on a couple hours of distraction.

Nothing is left to chance in a modern casino. Every possible element, from the design of the wallpaper to the thickness of the carpet, is there to draw you in and keep you gambling as long as possible. All the colors, sights, sounds, and sensations serve one purpose: to make you happy — even when you lose.

Accepting the odds: The house rules

The casino's first commandment is "The house shall always win." A couple of games permit sharp players to break even or eke out a small edge occasionally. But casinos are in business to make money, so for most players, winning is a losing proposition.

Why? Here is a reason, stated three different ways:

>> The house charges a *vigorish* (commission) in some games, such as sports betting.

>> In many games, the casino doesn't pay out *true odds*.

In roulette, for example, there are 37-to-1 odds of guessing the right number. But if you win, the payout is only 35 to 1. This difference may seem small, but that discrepancy actually gives the house one of the biggest edges in the casino. (Refer to Book 6, Chapter 2 for an explanation of *true odds* and Book 6, Chapter 7 for more info on roulette.)

» The casino has a *house edge* — a mathematical advantage over the player in any game. Throughout the casino, players must overcome odds that aren't favorable to winning. (Read more about the edge in Book 6, Chapter 2.)

REMEMBER

Your goal is to find games where the casino has the lowest edge. Craps is a great example. This fun, exciting game offers great odds — if you stay away from the *bad* bets. We explore craps in Book 6, Chapter 6.

Protecting your money with a plan

TIP

For most people, developing a strategy for doling out their gambling bankroll can keep them out of serious trouble. Set a budget and stick to it. Consider contingencies (such as losing your bankroll in the first few minutes of your visit) and know how to respond when your wallet gets whacked.

Your strategy, however, is only as good as your willpower. Nothing jacks up casino profits faster than undisciplined gamblers. If you're an impulsive type, then gambling may leave your bank account looking like it just went 15 rounds with a heavyweight boxing champion. (Refer to Book 6, Chapter 3, where we discuss important money-management issues.)

Now, it's certainly true that most people can save their money by avoiding casinos altogether. So the best advice we can give to folks who don't want to lose money is simple: Don't gamble! But the conservative and prudent path in life isn't the only choice. Gambling can be a great way to spice up a vacation and break out of a boring routine. Gambling is all about taking a risk — exposing yourself to a chance of loss.

WARNING

However, don't overdo it. Government studies show that as many as 1 in every 25 adults has a problem with compulsive gambling. Think about that the next time you sit down at a blackjack table. Several people in the pit probably shouldn't be there.

Identifying the colors of the rainbow

Knowledge is power and is your only ally against the formidable forces that threaten to separate you from your hard-earned cash. One piece of knowledge you definitely need, particularly if you're going to wade into the shark-infested waters of table games, is to be able to identify the varying colors and matching denominations of standard casino chips.

REMEMBER

The casinos make this bit easy for you because the chips also have a denomination printed on them so you know the red chip, for instance, is worth $5 and the green chip is worth $25. The following is a comprehensive list of common casino-chip colors, as well as their corresponding values:

>> White: $1

>> Red: $5

>> Green: $25

>> Black: $100

>> Purple: $500

>> Burgundy: $1,000

>> Brown: $5,000

Navigating the Casino Maze

From Monaco, the Las Vegas of Europe, to any modern-day cruise ship, most casinos of the world are laid out in a similar floor plan. Even at the smaller clubs, you recognize many of the same aesthetic and functional characteristics found at the megaresorts. This common design is no accident — casino owners have an intimate knowledge of the gambler's mind, and they design the interiors to make their guests comfortable with parting with their cash.

This section takes a stroll through a typical casino to prepare you for the sights and sounds you encounter when you walk through those neon-bathed doorways. Preparation is the key for maintaining control. You'll understand what we're saying when you find yourself subconsciously reaching for your wallet before you finish the chapter.

TIP

Remember that gambling is the ultimate impulse buy. The casino's layout encourages this impulse. Taking away the mystique is your first step toward improving your odds and coming out a winner. We suggest that, in addition to the virtual walk-through you get by reading this chapter, you do the same in every brick-and-mortar establishment you visit before you drop your first dollar on the table or pump a coin in a slot. Prepare yourself: Stand still, take a deep breath, and look around.

Getting in is the easy part

It may surprise you how fast you can find yourself in the middle of the sensory hurricane on the casino floor. In less restrictive states, such as Nevada and New Jersey, you can walk in off the street or get dropped off by a taxi and find yourself a few feet away from the gaming areas. You're practically holding the door for your significant other with one hand and rolling the dice with the other. After all, casinos want as little as possible to stand between you and your favorite game.

But most casinos give you a chance to catch your breath and do some mental stretching prior to plunging into the action. When you walk in, you often find yourself in a lobby or foyer. Remember that most casinos are also hotels, so you may see familiar sights, such as the concierge, bell desk, and check-in counter. People bustle about and crowd together before they find the destinations suited for them. While some gamblers are anticipating the excitement just steps away, others are exiting with delirious grins on their faces — or expressions of shock and awe.

This bottleneck is no accident; it's part of the calculated marketing strategy to lure you ever closer to the games. At the threshold of the gaming floor, the sounds, colorful lights, and crowd energy all go to work on your senses, even from a distance. Just like an infant reaching for bright colorful objects, casino visitors gravitate to the sights and sounds of the casino floor.

Interior design is to a casino floor plan what aerodynamics is to automobile manufacturers; forward movement is a result of an ever-expanding array of enticements including colors that dazzle, lights that entice, and a temperature scientifically controlled for maximum comfort. You quickly find that every destination in a casino — the guest elevators, the bathrooms, or the buffet — requires that you walk through (or dangerously near) the gaming areas.

Slot machines and video poker stations are positioned just inside the casino entrance. The boys in marketing put them here so you can test the waters and feel the rush a quarter at a time — getting your feet wet right at the casino entrance. Up ahead you see the casino proper, a virtual indoor carnival buzzing with excitement. You can almost feel the energy pulsing.

Slot machines: Place them and they will come

As you enter the casino proper, you see hopeful gamblers feeding tens, twenties, or payout tickets into slot machines, hoping to reap spitting, buzzing payoffs. You operate a slot machine by pushing the buttons or yanking down on the lever to the side. Larger casinos hold aisle after aisle of slots, like rows of corn.

REMEMBER

Casinos typically place the most profitable slot machines within easy access to the main traffic aisles, such as the foyer, restaurants, and bars, and are extremely careful to place high-hit frequency slots within earshot of the thronging masses.

If you venture farther onto the casino floor, you can see this philosophy in action. Clusters of people sit at the corner slots, sometimes two-deep as the individuals standing in line patiently await their turn to enjoy the payoffs. As you venture down the aisles of slots, you may find a few open machines, but not many. As one row ends, another aisle begins. Some of the most popular machines are Double Diamond and Wheel of Fortune. (See Book 6, Chapter 8 for more slot info.)

Table games: Penetrating the inner circle

Just as the sun is the center of the solar system, the table games rest in the middle of the casino system, attracting visitors ever inward and at the same time providing the main source of energy and vitality to the floor. Table games are grouped together into areas known in casino lingo as *pits*. The pits are separated from slot machines, restaurants, and other casino functions by a wide aisle, allowing nonplayers to watch the action and vicariously enjoy the thrill of turning over the winning card or nailing the winning roll.

Table games you can play include

>> **Baccarat:** The classic card game is often played in a separate room to create a more civilized and secluded atmosphere; see Book 6, Chapter 6.

>> **Blackjack:** Determine your own fate with smart decisions and timely double downs; see Book 6, Chapter 5.

>> **Craps:** Roll the dice and hear the crowd roar in the most boisterous game on the floor; see Book 6, Chapter 7.

>> **Poker:** It's just like your neighborhood game, except you never have to shuffle; see Book 2.

>> **Roulette:** Pick a number, place your bet, and then watch the spinning wheel go round and round; see Book 6, Chapter 8.

REMEMBER

If you're a high roller, the most exclusive gaming tables with the highest betting limits are often in adjoining rooms, separated by glass from the other tables. They feature fancy amenities, such as private cocktail servers or a bar.

But most table games are designed for moderate bettors. The loud, boisterous call of a lively crowd gathered around the craps table can seem like a siren song to players tempted to leave the boredom and repetition of the slots, and that's no accident. The intimate nature of the poker table beckons would-be strategists, while the smoky haze surrounding a blackjack game cries out to the novice with its lack of intimidation.

The bar: Quiet escape — or not?

Most casinos have a bar that's central to the main action. A large casino may offer numerous bars interspersed throughout the floor, each with a unique theme. Some feature live music, and some are simply service bars where you can take a quick pit stop away from the flow of traffic. But if you're picturing a quiet setting of soft music, hushed whispers, and clinking glasses, you're going to be disappointed. There's no escaping the games: Casino bars are in the midst of the lively pits.

REMEMBER

Casinos profit from the fact that alcohol lubricates the ATM card. But no casino wants drunk patrons, so the line they walk is a delicate one, and the policy on pushing alcohol consumption may vary from place to place. In addition, every state has different laws governing alcohol consumption inside its casinos, so there is no single unifying rule about how alcohol is handled inside betting areas. Some tribal casinos don't serve it at all, so if sipping on a stiff one as you play is important, make sure you do your homework before you leave home. The bottom line: The drinking environment varies widely, so the smartest play is to find a scene that suits your tastes, and always strive to stay in complete control.

TIP

If you don't feel like leaving your table to head to the bar, most casinos have servers who take drink orders. You can pay and tip them with chips from the casino or cash. However, if you want to eat, most casinos don't allow eating at the table. You need to visit one of the many restaurants to chow down.

Cashing out: Heading to the cashier's cage

The cashier's *cage* is where you redeem your *markers* — the chips the casino uses to represent cash — for hard cash and where you redeem your slot payout ticket. (You must buy your chips at the tables, and you must cash out at the cashier's cage.)

Every casino has cashier's cages — the larger the casino, the more cages you find. If the slot machines and gaming tables are the arteries that circulate a casino's input and output, the cashier's cage is the heart that pumps the casino's lifeblood: money. Highly trained and supremely trusted casino employees handle more cash each shift than most people see in a lifetime.

Cashier's cages are easy to find. Casinos typically locate them along the sides of the rooms to allow the more valuable floor space for games. Here, much like at a bank, one or more tellers deal with the public through a window.

CASINO CASHIERS: BEHIND BARS NO MORE

In the old days, the cashier's cage earned its moniker because it was, as the name implies, behind bars. Today's technology and construction make the modern cashier's cage much more inviting, providing maximum security without looking like Fort Knox. You can usually find casino cashiers in the core of the casino layout, as far from any exit as possible, which means the casino's money is more secure. This location also offers a beneficial side effect that casinos are happy to take advantage of. Their centrality means the cashier's cage is often in the lion's den of the most enticing betting areas, tempting many recent winners to *recycle* their bills by turning them right back into chips at a nearby table.

REMEMBER

If you're worried about leaving with your big winnings, you can request a check or get a safety deposit box in most casinos.

TIP

In addition to the cashier's cage, casinos usually offer a credit office. Depending on how big a player you are and the type of games you want to attack, you may want to ask for a line of credit. You can also get change, receive incoming money via a wire service, and even receive bank wire transfers (with proper ID, of course!). If you're interested in a line of credit, check out Book 6, Chapter 3, where we provide all the pros and cons.

Meeting the Casino's Cast of Characters

A vast and sometimes complicated hierarchy of employees with a variety of titles, responsibilities, and even different styles of dress populates a casino. These workers simultaneously cater to the needs of the guests and the casino owners. No matter who they are, the casino employees all have one goal in common: to provide you with ample opportunities to try your luck against the unevenly stacked house odds.

Casino employees are usually pleasant, professional, and well-trained individuals (after all, if you're treated with courtesy and respect, you're more likely to stay — and spend — longer). In this section, we introduce you to the pleasant cast of characters you may encounter, and we explain their unique roles. With this knowledge, you're better equipped to take advantage of their services — to *your* advantage.

In the pits: Serving the table players

As you explore the responsibilities of the various casino personnel, it helps to split the casino into two parts:

>> The area where slot machines appear in endless rows (see the section "Slot employees: The reel dealers").

>> The area where you play table games, such as blackjack, craps, or roulette.

The casino arranges the tables in clusters, similar to wagon trains encircled to protect against an attack. These groups of tables are known as *pits*. Each pit is designed to be an autonomous, fully functioning business, equipped with a variety of table games and a small community of casino personnel that is always willing to usher your dollar bills into the casino coffers.

Pit bosses

Pit bosses are smartly attired, experienced professionals who are responsible for all the gaming operations in their assigned pits. As the name implies, pit bosses are just that: bosses. They supervise floorpersons (see the next section), dealers (see the section "Dealers"), and the players within their pit. Theirs is a very detail-oriented job, requiring not only intimate knowledge of all aspects of the games but also the ability to keep track of thousands of dollars flowing through their spheres of influence. Even though the average gambler probably doesn't have much contact with a pit boss, in the event of a serious dispute, the pit boss is the one who steps in to settle matters.

Among other tasks, pit bosses monitor *credit markers,* or the amount of credit extended to you (we explore credit markers in greater detail in Book 6, Chapter 3), and they dispense *comps,* such as free meals or shows (see "Casino hosts" later in this chapter for the lowdown on comps), doled out according to an elaborate formula based on the number of hours you play and the amount of money you wager.

Winning or losing vast sums of money often ignites supercharged emotions. Another responsibility of the pit boss is to make sure those emotions don't explode into conflict. The pit boss is there to congratulate as well as to calm, to soothe as well as to strong-arm. The pit boss's job is part security staff, part supervisor, part gambling expert, and part public relations manager.

Floorpersons

Reporting to each pit boss (see the previous section) are several other *suits* known as *floorpersons*. The main difference from pit bosses is that floorpersons are in charge of only a couple of tables in the pit and report directly to the pit boss. They dress and act like the pit boss, and you typically can't distinguish between the two without asking. Both of them make sure that proper casino procedure is followed. These procedures include refilling dealer chip racks, monitoring markers, and handing out comps, all while remaining cool and calm.

Dealers

For most people, gambling is a social sport. Because the machine games are a more solitary venture, many players prefer the camaraderie of table gaming. *Dealers* are at the center of this emotional wheel of fun. Excellent customer-service skills are a requirement; after all, dealers stand on the front line when it comes to irate, belligerent, or inebriated gamblers. Even during high-pressure situations, dealers must promote a relaxed and pleasant atmosphere.

Dealers have their fingers on the pulse of the casino — figuratively and literally. Their hands, after all, deal the blackjacks and the full houses and take the money you lose or pay off your winners. Theirs is a high-pressure job with a demanding audience. Overseeing several players at a table, dealers must be confident in their gambling knowledge. They must know who wins, who loses, and how much to pay out on each hand. Many players mistakenly believe that dealers simply shuffle and deal cards, but dealers must also handle dice, chips, and money — accurately and quickly.

REMEMBER

Dealers have a wide range of personalities. Some are polite and ebullient, others efficient and brusque. Although finding a compatible dealer doesn't change the cards or the size of your winnings, it can make your gaming experience more enjoyable and, sometimes, that's as much as you can ask for. You can spot a good dealer by his or her smile, humor, demeanor, and often the size of the crowd at the table. When you find one you like, sit down, but remember the dealer has no control over the outcome. Most dealers prefer that you win because they make their money primarily from tips.

Slot employees: The reel dealers

The average American casino makes nearly two-thirds of its profits from its various slot machines. Much is at stake along the rows and rows of cling-clanging slot machines and electronic games. Therefore, casinos are diligent when it comes to maintaining and stocking them for long-term play. Just like the pit bosses and dealers who watch over the table games (see the previous section), the staff members assigned to the slot machines — the slot attendants and the slot supervisors — keep a careful eye on their vast realm.

Slot attendants

The person you're most likely to deal with if you have a problem or question about your machine is a *slot attendant.* Slot machine attendants are on constant vigil, ever watchful for the next jackpot or flashing light requesting service. The attendants, who are usually in uniform, are the perfect people to ask if you're not sure how to play a particular machine; they know every bell, cherry, and bar like the back of their hand.

REMEMBER

If you need assistance with a game, summon a slot attendant, who's usually at your beck and call. However, if a machine needs repair, the slot attendant calls a slot technician.

Slot supervisors

The slot supervisor rules the realm of the slot machines, managing employees and overseeing the maintenance and upkeep of the machines. The slot supervisor generally has several slot attendants as direct reports. Casual gamblers generally won't interact with slot supervisors.

Management: Running the tables

In addition to the employees who ensure the smooth-running operations on the floor, a host of other casino personnel contribute to the success of the house. As a beginning casino player, you may not come into contact with any of these people. However, if you do, management employees, such as the casino host, may become familiar (and friendly) faces.

Casino hosts

Modern casino hosts best resemble a successful hotel concierge: They're both at your service. Whether dealing with new guests, loyal customers, or high rollers, the casino host focuses on service, service, and more service.

A typical casino host is an affable and professional employee whose mission is to serve your every need. Hosts are hands-on people who greet VIP guests at the door and pamper them throughout their stay. Depending on the size and popularity of the casino and the thickness of your wallet, a casino host may

>> Comp your rooms

>> Arrange for greens fees at the golf course

>> Get tickets to sold-out shows

>> Give away free meals

If it's your first time in a casino, don't expect to have the keys to the penthouse at Caesar's Palace handed to you. But even low rollers can make a relationship with the casino host profitable. Keep the following in mind:

>> **Join the club:** The casino host expects you to be a casino loyalty club member before you're offered many comps. And don't forget to use your club card whenever you play.

>> **Express yourself:** Don't wait for the host to find you in the penny slots area; go introduce yourself to the host.

>> **Be loyal:** Find your favorite gambling locale and stick to it. Even small-scale visits can make you a valuable customer if they're repeated regularly.

>> **Just ask:** The players who get comps are the ones who ask the casino host. Don't be rude or demanding, just ask politely and see what benefits you qualify for.

Player development is all about forming relationships. Casino hosts are eager to wine and dine you if they believe they can create player loyalty through these lavish perks. Although player-development departments often employ telemarketers or other representatives to reach out to players through databases, casino hosts achieve their goals on a one-on-one basis by working their cellphones and roaming the casino floors, seeking ways to make their clients' gaming experiences more enjoyable.

Other managers

As in other walks of life, every casino employee has to report to somebody, and those somebodies are the *shift managers.* The shift managers then report to the casino manager. As the name implies, shift managers are responsible for their areas of casino expertise (such as slots or table games) during a particular shift (day, swing, and graveyard). Most land-based casinos are 24/7 operations, so shift managers must be prepared to work weekends, holidays, and late-night shifts.

When player disputes arise, money needs to be accounted for or items need to be authorized; the shift manager takes on these duties as well. Shift managers are responsible for employee schedules, customer service, comps, credit, and a host of other duties that make for a mind-boggling job.

The only position above the shift manager is the casino manager. You rarely see this head honcho on the floor, but he's the ultimate decision-maker for most gaming operations. As a beginning casino player, you aren't too concerned about who the casino manager is. The only time you may ever interact with the manager is if you win enough money to buy the casino.

Maintaining a Safe and Secure Environment

In today's massive casinos, five-star hotels merge with gargantuan, themed buildings, encompassing entire city blocks and housing restaurants, bars, theaters, nightclubs, gaming tables, slot machines, ATMs, snack bars, gift shops, and even the occasional theme park. A casino's security division, therefore, must function much like the police department of an entire town.

This section explains who the security personnel are, lets you in on who's watching you, and details how you can be proactive to protect yourself when betting your hard-earned money.

Security personnel: The human touch

In the old days, casinos simply had hired muscle watch after the owners' millions. These days, casino security folks are considered important members of a casino's floor team. Because it's a dynamic and demanding job, casino security has become a true career; casinos offer competitive salaries and benefits so they can hire people who are mentally *and* physically fit.

REMEMBER

Security staffs have a two-pronged task:

>> Protect the casino's property

>> Safeguard the casino's guests

Unfortunately, a security employee's job is made less agreeable by the fact that one task doesn't always go hand in hand with the other. For instance, some guests are also out to separate a casino from its money, either through cheating or through faking an injury in crowded conditions.

The responsibilities of security employees range from viewing the rows of surveillance cameras in high-tech rooms to patrolling the casino floors, constantly on vigil for fights, thieves, drunks, and other disturbances. Surprisingly, security also keeps a close eye on the help — casino employees have initiated many cheating scams over the years.

You can easily spot the security staff; they're always available to help you resolve a conflict or point you in the right direction. Even though every casino is different, security staff typically wear a uniform that is quasi-military, with a shirt that says *SECURITY* or at least a nametag or badge that identifies them as such. Other identifying features include a walkie-talkie, a badge, and possibly a gun.

Bigger hotels can have several dozen security officers working at the busiest times of day and a supervisor in each major area of the casino who manages the team. Security supervisors must wear many hats, including the hat of a diplomat. Their staff is on the front lines, both protecting and ejecting guests, and when the occasional temper flares or a misunderstanding arises, the security supervisor must wade in to render an on-the-spot verdict.

Surveillance: The eye in the sky

On-site security personnel at a casino can only see so much when trying to protect the casino and its guests. To assist them in their daily rounds, security personnel rely on electronic surveillance — *the eye in the sky.*

One-way glass conceals thousands of digital cameras in any casino. Some are hidden where you least expect them. Others are prominent, large, and noticeable to serve as warnings. Technology is such today that sophisticated cameras can see not only a player's face but also the cards in his or her hands and even the serial numbers on dollar bills. On-site security personnel can view banks of television screens to identify cheats and save casinos millions of dollars each year.

REMEMBER

Although most surveillance is for the detection and prevention of cheating and swindling, the eye in the sky also protects honest gamblers from slick crooks prowling the casino for easy prey. The newer casinos have cameras outside the building, such as in the parking garages, to cast the safety net farther for you.

Taking safety into your own hands

The modern casino should be a carefree environment where you forget your troubles, spend money, and — with hope — win some money back. Although winning isn't always possible, at the very least you expect a safe environment in which to gamble. Unfortunately, where innocent, naive, and trusting people congregate in great numbers — surrounded by huge amounts of disposable income — the predators of society gather as well. Thieves are on the prowl for ways to separate you or even the casinos from hard-earned cash.

TIP

Although casinos implement the most stringent security measures and the latest in state-of-the-art surveillance technology, you, as a prudent casino guest, should assume responsibility for your own safety. The following tips can help you avoid becoming a victim of a casino predator:

>> Tuck your wallet in a safe, hard-to-access spot, such as your front pocket.

>> If you carry a purse, take a small one that you can wear close to your body, preferably under a jacket or wrap.

>> Guard your chips or slot payout tickets; these work the same as money, so treat them accordingly.

>> If you go to the casino solo, be cautious about the overly friendly people you meet. Maintain tight control of your personal information, get your drinks straight from the cocktail servers, and keep your big wins to yourself so you don't become a target.

Chapter 2

Probability and Odds: What You Need to Succeed

Some people think gambling and casino games are only for dummies, something along the lines of "a fool and his money are soon parted." Although it's true that most people who gamble do lose, the *real* dummies are the ones who take on the casinos without first educating themselves — especially on concepts about probability and odds, understanding the house edge, and identifying which games offer the best chance for success.

Sounds like the intro to a lecture in higher mathematics? Don't worry, this chapter is brief — just enough to prepare you to walk through those casino doors and make sound gambling choices.

Defining Luck: A Temporary Fluctuation

Unfortunately, too many newbie gamblers rely on luck to guide their experiences. Casinos can be an easy place to burn through money, so your best chance for hanging on to that hard-earned cash is through a little dose of knowledge. But, you wonder, when it comes to striking it rich in the casino, isn't there such a thing as luck? Technically, the answer is *yes* — but don't count on your rabbit's foot to keep you on the path to riches over the long haul. The term *luck* can describe many situations, especially in gambling. Someone may have a lucky run at the blackjack table, or maybe your Aunt Rosemary plays a lucky slot machine that never loses.

REMEMBER

But to have a realistic perspective of your chances in the casino, you need to view luck in rational and mathematical terms: *Luck* is a temporary fluctuation or deviation from the norm. In the short run, you may perceive that you got real lucky when the dealer busted eight hands in a row at blackjack. But in reality, such an event is just normal fluctuation — also known as a *random walk* — such as when the stock market drifts one direction or another.

For example, in Caribbean Stud poker, for every $100 you wager, you can expect to lose about five bucks. Yet over the short run, anything can happen. You may get lucky and finish the day ahead— or you may get unlucky and lose far more than $5.

In a purely mathematical sense, neither of these results has anything to do with luck. They are simply the normal consequences of fluctuation. For example, try flipping a coin. Half the time it should be tails and half heads. But over a short-term sampling, it can veer far away from 50 percent.

Understanding the Role of Probability

Millions of merry gamblers frequent casinos all over the world every day without a clear understanding of one important concept — probability. Mastering one of the more complex branches of mathematics isn't necessary for successful gambling. But an elementary understanding of probability is certainly helpful in making sound gambling choices.

REMEMBER

Probability is the study of the laws of chance, the identification of how often certain events can be expected to occur. For example, to express the probability that a coin will turn up heads, you can give the result in numerous ways, such as a

>> **Ratio** — 1 in 2 times

>> **Fraction** — ½ or half the time

>> **Percentage** — 50 percent

>> **Decimal** — 0.50, which is the same as 50 percent

>> **Odds** — 1 to 1

> *Odds* expresses the number of times something *won't* happen next to the
> number of times it *will* happen. So, 1-to-1 odds means the event is an even
> money event; it has an equal chance of occurring or not occurring.

(If you're biting at the bit to find out more in-depth info about probability, check
out *Probability For Dummies* by Deborah Rumsey, PhD, [John Wiley & Sons, Inc.].)
This section looks a bit closer at probability's role in casino gambling.

Identifying independent events

Another important term to understand here is *independent* outcomes. Being independent has nothing to do with successfully ditching your loser boyfriend in the
keno lounge. In gambling, independent refers to events (such as roulette spins or
dice throws) that aren't affected by any previous results. Craps and roulette are
great examples. The dice and roulette table ball don't have a tiny brain inside, so
each new throw or spin is independent of all previous turns. In other words, the
dice or ball doesn't know what numbers are running hot or cold, so the probability
of outcome for each and every spin is exactly the same.

Slot machines are also independent. Recent jackpots do *not* change the likelihood
of the same combination coming up again. If your chances of lining up three cherries are 5,000 to 1 and you just hit the jackpot, the three cherries have exactly the
same chances of appearing on the very next spin.

Recognizing dependent events

So you may be asking yourself, what constitutes a nonindependent or dependent
event? *Dependent* events are occurrences that are *more* or *less* likely based on the
previous occurrences. Imagine a bag of five black balls and five red balls. *Before*
you pull a ball out, you know you have a 50 percent chance of pulling out a black
ball and the *same odds* of pulling out a red ball. Then you reach in and pull out
one red ball and toss it aside. Now *the odds have changed* — you no longer have a
50 percent chance of pulling either ball. Your chances of pulling out a black ball
are now *greater* (56 percent).

So in some situations, the past does affect the future. Another classic example
is the game of blackjack. Because cards are removed after they're played, the
remaining composition of the deck changes. For example, your chances for getting a blackjack drop dramatically when a disproportionate number of aces are
used up.

REMEMBER

Almost all casino games consist of cards, dice, spinning wheels, or reels. These games almost always yield independent events. Blackjack is the rare exception, which is the main reason for its popularity.

Factoring in the odds

REMEMBER

To be a successful gambler, you must understand the intersection of statistics, probability, and odds. In simple terms, that means you need to understand how likely something is to happen (*statistics*), how likely that it can happen to you (*probability*), and what you're going to get out of it, if it does happen (*odds*). With a grasp of these concepts, you're ready to tackle the casino with realistic expectations, and you can understand why some games should be avoided.

The best example to start with is the coin flip. You probably know that heads and tails each have a 50-50 shot at turning up. As we say in the previous section, you can communicate the probability of the flip in terms of odds. In the case of a two-sided coin, your odds of flipping heads are 1 to 1. In other words, with two possible events (outcomes), you have one chance to fail and one chance to succeed. Clear as mud? Here's another example. Consider the roll of a six-sided die. What are the odds that you'll roll a 3? The ratio is 1 in 6, so the odds are 5 to 1.

REMEMBER

Odds are, you'll hear the word *odds* used in other contexts. For example, the amount of money a bet pays compared to the initial bet are sometimes called *odds* too. But don't confuse *payout odds* with *true odds*. True odds refer to the actual chance that a specific occurrence will happen, which is usually different from the casino payout odds.

Examining How Casinos Operate and Make Money: House Edge

The seasoned gambler can count on true odds to dictate the chances of winning a particular game, right? Not exactly. Casinos aren't in the charity business — they exist to make money. And like all successful enterprises, they follow reliable business models. With their intimate understanding of probability and odds, casino owners guarantee themselves a healthy bottom line.

REMEMBER

So you can't beat the odds when the house arranges them in its favor, but you can understand the odds of winning inside a casino by arming yourself with information about the *house edge*. The house edge (sometimes known as the *casino advantage* or *house advantage*) by definition is the small percentage of all wagers that the casino expects to win. Every game has a different house edge, and even certain bets within a single game have a better house edge than other bets.

To put it a different way, casinos expect to pay out slightly less money to winning bettors than they take in from losing bettors. The laws of probability tell casinos how often certain bets win relative to how often they lose. Casinos then calculate the payout odds based on the winning probabilities, or true odds. The payouts are typically smaller than the true odds, ensuring that, with enough betting action, the casino will take in a certain amount with every dollar wagered.

Table 2-1 shows the house edge for popular casino games and how much you can expect to lose for an average three-day weekend of betting for gamblers playing $10 a hand at table games. As you can see, the higher the house edge, the more you can expect to lose. For example, you cut your losses by 80 percent if you switch from roulette to baccarat!

TABLE 2-1

The House Edge for Popular Casino Games

Game	House Edge	Loss per $8,000 in Total Bets
Baccarat	1.06 percent	$85
Blackjack	0.50 percent	$40
Craps	1.36 percent	$109
Caribbean Stud Poker	5.22 percent	$418
Let It Ride	3.51 percent	$281
Pai Gow Poker	2.54 percent	$203
Roulette	5.26 percent	$421
Three-Card Poker	3.37 percent	$270
Video Poker	0.46 percent	$37

This table assumes you only make the most optimal bets at games such as baccarat and craps. Also, the edge for many games, such as video poker or blackjack, varies depending on the particular type and version you find and on how skillfully you play. This next section looks at the three methods that casinos use to assist themselves in performing profitably.

Charging a fee

With some games, casinos charge a fee, or commission. Baccarat is a perfect example. If you bet on the banker's hand and win, a 5 percent commission is deducted from your winning bet. This fee tilts the odds slightly in favor of the house and ensures that the casino makes a profit at this popular table game. Another example of fees is in sports betting. The house adds what is called *vigorish* or *vig* (a commission) to every wager.

Paying less than the true odds

Another way the casino makes money is to pay out less than the true odds (see the earlier section "Factoring in the odds"). Take roulette: With 38 numbers on the wheel, your odds of guessing the winning number are 37 to 1. So you bravely place a $100 bet on a single number and hit it. Congratulations! After you quit jumping up and down and kissing the cocktail server, dealer, and anyone else who couldn't quickly escape, you collect $3,500.

But, wait a minute. $3,500 means a payoff of 35 to 1. What happened to the true odds of 37 to 1? The fact is, even though you win, your payoff is less than the true odds. The bottom line? Casinos take $200 out of every $3,800 wagered, which leaves the house with a hefty edge of 5.26 percent.

Muddying the odds

Casinos offer three types of games — games with fixed odds, games with variable odds, and games where skill can affect the odds. They all have different styles of play and appeal to different kinds of gamblers. Although you should naturally gravitate toward the games that are the most fun for you, you need to be clear on the three classes of games. This section looks at the three types more closely.

Games with fixed odds

When the odds are *fixed* (not subject to change), the bean counters in the back room can calculate exactly how much each of these games wins for every $100 gambled. That's because, no matter how much gamblers vary their play, the casino has the same edge. The house seldom has a losing day on games with fixed odds, such as

>> Slots

>> Craps

>> Keno

>> Roulette

Even though the profits fluctuate each day (due to short-term luck), casinos can easily forecast for the long run because they have hundreds of machines and tables all operating at once.

Games with variable odds

In this classification, the odds change, depending on how well gamblers play their cards or place their bets. Several of these games may yield better odds for smarter players. But the gain in these games can only go so far because over the long run, the odds still strongly favor the house. In other words — even if you play better than anyone else at the table, these games can't be beaten.

Some examples of these games include

>> Pai Gow poker

>> Three Card poker

>> Let It Ride

Games where skills affect the odds

A few games reward skillful play and allow a tiny minority of gamblers to get an edge over the house. These games are variable-odds games, but they offer an advantage that the others don't: Gamblers actually have a chance to win money in the long run. But don't think you can walk in off the street and start pocketing Ben Franklins. Winning requires study, discipline, patience, and practice. Here are the games where skill can get you over the hump:

>> Blackjack

>> Video poker

>> Regular poker

>> Sports betting

>> Horse racing

Calculating the Odds in Casino Games

If you're good at math, you often can detect when the casino payout odds are lower than true odds (see the section "Factoring in the odds" earlier in this chapter). With dice, for example, you have 36 different combinations, and the odds are

35-to-1 for each combination. But with other games, the odds can be impossible to calculate. Take slots, for example: The thousands of possible reel combinations and ever-changing progressive jackpots make it difficult for anyone to calculate the odds of winning.

REMEMBER

One of the most confusing aspects of odds is the difference between *for* and *to*. For example, in video poker a flush pays 6 *for* 1, which means your win of six coins *includes* your original wager. So your actual profit is only five coins. However, if the bet pays 6 *to* 1, your odds are better. Your profit is six and your total return is seven (your win *plus* your original wager). This small detail may seem like a silly case of semantics, but it can make a big difference in your payout.

This section ties together the joint concepts of payout odds and true odds that will get you on the road to understanding the house *edge* (or advantage). Armed with a full understanding of that key statistic, you'll be able to discriminate between good and bad bets in a casino.

Identifying payoff odds

In almost all cases, the payoffs favor the house, and you lose in the long run. However, some unusual situations arise that give astute gamblers an edge.

Zero expectation

A *zero expectation* bet has no edge — for the house or the player. This balance means that both sides can break even in the long run. For example, if you remove the two extra green numbers (0 and 00) from the roulette wheel, the game now becomes a zero expectation game because it has 36 numbers, 18 red and 18 black. Any bet on red or black would be a zero expectation bet. In other words, when you bet on one color, your chances for winning and losing are equal, just like flipping a coin.

Negative expectation

However, casinos aren't interested in offering zero expectation games. In order to make a profit, they need to add in those two extra green numbers to change the odds in roulette. Now, when you bet red or black, your odds of winning are $18/38$ rather than $18/36$. So your even money bet moves from a zero expectation to a *negative expectation*.

REMEMBER

Whenever you're the underdog (such as in roulette), your wager has a negative expectation, and you can expect to lose money. It may not happen right then. You may defy the bad odds for a while and win, but over time you will lose.

Most bets carry a negative expectation because the house doesn't give true odds for the payouts (as is the case for roulette). Craps provides another good example. Say you bet that the dice will total seven on the next throw. If you win, you are paid 4 to 1. However, the true odds for this occurrence happening are 5 to 1 ($^6/_{36}$).

That difference may not sound like a major change, but the house edge on that bet is a whopping 16.67 percent! And a negative expectation bet for you is a positive for the casino. (The casino makes an average of $16.67 on every $100 bet in the previous craps example.)

Positive expectation

In a *positive expectation* bet, the tables are turned on the house so the players have the advantage. Most people can't believe casinos actually allow a positive expectation for the gambler, but surprisingly, some are out there. One example is in tournaments, where, in many situations, the casino pays out more money than it takes in.

Getting an edge on the house edge

It's a fact: In most casino games, the house has the edge. But *you* can get an edge over the casino in two ways:

>> **Using match play coupons to double your fun.** You can often find match play coupons in the free fun books distributed by many casinos. Rip these coupons out and tuck them underneath your bet. In most cases, they essentially double your wager without having to risk any more money.

>> **Taking advantage of promotions.** Promotions can be the best way to secure a positive expectation. Here are a couple of examples: We have played at several casinos where they changed the rules for a short period of time and paid out 2 to 1 on all blackjacks. This change tipped the odds enough so even basic-strategy players had nearly a 2 percent edge over the house.

Another great promotion was when the Pioneer Casino in Laughlin, Nevada, offered *Double Jackpot Time* on some slot machines. Twice an hour, for a short period of time (approximately 30 seconds), they generously doubled the payout on certain jackpots. Most people shrugged off this opportunity as just another marketing gimmick, but it was very lucrative. A friend of mine made six figures a year there playing only a few minutes every hour.

Finding out about these great deals isn't easy. However, one helpful resource for casino promotions and coupons is the *Las Vegas Advisor*. Another tactic is signing up for casino e-newsletters to keep abreast of upcoming special events.

Chapter 3

Managing Your Money in a Casino

n accountant we know shares this favorite saying with clients who want to push the envelope: "Pigs get fed. Hogs get slaughtered." This adage is probably more applicable to gamblers tackling the tables than taxpayers dealing with the IRS. Greed and gambling are two words that go together like peanut butter and jelly, and they're just as likely to get you into a sticky mess.

When blinded by the possibility of winning more, you can easily end up blowing your gambling *bankroll* (money set aside just for gambling) in one evening — or faster. The prospect of striking it rich in the casino may make you forget that you have other financial obligations — paying the mortgage and feeding your children, to name a couple. We've heard and seen too many horror stories about individuals whose dream vacation to a gambling destination turned into a nightmare when they frantically began throwing good money after bad to make up for their losses early in their getaway.

In this chapter, we address nothing more than practical, pragmatic approaches to your money — the cash you come with and (hopefully) the money you win as you go along. We arm you with the same sort of no-nonsense advice your accountant or a financial counselor may offer to help you manage your budget.

Setting a Budget and Sticking to It

REMEMBER

To enjoy your gambling experience, you must *control* your gambling experience, which means setting — and sticking to — a budget. Whether you're taking a weekend backpacking tour in a nearby state park or a once-in-a-lifetime trip to the Galapagos Islands, you decide what you're willing — or can afford — to spend, and then you make your plans. The same goes for a gambling getaway. First you budget for the transportation to your destination, your hotel and food expenses, entertainment tickets, and sightseeing excursions — and how much you plan to spend on gambling.

If your main priority is to retain all of your money, the best advice we can offer you is not to gamble at all. Assuming you don't want to hear that bit of wisdom, our next-best suggestion is to firmly decide, before you walk through the doors of the casino, how much you're willing to spend (translation: *lose*).

Casinos are fantastic places where you can check reality at the door. Gambling should be a fun experience, a chance to get away from your daily stress and enjoy the escape that risk and winning can bring. But when the lines between reality and fantasy blur, when you buy into the dream and forget the budget, you can run into problems, and your money can quickly head south.

This section helps you predetermine exactly how much money you're willing to spend on your gambling venture. You also discover how to stick to your budget and avoid the kind of fun the casino wants to have — at your expense.

Playing within your means

For most people, gambling isn't a lifestyle. It's an escape from reality that has the same components of thrill, sizzle, and excitement as other forms of entertainment — well, maybe a little less than skydiving and a bit more than the opera.

A good starting point to determine your gambling bankroll is figuring out how much you spend on different types of entertainments and vacations, such as theme parks, ski resorts, or other sightseeing destinations. Knowing this information can help you compare your casino budget to the cost of last summer's beach vacation or that week in Paris.

REMEMBER

Your gambling bankroll needs to reflect fiscal reality. If your other vacations cost $1,000, why should your gambling vacation cost two or three or even four times as much? Like all trips, hobbies, or flights of fancy, gambling is a form of entertainment. And, just like that Caribbean cruise, your gambling losses shouldn't affect your day-to-day lifestyle or your ability to pay bills for the rest of the month, after the vacation is over.

As you calculate the cost of your gambling trip, consider its value to you in terms of fun and entertainment. If you perceive your casino gambling adventure as a form of entertainment similar to, say, dinner at a fine restaurant and an evening at the theater, you can begin to put a price on its value. Would such an evening cost you $500 for two? Possibly. Would you pay $1,000 for it? Possibly again, although sticker shock may be setting in.

WARNING

Okay, we may sound like credit counselors, but the money for your gambling vacation should come from your entertainment budget. In other words, don't cash in a savings bond, dip into the kids' college funds, or take out a new credit card to bankroll the trip. And by all means, don't budget with money you *plan on* winning during the trip!

Determining your daily limits

After you figure out your budget for your gambling adventure (whether a five-day trip to Vegas or just a quick jaunt to a riverboat casino), you need to break down that budget into how much you can spend each day. Take your predetermined trip bankroll, and then divide that amount by the number of days you're going to be in the casino. For example, say you set aside $1,200 for gambling on your three-day getaway weekend. You have $400 to play with each day, separate from the money you budget to feed, house, and otherwise entertain yourself.

REMEMBER

From day to day at the casino, you're either up or down. For example, on Friday, the first day of your three-day venture, you enter the casino with four crisp $100 bills in your pocket and finish the day with $600 for a $200 win. Congratulations! But how does your success affect your game plan? It doesn't. The next day, you should stick to your budget and still only gamble with $400. However, Saturday is a disaster and you lose every last penny of the $400 budgeted for that day. The carnage continues on Sunday, and once again you burn through $400. But because you stuck to your budget, you return home with $600 of your original $1,200 bankroll, which is a lot more money than less-disciplined gamblers (who never had a starting plan or failed to follow it) have at the end of their trip.

TIP

If you lose your $400 (or whatever the amount of your daily budget) early in the day, do something else. The free activities in and around casino towns can be pretty entertaining. Discover the mountain trails of Lake Tahoe, stroll the boardwalk in Atlantic City, or just hang out at the hotel and enjoy the swimming pool or workout room. A big mistake many people make is getting so engrossed in gambling that they miss out on the attractions of a beautiful resort.

Sizing up your bets

After splitting your bankroll into daily increments, the next step to budget your gambling is *bet sizing,* or breaking down your budgeted bankroll into the amount you allocate for each bet.

REMEMBER

A general rule (for most table games) is to have a bankroll with at least 40 times the maximum bet you plan to make. So if you decide to ration your trip bankroll into daily allotments of $400, your betting units are $10 per hand. Proper proportional betting reduces your risk of *tapping out* (going home flat broke).

Keeping your bets consistent

Unless you're a professional card counter, you don't benefit from changing the amount of your bets. The simplest and safest strategy in most casino games is to bet the same amount each time. For slots and video poker, that may mean playing the max number of coins or credits each time if you are playing a progressive machine (see Book 6, Chapter 8 for more on slots).

REMEMBER

Most players change the amount they bet on each play — typically increasing the bet size — because of two circumstances:

>> They've been losing, so now they're desperately attempting to regain that money. Consequently, they *steam,* or increase the size of their bets.

>> They've been riding a hot streak and are playing on *house money* (funds they've won from the casino).

Although games do run in streaks, you can't know when those streaks begin or end. After you have the money, it's yours. How you obtained it doesn't matter, but you still need to be judicious about how you spend or bet the money.

Limiting your losses

In addition to establishing a budget and portioning it out on a daily — and bet-size — basis, you can employ some simple strategies that help you stay within the framework of your budget. This section contains a few time-honored methods of limiting your losses.

Stop-loss limits: Covering your own butt

You may be familiar with *stop-loss limits* from the stock market. Stop-loss limits protect your shares from a severe downturn by instructing your broker to sell if a stock falls to a certain price.

You can apply the same rationale to gambling. An example is our earlier recommendation to decide in advance how much you're willing to risk per trip and per day (see the section "Determining your daily limits"). When you lose your preset amount, stop, head for the door, and spend the rest of the day golfing or sightseeing.

Big comebacks — erasing your gambling debt by winning big — are the stuff of legends. And that's where those stories belong. You're not gambling in the casino to make a living or pay off your bills. Treat gambling like a vacation, and leave the dreams of making a fortune in the casino for Hollywood movies. (Check out "Resisting the urge to chase losses" in this chapter for more about how this strategy can get you in trouble.)

Time limits: Knowing when you've had enough

Another good restraint is to set limits on how long you play each day. Marathon sessions at the tables usually spell disaster. The longer you play, the more likely you are to lose your focus and perspective.

TIP

Don't play for more than two hours at a time, and don't go play for more than four to six total hours a day. Casinos are tough enough to beat anyway, but when you're mentally foggy or hungry, you add an extra burden to the job.

Figure out how to take breaks because they can help you clear your head and protect your bankroll. Stopping for lunch or dinner may seem obvious, but the number of players who totally forget to eat when they're gambling is amazing. Reasons to take breaks abound. Here are just a few:

>> **Visiting the bathroom:** Drink plenty of water so you have to take frequent trips to the powder room. Those short walks stretch both your legs and your bankroll.

>> **Exercising:** Even if it's just a brisk walk around the casino floor, do something to get your circulation going. Even better is a real workout at the hotel gym.

>> **Calling your loved ones:** Your significant other and family appreciate a check-in call every once in a while. A check-in call can also provide additional restraints for sticking to your budget. You can easily lose touch with reality while gambling, and a quick phone call can remind you of what's important in life.

Win limits: Winning something is better than losing

Everyone wants to walk away a winner. Cashing out a winner is one of the greatest feelings in the world, and it's the ultimate goal of everyone who gambles. But remember — one of the worst feelings is dumping all your winnings back when you're up a lot and then losing for the day. So quitting when you win a predetermined amount ensures that you have some winning days during your visit.

Some people set up target goals, such as quitting when they get ahead of their daily bankroll by 50 percent or 100 percent. If you wisely add your profits back into your bankroll (rather than spending them), you have a larger buffer to withstand future negative swings.

REMEMBER

Keep in mind that quitting early never helps you in the long term because you have absolutely no way of knowing when the cards are going to turn for the day. But you reap a tremendous psychological benefit if you stop playing when you win a certain amount.

Looking at Casino Credit and Its Risks

Most people feel safer using credit cards rather than cash on vacation because, if stolen, credit is easier to replace than cash. But you have to turn that strategy on its head on gambling vacations. If you want to play it safe when gambling, always use cash instead of credit.

REMEMBER

The more credit you use (or perhaps *abuse*), the more you have to replace when you get home. For example, if you set a personal loss limit of $400 and blow your $400 in cash, stopping is easier because you're out of money. But with a $2,000 credit line, after you burn through the first $400, you can still tap into more funds, which can ultimately lead to serious debt trouble.

This section explains the downside of relying on casino credit. But there are also some advantages to casino credit, so we explain how to set it up and when to use that credit in a positive way.

Grasping casino credit

To understand the lure — as well as the danger — of casino credit, you first need to understand it. Casino credit is no different from store credit, something most people take advantage of every day. To make shopping easier, many department stores offer customers a little plastic card with a line of credit. Similarly, the casino offers you a line of credit based on your credit report and the size of your bank account. This line of credit allows you to borrow money from the casino in order to gamble — either because your funds have run out or because you just prefer not to carry cash.

REMEMBER

The whole casino industry is designed to make you forget that you're playing for real money, which is why casinos use chips rather than cash at the tables. And taking the next step — playing against your line of credit — can move you one step further from the harsh reality that eventually you have to pay the piper.

Credit is convenient, yes. But, it's also a very risky venture. First, access to credit tends to make some people spend more money than they otherwise would — both in gambling and in the real world. But with casino credit, the problem is compounded. If you buy a $300 sander from the local home-improvement center on your credit card and your spouse promptly persuades you that you don't *need* that item, you can usually return it and get your $300 back. But when you borrow $300 from your favorite casino and lose it at craps, it's long gone. Even worse is when you lose that $300, followed quickly by $600 more, and return home with bigger debts than you can handle.

TIP

Definitely steer clear of casino credit if you have an impulsive nature. Can't stop eating potato chips until the bag is empty? Then casino credit may be another bag you don't want to dip into.

Crediting yourself with an account

Recognizing that borrowing from the casino can lead to gambling debt is a critical step as you consider managing your bankroll. Yet credit can benefit people who are extremely disciplined inside the surrealistic confines of the casino. And casino credit does offer the following clear advantages:

>> Makes you a prime target for attractive comps (free meals and entertainment, for example)

>> May lead to invitations to big casino events

>> Allows you to cash personal checks at the casino cage instead of using the ATM or borrowing on your credit card, which can result in additional service fees

>> Allows you to gamble without the risk of carrying large amounts of cash

Establishing a line of credit is easier than you may think because the casino doesn't want to make borrowing money hard for you. You can set up a casino line of credit in one of two ways:

>> At the cashier's cage upon arrival

>> Online prior to your visit

Because credit approval may take a few days, visit your preferred casino's website and fill out an application form in advance. That way your line of credit is available to you as soon as you arrive.

Using markers against casino credit

After you establish your line of credit, don't expect to get a plastic credit card with the casino logo on the front. Instead, you use *markers* at the tables to tap into your line of credit. (A marker is basically a check or I.O.U. that you sign at the gaming table.)

Keep this fact in mind as you sign a marker for that next baccarat game: Chips and now markers serve as tools to distance you psychologically from the reality that you're spending your hard-earned money. And when you don't have to reach into your wallet when you're losing, continuing to play is a whole lot easier. If you choose to ignore our advice about sticking to cash while gambling, then be sure you're constantly aware of where you stand with the house, and never lose sight of the fact that payback will occur before the end of your casino stay.

At the end of your visit, the casino expects you to write a check to cover the cost of any losses you incurred during your visit. If you refuse to pay, the casino has the right to post the outstanding markers with your bank for collection from your account.

You use markers only after you've established a line of credit with the casino. And a line of credit is good only at the casino where you applied. In other words, you can't borrow money at the club across the street unless the same company owns both casinos.

THE TRUE COST OF AN ATM

Don't like the cut your bank takes when you use the ATM at home? Try using one at a casino! Not only are the odds at a casino stacked against you, but so are the ATM fees. In addition to the standard bank charges for using the ATM, the casino hits you with a stiff fee at the terminal. How can you avoid both fees? Simple: Bring a set amount of cash and spend only what you bring.

Figuring Out When Enough Is Enough

Gambling, by its very definition, implies risk, something many people aren't used to dealing with. In your work life, you eliminate uncertainty by accepting a job with a fixed salary. In your daily life, you protect against disaster through a spectrum of safety precautions, from smoke detectors to seat belts.

When you walk into the casino, the house is betting that your unfamiliarity with risk will work in its favor. (Look at how easy establishing a line of credit is and how quickly the little extras, such as comps, make you amenable to spending and risking more money.)

By following the advice in this chapter, you're taking the appropriate steps to reduce your risk of gambling-related problems when you enter the casino. But you're wise to continue looking for signs of trouble during, or even before, your casino visit. These problems can take many forms beyond simple financial issues; they can affect your relationships as well as your health. This section helps you identify the warning signs so you can walk away before it's too late.

Knowing the odds of failure

REMEMBER

The best protection you can offer yourself in a casino is knowledge. Having a full understanding of the odds involved with every game allows you to set realistic limits in your play. You can know when pushing a little harder and continuing to play is okay, but you can also have a solid grasp on when it's time to tuck your tail between your legs and go home. Without a basic understanding of your chances, you won't be able to recognize when you've taken one step too far.

Because the casino does everything in its power to help you step off the plank and into the ocean of risk, is it any wonder some people get in over their heads before they even realize they're in deep water? Book 6, Chapter 2 looks more closely at odds, and each chapter on the specific games examines the odds and explains whether the game is worth playing or not.

Knowing thyself

You may have packed light for your long-weekend gambling getaway. But, trust us, you're carrying more baggage than you realize — all that other stuff that defines who you are and how you react to certain situations. So be realistic about your own personality and temperament.

TIP

If you tend to get a little out of control when things go wrong, then bring along some safeguards in the event you start to lose. Have a friend hold your wallet, or simply leave access to money (beyond your bankroll) behind and carry nothing but cash. Above all else, be honest about how you've gambled in the past. Just because you haven't been a perfect angel doesn't mean you can't go, but you do have to be more careful than other gamblers.

Are you a disciplined type? Is adopting positive behaviors, such as daily exercise and saving money, easy for you? If you're cool, calm, and rational in your daily life, you're likely to be a good candidate for video poker or the blackjack tables. Or are you impulsive and undisciplined? Does a trip to the mall for a package of socks turn into a shopping spree that sets you back a couple of paychecks? Do you struggle to stick to a diet? If you lack control in everyday activities, such as shopping and eating, then casinos can become a dangerous diversion. We're not suggesting that you swear off casino visits if you can't stop yourself from eating just one more chocolate chip cookie. But understanding your nature and taking precautions to protect yourself from "cleaning out the cookie jar" is important.

TIP

If you choose to partake in the pleasures and excitement of a casino visit, then, in addition to strictly following the money-management advice in this chapter, you may want to take extra steps to curtail your impulsive side. For example, try traveling with someone who's more disciplined than you are and willing to serve as the designated banker.

Resisting the urge to chase losses

Even if you're a highly disciplined soul, the hypnotic sway of the casino can seduce you into uncharacteristic behavior. One typical lure that pulls gamblers off the cliff of control is *chasing your losses.* For example, say you've lost more than you intended. But, you think, if you could just win one big bet, your problem would be erased. So chasing your losses is tempting, especially in a casino where people seem to be winning all around you.

The sad fact is that most people lose when gambling. And when people lose, they tend to want to get their money back. Even though it's almost always a quick path to ruin, the urge to chase losses is a phenomenon that seems to sweep over casinos from the Mississippi River to Monte Carlo.

TIP

Don't fall victim to chasing your losses! When you seek to retrieve that lost money, you start throwing good money after bad, hoping to win it all back. To avoid losing even more of your gambling bankroll, treat a loss as just that: a loss. Say *no* to the next hand or play, and say *yes* to some other activity.

Sipping, not sinking

Part of the casino experience is enjoying the festive atmosphere, bright lights, and free drinks. But enjoying and exceeding are two different events, and the quickest way to short-circuit your budget is to overindulge at the bar.

Overindulging is tempting, of course, with cocktail servers adeptly appearing just when the game gets tense, graciously slipping a fresh cold drink next to your elbow. As you sweat a little more, the next drink goes down more quickly. And before you know it, you've lost count of how many drinks you've had, not to mention how much money you've lost.

TIP

Monitor your drinking as closely as you manage your budget. If your game of choice requires strategy, then you play better with a clear head. And even if the game doesn't require player expertise, you're still better off without the excessive alcohol muddying your thoughts or encouraging you to go for broke when you're in the hole.

Recognizing a gambling addiction

Exceeding your established gambling budget by a few hundred dollars on a trip to Vegas or your nearby riverboat casino is one matter. Getting yourself tens of thousands of dollars in debt over the course of time is another matter entirely; this sort of trouble is a serious gambling problem. Gambling addiction is a complex problem far beyond the scope of this book. But we'd be irresponsible *not* to address it in a chapter about managing your gambling money.

Gambling debts almost ruined Edgar Allan Poe and Thomas Jefferson and have devastated many families. Whether you're a beginning gambler, an occasional gambler, or a regular bettor, you need to know the signs of gambling addiction. A few signs include

>> Trying to escape other problems in your life by gambling

>> Lying to others about the frequency or amount of your gambling

>> Falling behind on basic payments, such as rent or other bills, to feed your gambling habit

>> Asking to borrow money from friends and family to cover your gambling debts

If you suspect you have a serious problem with gambling, you're not alone. Some excellent sources and support groups are available to help you fight your addiction and find ways to overcome debt and other related problems. You can start with an excellent website, www.gamblersanonymous.org, for answers and help.

IN THIS CHAPTER

Showing off your best table (and slot) manners

Handing out tips to casino personnel

Fighting off the temptation to cheat

Chapter 4

Minding Your Gambling Manners

K nowing how to play the games is one critical component of success in casinos. But minding your gambling manners is equally important, no matter how you cut the deck. *Manners*, you ask? You're seeking tips on how to win at cards, chips, and chance, and we're pulling a Ms. Manners on you? What's next? Instructions on holding your cards with your pinky fingers extended? Admonishments for ladies to draw first?

We stand by our pronouncement, but in this context, we broaden the definition of *manners* to encompass your *manner* in the casino: how you conduct yourself and behave with players, dealers, and the casino staff. Manners are frequently defined not only as a way of behaving according to polite standards but also as the prevailing way of acting in a specific culture or class of people. And, indeed, a casino exudes its own unique culture, with a social (not to mention legal) code of conduct. In order for you to fit in and maximize your casino experience, you need to know the code.

Most gambling etiquette harkens to two issues: respecting other players and discouraging cheating. In this chapter, we reveal the keys to the casino code of conduct, which encompasses those issues. But it's not just about following rules. You also need to know how to fit in, so we also offer advice for tipping dealers and casino personnel.

Playing Well with Others: Minding Your Table Manners

Most of your interaction with other players comes within the context of the games themselves. So whether you're playing Poker, Blackjack, Baccarat, or Roulette, you want to know how to play the game, and you want to have an understanding of the house rules that dictate your conduct before, during, and after the game. House rules help ensure respect and sensitivity to all players participating, and they protect against cheating.

Knowing your limits

Before you cash in your money and make any bets at a table game or slot machine, be sure you know the rules and parameters of the game you're about to play. Even popular standards, such as Blackjack and Video Poker, may have weird variations or unusual rules. Avoid disrupting other players — and save yourself some embarrassment — by confirming that you're playing the game you *think* you are before you join in. Just ask the dealer (while she's shuffling is the best time) to give you a quick overview of the game. But most specialty or unusual games have their rules printed at the table, so you can typically read them before you play.

TIP

Always check the *table limits* — the betting minimums and maximums — before you sit down. Casinos usually print the limits on a small, colored placard on the table to keep you from inadvertently joining a high-limit game where you can't afford even the minimum bet. Making a $5 bet only to have the dealer point out that you're sitting at a $100-minimum table can be humiliating.

Joining a game

Sitting down at any table or slot machine that has an empty chair is acceptable, but remember these caveats when joining a game:

>> Ask at a crowded table if a position is open. (For example, someone may have run to the restroom.) Craps doesn't have chairs or stools, so sometimes you can't easily determine whether the table has room for you. If in doubt, ask the dealer closest to you or the stickman if the table has room for one more. Some Blackjack tables have a sign saying *No midshoe entry*. At these tables, you need to wait until the shuffle before you can play.

As you discover in Book 6, Chapters 5 and 6 (on Blackjack and Craps, respectively), some games are played in natural cycles. If the table you want to join has any big bettors, you should politely ask before jumping in midshoe or in the midst of a hot roll. Many players are superstitious, and if they have great runs going, they often prefer you wait. In Blackjack, you hold off until the shuffle so you don't break up the *sacred order* of cards. In Craps, you wait until the next come-out roll.

REMEMBER

>> When you do sit down, you need to *buy in (*convert money to chips), unless you bring chips with you from another table. To do so, place your money on the table (but outside any betting areas) for the dealer to exchange into chips.

Thou shall not touch. . .and other table commandments

In many games, what you can do with your hands (the ones on the end of your arms, not the ones made of playing cards) is strictly defined, and the reason is simple: The casino wants to minimize your opportunity to disrupt the game or, worse, cheat. You can discover the protocol of specific games in the respective chapters of this book, but for now, be aware that casinos are sensitive about how you handle all gaming material, such as chips, cards, or dice.

>> In Craps, don't touch the dice unless you're the *shooter.*

>> In table games, if the cards are dealt face-up, don't touch them after they hit the felt.

>> After you place a bet and play has begun, you aren't allowed to touch your bet again, even to tidy up a toppled stack of chips. (There are a few exceptions to this rule in craps.)

>> Use only one hand to touch your cards. This is primarily because cheaters use two hands to switch cards.

>> Understand and use all hand signals or gestures that are part of the game. (Although the dealer or the other players may help you, you need to know the rules before you sit down to play.)

>> Don't do anything to mark or damage the cards in any way, such as bending, warping, or scraping with your fingernail.

>> Don't give unsolicited advice to other players. Even if you're offering good strategy, players aren't likely to accept it in the generous spirit in which you gave it. And if they do take your advice and lose, guess who they'll blame?

>> If you bring a friend to cheer you on, remember that the chairs are only for players. However, if the casino isn't crowded, nonplayers usually can sit in a chair as long as they're prepared to vacate when the table begins to fill up.

- » At the end of the hand, place your cards in front of you; don't hand them to the dealer.

- » Some slots and Video Poker fanatics play more than one machine at a time. Before you sit down at a machine, make sure someone isn't playing the machine; arm pullers can be very territorial.

- » Casinos are sensitive to any kind of electronic devices around the gaming areas. In some places, you aren't allowed to snap pictures or talk, text, or do an Internet search on a cellphone.

Enjoying a Smoke and an Adult Beverage

One of the attractions of gambling in a casino is the ability to legally smoke and drink while playing table games or slot machines. Not many places these days allow you to enjoy these pleasures together in public anymore. However, because not everyone indulges in tobacco products or alcohol, you should be aware of some social niceties; by following these, you improve the odds of keeping the peace among other players at the table or nearby machines. The following sections give you the lowdown.

Smoking permitted (sometimes)

In contrast to almost every public venue, most casinos allow smoking throughout their many public areas and offer only token nonsmoking arenas. For many gamblers, their entire casino experience depends on the ability to puff while playing. If you're in that camp, you'll find yourself among friends virtually everywhere you go in a casino. However, you should always check first before you light up, just in case you stumble across a nonsmoking table game or find yourself in a smoke-free section of the casino. You can also show good manners by asking other players at the table if they mind your firing up a cig or stogie.

As more casinos restrict smoking, do your research and make sure you're visiting a place that allows smoking before you find out the hard way. In addition, casino restaurants and bars may also have nonsmoking policies or sections, so look for the signs, or ask a casino employee about the smoking policies.

REMEMBER

If you're not a smoker, don't automatically assume the advanced filtration systems will remove all secondhand smoke from the casino air. If you're playing in an older casino that has low ceilings and allows smoking, you're essentially playing in smog. For the occasional visitor, a few days won't bother you. But if you have any medical conditions (such as asthma) that bad air may aggravate, don't expect a smoke-free table in a smoke-filled casino to do you much good.

Like just about everything else in a casino, smoking has its own set of unspoken rules for nicotine fiends to be mindful of, including the following:

>> Casinos that allow cigarette smoking may have a prohibition on cigars, so double-check before you fire up that stogie.

>> Cocktail servers are often able to buy packs of cigarettes for you; just be prepared to pay higher prices and make sure you tip generously for going the extra mile.

>> Dealers for some games ask you to take extra care with a lit cigarette. For example, if you're playing Craps, never hold your cigarette over the rim where ashes could drop on the table.

Drinking encouraged

Drinking and gambling seem to go hand in hand, so you shouldn't be surprised to find out that drinking at the tables, slots, restaurants, clubs, and shows isn't only permitted but also — many would argue — encouraged. After all, how many places aside from casinos offer free drinks on the house with cocktail servers coming to your table to take and deliver your orders? Drinking doesn't get any easier: however, in some casinos, drinking isn't free or allowed, especially on Indian reservations.

Keep in mind that, from the casino's perspective, alcohol is a lubricant that helps loosen your inhibitions — translation: purse-strings or wallet clips. If you've had a drink or two, you're more likely to take risks with your money. So, yes, many casinos encourage alcohol consumption — as long as you're of legal age, that is. Don't be surprised if you have to provide proof of age before you can place your drink order. Keeping your identification with you is a wise idea.

REMEMBER

You'd be smart to control the amount you drink while gambling. A sober head not only helps you play better but also keeps rein on your emotions and your mouth. Loss of either may lead to trouble with the dealer, other players, and casino security.

Giving Gratuities to Dealers and Others

Most people view gaming as a form of entertainment. And just as you tip a restaurant server, valet, coat-check assistant, or cashier at your favorite coffee shop, offering gratuities to the service staff you encounter in the casino is customary.

REMEMBER

Most casino employees, like other workers in the service sector, rely heavily on the generosity of the people they serve in order to supplement their wages. Hard-working dealers, cocktail servers, bellhops, and the like depend on your support, so offering tips — or *tokes*, as they're known in gambling lingo — is a customary practice in the casino.

Although some people feel that casino staff have become jaded — eagerly expecting (if not outright demanding) a tip whether or not their service justifies it — most staffers genuinely strive to serve and make your casino experience a pleasant one. So be prepared to tip your service providers; maybe you'll increase your odds of generating positive casino karma!

Tipping your dealer

Servers, valets, bartenders, housekeepers — you're already familiar with tipping many of the service personnel you encounter on a daily basis. But dealers are unique to the casino world, so tipping can pose a dilemma to the gambling novice. When do you tip? How much do you give? How exactly does the money change hands? This section helps pare down when tipping your dealer is appropriate and how to tip correctly.

Spreading the wealth

Dealers make most of their income from tips. But casinos don't work the way a restaurant works. When your food comes on time and your server remembers to put the horseradish on the side, the extra buck you toss him goes directly into his pocket. However, casino tips are almost always pooled, and with good reason.

>> Pooling eliminates any direct incentive for a dealer to cheat on behalf of a player.

>> Pooling provides equality for dealers, some of whom deal at low-end tables while others get the high-rollers who toss black $100 chips around like they were nickels.

Tips are usually pooled based on shifts, which allows for a simple daily calculation for everyone who worked at the same time.

If you think you can get by without tipping your dealer, you may be surprised to feel the overt pressure to tip at the table. Some dealers are out-and-out rude if a winner fails to share his good fortune with them.

TIP

So the first question is, under what circumstances is a tip to the dealer customary? The standard practice is to tip when you're winning, but winning or losing has nothing to do with the dealers. Tipping is a way of showing appreciation, but it doesn't change the odds, help you in the future, or give you better cards. Tipping only changes the way dealers, players, and pit bosses treat you while you're sitting at the table. So if you want to be loved, tip generously whether you win or lose.

How to tip the dealer

The most common method of passing a tip to your dealer is placing an extra bet in front of your regular bet. You also can place any amount on top of your bet for the dealer. Adding to your bet basically makes your dealer a *partner* with you on that hand. Dealers usually enjoy being able to participate in the game.

REMEMBER

Giving the dealer a chip or two when you leave the table after collecting your winnings is also common. Dealers often have you *color up* (exchange your many smaller denomination chips for chips of higher value) before you leave a table, so make sure you set aside some small chips for the dealer before this process.

How much to tip (or not)

Casinos have no universal tipping standards such as those recognized for valets or bellmen. Most dealer tips are based on how much you're betting or how much you're winning. Unfortunately, most gamblers tip far more than they realize — and win far less than they think.

For example, suppose you bet $10 every hand at a full Blackjack table (typically six players). You decide to tip only when you get a Blackjack (an ace and a face card, or 10). Because a Blackjack pays you an extra $5 (at 3-to-2 odds), you share that bounty with the dealer by placing a $5 bet for her on the next hand. That action translates into approximately $15 worth of tips for the dealer every hour (or one tip every 20 minutes).

Your expected loss during that same time period is $6.70 (assuming that you master the condensed basic strategy for Blackjack in Book 6, Chapter 5). So your modest tipping actually gives the dealer more than twice as much money as you lose to the casino. If everyone at your table follows this same tipping practice, the dealer averages close to $100 an hour in tips!

TIP

Now that I've told you how *not to* tip, you may still be wondering how *to* tip. Keep these few guidelines in mind when tipping:

>> **Think of tips like dog treats.** The quantity of cheddar cheese is less important to Fido than the frequency. He'll roll over just as enthusiastically for a sliver as he will for a chunk. So spread out your tips and make them in small amounts.

>> **Start off on the right foot.** Making a small bet for the dealer when you first join a table is always appreciated.

>> **Make amends.** If you're getting bad service or you're playing with a rude or indifferent dealer, a tip is a good way to end the cold war and get the dealer back in your corner. But if that's not your style, or if you simply don't think he deserves it, by all means don't hand over a gratuity.

>> **Keep track of your tips.** Most important of all, keep a very rough estimate in your head of how much you've tipped. The number may surprise you.

Tipping doesn't have any hard-and-fast rules. A casino or dealer will never kick you out or ban you for refusing to tip. Remember that these guidelines are simply that — guidelines. Observe how more-experienced players at your table give gratuities and make note of the rapport they build with the dealers. Before long, you can develop a feel for what's appropriate and what isn't. Just as important, you get a feel for what kind of tipping pattern fits your personality and budget.

Tipping other casino employees

From the valet who parks your car to the cocktail server who delivers your complimentary drinks to the hotel housekeeper who turns down your bed, you encounter plenty of casino employees who anticipate a gratuity of some sort. Some services — waitresses and concierges — are universal, and others — slot attendants — are unique to casinos.

This section provides a quick rundown of tip situations you can expect to encounter on your casino adventure. Table 4-1 breaks down the customary tip amounts for all the different service workers who may serve your needs.

TABLE 4-1 **Tips for Proper Tipping**

Occupation	Standard Tip	High-Roller Tip
Bartenders	$1 per round	$5 per round
Casino cocktail servers	$1 per round	$5 per round
Dealers	$2 to $10	$25 to $100
Hotel bellhops	$1 to $2 per bag — more for heavier bags	$3 to $5 per bag — more for heavier bags
Limo drivers	Minimum of $5	Minimum of $10
Maids	$1 per night	$5 per night
Room service personnel	15 percent of check	20 percent of check
Servers in restaurant	15 percent of check	20 percent of check
Keno runners	$1 to $5	$10 to $25
Taxi drivers	Minimum of $2	Minimum of $5
Valets	$1 to $2	$5 to $20

Pay attention to the following tips for tipping the different casino personnel and hotel, restaurant, and bar staff in a casino hotel:

>> **Cocktail servers.** Many casinos provide free drinks while you're playing any game in the house. Like most other casino employees, cocktail servers receive low wages and count on your tips. Depending on your first few tips, cocktail servers can leave you either high and dry or refreshed and relaxed. A standard tip is $1 for every one or two drinks, and you can always use chips for tips.

REMEMBER

Servers record what you order based on where you sit in the casino. They work by sections, and each server stays in her area. Therefore, if you move, don't expect your server to find you and deliver your drink.

>> **Other hotel workers.** Just as in any resort hotel, the service personnel at a casino hotel expect a commensurate gratuity, more or less, depending on the level of luxury and hoopla provided by the house. Therefore, even though you only pay $1 to park your 1998 olive-green Chevy at your hometown country club, consider upping that amount to at least $5 if you've rented a Ferrari and pull into the driveway of Caesars Palace. The same goes for your other service providers.

TIP

Be prepared to tip the cast of characters by having plenty of one-dollar and five-dollar bills handy before you arrive.

Avoiding the Appearance of Cheating

Cheating in casinos is a subject worthy of its own book because it has a long and not-so-distinguished history. But as a novice casino visitor, you need to understand some basic facts about the subject and how it affects you.

With so much money flowing, casinos are an inevitable target for cheats. But put your mind at ease because the casino virtually can't cheat you. Gaming commissions and competition ensure fair games these days, and besides that, casinos don't *have* to cheat. Probability theory guarantees them long-term profits on the games. Nevertheless, some cheating still goes on — from both sides of the table — just not in the way you may think. Casinos catch dealers cheating from time to time, but the dealers' targets are rarely the gamblers at their tables. The few dishonest dealers try to swindle the casino by palming chips, overpaying an accomplice, or some similar technique.

You may not be able to imagine yourself cheating in any shape or form to win. But if you devote any good amount of time to gambling, chances are you'll be confronted by temptation. A dealer may overpay you, or your slot machine may malfunction and spit out extra coins.

You may also experience casino protocols that, on the surface, seem irrelevant but are actually in place to avoid situations that can be interpreted as attempts to cheat. One example is the marking of cards. Of course, you didn't mean anything by getting your chili-cheese-fry fingerprints on the ♥Q in the last hand. But you find that casino personnel are very unsympathetic to your tragic lack of a napkin.

WARNING

Make no mistake about it: Cheating when gambling is an extremely serious offense. If a casino catches you cheating, jail time is in your cards!

Following are some efforts made by casinos to eliminate cheating among players. Some examples appear elsewhere in this chapter, but they bear repeating.

» Casinos typically have the legal right to ask anyone to leave their premises at any time for any reason. If casino employees suspect a customer of cheating, they can detain the person and possibly arrest him or her.

» Even though casino personnel do their very best to be polite about it, touching taboos are taken very seriously. Casinos expect neophytes to accidentally violate these rules from time to time, but repeat offenders are eventually asked to leave.

>> Theft is a problem that casinos take seriously even though they aren't directly in harm's way. Gamblers are caught snagging chips from stacks of other players every day. You're especially vulnerable at Craps and Roulette tables because attention is so often focused away from your stack.

>> Casinos are also sensitive to violating interstate gaming laws, so they're wary of cellphone use in certain areas. For example, don't make or take calls while you're in the race and sports book.

>> Casinos invest millions of dollars in security technology to protect themselves against cheaters. You can use this technology to your advantage as well. For example, if you believe a dealer made a mistake, the tape can be rolled back to see what really happened. And the lens doesn't lie.

Chapter 5

The Easiest Game to Beat: Blackjack

Blackjack is the most popular table game in casinos because it offers the best chance for beating the house. Rather than relying on the cold, mechanical whim of slot machines, you make decisions at Blackjack that help determine your fate. Each hand of cards at the Blackjack table offers several options, and the choices you make with your cards affect whether you return home a winner or a loser.

You may have avoided Blackjack in the past — because you felt as out of place as a ballerina at the Super Bowl. But Blackjack is a fairly simple game to understand, and with just a few lessons and strategies, you can feel comfortable and confident at the tables. This chapter lays out the basics and gives you the tools you need for your first venture into the world of Blackjack.

Dealing Out Blackjack Basics

Blackjack, or 21 as it's also called, is a card game with a very clear-cut objective: You try to beat the dealer. Not your neighbor to the left. Not everyone else at the table. Just the dealer. And you have three — count 'em, three — ways to win:

>> The dealer deals you a *Blackjack,* any starting hand consisting of an ace and a 10 (10s and all face cards — jacks, queens, and kings), equaling 21 points. However, this is a tie if the dealer also has a Blackjack.

>> The dealer's hand *busts* — or exceeds 21 points — and your hand doesn't.

>> Your hand — which doesn't exceed 21 — is higher than the dealer's hand. For example, you have 19, and the dealer has 18.

The news gets even better — the dealer must stick to some restrictive rules that favor the players. (I explain these rules in "Drawing the dealer's curtain" later in this chapter.) And following a number of simple strategies helps you improve your odds of beating the house.

In this section, we set the stage for your game of Blackjack. We explain the arena in which you play and the cards' values. We also provide a brief *script* on how to play the game.

Setting the scene

You play Blackjack on a semicircular felt table that seats up to seven players on the curved side of the table, while the dealer stands opposite (see Figure 5-1). These Blackjack tables are clustered together into *pits,* which you usually find in the middle of a casino. The only other accoutrements to the game are the cards — the game uses anywhere from one to eight decks (more about that in "Dealing what's in the cards" later in this chapter) — and the chips, which you use to make your bets. In addition, small placards indicate the table limits and minimum and maximum bets allowed. (Check out "Eyeing table bet levels" later in this chapter for more information about bets.)

Valuing your cards

In Blackjack, the cards are normally worth their face value, or their *pip number.* A 4 counts as four points, an 8 is equal to eight points, and so on. The only exceptions are that 10s and face cards all are worth 10 points, and an ace can count as either 1 or 11 points, depending on how you want to use it. The ace is also the most important card in the deck — the combination of an ace and any ten-point card (10, jack, queen, or king) on your original two cards results in a *natural,* or a Blackjack.

Blackjack

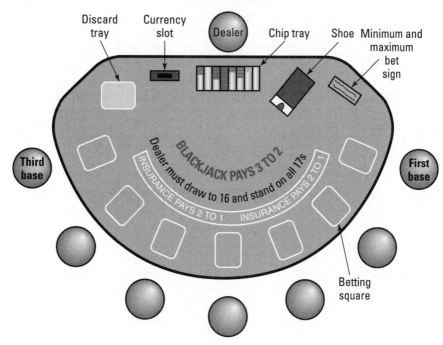

FIGURE 5-1:
A Blackjack table.

© John Wiley & Sons, Inc.

REMEMBER

Unlike games like poker, individual suits — clubs, hearts, spades, or diamonds — make no difference whatsoever in Blackjack.

Preparing to Play

Yes, understanding the basics of Blackjack is relatively easy. But before you can walk away a winner, you need a deeper understanding of the nuances of the game and casino protocol. In the previous section, we briefly discuss how you play Blackjack. In this section, we delve a little deeper and plumb the many facets that, when mastered, lead to Blackjack success. We begin with the warm-up acts — getting seated, purchasing chips, and placing bets — all of which are important steps before you actually begin playing the game.

Finding a table: Strategic seating

Blackjack begins by selecting a seat at the table. Typically, a Blackjack table allows for five to seven players. Whenever you see an empty seat at a Blackjack table, you may assume it's for your taking (unless chips or a coat are holding the spot for a player who just stepped away for a moment or unless some player is playing two hands). In most cases, joining a game in progress is okay, although some tables have a *No-Midshoe Entry* policy (usually marked by a sign at the table), which means you have to wait until the shuffle before playing.

TIP

For your first trip to the tables, you're better off finding a nearly full table. Although the number of players at the table has no effect on the odds on your hands, the game is much quicker with fewer players. A fuller table gives you more time to think about each hand without being rushed or pressured.

The following sections provide a few more pointers to keep in mind when looking for a seat. Ideally, you want to search for a table with fewer decks and favorable rules.

Seeking single-deck tables

Without getting into a lot of math, here's a good rule to follow: The fewer decks the casino uses, the better for you. Your chances for success increase if you can find a single-deck game. Most casinos worldwide have gone to six or more decks in an attempt to thwart *card counters* (skilled players who keep track of cards). But some places still deal Blackjack the old-fashioned way — with one deck of 52 cards. Most of the casinos in northern Nevada (Reno, Lake Tahoe, and Wendover) still use one deck of cards at many of their Blackjack tables. If you aren't sure how many decks the casino is using, just ask.

Spotting tables with favorable rules

When searching for your table, you also want to know which rules favor you. Some rule changes are beneficial and help players — dealer standing on *soft* 17 and *surrender* are good examples (look at "Homing in on house rules" later in this chapter for specifics on these rules). Sometimes these rule variations are spelled out at the table, but if you're unsure, just ask the dealer what the specific rules are.

ABRACADABRA: CAN A CERTAIN SEAT GIVE YOU AN EDGE?

Unfortunately, nothing is magical about seat selection. Despite some popular myths, no spot at the tables gives you more of an edge over other seats. Some players like to sit in the last spot (commonly called *third base*), thinking that they can somehow control the cards right before the dealer acts. But unless they're psychic, this position won't improve their chances of winning.

STAYING ORIGINAL

Blackjack has undergone many revisions and changes over the years. Some of these variations have stuck, and others have disappeared. Our advice: Steer clear of the hybrids and stick to plain, old basic Blackjack. One of the more popular hybrid games is called *6-5 Blackjack*. It may look like a normal game, but, because it pays only 6 to 5 on Blackjacks ($12 for every $10 bet), this variation doesn't provide the return that a traditional game offers. Stay clear of it.

Other more-common new breeds of Blackjack are *Spanish 21, Super Fun 21,* and *Double Exposure.* If you're ever unsure of the rules at your favorite casino, just ask because games and rules often change.

Eyeing table bet levels

REMEMBER

Before you actually sit down, look for the table's minimum and maximum betting limits. Every table has these fixed limits, which the casino usually posts on a small sign located on the table to the right of the dealer.

For example, you may sit down at a table where the placard says $5–$500, which means you have to bet at least $5 on every hand and can never bet more than $500 on any one spot. Typically, the higher the minimum starting bet, the higher the maximum bet for that table. (Check out "Eyeing table bet levels" later in this chapter for more about bets.)

TIP

When you're starting out, find the lowest minimum table in the casino and begin there. Making smaller bets keeps you out of trouble until you understand the game better — and you're less likely to end up sitting next to a high roller (who may not appreciate a novice at his table).

Purchasing chips

After you select your seat, you need to buy chips from the dealer. Select the amount of money you want to start with and lay your cash on the felt in front of you. The dealer changes your cash into chips and slides them across the felt to you.

WARNING

Don't hand your money directly to the dealer; doing so is a breach of etiquette and brands you as a greenhorn.

After you receive your chips, leave them on the table in front of you. Chips come in several denominations and are color-coded. Although every casino uses distinctive chips, most colors are standard. (Check out Book 6, Chapter 1 for a list of the different color chips and their values.)

TIP

Start off with a small amount of chips. A good approach is to cash in no more than 25 percent of your daily bankroll for chips. For example, if you budget $400 for the day, buy in for no more than $100 to start. This way, when you're losing, you minimize the temptation to bet more than you planned. You can always buy more chips later if necessary.

Homing in on house rules

Blackjack rules are fairly similar worldwide — with a few variations. Sometimes a small placard sitting on the table indicates where the casino stands in regard to certain scenarios. If you don't see a placard, you may ask the dealer what the house rules are, even when you're in the middle of a hand.

Does the dealer hit on a soft 17?

A *soft hand* is any hand that counts an ace as 11 rather than 1. The hand is soft because it can't bust on the next card. For example, if you hit (take another card) a soft 18 (an ace and a 7) with a 6, the ace automatically reverts to 1 (rather than 11), and the hand total is now 14 (rather than 24, which would be a bust).

Whether a dealer hits or stands on a soft 17 is usually spelled out in bold white letters right on the felt.

Is doubling down restricted to certain card combinations?

In Las Vegas, casinos typically allow *doubling down,* an option that allows you to double your bet, on any two cards, but other places may restrict this move to just totals of 10 or 11. The placard probably won't list restrictions to doubling down. If you aren't sure whether restrictions are in place, don't be afraid to ask the dealer, even if you're in the middle of a hand.

Can you surrender?

A playing option known as *surrender* is an extremely profitable option for you as a player, but not many casinos offer it. When you surrender, you lose half of your initial bet and give up your hand. For example, if you bet $10 and are dealt a 16, you can surrender and only lose $5 (half your bet) rather than risk the entire $10 on a bad hand. Once again, the placard may not readily advertise this rule variation, so always ask if surrender is available.

CUTS AND BURNS: ENSURING SHUFFLING SAFETY

Cutting the cards is a time-honored tradition in gambling that helps protect the honesty of the game. In Blackjack, the dealer places the shuffled deck or decks in front of one of the players to cut the cards. (This job rotates, and you can decline.) You cut the cards by placing a plastic cut card into the middle of the deck or decks. The dealer then takes the bottom section of cards and places it on top of the other half.

To further ensure the integrity of the game, the dealer takes the top card, known as the *burn card,* and removes it from play.

Dealing what's in the cards

All right, you're situated at the table, you've made your bet in the betting box, and your heart is pumping like a jackhammer. The dealer flashes you a warm smile, wishes you good luck, shuffles the deck, and asks you to cut the cards.

REMEMBER

If you're playing a one- or two-deck game, the dealer holds the cards in his hands and deals you two cards face-down. You can pick up these cards, but make sure you only hold them in one hand.

However, the majority of Blackjack games today use six or eight decks. In these cases, the dealer deals your two cards face-up from a *shoe* (a boxlike device that houses the cards).

Whether your cards are dealt face-up or face-down really doesn't matter — dealers follow strict rules, and seeing the values of your cards doesn't influence them. Dealers' hands always start off with one card exposed and one card hidden, regardless of the number of decks.

Betting Your Bottom Dollar

On the felt in front of you is a *betting circle* or *betting box*. Place your chips in this spot to indicate how much you want to bet on the upcoming hand. You must make all bets before any cards are dealt.

After you make your bet, you aren't allowed to add, take from, or touch the wager again. After the hand is *resolved* (the dealer has paid out the winners and collected chips from the losers), you may change the amount you wager for the next hand.

Ah, but of course, exceptions apply to every rule. And in Blackjack you *may* alter your bet in two ways:

>> **Doubling down:** You double your original bet.

>> **Splitting:** You break your original hand into two separate hands.

For more information about these two lucrative options as well as other playing options, check out the next section, "Playing Your Hand."

Playing Your Hand

After dealing, the dealer addresses the players from left to right, asking them to take action. At last — the moment of truth. Now your skill and understanding can improve your chances of beating the dealer.

Unlike many of the casino's games, Blackjack isn't based entirely on luck. Skill and strategy play a significant role in who wins at the Blackjack tables — and part of the fun and challenge is weighing the various options you can use in a hand.

Exercising your options

Depending on your hand and the dealer's *upcard* (the one you can see), you have a number of options to consider. The great appeal of Blackjack lies in the many decisions available to you, and each hand presents a wide range of choices. The two most common ones are the following:

>> **Hitting:** Taking another card to improve your hand.

>> **Standing:** Passing up the opportunity for another card if you're satisfied with the total you already have.

The following sections explore your other options. (You can also check out "Identifying Common Mistakes" later in this chapter for help with some specific Blackjack circumstances.)

Act natural: Holding 21

If your first two cards total 21 (an ace and a 10 or a face card), you're the proud owner of a natural, also referred to as a *Blackjack*. A natural is as good as it gets — you no longer have any agonizing decisions over whether to hit or stand. (Check out "Drawing the dealer's curtain," later in this chapter to find more information about whether you win.)

Stand and deliver: Staying put when your total is high

If you don't have 21, but your total is still pretty high — 17 or more — your best strategy normally is to stand.

Communicate that you're standing by waving your hand over the top of your cards in face-up games or by tucking your cards gently under your bet in face-down games.

Hit me, baby: Asking for another card

If you don't get a natural and your hand total is very low — say a 5 and a 4 for a total of 9 — you should hit. Even if you get a 10, you won't bust, so you're safe to request another card. Signal you're hitting either by motioning with your finger in face-up games or by scratching your cards on the felt behind your bet in face-down games.

Anytime your hand totals 12 or higher, there is a risk in adding another card. If your hit card is a face card, your hand now exceeds 21 and you lose, regardless of what happens to the dealer's hand. (I provide correct basic strategy for all hands in "Strategizing in the computer age.")

Get two for one: Splitting pairs

If you hold two cards of equal value — such as two 8s — you have the option of *splitting*, or making two separate hands from the pair. With this tactic, you must match your original bet. In other words, if you bet $10, you increase your bet by $10 more for the new hand. You then play two separate hands, each starting with one of the original 8s. You play these two hands out, one at a time, with the normal options of hitting, standing, splitting, or doubling down. Splitting is one of the rare opportunities you have to alter your bet in the middle of a hand.

Double the fun: Increasing your bet

Doubling down is an option that allows you to double your original bet. The tradeoff is that you receive only one more card, which the dealer traditionally deals face-down. Most casinos permit doubling down on any first two cards.

Going beyond Lady Luck

Most new players have two primary goals for their first session of Blackjack: Win money and avoid looking like a rookie at the table. But to become a successful Blackjack player, you need to master the principles of basic strategy. And relying on Lady Luck or a rabbit's foot isn't a basic strategy that works in Blackjack.

In this section, we simplify and condense basic strategy down to six bite-sized blocks — tactics that help you reduce the house edge to approximately 1 percent. If you want even better odds, then we suggest you skip this simplified version and learn regular basic strategy (see the section "Strategizing in the computer age").

Basic strategy for double downs

Doubling down permits you to double your original bet but restricts you to receiving just one more card. The following are the best times to use this strategy:

>> On 11, double if the dealer's upcard is a 2 through 10; otherwise hit.

>> On 10, double if the dealer's upcard is a 2 through 9, otherwise hit.

A starting total of 10 or 11 is the best time to double down because you have approximately a 30 percent chance of receiving a 10 or a face card.

Basic strategy for pair splits

When you hold two cards of equal value, you can split your cards and make two separate hands from the pair by matching your original bet. You play the hands out one at a time.

Keep the following strategies in mind for pair splits:

>> **Always split aces and 8s.** Aces are great to split because of the chance to make 21; you split 8s more for defensive reasons (16 is a poor starting hand).

>> **Never split 5s or 10s.** Never split 5s and 10s because their totals (10 and 20, respectively) are great starting hands.

Basic strategy for stiff hands

Stiff hands are any hard totals between 12 and 16. Stiff hands are obviously your worst nightmare because any 10 busts your hand. Follow these strategies for stiff hands:

>> Stand when the dealer is weakest (upcard of 2 through 6).

>> Hit whenever the dealer is strong (upcard of 7 through ace).

Basic strategy for pat hands

Pat hands are any hard hands of 17 to 21. Because of their high starting total, pat hands deliver most of your winnings. Whenever you have a hard hand of 17 or more, stand.

Strategizing in the computer age

After you have a little experience under your belt at the Blackjack tables, I recommend studying the complete version of basic strategy in this section. Mastering basic strategy definitely takes a little work, but the additional gain is very worthwhile. Following basic strategy (rather than the simplified strategy offered earlier) cuts the casino edge against you in half — to a half percentage point or less — by far the best odds of any table game played against the house.

TIP

If you aren't able to memorize Tables 5-1, 5-2, and 5-3 right away, you can always buy a basic strategy card at most casino gift shops and use it right at the tables.

THE FOUNDING FATHER OF CARD COUNTING

Once upon a time, craps was king of all casino games, and Blackjack lagged far behind in popularity. That pecking order changed dramatically when Dr. Ed Thorp, a professor from MIT, developed a system for counting cards in 1961. His work showed that Blackjack is a game of skill; how you play the cards and vary your bets can dramatically affect the outcome. Thorp's powerful pen set off a stampede of players eager to make their fortune at the Blackjack tables. Unfortunately, very few got rich. The reason they failed was simple: Most of them couldn't master Thorp's complicated strategy.

This history lesson should provide one clear insight — players can beat the game of Blackjack, but the complexity often proves more than players can comprehend. Far too many gamblers still don't know how to correctly play their hands. Therefore, the first step for any budding Blackjack pro is to study *basic strategy*, a computer-simulated model, for the optimal way to play each and every hand of Blackjack.

There's only one way to consistently win at Blackjack — by learning to count cards. Anyone with average aptitude can become a card counter — but this skill takes discipline and drive, and most players don't want to get that serious about their hobby.

TABLE 5-1   **Strategies for Hard Hands**

Hard Hand	Playing Strategy
8 or less	Always hit.
9	Double versus 3–6. O/W (otherwise) hit.
10	Double versus 2–9. O/W hit.
11	Double versus 2–10. O/W hit.
12	Stand versus 4–6. O/W hit.
13	Stand versus 2–6. O/W hit.
14	Stand versus 2–6. O/W hit.
15	Stand versus 2–6. O/W hit.
16	Stand versus 2–6. O/W hit.
17 through 21	Always stand.

TABLE 5-2   **Strategies for Pair Splits**

Pair Split	Playing Strategy
A-A	Always split.
2-2	Split versus 2–7. O/W hit.
3-3	Split versus 2–7. O/W hit.
4-4	Split versus 5–6. O/W hit.
5-5	Never split.
6-6	Split versus 2–6. O/W hit.
7-7	Split versus 2–7. O/W hit.
8-8	Always split.
9-9	Split versus 2–6, 8–9. Stand versus 7, 10, A.
10-10	Always stand.

Making a side bet

Occasionally you may sit down at a Blackjack table that offers *side bets.* You can make these bets in addition to your basic wager (typically before the hand is dealt) in a separate, distinct betting box. The appeal of side bets is their huge payoffs for certain card combinations (up to 1,000 to 1 in *Lucky Ladies*, for example).

TABLE 5-3   **Strategies for Soft Hands**

Soft Hand	Playing Strategy
A-2	Double versus 5– 6. O/W hit.
A-3	Double versus 5–6. O/W hit.
A-4	Double versus 4–6. O/W hit.
A-5	Double versus 4–6. O/W hit.
A-6	Double versus 3–6. O/W hit.
A-7	Double versus 3–6. Stand versus 2, 7, 8. Hit versus 9, 10, A.
A-8 or A-9	Always stand.
A-10	Always stand.

Although several popular Blackjack side bets exist (you may have heard of some, such as *Super Sevens* and *Royal Match*), only one — *insurance* — is generally available at all Blackjack tables. Insurance is a hedge bet you can take whenever the dealer's upcard is an ace. You wager up to half of your original bet that the dealer's hole card is a ten (that the dealer has Blackjack). If the dealer does have Blackjack, your side bet pays back 2 to 1.

WARNING

Side bets are almost always bad, and you should avoid them. Unless the bean counters in the backroom make an error on their slide rules, every side bet in a casino favors the house with odds far worse (for you) than regular Blackjack. The insurance bet is a good example; it's just another tactic to separate gullible gamblers from the contents of their wallets.

Drawing the dealer's curtain

Now the dealer. . .drum roll, please. . .reveals that mysterious face-down hole card that can make or break your successful outcome (see Figure 5-2).

The following possible scenarios can result:

>> If the dealer has a natural (21), the game is over — you lose (unless you also have a natural; then you tie).

>> If the dealer's total is 16 or less, the dealer has to hit.

>> If the dealer busts (exceeds a total of 21), the game is over — you win if you haven't also busted.

>> If the dealer's hole card reveals a total of 17 or more, the dealer must stand. Your hand must beat the dealer's hand to win.

FIGURE 5-2:
The dealer's hand is revealed.

© Lynn Goldsmith/Corbis

REMEMBER

The dealer is bound by these rigid rules. For example, if the dealer has 15, she can't choose to stand, even if doing so is beneficial, because she must always hit until reaching 17 or higher. And the dealer doesn't have the options that are available to players, such as doubling down or splitting.

Looking at payouts

After the dealer has completed her hand, you know whether you win, lose, or tie. The following are some of the payout possibilities:

>> **You're dealt a natural** (your first two cards equal 21). The house pays you 3 to 2 — at least in most casinos — which means that a $10 bet wins $15 ($25 total, for a profit of $15).

>> **You bust, exceeding 21.** You lose, no matter what happens with the dealer's hand, and the casino wins your $10 bet (a loss of $10).

>> **Your hand is higher than the dealer's hand.** For example, your hand totals 20, and the dealer has 18. You win even money on your wager — $10 for every $10 bet ($20 total, for a profit of $10).

>> **Your hand is lower than the dealer's hand.** For example, you have 17, and the dealer has 19. You lose, and the dealer keeps your chips (a loss of $10).

>> **You and the dealer tie, or have a *push*.** Nobody wins, and no money changes hands.

REMEMBER

Mathematically speaking, the casino game of Blackjack is the best table game to play because of its favorable odds. The small house edge comes from the simple fact that the dealer goes last and that many players bust out and lose their money before the dealer even acts on his hand.

Blackjack protocol: How to avoid trouble

When playing Blackjack, you want to ensure that you don't make any faux pas. Just like in other casino games, etiquette is important when playing Blackjack (check out Book 6, Chapter 3 for general casino etiquette). Blackjack is a fairly social game, and talking openly about your hand with other players is common. But make no mistake, Blackjack — along with poker — boasts a long history of innovative or desperate players who cheat in order to get an edge. And modern casinos are vigilant about stopping any suspicious activities that suggest card-marking or other nefarious techniques. Consequently, you want to be careful, especially as a rookie, how you handle yourself — not to mention your cards and chips. For example, you can easily bend cards without realizing you're doing anything wrong.

Here are some tips to help you be a good citizen of the Blackjack table:

>> If you're uncertain as to what behaviors draw suspicion, explain to the dealer that you're new to the game and ask him to inform you if you're making any mistakes.

>> Follow the game protocol by turning over your cards when you bust or have a natural (in a face-down game).

>> Remember that you aren't competing against other players at the table, so don't feel like you have to hide your cards like you do in poker.

>> Lastly, don't give any advice. Although you have good intentions, other players rarely welcome your help, which can backfire if they follow it and lose. Telling other people how to play or how to spend their money is also poor etiquette.

Identifying Common Mistakes

In order to help you play your cards correctly and understand basic strategy principles, Table 5-4 includes six examples of common mistakes and the rationale for how to avoid them.

TABLE 5-4   **Common Blackjack Mistakes — and How to Avoid 'Em**

Common Mistake	Scenario	Strategy	Explanation
Hitting with a stiff hand when the dealer's card is low	You have a 12 (a 5 and 7), and the dealer's upcard is a 4.	Stand	A general rule for these troublesome stiff hands is to stand against a dealer's upcard of 2 to 6 and hit against a dealer's upcard of 7 or higher.
Standing with a soft hand, ace and 6 or less	You have an ace and a 4.	Hit	Always hit or double down on soft 17 or less (when you hold an ace and 2 through 6).
Not splitting when you have two 8s	You have two 8s and the dealer's upcard is a jack.	Split	Splitting the 8s considerably reduces the house edge on this difficult hand. If you chicken out and don't split, the dealer has an advantage higher than 50 percent against you.
Splitting two face cards	You have a queen and king.	Stand	Close to 70 percent of your gain in Blackjack comes from being dealt either 20 or 21, so don't be too quick to part with your gift horse.
Not doubling down on 11 when the dealer has a 10 up	You hold a 5 and a 6 and the dealer's upcard is a 10 or face card.	Double down	The odds favor the brave in this scenario, and you'll make more money over the long run by taking the extra risk and doubling down.
Not taking advantage of a weak dealer upcard	You hold a 5 and a 5, and the dealer's upcard is a 2.	Double down	When the dealer has a small upcard (2–6), you typically want to go gangbusters and double down or split whenever you can. Against the bigger upcards (7 through ace), you tend to split and double down less often.

If you can avoid these six common mistakes, you're ahead of 95 percent of the players in the casino. Very few gamblers understand that a correct way exists to play each and every hand of Blackjack. After you acquire that knowledge, you can whittle the odds against you down to nothing at a good single-deck Blackjack game.

Chapter 6

Not Just For High Rollers: Baccarat

The camera pans through a luxurious casino in London and then zooms in on two high rollers at the chemin de fer table (a European version of Baccarat). A gorgeously dressed woman turns to the dapper-looking gentleman in a tuxedo and says, "I admire your luck, Mr. . . ." "Bond," he replies as he coolly lights his cigarette, "James Bond."

The year 1962 was the first time the viewing public saw Sean Connery as Ian Fleming's secret agent in *Dr. No,* and, even today, people still know Baccarat as James Bond's game. With all its mystique and opulence, Baccarat has become *the* game for millionaires, princes, celebrities, and, of course, those in the espionage business.

If you haven't tried Baccarat, I can guess why: You think that because you're not a millionaire, royalty, a movie star, or a spy, you don't deserve entree into the glamorous game. The tuxedoed dealers, the chandeliers, and the thick, red-velvet ropes that seem to warn "Commoners, keep out" can intimidate many a player.

Don't be cowed, though. The formality is just for show, and behind its elegant veneer, the game itself is surprisingly easy to play — and offers some of the best odds in the casino. Baccarat isn't so much a game of skill as a game of luck. Playing Baccarat is sort of like betting the red or the black on a roulette wheel or hitting the *spin* button on a slot machine — except that if you bet evenly and consistently, your bankroll lasts much, much longer.

In this chapter, we coach you through the game of Baccarat and explain just how to bet evenly and consistently. We identify the two most common versions of Baccarat, explain the odds, and offer plenty of tips to help you convince everyone at the table that you're as suave and sophisticated a player as the world's most beloved secret agent.

Counting Down the Baccarat Basics

Baccarat is a simple card game: In the regular version of Baccarat (also called *formal, traditional,* or *big Baccarat*), the *croupier,* or dealer, deals only two hands, no matter how many players are seated at the table — and as many as 14 can play. One hand is the *player's hand,* and the other is the *banker's hand.* The object of the game is to bet on which of the two hands will come closest to a total of 9 points, also called a *natural* (a total of 8 points is also a natural, but it loses to 9). Players make all bets before the croupier deals the cards, and unlike blackjack, you can't make additional bets, such as doubling down, splitting, and so on. You have only three bets to choose from in Baccarat. You can bet on

» **The player's hand:** A winning bet on the player's hand pays *even money* (1 to 1). So a winning bet of $10 would receive another $10.

» **The banker's hand:** A win on the banker's hand also pays even money, *minus a 5 percent commission* (the casino charges a commission on this bet because the banker's hand has a better mathematical chance of winning, so the 5 percent commission helps even up the odds between the two bets, although even with the added commission, the banker's hand is still the best of the two bets). The dealer keeps track of these commissions (they aren't actually taken from each bet) and settles up either at the end of the shoe or when you're ready to leave. So a winning bet of $10 would actually end up netting only $9.50. However the croupier only charges this 5 percent commission on winning bets.

» **A tie:** A winning wager on the tie bet pays 8 to 1.

WARNING

The tie bet isn't a smart bet because the house has more than a 14 percent advantage (meaning the casino wins approximately $14 for every $100 you bet), and one that sober people shouldn't even *think* about making. However, at some clubs the house pays 9 to 1 on tie bets, which reduces the edge to less than 5 percent, but it's still not a wise bet.

Both hands start with just two cards, and depending on the starting total, the banker or player hand sometimes draws one more card. Whichever hand comes closest to 9 wins. Because 9 is the highest score, any amount of 10 or more automatically subtracts 10 points; 10 is actually worth 0, 11 is 1, 12 is 2, and so on. After the total reaches 10 or more, simply drop the first digit, and that's the score of the hand. If the player's hand consists of an 8 and a 9, the hand's score is actually 7 (8 + 9 = 17 − 10 = 7). So that's a pretty cool feature of Baccarat — ensuring that you can't bust out like in blackjack.

Remembering the following pointers about Baccarat basics can improve your chances of winning:

>> Two hands are dealt — the player's hand and the banker's hand.

>> Each hand starts with two cards.

>> Whichever hand has the closest to a total of 9 wins.

>> Each *pip card* (cards 2 through 9) is worth its face value; the 2 equals two points, the 5 equals five points, and so forth.

>> Aces count as one point.

>> Tens and royals (kings, queens, and jacks) are worth nothing. In fact, the name of the game is similar to the Italian word *baccara*, meaning *zero*.

>> Suits (clubs, spades, diamonds, and hearts) are meaningless.

TIP

With the exception of blackjack and certain bets in craps, Baccarat is one of the best table games to play in a casino. The house edge on the player's hand is 1.24 percent and 1.06 percent on the banker's hand!

CAN YOU SAY "BACCARAT"?

Pronouncing the name of the game may just be one of the most difficult things about Baccarat. But you don't need to speak a foreign language to play this game. The name is simple to say. Don't pronounce the "t" at the end, and let it roll off your tongue; just say "*bah*-cah-rah" and not "back-uh-rat."

The history of the game is a little unclear. Some think Baccarat evolved from Tarot cards or the French game of vingt-et-un (a forerunner of blackjack). Whatever its roots, Baccarat spread from Italy to France to Great Britain between the 15th and 19th centuries. Its appearance in the New World is far more recent; it has only been a staple of American casinos for the last 50 years.

Of course, more nuances distinguish the novice players from the pros in Baccarat. When you step foot in a casino and decide to try Baccarat, you need to know that you can play two types of Baccarat in most casinos in the United States: formal Baccarat, also referred to as *traditional* or *classic* Baccarat, and Minibaccarat. Although both games follow the same set of rules, each has its notable distinctions. The following sections explain the main differences.

Formal Baccarat: High stakes, high rollers

Many high rollers are more interested in testing their luck than exercising their math skills. So Baccarat is often the high-stakes game of choice for the wealthiest gamblers. Minimum bets vary greatly from club to club, but posted maximums are typically $2,000 to $4,000. However, the larger casinos often extend higher limits to premium players, and the maximum bet can reach six figures — depending on the high roller's credit line and how much risk the casino is willing to take.

Playing in a room apart

In the biggest games, you find a cast of characters that could populate the *Dr. No* film set — and their wagers reflect their glittering diamonds and gold cigarette cases. Because of the large amounts of money bet on Baccarat, the game is sometimes played in an area that's private (open only to premium players or VIPs) and tucked away from the noise and crowds of the casino. This seclusion also allows the casino to provide a measure of security for its high rollers. Sometimes millions of dollars change hands each night at the high-stakes Baccarat tables in the biggest casinos.

Setting a table for 14

Baccarat's upscale clientele isn't the only aspect that sets it apart. Play takes place on a large table that seats from 1 to 14 players, as Figure 6-1 shows. (You may notice the absence of seat 13 in this illustration; most casinos skip that unlucky number at their tables.)

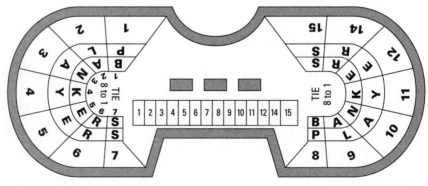

FIGURE 6-1: The formal Baccarat table for 14 players.

© *John Wiley & Sons, Inc.*

Dressing to the nines

Because of the elegance of Baccarat, most players honor its tradition and dress accordingly. Of course, the level of dress varies from casino to casino and is becoming less formal, but you're safe to assume that Baccarat is the place to wear that long-neglected tuxedo or parade that sparkling evening gown.

Dealing and calling

Three croupiers serve the formal or regular Baccarat table. The caller, one of the three croupiers, handles the game and announces the card totals and the winning hand. He may also use an elongated paddle to move cards and chips around the table. The two others stand on either side of the caller and pay off winning bets, collect losing bets, and post commissions (on bank hands).

Banking on the house

Most casinos use an eight-deck shoe to deal the cards in regular Baccarat games. And you and other players are part of that ritual! Every player gets a turn at handling the shoe and acting as the banker or dealer. You continue to deal as long as the banker's hand is winning; when the banker finally loses, a different player deals the cards.

You're the banker in name only, because dealing offers you no additional risk or advantage; it just makes the game more sociable. You can choose to participate in the ritual or decline and pass the shoe to the next player.

REMEMBER

When you're acting as the banker, you're expected — but not required — to bet on the house (banker's hand). If you'd rather bet on the player's hand, custom dictates that you allow the shoe to pass to the next player. But no matter which hand you bet on, you must be involved and have a wager for the upcoming hand (if you want to deal).

Minibaccarat: Less glitz, lower stakes

Is your tuxedo at the cleaners? Or is your betting bankroll a little low these days? If the formality and high stakes of the regular Baccarat table isn't to your taste, then Minibaccarat may be the game for you. With lower minimum bets ($2 to $5), this condensed version gives low rollers or the uninitiated a taste of Baccarat. It also offers the same low-house advantage of regular Baccarat.

Distinguishing differences

Minibaccarat follows the same rules as its upscale cousin, formal Baccarat. The following are the main features that distinguish Minibaccarat from regular Baccarat:

>> Play takes place on a smaller, semicircular table with places for only seven players, but just like regular Baccarat, the game can begin with only one player.

>> Just one *croupier* (called a dealer at this table) is present instead of three.

>> The dealer handles all the cards and deals them face-up.

For specifics on how to play formal Baccarat and Minibaccarat, check out the next section.

Relaxing at minibac

In most casinos, you find the Minibaccarat, or minibac, tables nestled in with the blackjack tables. And picking up on the relaxed and informal tone won't take you long. You can feel right at home at Minibaccarat even if you're dressed in shorts and flip-flops. Figure 6-2 shows you what a typical Minibaccarat table looks like.

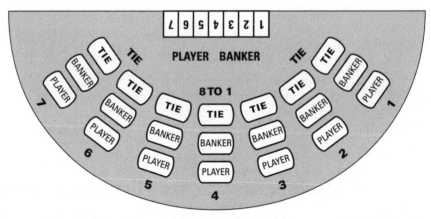

FIGURE 6-2:
The Minibaccarat table for seven players.

© John Wiley & Sons, Inc.

TIP

When playing minibac — or formal Baccarat, for that matter — tipping the croupier is perfectly acceptable. Just place a bet for the dealer as you do at other table games.

Stepping into Baccarat

Whether you play Minibaccarat or decide to dust off your evening wear and head for a high-stakes formal game, don't worry about any pressure. Baccarat is a no-brainer. But in case you're nervous and need to build your comfort level, the following sections walk you through a game one step at a time.

Positioning yourself to play

Feel free to sit in any open seat at the table — your position won't help or hinder your game in any way, nor does it matter how many people are playing. Then observe the unique aspects that distinguish a Baccarat table (formal and Minibaccarat) from any other gaming surface:

>> **A number outlined on the felt before each player.** The numbers indicate each player's position and run from 1 through 7 in Minibaccarat and 1 through 15 in regular Baccarat; most casinos skip the unlucky number 13.

>> **Three designated boxes.** These boxes or circles are located on the felt above each player's number. Closest is the *player* bet box. Next is the *banker* bet box, and farthest away is the *tie* bet box. Check out Figures 6-1 and 6-2 to see how the boxes may appear on both a formal and a Minibaccarat table.

On the formal table, you also see a boxlike device called the *shoe*, which houses the cards. At the beginning of a game, one of the three croupiers gives the shoe to a player, who acts as the banker and deals the cards from the shoe.

Betting the banker (or the player)

Before the banker deals the cards, the caller asks you to place your bets. So there you are — you haven't received your cards, and yet you must decide the winner: the player or the banker. Or will you have a tie?

REMEMBER

As we explain earlier in this chapter in "Counting Down the Baccarat Basics," you're betting on which hand — the player's or the banker's — you think will come closest to 9, the highest possible score, or if you think you'll have a tie. Baccarat is simply a matter of luck. No skill or card counting or complex mathematical formula can beat the house, but knowing that the odds favor the banker's hand can give you an edge.

Betting on the banker's hand offers the best odds (−1.06 percent) because of the simple fact that the banker acts after you each round. Baccarat rules are designed to provide a calculated split between the two hands. Statistical analysis shows the odds of the player's hand winning are about 44.6 percent, the banker's hand winning around 45.8 percent, and ties winning about 9.6 percent. Even after factoring in the house commission (5 percent on winning bets), the banker's hand is still your best bet. For example, if you bet $10 on the banker's hand, you'd push two $5 chips out into the second box or circle in front of you (the one marked Banker or Bankers).

Dealing the hand

If you're playing regular or formal Baccarat, as soon as the caller announces, "No more bets," the player with the shoe (known as the banker) deals out four cards. If you're the banker, follow these steps:

1. **Deal two cards, sliding one card face-down to the caller for the player's hand and slipping the second face-down under the corner of the shoe for the banker's hand.**

   Repeat this process with the third and fourth cards.

2. **Take the two cards you dealt for the player's hand and place them face-down in front of the player with the largest bet.**

   This player gets the privilege of taking the first peek at these cards and then turns them over. No advantage actually exists to seeing the cards first — just part of the pomp.

3. **Hand the caller the banker's hand when she requests you to do so.**

   Before you receive this request, the caller places the player's hand face-up in the center and announces the value.

   Then the caller places the banker's cards face-up in the center and announces the total.

Le petit is a natural of 8 points; a natural of 9 is *le grande.* If either hand draws a point total of 8 or 9 on the first two cards, the le grande wins. If the hands have equal value, then you have a tie. Either way, the game is over.

REMEMBER

When the player or the banker draws a total of 8 or 9, the hand stands, and the round ends. This rule is the *natural rule* and overrides all the other rules.

Drawing for another card

If neither hand has a total of 8 or 9, an additional card may be drawn on one or both hands, depending on the amount in the hand. The rules for drawing are clear-cut. Neither the player's hand nor the banker's hand has discretion but must follow predetermined rules. The following sections explain the rules.

Following the player's rules

To draw an additional card, the banker's hand is dependent on the total of the player's hand — the reason these rules are known as the *player's rules*. For example, the player's hand has two face cards, which equal 0. The banker's hand has a 9 of hearts and a 10 of diamonds, giving it a point value of 9, a natural. The banker's hand wins based on the natural rule, and the game is over. There are no gray areas, no decision making, no folding, no passing, no bluffing. Just the rules.

TIP

Don't worry if you can't remember these rules — the caller (and dealer in Mini-baccarat) directs all the action. Table 6-1 shows the three possibilities.

TABLE 6-1

Player's Rules

Value of Player's Hand	What to Do
8 or 9	Stands on a natural
6 or 7	Stands
0 to 5	Draws a card

REMEMBER

The banker's hand follows these same player's rules as long as the player's hand does *not* draw a third card. If the player's hand draws a third card, the situation gets a little more complicated, and the banker's hand must follow special *banker's rules*. The following section explains what happens when the player's hand draws a third card.

Adhering to the banker's rules

The banker's rules apply only to the banker's hand, and only in those situations when the player's hand draws a third card. These third-card rules are consistent for all variations of Baccarat around the world. Table 6-2 shows the banker's rules.

REMEMBER

Neither the player nor the banker will ever have more than three cards in their hand, but the goal is simple — whichever hand has the higher total wins.

Knowing when the banker follows the banker's rules

Once again, unless the player draws a third card, the banker must adhere to the player's rules for the two-card total. Only when the player draws a third card do the banker's rules come into play.

TABLE 6-2

Banker's Rules (When the Player's Hand Has Three Cards)

Value of Banker's Two Cards	Banker's Action
8 or 9	Stands on a natural
7	Stands according to player's rules
6	Draws if player draws a third card and player's new hand total is 6 or 7
5	Draws if player draws a third card and player's new hand total is 4 through 7
4	Draws if player draws a third card and player's new hand total is 2 through 7
3	Draws if player draws a third card and player's new total is 0 through 9
0, 1, or 2	Draws a card

You can refer to Table 6-3 as a resource for when the banker draws. In this table, the numbers across the top, 0 through 9, represent the player's hand total. The banker must stand or draw, depending on the player's hand point total and the banker's starting two cards.

TABLE 6-3

When the Banker Can Draw After a Player's Third Card

Banker's Score	Player's Third Card									
	0	1	2	3	4	5	6	7	8	9
7	S	S	S	S	S	S	S	S	S	S
6	S	S	S	S	S	S	D	D	S	S
5	S	S	S	S	D	D	D	D	S	S
4	S	S	D	D	D	D	D	D	S	S
3	D	D	D	D	D	D	D	D	S	D
2	D	D	D	D	D	D	D	D	D	D
1	D	D	D	D	D	D	D	D	D	D
0	D	D	D	D	D	D	D	D	D	D

S = STAND D = DRAW

Having trouble memorizing all these variations? Don't strain your brain! Remember that as a player you don't have to remember any of these rules — the dealer does all the work.

REMEMBER

Avoiding Baccarat Time Wasters

We've said it before, and we'll say it again: Baccarat is a game of luck. Yes, yes — if a smart guy like James Bond played it, then it has to require some brains or skill, or at least a good sense of fashion flare, right? The truth is that most of the advice we can give you has more to do with how to increase the enjoyment of your Baccarat experience than how to improve your winnings. But consider following these last bits of advice — about what *not* to do.

Wagering on ties

Don't *ever* bet on the hands to tie. Even though the payoff when you win is far better (8 to 1 instead of even money), ties occur only about once every 9½ hands, making the reward not worth the risk (house edge is a whopping 14.36 percent). This bet is a waste of your hard-earned money.

REMEMBER

Because a tie hand is a *push* (neither the player or the banker wins), your bet on either the player or the banker is also a push — and you won't lose any money for that hand.

Note taking and keeping score

Taking notes is a waste of time. Because of superstitious or misinformed players, casinos routinely stock score cards and pencils at Baccarat tables for players to keep track of how the hands are running. The past dozen or so hands are no indication of how future hands will play out, so the pencil and paper are more useful for your grocery list.

Counting cards

No successful card-counting system exists for Baccarat. Even though some studies have shown that the low cards favor the player's hand and high cards favor the banker's hand, statistically speaking, the margin is so small that card counting really offers no advantage.

Relying on instinct

Some people think they were born under a lucky star. They believe they have the uncanny ability to predict whether a coin lands on heads or tails with accuracy. Or perhaps their instincts at the tables tell them when a hot streak is about to begin . . . or end.

But our opinion on this matter falls into the rational and scientific camp: You have no way to turn negative odds into a positive expectancy game. Although Baccarat is definitely one of your best bets because the slow pace (especially in the formal version) and slim house edge combine to make it a good value for you, over the long run, you end up a slight loser despite the amount of mojo you think you have working for you. You may win in the short term, but no amount of guesswork can swing the odds in your favor.

TIP

Don't even try to rely on your instinct. Just drink in the pageantry and ambiance of this elegant game and enjoy the ride. And remember: Don't be intimidated by the posh crowd. You have every right to sit down next to the billionaires and try your luck at this historic game.

Chapter 7

Rolling the Dice: Craps

S tep into any casino and follow the noise — and you no doubt end up at the Craps table. Craps is loud. Craps is fast. And Craps is definitely where the action is. While the poker tables emit a restrained energy, the mood of the Craps corner is one of exuberance — irrational and otherwise. Above the jabbering of slot machines, whirring of roulette wheels, and *ca-ching*-ing of payouts, you can hear the Craps crowd cheering and moaning as luck shifts with each roll of the dice, the heart of the game.

Despite all its heart-pounding intensity, Craps can be one of the best games in the house. Depending on which bets you make, the house edge can be less than 1 percent. And even though Craps may seem incredibly complex, it's easy to play. After all, in essence, you're betting on the outcome of two rolled dice.

This chapter gives you the lowdown on Craps, including how you play and what your best (and worst) bets are. So let your ears lead the way. Listen for the roar of the crowd and get ready to rock — and *roll.*

Setting the Craps Stage

Craps is like no other casino game. The sheer variety of bets means you and other players at the same table may all be playing different games. A single dice roll may mean a win to you, a loss to another player, and absolutely nothing to a third.

Before you can start making your bets, you need to know how to play Craps. This section looks at the game's objective and its important props and characters. We also have a short section on how to properly behave at a Craps table.

Casting the dice

REMEMBER

The dice are the heart and soul of the Craps game. No doubt, you know a die (the singular form of dice) when you see it: that six-sided cube, one to six dots (or *pips*) marking each face.

In the game of Craps, the objective is to bet on the outcome of the roll. So you can help yourself by understanding the various combinations of dice throws. Take a look at Figure 7-1. A pair of dice has 36 possible ways to land on a given throw, which means that you have a 1-in-36 chance of rolling any single combination. But for the most part, the dice *total* is what matters in Craps. A 7 is still a 7, whether the dice come up 5 and 2, 6 and 1, or 3 and 4. Because some totals have multiple combinations, certain rolls are more likely than others.

Number Rolled							True Odds		
2							35	to	1
3							17	to	1
4							11	to	1
5							8	to	1
6							6.2	to	1
7							5	to	1
8							6.2	to	1
9							8	to	1
10							11	to	1
11							17	to	1
12							35	to	1

FIGURE 7-1: The possible dice combinations.

© John Wiley & Sons, Inc.

In Craps, you have the following possibilities of outcomes:

>> Six ways to roll a 7, or 16.7 percent

>> Five ways to roll a 6 or an 8, or 13.9 percent for each

>> Four ways to roll a 5 or a 9, or 11.1 percent for each

>> Three ways to roll a 4 or a 10, or 8.3 percent for each

>> Two ways to roll a 3 or an 11, or 5.6 percent for each

>> One way to roll a 2 or a 12, or 2.8 percent for each

REMEMBER

Don't think of Craps as a game of just dice rolls but as a game of dice-roll *sequences*. Craps is more than a toss of the dice; it's a series of tosses. Most bets win or lose based on numbers thrown in a certain order. Knowing the terminology can help you keep it straight: A *throw* is a single toss of the dice, and a *roll* is the series of throws that result in a win or loss for the main Craps bets. Sometimes you even hear the word *hand*, which refers to every *roll* (as in sequence of throws) a single *shooter* (see "Shooting for the whole table," later in this section) has before relinquishing the dice to the next player.

Surveying the lay of the table

REMEMBER

Before you can start to play Craps, you need to know the landscape. You play Craps on a long, narrow, felt-covered table (see Figure 7-2) that has a foot-high ridge running all the way around, making it the perfect mini-arena for tossing dice — or racing hamsters. The standard Craps table is large in order to accommodate up to 14 players at a time. Craps is a *stand-up* game — no chairs for you or the other players. At the top of the ridge is the *rail* with two grooves (the *rail rack*) perfectly sized to hold casino chips. But make sure you keep your drinks, purse, cigarettes, and everything else off the rail. A built-in shelf at your knees keeps your personal items safely out of the way of the game.

Depending on how you choose to bet, you place your bets in the designated area of the *layout* (the playing surface). Figure 6-2 shows the jigsaw puzzle of betting boxes. (We explain these boxes in "Relying on Strategy to Place the Best Bets," later in this chapter.) The layout consists of two parts:

>> The center section is for long-shot bets (see "Avoiding 'Sucker' Bets" for more on high-risk bets).

>> The left and right wings are for the main bets.

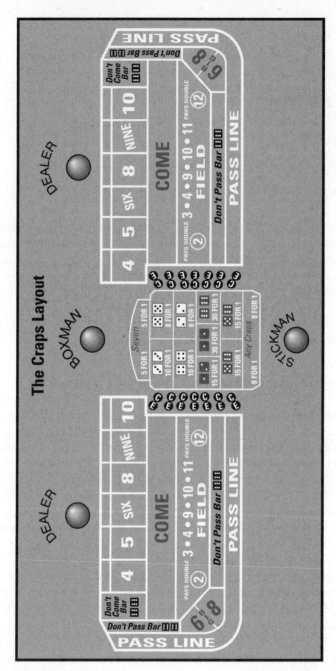

FIGURE 7-2:
The Craps layout.

© John Wiley & Sons, Inc.

The left and right halves of the table are identical to each other, so you can pick either one. Some space-constrained casinos have smaller Craps tables consisting of a center section and a single wing. But other than the truncated table (and reduced dice trajectories), game play at those tables is identical to play at full tables.

Getting to know the Craps crew

Before you start to play, you need to understand who's who at a Craps table. The following four people man a standard Craps table. (You can also check out Figure 7-2 to see where these people stand during play.) They're listed according to how much you interact with them during a session at the Craps table.

>> **Two dealers:** Each dealer covers one wing of the table. The dealer's job is to change your currency into chips, help place your bets, and pay off winners.

>> **Stickman:** The stickman, who stands at the middle of the table and opposite from the dealers, is in charge of the dice. His job is to retrieve and deliver the dice to the felt in front of the shooter by using a long, straight, putter-shaped stick. The stickman also makes the *call* (announcing the results of the roll to the entire table), oversees the central betting area (placing all bets in that area for players), and instructs the dealers to pay out winners.

>> **Boxman:** Sitting across from the stickman at the center of the table, the boxman is also the *bossman,* overseeing the entire game, releasing stacks of chips to the dealers, and collecting cash for the house. He watches the bets and keeps a wary eye on the dice, the other dealers, and you and the other players to make sure everything's on the up and up.

Shooting for the whole table

The *shooter* is a key character in Craps because she's the player who's rolling the dice. In Craps, *shooting*, or dice rolling, is a rotating affair. Each player gets a turn to roll for the entire table, and the honor moves clockwise around the table. When your turn comes around, the stickman pushes five dice toward you, and you select two. The only requirement to shoot is that you have a bet riding.

TIP

If you're a Craps newbie, you can refuse your turn to roll the dice, but we recommend you give it a try. Shooting is part of the experience of Craps. Even if your first roll goes completely off the table or lands in someone's drink, pocket, sleeve, mouth, or cleavage, the game continues, and nobody gets too upset. The stickman (when he's done laughing at you) calls, "No roll." Then the boxman inspects the errant die and gives you another shot at getting it right.

Minding Mr. Manners at a Craps table

REMEMBER

When you're playing Craps, most of the etiquette-related manners focus on the dice, so pay attention to where the dice are at all times. When the stickman yells, "Dice are out!" the shooter has permission to roll the dice. This is your signal to get your hands up and out of the way (assuming you're not the shooter).

The following are some of the simple do's and don'ts of Craps etiquette:

» **Keep drinks away from the rail.** And definitely don't hold your drink *over* the rail. Craps is a fist-pumping, back-slapping, wild game, so you're bound to get jostled and splash your whiskey on the felt.

» **Don't touch the numbers.** Craps dealers keep a lockdown on parts of the layout. Players are only allowed to place chips on the bets right in front of them: the pass-line and don't-pass bets, plus the come, don't-come, field, and Big 6/8. The unspoken demarcation line is the come box; any bet in the numbered squares requires a dealer's assistance. The same is true for all bets in the middle area; the stickman places those bets for all players. (Check out "Avoiding 'Sucker' Bets," later in this chapter, for more info about these bets.)

REMEMBER

» **Handle the dice with one hand only.** When your turn comes, never use two hands — and keep the dice where the crew can see them. Casinos are justifiably obsessed with cheaters who might sneak crooked dice into the game, so these rules limit those chances of cheating.

» **Do your best to toss a valid throw.** Toss the dice so they hit the far wall of the table and bounce off. This move ensures a random outcome and is considered a valid throw. Also, don't toss the dice too high or too soft, and keep the arc lower than the tallest player at the table.

>> **Leave the fancy pitches to baseball.** Don't fling the dice like a hotshot grounder to third — you're likely to leave piles of rubble in your wake and generate a dirty look from the boxman. As a dealer once said of dice, "They're small, light, and not made of dynamite."

Walking through Craps, Step by Step

Craps is definitely a luck-based game, but estimating the odds successfully does require some homework so you understand the chances of rolling certain number combinations. The good news is that your odds of coming out ahead of the house are some of the best in the casino if you stick to the basic bets (despite the numerous fancy bets available).

Before you decide to join the game, make sure you've read the previous section, "Setting the Craps Stage," for the lowdown on a Craps table layout and the important members of the cast and crew.

Buying in

The game cycle starts as you place chips — or have the dealer place them — onto the marked betting boxes on the table. Minimum Craps bets typically begin at $5. (The table minimum and maximum appear on the standard casino betting-terms placards on the inside wall of the table in front of each dealer.)

After you elbow your way in and claim a spot at the rail, you need to get some chips to play with. Wait until after the dealers pay out the winning bets and the dice are sitting idle at the center of the table in front of the boxman. Then ask the dealer for chips by saying "Change, please."

REMEMBER

Dealers can't take money directly from your hand, so drop the bills on the table. If the dealer is busy doing something else, just wait a few seconds. The crew has its own ways to keep track of all the players. After the dealer notices your bills, she takes them and slides a stack of chips back to you. Pick them up and put them in your *rail rack* — the two grooves on the rim of the table that act as trays for your casino chips.

Coming out: The first roll in Craps

Before the game starts, most players at the table place *line bets*, which means they put money on the pass line or the don't pass (see "Relying on Strategy to Place the Best Bets," later in this section, to understand what these actual bets mean). The action begins when the stickman pushes five dice to the shooter, who selects two for the throw. The shooter tosses the dice to the opposite end of the Craps table for the *come-out roll*, the first step in the game sequence. Although this throw looks like any other, certain rules apply for come-out rolls that are different from subsequent rolls.

REMEMBER

If the come-out roll is 7 or 11 (a *natural*), all bets on the pass line win even money. If the roll is a 2, 3, or 12 *(Craps)*, then all pass-line bets lose. For example, a player sets a $25 chip on the pass line and the shooter throws a 3 and 4 on the dice (to make a 7 for a natural). That player's bet wins, and he is paid immediately; the dealer on his side of the table places a $25 chip next to his original bet. Had the shooter rolled a 1 and 1 for a total of 2 (Craps), the pass-line bet would lose, and the dealer would remove the player's $25 chip.

Making a point

If the come-out roll is a 4, 5, 6, 8, 9, or 10, that number becomes *the point*. The line bets are neither paid nor raked if a point number is rolled on the come-out; the fate of those bets now depends on the next roll.

As soon as the point is established (assume it's the number 9), the shooter is no longer coming out. Instead, he now makes point rolls: throwing the dice until he either hits the number 9 again *(makes the point)* or throws a 7. If he makes the point by rolling a 9, the sequence starts over — the table reverts to a new come-out roll with the same shooter. However, if he throws a 7 before a 9, then the roll is a loser, the shooter's turn is over, and the dice move to the next shooter.

TIP

If you make your way to the edge of the action in the middle of a game, you can quickly tell what type of roll it is by looking for the *marker puck*, a small plastic disc. If the roll is a point roll, the puck sits white-side-up in the square above the point number on the felt. During the come-out roll, the puck sits black-side-up in the *don't-come area* (see Figure 6-2), and the dealer moves it as soon as the point is rolled. For example, if you see the white puck over the 4, you know that the table is currently in the point roll, and the shooter continues to roll until she hits a 4 *(makes the point)* or throws a 7 *(sevens out)*.

Relying on Strategy to Place the Best Bets

Craps offers more than 100 different kinds of bets. The table layout (Figure 6-2) gives a mere hint of all the betting options to consider, from bets that depend on a series of rolls to one-roll bets that hinge on only the next throw. But with a variety of bets comes a variety of odds. Many of the bets in Craps tilt too heavily toward the house to be worth considering.

REMEMBER

Before you toss down your cash and buy in at a table, make sure the table betting minimum is within your budget so you don't make a quick exit. Minimum bets are as low as $5, sometimes even $3, but during busy times or at ritzier clubs, the minimums rise accordingly, with many tables sporting $25 or $100 minimums.

You may have a good understanding of how to play Craps if you've read the previous sections in this chapter. (If you haven't, we suggest you check them out to get a good foundation of how to play Craps.) If you do understand the very basics of Craps, then this section is for you. Here we focus on betting and how you can use strategy to make the best bets.

You don't need to understand every single bet on the table to become a good player. In fact, some bets have such poor odds that you're better off avoiding them altogether. With so many options, you want to concentrate on the most advantageous bets. If you're fairly new (or even an old pro) at playing Craps, we suggest you focus on the following bets.

The pass-line bet

The main wager in Craps is the *pass-line bet*, also called the *front-line bet*. The pass-line bet is popular because it offers eight ways to win and only four ways to lose, yielding a low house edge of only 1.41 percent (the casino wins an average of $14 out of every $1,000 bet). The pass-line bet works as follows:

>> On the come-out roll, a 7 or 11 wins.

>> A come-out roll of 2, 3, or 12, known as a *Craps,* loses.

>> If the come-out roll is a 4, 5, 6, 8, 9, or 10, that number becomes the point, and the next sequence of rolls is point rolls.

>> A 7 is a loser after the point is established.

During point rolls, all pass-line bets can still win if the point is rolled before a 7, which can happen on the very next roll. However, the shooter may have to throw the dice dozens of times before the bet is resolved by either a 7 or the point number coming up on the dice. If the shooter *sevens out* — rolls a 7 before the point — all the pass-line bets lose. For example, if the come-out roll is a 10, the dealer moves the puck white-side-up into the 10 square. For the next roll or sequence of rolls, your pass-line bet wins if the roll is a 10 but loses if it's a 7. All other numbers rolled will be meaningless (at least for the pass-line bet).

You aren't allowed to *take down* (remove your pass-line bet) after the point is established, but you may increase it with an *odds bet,* which we discuss later in "The odds bet" section.

Most casinos allow you to make a pass-line bet (called a *put bet*) after the point is established. Some gamblers place these bets if they walk up to a table in the middle of point rolls. This move lets them play immediately instead of waiting for the next come-out roll. But put bets aren't smart moves, even if they look attractive when the point is 6 or 8. The better play is to make a come bet. (See the next section for more on the come bet.)

The come bet

After the point is established on a come-out roll, only the point and the 7 can affect bets on the pass line. Because it can take a dozen or more rolls to hit one of those two numbers, the *come bet* offers extra playing excitement to bettors. With a come bet, *every* point roll can be an independent come-out roll.

You can place come bets only after a point has been established for the pass-line bettors. To place a come bet, slide a chip to the large area on the layout marked *Come.* Make sure you slide the chip directly in front of you so the dealers know it's yours. Now you're betting on the next throw of the dice. Just like a pass-line bet,

>> 7 or 11 win outright.

>> 2, 3, or 12 loses.

>> If a 4, 5, 6, 8, 9, or 10 is thrown, that number becomes your point number. You win if that point number is thrown again before a 7, but you lose if a 7 is rolled before the point number.

So, for example, you have a pass-line bet on the board and the established point is a 6. That bet is only resolved if a 6 (win) or 7 (loss) is thrown. Before the next throw, you place a new bet in the come area, subject to the same minimum betting rules as the pass-line bet. Now the shooter throws a 2. Your original pass-line bet is unaffected, but you lose your new come bet. You put another chip on the come area, and this time the shooter throws an 8. The dealer moves that come bet to the 8 square. Now you're rooting for two different numbers, the 6 and the 8. If either number appears, one of your bets will pay off. Of course if a 7 appears, you lose both the original pass-line bet and the come bet on the 8.

When you hear about players going on great Craps rolls, some time period is usually associated with it . . . 30 minutes, 45 minutes, an hour. You lose your turn only when you *seven out*, or throw a 7 after the come-out roll. Only on seven outs does the whole table lose all its pass-line and come bets. So for a hot shooter to roll the dice over and over, she must be hitting point after point after point.

The don't-pass line bet

The *don't-pass line bet*, or *back-line bet*, plays the opposite of the pass-line bet. If you make this bet, you're called a *wrong-way* bettor. But don't worry, it's not immoral or against the rules to bet this way. The word *wrong* just means you're betting opposite the dice, or opposite the way most people bet. How you win your bets is also opposite. If the come-out roll is a 2 or 3 (Craps), the *don't-pass bet* wins even money. But if the shooter throws a 7 or 11, the bet loses. The don't-pass line bet is fairly safe, yielding a house edge of 1.36 percent, which is slightly better than the pass-line bet.

REMEMBER

You can only place chips on a don't-pass bet before a come-out roll. As soon as a point has been established and the shooter is throwing point rolls, the don't-pass bet is off-limits.

As a don't-pass bettor, you want the opposite of what pass-line bettors want. You don't want to see a 7 or 11 on the come-out roll (automatic loser). Instead you're rooting for a 2 or 3 (automatic winner) and are indifferent to a 12. If a point is established, you're hoping a 7 appears before the point number is rolled again. If that happens, your don't-pass bet wins.

People who play the don't pass are typically in the minority at a Craps table. Playing against the dice goes against one of the major appeals of the game: its community spirit. You cheer as the others are shaking their heads and cursing. But because the odds are slightly better, playing the wrong way is absolutely fine. Some people prefer the dark side approach, and over time the don't-pass bets keep more money in your wallet than the pass-line bets.

REMEMBER

In a pass-line bet, the 12 (along with the 2 and 3) means Craps. But, even though the 2 and 3 win even money in a don't-pass line bet, wrong-way bettors *tie* (no money is won or lost) if 12 is rolled. (The don't-pass rules can't be completely opposite the pass-line rules or the wrong-way player would have the same slight statistical advantage that the casino enjoys with the pass-line. So one number, usually the 12, becomes the odd man out.) Two dice of 6s (*box cars*) appear on the table in the don't-pass space to indicate that the don't-pass line *bars* the 12, preserving the advantage for the casino. Even with this negative feature, the don't-pass line is still a good bet.

The don't-come bet

You make a *don't-come bet* after a point has been established for the pass-line bet. But like don't-pass bets, these bets are wrong-way, too. The don't-come bets are at risk on the first throw — they lose if a 7 or 11 is thrown, but they win outright on a 2 or 3. The 12 is a *push* or tie — the same as the don't-pass bar. After the don't-come bet gets safely on base, it wins if 7 is rolled before the come-point is repeated, and it loses if the come-point is thrown before the 7.

The don't-come bet is to the wrong-way bettor what the come bet is to the regular Craps bettor. The bet allows him to have more numbers *working* instead of having to wait for a new come-out roll.

The odds bet

One of the best bets in the entire casino is the *odds bet*, offered on pass-line and come bets. The odds bet is also advantageous for wrong-way bettors playing the don't-pass and don't-come bets, although the payout is less. Because taking odds is such a good deal, casinos sometimes don't advertise this option. But if you look carefully, you can see the odds limit posted on the end zone under the rim where the dice bounce. If your bankroll can afford it, you should almost always take the odds bets.

BETTING AGAINST THE DICE

Craps players come in two basic flavors: right-way bettors and wrong-way bettors. Most players bet on the pass line and follow up with come bets. In other words, they bet *with* the dice. On the opposite side are the wrong-way bettors. They bet on the don't-pass bets and follow with don't-come bets — betting *against* the dice.

In addition to their polar-opposite strategies, right-way and wrong-way bettors hold another important difference: The right-way bettor must stick with the bet, while the wrong-way bettor can take down the bet at any time. Because wrong-way betting has the advantage of the bet after the point is established, the wrong-way bettor has no reason to ever take down the don't-pass bet.

Wrong-way bettors enjoy the thrill of bucking the crowd and betting the "don't." But you're definitely not going to win friends around the table when you win and everyone else loses.

TIP

You have no designated spot or box to place your odds bets, but the standard practice is to tuck them in right behind your pass-line bet. (See Figure 7-3.)

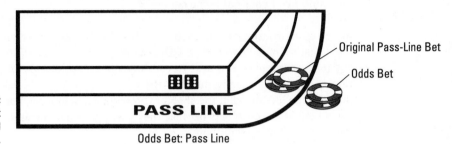

FIGURE 7-3:
The pass-line bet with odds placed behind it.

Original Pass-Line Bet

Odds Bet

PASS LINE

Odds Bet: Pass Line

© John Wiley & Sons, Inc.

Taking odds on pass-line and come bets

After a point is established for the pass bet, you can take the next step and *take odds.* All you need to do is place your odds bet directly behind your pass-line bet (this is done between dice rolls). As long as your pass-line bet is still alive (whether it's right after the point was established or ten rolls later), you're free to take odds or *back your bet.* The amount allowed on this bet varies from casino to casino and can range from 1 to 3 times the norm — or up to 100 times the odds in rare instances.

For example, three times the odds means you're allowed (but aren't obligated) to bet up to three times your original pass-line bet or come bets with an odds bet. Some casinos vary the amount of odds you can take from number to number, allowing several times more on the 6 and 8 than they do on other points. If in doubt, just ask your dealer about maximum odds allowed.

REMEMBER

Odds bets are called *free odds* because the house has no advantage over the player — the bet is a break-even proposition. By taking odds, you can reduce the house edge to less than 1 percent, so the bet is definitely worth making. If the point is rolled before a 7, you win both your pass-line bet and your odds bet. But if the 7 comes first, you lose both bets.

Say you put $5 on the pass line before a come-out roll in a casino that allows 3× odds. The shooter then throws a 4, a tough point number to hit because the shooter is twice as likely to throw a 7 before he throws a 4 (refer to Figure 6-1 earlier in this chapter for outcome possibilities). Not only is the house more likely to win the bet, but even if a 4 *is* thrown, your pass-line bet only pays even money, putting you at a serious disadvantage.

During the 10 to 20 seconds between dice throws, while other bettors place additional bets, you reach down and place $10 in chips behind your $5 pass-line bet. (You could have placed $15 because the casino allows 3× odds, but it's fine to place any multiple of your pass-line bet.)

As the game continues, the shooter tosses the dice and, sure enough, it's Little Joe! (That's Craps lingo for a 4.) The casino pays your pass-line bet even money ($5 for $5) and puts $20 next to your odds bet. Payout odds on a 4 are 2 to 1, a reward level that exactly matches the bet's risk. Your odds bet did nothing to improve the likelihood of the shooter throwing a 4 before a 7, but you should take advantage of the odds bets because they vastly improve the amount you're compensated for hitting your point.

Although the pass-line and come bets pay even money, the payouts for taking odds are as follows:

» When the point is 4 or 10, the odds bet pays 2 to 1.

» When the point is 5 or 9, the odds bet pays 3 to 2.

» When the point is 6 or 8, the odds bet pays 6 to 5.

REMEMBER

Always make sure you place odds bets in increments the casino can easily pay off. At $5 tables, the odds cause minor problems when players take single odds on pass-line and come bets. For example, if the point is 5 or 9, your odds bet should be an even number (such as $6 or $10, rather than $5), so the dealer can quickly pay out the 3 to 2 on winners.

Laying odds on don't-pass and don't-come bets

The wrong-way bettor can *lay odds* on don't bets just like the right-way bettor takes odds on the pass-line and come bets. However, the *don't* bettor (a wrong-way player who bets on don't pass and don't come) gets only a fraction of his odds bet when he wins. For example, he has to risk $40 to win $20 with odds on the 4 or 10. Even though the numbers may not look like it, these are actually true odds; laying odds reduces the house advantage to less than 1 percent over the player, which makes laying odds a good option for players. (Check Figure 7-4 to see what this bet spot looks like on the layout.)

REMEMBER

Unlike the come-bet odds, which are temporarily suspended during come-out rolls, the odds bets on don't-pass and don't-come bets are always *working* or *on.*

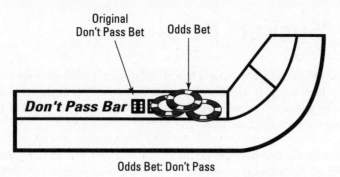

Original
Don't Pass Bet   Odds Bet

Don't Pass Bar

FIGURE 7-4:
The don't-pass
bet with an
odds bet.

Odds Bet: Don't Pass

© John Wiley & Sons, Inc.

The payouts for laying odds are as follows:

>> When the point is 4 or 10, the odds bet pays 1 to 2.

>> When the point is 5 or 9, the odds bet pays 2 to 3.

>> When the point is 6 or 8, the odds bet pays 5 to 6.

The odds calculation is slightly different for wrong-way betting. Use the example of placing a don't-pass bet of $5 and the point number 10. When you lay odds (place odds behind a don't-pass or don't-come bet), you calculate based on what you would win. At a double odds table, the most you could win is twice your $5 bet, or $10. To win that $10, you'd place $20 behind your bet because the odds pay 1 to 2 when the point is 10.

Taking the maximum odds

TIP

After the point is established, you usually want to take the maximum odds that you can safely afford on your bets. Most casinos offer single or double odds, but you can occasionally find a table that offers up to 10 times — sometimes even up to 100 times — the odds for games with low table minimums. If the table limit sign indicates "3x — 4x — 5x odds," the maximum allowed bet is three times the odds on the 4 or 10, four times on the 5 or 9, and five times on the 6 or 8. The house edge decreases as the odds increase, making the odds bet one of the best plays in the casino.

Avoiding "Sucker" Bets

Like any casino game, Craps has bets that have better odds for you as well as bets that have a higher edge for the house. In Craps, bets of the one-roll variety aren't player friendly — you win or lose depending on the next roll of the dice, and the odds are poor on these bets.

Most of the *bad* bets are in the center box in front of the stickman, but — be warned — danger is everywhere, and some of the riskiest (translation: "sucker") bets are oh so close to you. In this section, we tell you about some of the not-so-good bets and show why they're not the best way to make money at a Craps table.

Resisting the lure of Big 6 and Big 8

WARNING

A bet on the *Big 6* or *8* (found in the corner of the layout, temptingly close to you and next to the pass-line bet box) is a wager that the shooter rolls a 6 or 8 before a 7. This bet pays only even money and has a whopping house edge of 9.1 percent. (In other words, it's a horrendous bet to make because the casino wins an average of $91 out of every $1,000 bet.)

If you want to play something with a 6 or 8 in it, just mere inches away from the Big 6 and Big 8 is the more advantageous *six or eight place bet*, which pays 7 to 6 and has a house edge of only 1.52 percent!

Swearing off the place bets

REMEMBER

A *place bet* on one of the point numbers (4, 5, 6, 8, 9, or 10) is a wager that the shooter will roll that number before a 7. For example, you can place this bet at any time by saying to the dealer "I want to place number 5" and dropping your chips in the come area. The dealer then moves your chips to the appropriate number box. Place bets are identical to established come bets in how they win or lose. But their payout odds are different, and you have the option of taking them down and getting your chips back, should the whim hit you. Place bets are *off* on the come-out roll unless you ask for them to be *on*.

The house pays place bets at slightly less than correct odds, giving the house an edge of 4 percent on a 5 or 9 and a 6.67 percent edge on a 4 or 10.

The following are the payouts for a place bet:

>> A winning place bet on a 4 or 10 pays 9 to 5 (bet $5 and get paid $9).

>> A winning place bet on a 5 or 9 pays 7 to 5 (bet $5 and get paid $7).

>> A winning place bet on a 6 or 8 pays 7 to 6 (bet $6 and get paid $7).

Steering clear of buy bets

Buy bets resemble place bets but with one difference — they pay out at true odds in exchange for a 5 percent commission. Remember, the house normally reduces payout odds slightly, so the player isn't compensated in proportion to the risk level of his bet. (*True odds* means the house pays in exact proportion to the actual risk of the bet.) Buy bets are *off* by default on the come-out roll, meaning they're in suspended animation: They can neither win nor lose, no matter what's rolled. Bettors are also free to bet or remove buy bets at any time. For example, the 4 or 10 buy bet is slightly more advantageous to the player than the 4 or 10 place bet because the buy bet has a 4.76 percent house edge versus the place bet's 6.67 percent house edge.

REMEMBER

Be sure to factor the 5 percent commission into your bets ($1 on a $20 bet, for example). The 4 or 10 buy bet is the only buy bet worth making; for the 5, 6, 8, and 9 numbers, you're better off making a place bet. Nevertheless, players often use buy bets as a way to simplify their betting; they pay the commission and then enjoy correct odds on all their bets. Of course, the money all comes from the same place, but, as they say, "Different strokes . . ."

Laying off lay bets

A bet on one of the point numbers (4, 5, 6, 8, 9, or 10) is to lay odds that the 7 rolls before the point number — the opposite of a buy bet (check out the previous section for more info on buy bets). But like the buy bet, you can place or remove a *lay bet* at any time, and it's always *working* — which means the bet is active and can win or lose even on the come-out roll. Because the 7 is more likely to appear before the point number, lay bets have a better-than-even chance to win and, therefore, pay less-than-even money: A 4 or 10 lay bet pays 1 to 2; a 5 or 9 lay bet pays 2 to 3; and a 6 or 10 lay bet pays 5 to 6.

The casino takes a 5 percent commission on a win (not on the bet). So if you bet $60 on a 9, your net win is $38 ($40 minus $2 — or 5 percent of the $40 you win, not of your $60 original bet). To place these bets correctly, you need to lay $41 to win $20 on the 4 or 10 (your best bet), lay $31 to win $20 on the 5 or 9, and lay $25 to win $20 on the 6 or 8.

Passing up field bets

You can find *field bets* in the middle of the layout. These one-roll bets consist of the numbers 2, 3, 4, 9, 10, 11, and 12. They pay even money, except for 2 and 12, which pay 2 to and sometimes 3 to 1. The house edge on field bets is 5.56 percent and is popular with inexperienced players because it's a one-time roll that's simple to understand. But you rarely see Craps experts placing field bets because of the ugly house advantage.

Saying no to proposition bets

Proposition bets (also known as *center bets*) are one-roll bets you place on a 2, 3, 7, 11, or 12, and they're bets you can make on any roll of the dice. You can see the *prop* bets in the center of the table layout (check out Figure 6-2 earlier in this chapter). The stickman places these bets for you.

REMEMBER

Some proposition bets indicate the bet pays 30 *to* 1, while another table layout may state the payoff odds as 30 *for* 1. Be careful because these two types of bets are different. A bet that is 30 *to* 1 is paying 30 times the bet — but a bet offering 30 *for* 1 pays 29 times the bet. Although *for* seems like an innocent little word, don't let semantics fool you into thinking a bet pays more than it really does!

The smartest and simplest strategy is to ignore all bets in the center of the table (see Figure 7-5). If you feel an urge to play these bets, go for it. Just remember that we're offering you expert advice because we want to help you keep your losses at a minimum. The following proposition bets can suck your wallet dry:

>> **Any 7:** A one-roll bet that pays if the next roll is a 7 and loses if any other number appears. Although the probability of rolling a 7 is 5 to 1, this bet pays only 4 to 1 (or 5 *for* 1, which is the same thing). The casino's edge is 16.7 percent. Can you say ATM?

>> **Craps-eleven:** A one-roll bet on any Craps (2, 3, or 12) or the 11, represented by all those circled *C* and *E* initials on both sides of the center box. The payout is the same as for the bets for any Craps (8 for 1) or the 11 (16 for 1). House edge is more than 10 percent.

>> **Horn bets:** A one-roll bet that pays out if the next roll is 2, 3, 11, or 12 and loses if any other number appears. Horn bets may not even appear on all center-box layouts, but it's the same as Craps-eleven. You make a wager with four chips as if you're making four individual bets; you're paid 16 for 1 (for the 3 or 11) or 31 for 1 (for the 2 or the 12) — but you also lose the other three wagers. House edge is 12.5 percent.

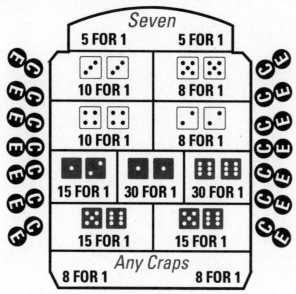

>> **The 2, 3, 11, or 12:** One-roll bets in the center box offering typical payouts of 16 for 1 on numbers 3 and 11 and 31 for 1 on numbers 2 and 12. (Some casinos may offer 30 for 1.) The house edge on these bets ranges from 11 to 14 percent.

>> **Any Craps:** A one-roll bet that pays if the next roll is a 2, 3, or 12 and loses otherwise. A box is available for this bet at the bottom of the center-bet layout. A win on any Craps pays 8 for 1, and the house edge is a stiff 11 percent.

Finding out the hard way

Four different *hard-way* bets are available to players on the following numbers: 4, 6, 8, and 10. A bet placed on a hard way wins if that number is thrown as a pair (for example, a dice roll of two 4s is a *hard 8*) and loses if that number comes *easy* (for example, a 6 and a 2 is an *easy 8*). You also lose the bet if any 7 is rolled.

The bets are placed in the center of the table, but, unlike the proposition bets, they aren't single-roll wagers; they remain on the board until resolved one way or the other. Hard-way bets are some of the worst bets on the table with the house edge a hefty 9 to 11 percent.

Chapter 8

Spinning Wheel Goes Round 'n' Round: Roulette

The Roulette wheel is a readily recognizable casino icon, conjuring up images of tradition and nobility, creating an ambience of luxury and elegance. In fact, Roulette is the oldest of all the casino games and is still around for two good reasons: It's fun, and it's easy to play. Roulette is probably the best place for you as a novice to start your gambling experience (although not always the smartest because of the odds).

The centerpiece of this age-old game is the beautifully crafted wheel in which a small white ball spins around a groove and drops down into one compartment, or *pocket,* on the wheel. Over the centuries, a number of scientists and mathematicians have tried to figure out how to beat the wheel, but such systems and theories always end in failure.

The fact is that where the Roulette wheel stops is a matter of chance. And chance rarely favors the players because the stiff house odds virtually ensure a profit for the casino. So playing Roulette isn't the likeliest route to becoming independently wealthy.

The game still has a seductive appeal, and if you catch on to some time-tested betting strategies, you can manage your gambling bankroll and stretch it into an enjoyable casino pastime. In this chapter, we explain the game's basics, some important betting tips, and some helpful strategies.

Getting the Spin on Roulette Basics

The basics of Roulette start with placing piles of colored chips on a long, rectangular table. After all the bets are made, the *croupier* (dealer) spins a large, bowl-shaped wheel with corresponding slots marked by colors and numbers in a counterclockwise direction, and then she releases a small, white ball in a clockwise direction. Anticipation builds as the ball and wheel spin, whirr, and slow. You wait for the ball to drop into one of the numbered pockets (hopefully in one of the spots you bet on!).

The goal of Roulette is basically to guess where the ball will land when the wheel finishes spinning. But, of course, you need to know a little more than that. This section takes a look at the wheel and the table betting area, walks you through a step-by-step Roulette play, and explains the role of the croupier.

Starting with the wheel

The first step toward understanding the game of Roulette is to decipher the Roulette wheel — the most recognizable casino gambling symbol in the world. Beautiful and flawless, the wheel is a finely crafted device weighing in at 100 pounds (45 kilograms) and costing thousands of dollars. A Roulette wheel has the following distinguishing characteristics:

>> The outside rim of the wheel is divided into numbers in alternating pockets of black and red.

>> The outside rim also has one or two pockets in green (0 and 00).

>> The numbers on the wheel are mixed up — they don't run consecutively or in any discernible pattern, such as alternating odd and even.

And how many number segments are on the wheel? The answer depends on where you're playing Roulette.

>> **United States:** If you're playing in Las Vegas, Atlantic City, or anywhere else in the United States (including cruise ships and Indian reservations), the Roulette

wheels you encounter most likely have a total of 38 numbered slots, or pockets, containing numbers 1 through 36, and two green compartments, one with a single zero and the other with a double zero. (This wheel is often referred to as the *American wheel.*)

>> **Europe and South America:** If you're gaming in Monte Carlo or another location in Europe or South America, your Roulette wheel (often referred to as the *European* or *French wheel*) has one pocket less than its American counterpart (it doesn't include the double-zero pocket).

Check out Figure 8-1, which shows the major differences between the American wheel and the European wheel.

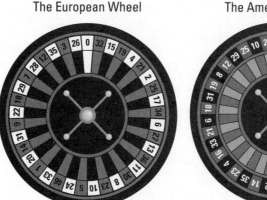

The European Wheel   The American Wheel

© John Wiley & Sons, Inc.

FIGURE 8-1:
The European
wheel with a
single zero (left)
and the American
wheel with zero
and double zero
(right).

REMEMBER

Roulette is more popular in Europe than in the United States mainly because the European wheel offers better odds with one less possibility to bet on (no double zero). But don't buy that plane ticket to Paris quite yet. Although most of the wheels in the United States have 38 pockets (two green numbers), you can find European wheels in some upscale American casinos.

Taking in the table layout

The other key component to a Roulette game is the *betting table* where the players place their chips for wagering. The betting table is situated adjacent to the wheel and is inlaid with a variety of squares and bars. Take a look at Figure 8-2 as we dissect the Roulette table to make some sense of it.

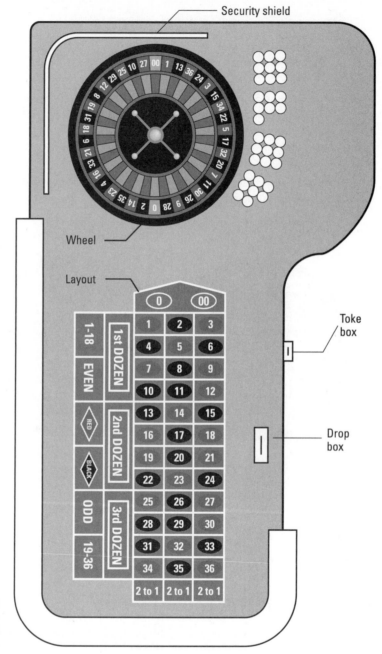

Security shield

Wheel

Layout

Toke box

Drop box

FIGURE 8-2: American Roulette wheel and betting layouts.

© John Wiley & Sons, Inc.

Two sections make up the Roulette table:

>> **Squares showing numbers and colors corresponding to the number and color pockets on the Roulette wheel.** These squares take up the most space on the layout. Unlike the wheel, the numbers on the table run in sequential order in rows of three. For example, in the third row from the top in Figure 8-2, you find the number 8 in black between 7 and 9. This betting spot corresponds to the black 8 pocket on the wheel, and it's where you place your chips if you want to bet on the 8.

>> **Bars wrapping around the outside of the rows of sequential numbers.** For example, you can see in Figure 8-2 bars containing the words *odd* and *even* and diamonds containing the words *red* and *black.* As you may guess, you place chips in these areas to bet on other aspects of the wheel outcome. For example, placing chips on *odd* is a bet that the ball lands on an odd number — *any* odd number.

I explain more about these various betting areas in the section "Betting: The Inside (and Outside) Scoop." *Inside bets* are bets you place on any of the columns of numbers; *outside bets* are — no surprise — bets you place in the outside areas.

TIP

The table normally accommodates up to six players, but some double table layouts can handle a dozen or more players. Try to get a seat right in the middle so you can place a bet in any area on the table. If you're stuck sitting at the end of the table or standing, you must slide chips toward the croupier and ask her to place bets on any area that you're not able to reach.

Betting with chips of a different color

You make bets by placing chips on the squares that correspond to the numbers or colors on the Roulette wheel. Roulette doesn't use normal casino chips, however. Instead, it features special color-coded chips unique to each player at the table and the particular Roulette table you're playing at. You can't play the chips you use at one Roulette table at a different game because the chips have no value marked on them.

Each player gets a different color of chip, allowing the croupier to distinguish one player's bet from another's. For example, your orange chips may be worth $5 each, while another player's blue chips may be worth $1 each. The distinctive chip color allows all players to have bets on the table without fear of mixing the bets up. In other words, if the player next to you places a stack of blue chips on your favorite number, go right ahead and stack your yellow chips on top of his.

When you join the game, or *buy in*, you generally ask for a *stack*, which consists of 20 chips. Let the croupier know what value you want assigned to the chips. The croupier keeps track of the value by placing a marker called a *lammer* on your color in the chip stacks. (Although at smaller casinos or when everyone is playing the same-value chips, lammers may not be used.) When you leave the table, the croupier exchanges your Roulette chips with casino chips, which you take to the cashier's window and cash out.

Dealing with the croupier

In the game of Roulette, the dealer is called the *croupier* (pronounced croop-ee-*ay*) and performs a variety of tasks to facilitate the play. When you're playing Roulette, just remember that the croupier does all of the following:

>> Converts your cash or casino chips to the colored chips unique to Roulette.

>> Places your chips on the table if you're unable to reach the spot on the table where you wish to bet them.

>> Spins the wheel counterclockwise and releases the ball clockwise, even as you continue to put down bets. Players may place bets until the croupier announces, "No more bets" and waves a hand over the table.

>> Announces the winning number and color as soon as the Roulette gods determine the ball's fate. Then the croupier places a marker (it looks like a chess piece) on the corresponding winning number on the table.

>> Rakes in losing bets and pays off winning bets (starting with those players farthest away). Don't grab your chips or place any new bets until the croupier completes paying off everyone. And be sure to pick up your winning chips if you don't plan on betting them again on the next spin.

Betting: The Inside (and Outside) Scoop

As we discuss in the previous section, the Roulette table layout breaks betting down into two sections: the inside bets and the outside bets. Inside bets involve betting specific numbers on the wheel; a winning bet on a single number pays 35 to 1. The outside bets are outside of the numbers on the table layout. They pay either *even money* (1 to 1) on red/black, high/low, or odd/even, or 2 to 1 on *columns* and *dozens*. (Check out "Making outside bets: Better odds but lower payouts" later in this section for more on columns and decks.)

Although you know what the bets mean, that information doesn't help much if you don't know how to make them. This section gives you the lowdown on identifying the table limits and placing your bets.

Knowing your (table) limits

Most games establish a minimum wager of, say, $1. In addition, inside bets may require a minimum *spread* — $5, for example. You can achieve a spread by making five different $1 bets (betting numbers 2, 13, 21, 28, and 33 for example), or by making one $5 bet (on just a single number). Basically a spread is the total of all your bets.

REMEMBER

The Roulette table usually has a sign displaying a table minimum and a chip minimum, but you can't mix and match inside and outside bets. For example, at a $5 table with a $1 chip minimum, you must place a minimum bet of $5 on the outside bets, or you can place five $1 number bets on the inside bets. You aren't allowed to bet $2 on the outside and $3 on the inside.

Making inside bets: Long shots and big payouts

Inside bets (betting on single numbers or a combination of numbers) have just the right elements for drama, nail biting, and impressing others. After all, when you set your chips down on a single number on the inside of the table, you're basically betting that, of all the 38 (or 37 on the European wheel) slots on the Roulette wheel, the ball will land in that particular number. But players typically bet on more than one number at a time to increase their chances of hitting a winner.

TIP

Although most croupiers review the layout and point out any ambiguous bets before dropping the ball in the track, make sure the croupier properly places your bets, and watch that other players don't accidentally knock your bet onto a different spot. You don't want the croupier to have to eyeball an imprecisely placed wager and tell you that your winning three-number street bet (paying 11 to 1) is so far out of place that it looks like a six-number line bet (paying 5 to 1).

Take a look at the circles on Figure 8-3. The following are examples of bets that players can make on the inside:

>> **Straight up:** This bet is on an individual number, such as 21. If the ball drops on this number, the bet pays 35 to 1. For example, if you bet $1, you receive 35 times your bet, plus your original bet, for a total of $36. (See Circle A in Figure 8-3.)

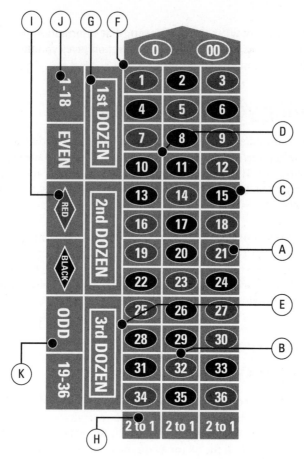

FIGURE 8-3:
Zooming in on
the table.

© John Wiley & Sons, Inc.

>> **Split:** This bet is on a line between two adjacent numbers, such as 29 and 32. If the ball lands on either number, the bet pays 17 to 1. (See Circle B in Figure 8-3.)

>> **Street:** This bet is on the outside line of a row of three numbers, such as 13, 14, and 15. If the ball lands on any one of these numbers, the bet pays 11 to 1. (See Circle C in Figure 8-3.)

>> **Corner:** This bet (also called a *quarter* or *box bet*) is on the corner of a group of four adjacent numbers, such as 7, 8, 10, and 11. If the ball lands on any one of these numbers, the bet pays 8 to 1. (See Circle D in Figure 8-3.)

>> **Line:** This bet is on the end, on the intersecting lines of a group of six numbers, such as 25, 26, 27, 28, 29, and 30. If the ball lands on any one of the six numbers, the bet pays 5 to 1. (See Circle E in Figure 8-3.)

>> **Five-number bet:** This bet is on the end of the line of the zero, double zero, one, two, and three boxes. If the ball lands on any one of the five numbers, the bet pays 6 to 1. (See Circle F in Figure 8-3.)

WARNING

Just say *No* to five-number bets! They have the distinction of being the worst bet on the table. The problem lies in the improper payout of 6 to 1 — less than the *true* odds (actual odds of bet hitting) — leaving the house with a hefty edge of 7.89 percent and making this bet extremely hazardous to your bankroll.

Making outside bets: Better odds but lower payouts

The outside bets involve the designated spots on the table that are *not* numbers — the ones on the rim of the table layout, nearest you and the other players. These bets are more likely to come up than the inside bets, but the payoffs are much less (either even–money or 2 to 1). However, if the ball lands on a green number (0 or 00), all of the following outside bets lose.

The corresponding circles (G through K) in Figure 8-3 indicate outside bets:

>> **Red/Black:** This bet says the winning number will come up either red or black. A win is paid at even money, or 1 to 1. For example, if you have a $10 bet on red and the ball lands on red 21, you win $10, plus the return of your original bet, for a total of $20. (See Circle I in Figure 8-3.)

>> **High/Low:** This bet says the winning number will be in the low half (1 to 18) or the high half (19 to 36), excluding 0 and 00. The house pays a win at even money. (See Circle J in Figure 8-3.)

>> **Odd/Even:** This bet says the winning number will be odd or even, excluding the 0 and 00. The house pays a win at even money. (See Circle K in Figure 8-3.)

>> **Dozens:** This bet is on the first, second, or third dozen numbers, excluding 0 and 00. The dozens are 1 to 12, 13 to 24, and 25 to 36, and each dozen contains six red and six black numbers. If the ball lands on one of the numbers in your dozen bet, the house pays the win at 2 to 1. (See Circle G in Figure 8-3.)

>> **Columns:** This bet is on one of three columns of a dozen numbers, excluding 0 and 00. If the ball lands on a number in your column bet, the house pays the win at 2 to 1. Note that Column One contains six red and six black numbers, Column Two has four red and eight black numbers, and Column Three has eight red and four black numbers. (See Circle H in Figure 8-3.)

Reciting Roulette Etiquette

Roulette attracts a polite, dignified gambler who enjoys a laid-back, casual game, as opposed to the frenzied atmosphere of, say, a craps game. (For a sense of how crazy craps can be, check out Book 6, Chapter 6.) And, as with any table game, understanding a few social niceties helps you fit right in with the suave Roulette crowd. This short section provides key points you need to remember when playing Roulette.

>> Place your money on the table when asking for chips — the croupier isn't allowed to accept it directly from your hand.

>> Bet with regular casino chips if you aren't going to play very long, especially on the outside bets, where plenty of room exists for lots of chips. If you want to make inside bets with casino chips, make sure to keep track of them so another player doesn't claim them in case of a win. In the case of a dispute, the croupier may call the pit boss to resolve the matter (see Book 6, Chapter 1 for more on the pit boss).

WARNING

>> Wait until the croupier removes the win marker from the layout — the signal that you can begin betting again. Placing new bets before the croupier finishes paying off bets from the previous spin is easily the biggest gaffe that new players make.

>> You can join a game anytime after the ball has landed and the croupier has finished paying off the winning bets.

>> Remember that favorite numbers, such as birthdays, anniversary dates, children's ages, high school boyfriends' IQs, and so on, possess no magical powers for winning, although they can make gambling more fun.

Improving Your Odds

Remember to stay realistic about the long odds on this popular game of chance. Approach Roulette with the sober realization that, with a house advantage of 5.26 percent on the American wheel, Roulette is among the worst bets in a casino. Despite the odds, you can still use some simple strategies to stretch your Roulette bankroll and enjoy the thrill of the spin. This section contains a few tips that can help you improve your chances of winning.

Roulette is a drain on your wallet simply because the game doesn't pay what the bets are worth. With 38 numbers (1 to 36, plus 0 and 00), the true odds of hitting a single number on a straight-up bet are 37 to 1, but the house pays only 35 to 1 if you win! Ditto the payouts on the combination bets. This discrepancy is where the house gets its huge edge in Roulette.

Starting with the basics

Strategy is critical if you want to increase your odds of winning. The first time you play Roulette, the players sprinkling the layout with chips may look as if they're heaping pepperoni slices on a pizza. You can make many different bets as long as you stay within the table's maximum limits. Consequently, few players make just one bet at a time.

Of course, the more bets you make, the more complicated and challenging it is to follow all the action. Here are two possible plans of attack to simplify matters:

>> **Stick to the table minimum and play only the outside bets.** For example, bet on either red or black for each spin. This type of outside bet pays 1 to 1 and covers 18 of the 38 possible combinations.

>> **Place two bets of equal amounts on two outside bets: one bet on an even-money play and the other on a column or dozen that pays 2 to 1.** For example, place one bet on black and one bet on Column Three, which has eight red numbers. That way, you have 26 numbers to hit, 4 of which you cover twice. You can also make a bet on red and pair it with a bet on Column Two, which has eight black numbers. Again, you cover 26 numbers, and 4 of them have two ways to win. Pairing a bet on either red or black with Column One (or on one of the three dozens) covers 24 numbers, and 6 numbers have two ways of winning. Spreading bets like this won't make you rich, but it does keep things interesting at the table.

Playing a European wheel

If you happen to find a single-zero European wheel, you greatly improve your odds: The house edge is half that of Roulette with the American wheel — only 2.63 percent. You may see a European wheel at one of the posh Vegas casinos, such as Bellagio, Mirage, or Caesars Palace. If you can't find one on the floor, it's probably tucked away in the high-limit area along with the baccarat tables, so you may need to ask. You can also find the single-zero wheel at some other upscale casinos around the country.

REMEMBER

Because casinos set aside the European wheel for high rollers, you're likely to find a higher table minimum, say $25. But because the house edge is half that of a double-zero wheel, the European wheel is the better Roulette game to play for bigger bettors.

Avoiding Strategies That Don't Work

Again, Roulette is a game of chance — and in such games, you're at the mercy of the fates for the most part. Although you can follow some simple steps to stretch your money and improve your odds (for more, see the preceding section), no magic system can turn you into a consistent winner at Roulette. Steer clear of falling into these traps.

Basing your plays on history

WARNING

Each spin of the Roulette wheel is completely independent, or unrelated, from the past, so don't let previous numbers influence you. Most Roulette tables have a lighted scoreboard that displays the numbers that have hit over the last 20 rolls in two columns: red and black. However, players who try to guess what color will come up next by relying on history are wasting their time. The information means absolutely nothing. The wheel has no memory, and, although streaks of red or black for six or ten spins may occur, these streaks are no indication of the next result.

Blaming wheel bias

You don't have to watch for *wheel bias* — the casino beats you to it. The house regularly balances and checks and then rechecks Roulette wheels for any suspected favoritism to certain numbers.

Sometimes a wheel becomes *biased* because the mechanical wear and tear results in a less-than-random play. After all, the wheel consists of metal and wood. And certainly, after a quarter-million spins every month, all that activity may cause the wheel to wear down in certain strategic points. For this reason, casinos inspect Roulette wheels routinely and monitor the results statistically with software.

Buying into betting systems

The Roulette table attracts the largest number of players attempting to apply a betting system. The most prominent progressive betting system is the Martingale system, in which you double your bet after each loss. Another popular one is the Reverse Martingale, in which you cut your bet in half after each win.

We don't recommend using any progressive betting system because a streak of four or five bad spins can cripple your bankroll in less than ten minutes.

REMEMBER

Despite all the systems advertised for sale, no magic bullet can help you beat a Roulette wheel. Books on Roulette systems are scams to separate you from your money. Why does someone want to share her amazing supersecret strategy with you? If you'd written such a system, wouldn't you prefer to just make a quick fortune, buy a small island, and retire? So beware of Roulette *pros*. They make money by selling books, not by divulging a consistently winning Roulette system.

Chapter 9

Mastering the Machines: Slots

From its Wild West roots in San Francisco, the slot machine has evolved into one of the most diverse and high-tech games in the casino. In fact, slots are now the most popular feature in a casino, enticing players with an endless variety of colors, shapes, types, and styles. Yet, for all their gadgets and gizmos, slot machines are blessedly easy to play. You press the button. That's it — and that just may be the reason behind their popularity.

Even though slot machines are cash cows for casinos (generating nearly two-thirds of the revenue in most casinos), they're far and away the most popular game for gamblers. And, although there are several reasons for this appeal, the main one is spelled J-A-C-K-P-O-T! The chance to win life-changing money is the rainbow that draws many eternal optimists back to these machines, trip after trip, push after push, ever searching for their own pot of gold.

In this chapter, we focus on the most important facts about slots: how to play them and recognize different types and how to understand the odds and stretch your bankroll and how to take advantage of comps. After you read this chapter, you'll be ready for the one-armed bandits.

Understanding How to Play the Slots

The design of slot machines remained the same in the early years after they were developed, except for one detail: The reels expanded from 10 to 20 symbols, increasing the possible combinations from 1,000 to 8,000. By creating so many more ways to win, this new version stirred up greater excitement and promised a much bigger jackpot.

Although modern machines present several new twists and updates to the original game, the goal for gamblers remains the same: to line up identical symbols in a row. Machines vary: They may have five reels instead of three. They may have multiple paylines. They may have more options than one-coin-a-pop. They may have buttons to push rather than a handle to pull. But the concept hasn't changed — line up a row of identical symbols, up–down, left–right, or diagonal, and call yourself a winner.

Slot machines used to accept and dispense only coins. Today you'd be hard-pressed to find a machine that accepts coins. All machines accept bills of every denomination. You insert your paper currency (or a payout ticket) into a bill receptor, and then the machine shows a credit for the amount of cash you inserted.

This section shows you how to play slots and what you need to know about the inner workings of a slot machine. We also cover the all-important payouts and how technology has changed the way you play slots.

LOW MAINTENANCE AND HIGH PROFIT: A CASINO'S DREAM

Slot machines make the perfect employees. They require no wages, tips, workmen's comp, or insurance benefits. They never call in sick, show up late, or have to leave early. Slot machines are also easy to play, they're available 24/7, and their computerized operating system allows gamblers to feed in paper currency at a frantic pace — producing a high profit margin for the house.

Playing the game: Easy as pushing a button

Although hitting a jackpot is the biggest attraction for slot fans, the machines are popular for other reasons. One of the biggest pluses is their simplicity. With most machines, you don't have to master a complicated strategy or decipher some finicky rules. You simply put in your money and watch the reels spin. You could even play blind-folded because the machine automatically pays you on every winner — whether you realize it or not.

REMEMBER

Several buttons on the machine allow you to streamline your playing (translation: drain your wallet faster). Look for the following:

>> **Bet One:** Press this button when you want to wager just one credit.

>> **Bet Max:** This button permits you to play the maximum number of credits that the machine allows per spin (each machine has an established max).

>> **Line buttons:** Instead of playing just the line that runs horizontally across the middle of the reels, you can play lines that run every which way across the screen on some machines. The line buttons allow you to choose how many lines to play: 1, 5, 9, 15 — even up to 30. Of course, the more lines you play, the more money you bet.

>> **Play X per line buttons:** These buttons allow you to increase the number of credits you play per line. If one credit is 25 cents, two credits would be 50 cents and so on. Again, the more credits you play, the more money you bet.

>> **Service:** Push this button when you want to summon a slot attendant.

>> **Cash Out:** Ready to cash out and move on? Just press here to receive any unused credit.

Dissecting the innards: How slots work

Novice slots players may wonder if there is any strategy to pressing the button that increases the likelihood of a win. Unfortunately no strategy exists. You can press lightly or forcefully. You can blink three times, click your heels together, or say a little prayer. It makes no difference. After you make your move, the outcome is preordained.

The computerized *Random Number Generator* (RNG) chip determines the outcome of each spin. The RNG is always at work, cycling through millions of random numbers, even when the machine isn't being played. The moment you press the spin button, the generator freezes the current numbers and their corresponding stops on the reels.

REMEMBER

Because of RNG technology, nothing can be done to predict or change the outcome. Even if you play on an interactive machine that allows you to make some decisions, slot machines are cold creatures that can't be influenced by anything you do.

On newer machines, your eyes just see a representation of the old-fashioned spinning reels. The RNG chip has predetermined the outcome — the images flashing before you on the machine are just for show.

REMEMBER

Each spin is completely independent of any previous results. As its name suggests, the RNG is *random*. There is no pattern or cycle that repeats after it has run its course.

Getting wise to virtual reel-ality

Although the RNG is random, it does allow for some tweaking of individual machines. For example, although the machines *appear to have* only 20 different symbols on each reel, the RNG creates virtual reels that *actually have* many more possibilities. This option creates bigger jackpots, but it also allows casinos to adjust the odds (or payback) for each machine. So, two identical machines can sit side by side, yet their odds for winning can be different.

But don't misunderstand. The casino doesn't change the payouts at will. There is no magic switch that allows an evil slot supervisor behind the green curtain to crank back the odds when the casino is losing. Reprogramming the RNG chips requires a great deal of paperwork and effort, so this adjustment is rare after the machines are on the floor. The manufacturer usually sets the exact payback before shipping the machine to the casino.

Entering the coinless age: Cashout tickets

Paper ticket technology, called *TITO* (ticket-in, ticket-out), has swept through casinos across the country. This change has revived penny and nickel slots because gamblers don't have to carry rolls of coins and a $20 win doesn't require hauling 400 coins to the cashier's cage. (Refer to Figure 9-1 for an example of a payout ticket.)

TITO also cuts down overhead and employee costs for casinos because they no longer have the hassle of refilling machines with thousands of pounds of coins. Here's another important feature for the casino: Players can spin more reels per hour on a coinless machine because they don't have to stop and feed coins into the slot. The result? Higher profit. Talk about a win-win for the casino!

FIGURE 9-1:
A typical payout
ticket is a
bar-coded
voucher.

Typical cash ticket

© *John Wiley & Sons, Inc.*

TITO slot machines accept both cash and machine tickets to start play, so there's no need for a coin hopper (metal bin to catch coins). For psychological effects, however, the machines still provide that irresistible sound of clinking coins when a player hits a jackpot or cashes out his credits (that lovely *Dink! Dink! Dink!* as if real coins were pouring through the trough).

REMEMBER

The ticket also gives you, the player, more flexibility. For example, if you've played six or eight spins on a machine without hitting anything, you can move to another machine by *cashing out* (pressing the cash out button). The machine prints a new ticket with your remaining credit balance so you can take it to another machine, even one that uses a different denomination. After you're done playing, redeem your ticket at the cashier's window or a ticket redemption machine. (Ticket redemption machines work similar to ATMs. You insert your ticket, the machine reads the bar code on the ticket, and voila! The value of the ticket is dispensed to you, right down to the last penny.)

WARNING

Don't throw away or lose your ticket — make sure you cash it in before you leave. Some tickets are valid for up to six months. Just be sure to turn it in before it expires. Casinos earn hundreds of thousands of dollars a year on the revenue from unclaimed tickets (even though most of them are under $1).

Identifying Differences in Slot Machines

The brave new slot world of the 21st century means you no longer need to settle for three-reel, three-payout-line machines. Every conceivable flavor, shape, and color is now available to tempt gamblers. Literally hundreds of new designs reflect the public's insatiable appetite for video slot machines, especially those with interactive touch screens. Some machines are so versatile, they let you change the type of game without leaving your seat! Just make sure you check the payout schedules for the winning combinations and for any special quirks that particular game has.

Anyone can play a slot machine — no wonder it's a favorite indoor sport. This section takes a look at the basic types of slots that you may encounter in your friendly neighborhood casino.

Increasing wagers with multipliers

On most machines you're looking for identical symbols to come up on one line (cherry, cherry, and . . . cherry!). On a typical machine, you can play just one credit, or you can play up to five credits, meaning you're *multiplying* — increasing — your wager. However, there is no advantage to betting more credits because the payout is proportional. For example, hitting three cherries may pay $50 if you played one coin, $100 if you played two coins, $150 if you played three coins, $200 for four coins, and $250 for five coins.

REMEMBER

A variation is the *bonus multiplier,* which offers a bonus when you play maximum coins and hit the jackpot. For example, for the same three cherries, the bonus multiplier may pay $50 for one coin, $100 for two coins, $150 for three coins, $200 for four coins — but $500 for five coins (twice the normal multiplier). This type of machine encourages players to wager the maximum number of coins, and they have odds similar to those of regular machines. If you play a bonus multiplier, you should always play max coins to take advantage of the bonus.

Zigzagging for multiple paylines

Both traditional reel-spinning slots and newfangled video machines offer *multiple payline* games, which can pay on dozens of different lines. These lines may appear as straight or zigzag patterns on the screen. Each line bet you make — and you can make multiple selections — corresponds to one line on the screen: up, down, or diagonal.

If you want to play just one line, you can still bet one credit, but if the machine displays a winner on one of the lines you *didn't* bet, you don't win. Multiple paylines are very common on lower-denomination machines, such as the penny and nickel machines that are popping up all over the casino floor. (Check out Figure 9-2 for an example of a multiple payline machine.)

FIGURE 9-2:
The multiline,
multibet video
slot machine.

© John Wiley & Sons, Inc.

Tuning in to theme machines

The hottest trend in slots links the game to popular TV shows (such as *Game of Thrones*, *Star Trek*, and the *Wheel of Fortune*), traditional board games (such as *Monopoly*), movies, cartoons, and so on. These *theme* machines rely on familiarity and popular branding to entice loyal fans.

WARNING

But in most cases, we suggest you skip these theme machines, even if you're a big fan of Vanna White or Mr. Spock. The reason is simple: These machines have bad odds. Typically, the casino must agree to share the revenues from any slot connected to a celebrity, show, or cartoon. (You don't expect Vanna to let them use her face for free, do you?) Consequently, the pie has more slices — and smaller paybacks.

Working the progressive slots

The *progressive* slot machines are typically grouped together in a *bank* or a *carousel* with a large jackpot tally spinning feverishly above them. The progressives can be linked to slots in one casino or multiple casinos. (The Megabucks game, for example, is linked to several casinos throughout the state of Nevada.)

The jackpot is based on a small percentage of the money played at each machine in the group. Because progressive slots are linked together on a network, the jackpot grows, little by little, each time a player feeds the beast. The question is: Should you play a regular machine with its paltry little jackpot, or should you gamble at the neon-flashing progressive machine with the shiny sports car spinning on the platform above the slot carousel?

TIP

The answer depends on your goals: If modest wins are fine, then you have much better odds of hitting a small jackpot on a regular machine than winning the big jackpot on a progressive machine that has as many as four or five reels and thousands of potential combinations. But some players aren't satisfied with a lot of small wins — they want to go for the glory. *Note:* The odds are long, and the winners are few at the gigantic progressives.

MEGABUCKS HITS . . . AND MISSES

Less than a year after the Megabucks progressive slots were introduced, Californian Terry Williams made slot history by winning almost $5 million at Harrah's Casino in Reno on February 1, 1987.

(In case you ever wondered, the large cardboard check that winners struggle to hold up is just for camera time. Most MegaJackpots are paid out in 25 annual installments.)

On the other end of the spectrum, consider one of the saddest moments in gambling: A player miraculously hit all three symbols on a machine but failed to play the maximum credits needed to win the big jackpot. This life-crushing experience happened to Kirk Tolman on March 14, 2001. Distracted by a friend while playing in Wendover, Nevada, Tolman popped just two coins instead of three into a Megabucks machine. Sure enough, the three reels lined up for the jackpot. Although the 22-year-old won $10,000 for his two-coin play, he lost the chance to collect the $7.96 million prize, just because he was a buck short.

The moral of the story: If you want a jackpot, play max credits — every spin, every session.

Engaging in interactive machines

The new *interactive* slot machines have become enormously popular with gamblers. Interactive means the player gets to make some decisions (usually done with a touch screen) during the game. However, other than blackjack slot machines, most interactive slot machines have few (if any) choices that allow skill to enter into the equation.

But even if these interactive machines don't change the odds, they're still extremely popular. They're fast and fun to play, but they're also mesmerizing, seductive, and hard to tear yourself away from. They hypnotize you with their subtle chant: "Must. Have. Your. Last. Dollar." And they usually get it.

The advantage of interactive slot machines is that the manufacturers get really creative. These games often have increasingly challenging levels, and each step up the ladder offers more money to make the game interesting and the journey worthwhile.

Most players are hoping to reach these bonus rounds — where the fun really begins. For example, on one version the reels disappear, and animated characters pop up as the game progresses. You choose between several images and click on one to reveal the bonus hidden behind the icon. The object is to win additional credits before clicking on a character with no credits, which ends the bonus round.

TIP

The total amount you win in the bonus round depends on the number of coins you play, so it's important to play the maximum coins allowed on interactive machines. Some bonus rounds also award bonus spins, where you can double or triple your winnings and win additional free games.

Getting a Handle on Slots Odds

Before you decide to feed a dollar or twenty into a slot machine, you first need to understand the odds. Sad but true, coming up with a strategy to beat the odds — when they favor the house so strongly — is impossible. (Check out Book 6, Chapter 2 for more on house odds.)

The payout of slot machines generally falls somewhere between 90 and 95 percent. That means for every $100 you put into a machine, your average return is $90 to $95 (a loss of $5 to $10). This hefty house edge makes slots one of the worst games in the casino. When you factor in the speed of the games, you start to understand why slots are so profitable for modern casinos.

TIP

If you have the time and interest, you can search online for the payout rates for a given machine. Analysts have determined that that nickel slots tend to be the *tightest* (worst odds) machines, returning about 91 percent, while $1 and $5 slots are the *loosest* (best odds), returning about 94 to 95 percent.

WARNING

Generally, you find the best machines and odds where the competition is most fierce. Try the Las Vegas Strip, where casinos are clustered closely together, each of them vying equally hard for your gambling dollar. On the other hand, playing slots on the water often leaves you all wet. Because cruise ship casinos aren't under the jurisdiction of U.S. gaming laws, some have payouts as low as 80 percent. Consequently, you're better off tucking your money back into your purse or wallet and waiting until you're on dry land.

Stretching Your Money at the Slots

With literally hundreds of machine choices, perhaps the most difficult decision is which one to play. You want to choose the game that offers the highest theoretical return. Unfortunately, finding the best machine in a sea of slots can be a difficult task — and a bit like comparing apples to oranges. For example, one machine may pay 5,000 credits for its jackpot while another pays only 1,000. But the jackpots are only part of the equation: Your total return also depends on the other winning combinations and how frequently they hit.

Although you can't do much to change the odds of hitting the jackpot, you can take steps to extend your gambling bankroll. Think of it this way: When you make your money last longer, you're maximizing the value of your entertainment dollar at the slots. This section helps make your slot experience more memorable by explaining what you can do to make your money last longer.

Reading the paytable

TIP

The *paytable* (located on the top glass of each machine) provides the most valuable information about a slot machine. Be sure to read (what combinations will win, how many credits are required, and so on) and understand the paytables before you start playing. (Check out Figure 9-3 for an example of the glass-panel payout information.)

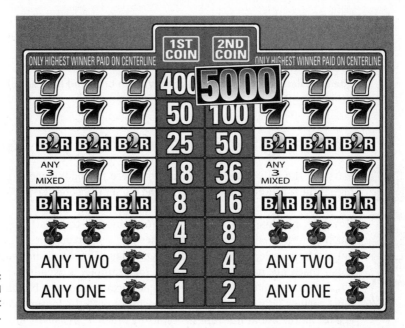

		1ST COIN	2ND COIN		
ONLY HIGHEST WINNER PAID ON CENTERLINE				ONLY HIGHEST WINNER PAID ON CENTERLINE	
7 7 7		400	5000	7 7 7	
7 7 7		50	100	7 7 7	
B2R B2R B2R		25	50	B2R B2R B2R	
ANY 3 MIXED 7 7		18	36	ANY 3 MIXED 7 7	
B1R B1R B1R		8	16	B1R B1R B1R	
🍒 🍒 🍒		4	8		
ANY TWO 🍒		2	4	ANY TWO 🍒	
ANY ONE 🍒		1	2	ANY ONE 🍒	

FIGURE 9-3:
The glass panel
gives the payout
information.

© *John Wiley & Sons, Inc.*

Machines that display a higher paytable usually have a greater number of symbols on each reel. For example, the older, three-reel slot machines have 20 symbols with 8,000 possible combinations ($20 \times 20 \times 20$), which means your odds of hitting the jackpot are 1 in 8,000. Likewise, a four-reel machine has odds of 1 in 160,000. The odds increase even more dramatically on a five-reel video machine: With 20 symbols, your chances of hitting the highest jackpot are about 1 in 3 million!

TIP

Having more reels and symbols doesn't necessarily make a machine any better or any worse. It just creates more potential combinations. You hit the jackpot more frequently on the three-reel machines, but the amount of money you win is typically much less than a jackpot on a five-reel machine. So which type of machine should you play? In the long run, it hardly matters. The casino has a sizeable edge over you on every slot machine in the house.

Choosing the type of machine

If you feel a need for speed, then you may want to try the traditional three-reel machines. These machines usually spin faster than video machines, which means you get more plays in an hour — and more opportunities to lose money. On the other hand, video slot machines have those cool bonus rounds that come up a couple of times in an hour; they can slow down the pace, stretching both your bankroll and your enjoyment.

The final decision is yours. You can try them both and then select the one you like the best.

Choosing the denomination you bet

REMEMBER

Slots are the only game in the casino where the odds depend on your bet. The higher the machine's denomination, the higher the potential payback — normally.

WARNING

However, returns vary from casino to casino, so the exact amount of payback (such as 91 percent for nickel machines and 95 percent for $5 machines) can be quite different depending on where you play. When a casino advertises that its dollar machines pay back 97 percent, for example, it usually means it pays *up to* 97 percent on *some* machines. These qualifications make a big difference because most casinos only have a couple of machines with the loosest payouts. The average for all the dollar machines is typically much less (usually around 93 percent), and there is no way to know which *special* machines are set to pay out at the higher rate (97 percent).

REMEMBER

Even though a dollar machine may pay back 95 percent and a nickel machine only 90 percent, you still lose less money with the nickels in the long run because you risk less money each spin.

Here's the math with five coins per spin: Dollar machines cost you 25¢ per pull ($5 times the house edge of 5 percent), and nickel machines cost you less than 3¢ per pull (25¢ times the house edge of 10 percent). So even though the house edge is twice as high on the nickel slots (10 percent versus 5 percent), the nickel slots are easier on your wallet (you only lose a few cents a spin on the nickel slots versus 25¢ each spin on the dollar machines).

Other potential budget-busters are the multibet, multipayline video slots that are so hot today — they can cost you a lot more money than normal machines. A nickel machine may cost a mere 5¢ for a single coin spin, but if you go with a max bet of 45 credits, your game actually costs $2.25 per spin. Some machines allow up to 90 credits, meaning you'd be betting $4.50 per spin! Surprisingly, even the max credit on the lowly penny slots can be 300 coins, or $3.

REMEMBER

Even at the lowest denomination, max betting can rapidly drain your gambling stake, and you may soon find yourself feeding another $20 bill into the penny slot machine — not what you intended. When coin options are sky-high, you're better off playing a dollar machine for one or two coins than a low-denomination max bet with worse odds.

THE COLOR OF MONEY

To avoid that "kid-in-a-candy-store" confusion around slot machines, you need to know what kind of "candy" you want, right? Well, keep this point in mind: The big light on the top of a slot machine is called a *candle*, and the rim color of the light tells you the denomination of the machine. In most casinos, you can check for the following colored candles to decipher the denominations of each machine:

- $1 machines are blue.
- 50-cent machines are gold.
- Quarters are yellow.
- Nickels are red.
- Pennies don't have a standard color.

By knowing these colored candles, you can instantly spot the denomination you want to play when you look across a casino.

Hitting an empty casino

If you're a sun-worshipper, you probably pursue your slot jackpot in the evening because you prefer to spend your afternoons at the hotel pool, sipping your favorite drink. But what's the best time to play the slots? Actually, the drowsy hour just before dawn is the deadest time in a casino. Light sleepers can grab an early morning cup of coffee and hit a nearly empty casino to enjoy a relatively peaceful playing time with the widest array of machines available. However, the odds never change on these machines, so don't expect to find looser slots just because they're lonely and looking for players.

Playing full credits on progressive games

REMEMBER

When playing a progressive machine, you need to keep one hard-and-fast rule in mind: Always play the maximum number of credits each spin. If you don't, you greatly dilute your odds because a big part of the payback in progressive machines is predicated on hitting the jackpot with max coins. If you don't have the bankroll to play the maximum number of coins, then play a non-progressive machine where the payback is unaffected by the number of coins played. See the section "Increasing wagers with multipliers" for more information.

Playing max credits does have its downside, though. Proficient players can easily get in 600 spins an hour on most machines. If you play the max number of credits each time, your money can vanish darn fast. An average loss can be $100 an hour — or more — at many dollar machines, which makes for a pretty expensive hobby.

If you're new to slots, your safest bet may be to stick to two-credit, single payline machines. Although they don't offer a large jackpot, they at least stretch your bankroll, enabling you to play longer and enjoy more of that one-armed bandit euphoria you sat down to experience in the first place.

Maximizing your fun

We're fairly negative about slots. These machines carry a high price tag for their fun. But we can't ignore the fact that there's something addicting to those whirring, humming sirens. And the fact that they're so simple to play makes them irresistible to most casino guests. So if you can't say *no* to slots, we suggest you keep the following tips in mind to enhance your relationship with these aptly named one-armed bandits:

>> **Leave your myths and superstitions at home.** Rid yourself of any myths or hunches about hot and cold machines.

>> **Do some investigative work.** Find out which casinos have the best paybacks on their slot machines before you take your trip. A good way to do your homework is by subscribing to *Casino Player Magazine* or *Midwest Gaming and Travel.*

>> **Stay within your means.** Never play a game that you don't understand or one that requires larger bets than you planned on making.

>> **Remember the odds.** Slot machines are *negative expectation* games. The longer you play, the more you lose. So take frequent breaks and pace yourself and your bankroll.

>> **Be realistic.** The odds of hitting the Megabucks jackpot are much worse than your chance of getting hit in the head by an asteroid.

>> **Slow down.** Savor your jackpots and enjoy the journey. Because of the high house odds, the faster you play, the more you lose.

>> **Double-check your payouts.** On your big wins, always make sure you get paid correctly *before* rushing to the next spin. Also, be careful to cash out your credits before you leave the machine.

You also want to make sure you bring your ID. You must have a valid driver's license or government ID to get paid on any large jackpot ($1,200 or more). And while you're at it, comb your hair. You want to look good for the paparazzi when they snap a photo of you holding your oversized cardboard check.

Honing Your Slot Etiquette

Etiquette in slots? You think we're joking, right? Actually, even though playing slots is a solitary activity, a few little courtesies can ensure that you keep the peace with the blue-haired lady to your left. This section focuses on the main do's and don'ts of slot-machine etiquette.

Saving a machine

How can you tell if a machine's been saved? Well, it doesn't shout, "Hallelujah, I've seen the light!" But, trust us, you definitely want to know if the seemingly unattended machine has been claimed by someone else. Otherwise, the wrath you incur just might feel like Judgment Day. There's no quicker way to turn a kindly old grandmother into the avenging angel than by *stealing* her favorite machine (especially when, after only a few coins, you magically win *her* jackpot).

REMEMBER

It's common practice in casinos for a player to save a machine for a short while when she needs a break. The length of time you can hold a machine varies, depending on the casino and whether you're a high roller; 10 to 15 minutes is rarely a problem. But expecting the machine to remain exclusively yours while you chomp down crab legs in the buffet for an hour may be pushing it. You can save a slot by leaving your coat on the chair or by tipping the chair forward so it leans against the machine.

Playing two machines at once: Double trouble

Many avid slots players like to play two machines at once. They do so by sitting in one seat and reaching back and forth between two machines. In those cases, you may think a machine is available because the seat is empty. Beware: Before you get a chance to slip in a dollar, you will get a stinging rebuke from the serious "I can't lose my money fast enough, so I play two machines at once" gambler in the next stool.

Minding your manners

Slots may be a solitary game, but you're still playing in an open environment, so be sensitive to your neighbors to your right and left. Consider these helpful tips for being a polite gambler and keeping the peace.

>> **If you aren't actually playing, stay out of the way.** If you're watching a friend or spouse play, make sure you aren't in the way of another player. Just like at the table games, nonplaying guests must give up the seat to a player who wants to play.

>> **If you find a slot card in a machine you want to play, be careful.** If the player is nowhere in sight, feel free to remove the card and play. But don't toss it in the trash; just put the card on top of the machine. Chances are, the player is already headed back to retrieve it and will be grateful for the gesture.

>> **Never covet thy neighbor's jackpot.** Slots are different from table games like poker. You're not competing against each other; everyone is competing against the house. So don't sulk when an adjacent machine hits a big winner. Cheer him on and help him enjoy the moment. Being a good sport won't change your luck, but it makes the overall gaming experience more enjoyable.

Playing for Comps

One of the best incentives for slot players is the generous comps that casinos bestow on them. Typically, the more you play, the more freebies you receive (comped meals, entertainment tickets, cashbacks, and other perks). There's just one drawback to playing for comps — it can become too enticing. Just like some people go crazy over frequent-flyer miles and take extra trips to get to the next level, some gamblers play longer and for more money just to score a comp to the buffet.

TIP

Slots can be very entertaining, but those free meals can end up being very expensive. Always stick to your budget when gambling, and never chase the comps. But hey, as long as you're there, feel free to enjoy the great side benefits that come your way.

This section focuses on how to take advantage of slot comps, including how to sign up for a slot club and how to cash in.

Taking advantage of the comps

Today's casinos use club cards to keep track of how much individual gamblers bet and how long they play. Slots are the perfect vehicle for this system because the machine automatically tallies every wager you make. The longer you play or the more you bet, the more club points you accumulate.

TIP

The main reason you should want a club card is to turn those points into *comps*. Comps come in many shapes and forms, from free hats to penthouse suites. But the premise is the same for all gamblers, whether high rollers or nickel slot players — the amount of time you play and the average amount you bet is tabulated to determine what comps you receive. A comp is truly a great benefit and can help defray your losses. Although formulas vary among casinos, the basic principle is this: A percentage of your theoretical loss is returned to you in the form of comps (such as free meals, shows, or complimentary hotel accommodations).

REMEMBER

You don't get comps only when you lose. The casinos never care whether you win or lose in the short run — they only want to see some action from you. Because they're *always* the favorite, they know they're going to win in the long run.

Some comps are immediate, although others may accrue over a few trips to the casino and finally bring you up to a new level, such as an invitation to a special event or a tournament. Because casinos want to develop a loyal customer base, they aggressively reward their best customers with little extras to keep them coming back.

Signing up for a slot club

Casinos strongly encourage new players to sign up for the slot club, and they make it simple. With just a few minutes of your time and a valid ID, you receive a shiny laminated card with your name on it (and usually a handy little key chain to fasten the card to your body). Also, be sure and ask if there are any sign-up perks. Many casinos offer special deals to attract new players.

When you play the slots, simply insert your card into a card reader on the machine; the computer automatically tracks how long you play and how much you bet.

TIP

If you ever lose your card, which is very easy to do, just go back to the desk where you first signed up and ask for a duplicate. Or you may want to ask for an extra card to begin with, especially if your spouse also wants to play under your account or you intend to play two machines at once.

Cashing in on cash rebates

What's even better than free meals? Free cash! Many contemporary casinos offer cashback programs (up to 1 percent) in addition to their generous comps. Of course, casinos can afford to be generous because slots are so profitable for the house.

Casinos normally figure your comps and potential cashback rewards on a point system. The more points you accrue (based on the machine denomination and how many hours you play), the larger your perks. Also, just like with grocery store coupons, you can get double or triple points on certain days of the month, putting you on the fast track to cashing in. Points are usually nontransferable and often have an expiration date.

Your cashback typically comes in two flavors:

>> You receive the cashback the same day you earn it.

>> You're mailed a cashback certificate, good for your next trip to the casino. This program is called a *bounce-back*.

Bounce-back programs typically require you to return within a certain time. If your favorite casino is within a short drive, that isn't a problem. But if you have to fly across the country to cash it in, your certificate becomes much less valuable.

Index

C

Calamity Jane (Black Lady; Black Maria; Black Widow; Slippery Anne) (in Hearts), 94, 98
Calculation, 20–22
calling
  defined, 127
  in Internet Poker, 298–299
  passive players, 259
  in Poker, 123, 143
  in Seven-Card Stud, 153, 162
  in Texas Hold'em, 206, 221, 226–227, 234–236
Canfield, 22–24
card counters, 456, 463, 479
Caribbean Stud Poker, 420, 423
cashback programs, 532
cashier's cages, 410
cashout tickets, 518–519
casino gambling
  alcohol, 410, 439, 445
  bankroll management, 406, 430–434, 437–439
  casino credit, 434–436
  cheating, 450–451
  chip colors, 406–407
  employees, 411–415
  gambling addiction, 439
  handling gaming material, 443–444
  house edge, 405–406, 422–425
  joining games, 442
  layout, 408–411
  marketing, 405
  match play coupons, 427
  probability and odds
    defined, 420–421
    dependent events, 421
    identifying payoff odds, 426–427
    independent events, 421
    luck, 419–420
    payout odds versus true odds, 422
    statistics and, 422
  promotions, 427
  psychology of design, 403–404, 407–408
  security, 416–418
  smoking, 444–445
  table limits, 442
  tips and gratuities, 446–449
Casino Gambling For Dummies (Blackwood), 2
casino hosts, 414–415
casino managers, 415
Casino Player Magazine, 528
casino Poker games
  advantages of, 133–134
  buying chips, 135
  dealing, 135
  defined, 409
  entering games, 134
  home games versus, 135–136
  pace of play, 134, 136
  players banks, 133
  selectivity of play, 136
  shuffling, 135
  tightness of games, 135–136
center bets (proposition bets) (in Craps), 498–499
center hand opponent (CHO), defined, 7
Chan, Johnny, 121
chat feature (in Internet Poker)
  abuse of, 292, 309
  controls, 296–297
  lingo and abbreviations, 303–306
Cheat, 112–114
checking
  defined, 127
  in Internet Poker, 297, 299
  in Seven-Card Stud, 153
  tells indicating, 264
  in Texas Hold'em, 206, 234–235, 250
check-raising
  aggressive players, 258
  defined, 127
  in Texas Hold'em, 234, 237–238, 242
Chicago (Black Mariah), 193
Chicago (four-deal Bridge) scoring method
  Bridge wheel, 396–399
  game contracts, 393
  general discussion, 391
  grand slam, 394–395
  partscore contract, 394

flushes
  in Omaha/8, 172–173, 175, 177–178, 180
  in Poker, 124–125
  in Seven-Card Stud, 155–156
  in Texas Hold'em, 166, 230–231, 235, 242–243, 245–246, 251, 274
folding
  in Internet Poker, 297–299
  in Omaha/8, 184
  in Poker, 121–123, 127, 136, 143
  in Seven-Card Stud, 152–153
  tells indicating, 264
  in Texas Hold'em, 200, 206, 227, 267
Foley, Ray, 35
Follow the Queen, 325
following suit
  defined, 10–11
  in Euchre, 67, 74
  failing to follow suit, 11
  in Hearts, 95
  in Oh Hell!, 59, 61
  in Rummy, 37
  in Spades, 76
forfeits (in Beggar My Neighbor), 104
foundations (in Solitaire), 16
four-deal Bridge scoring method. *See* Chicago scoring method
four-of-a-kind (quads)
  in Omaha/8, 179
  in Poker, 124–125
  in Texas Hold'em, 230
fourth street
  in Seven-Card Stud, 154, 161–162, 319
  in Texas Hold'em, 164–165, 202, 241–247, 316
free cards (in Texas Hold'em), 238–239
free odds (odds bets) (in Craps), 490, 492–493
freerolls (in Texas Hold'em), 232
French (European) Roulette wheel, 503, 511–512
front-line bets (pass-line bets) (in Craps), 489, 493–494
full house
  in Omaha/8, 179
  in Poker, 124–125

in Seven-Card Stud, 156
in Texas Hold'em, 230
Full Tilt (Internet Poker company), 284

G

gambling addiction, 439
game contracts (in Bridge), 393
game texture (in Texas Hold'em), 166–167
gapped cards (in Texas Hold'em), 167–168
gaps (spaces) (in Solitaire), 16
Gin Rummy
  dealing, 44
  going out, 45–47
  ranking card order, 6
  requirements for game play, 44
  tallying score, 45–48
Go Fish, 111
going all-in (in Poker), 128
grand slam (in Bridge), 394–395
gratuities. *See* tips and gratuities
groups. *See* sets

H

hands
  arranging, 8
  defined, 8
  looking at before deal is completed, 8, 13
  runs, 9
  sets, 9
hard-way bets (in Craps), 499
Harlan, Mark, 2, 199, 553
Harroch, Richard D., 2, 554
HCP (high-card points) (in Bridge), 389–390
heads up play
  in Poker tournaments, 328–329
  in Seven-Card Stud, 162
Hearts
  dealing, 92
  game play, 93–97
  misdeals, 93
  objective of, 92

R

rags (in Bridge), 363

rainbows (in Texas Hold'em), 203

raising
  aggressive players, 258
  defined, 127
  in Internet Poker, 298–299
  in Omaha/8, 182
  in Poker, 123, 129
  in Seven-Card Stud, 153–154
  in Texas Hold'em, 169–170, 206, 213, 221, 224, 227, 234, 236–237

raking, 200, 255

Random Number Generator (RNG) technology (in slot machines), 517–518

random walks, 420

ranking card order
  in Blackjack, 454–455
  in Bridge, 334
  in Cribbage, 6
  in Euchre, 6, 68
  in Gin Rummy, 6
  in Hearts, 95
  overview, 6
  in Pinochle, 6
  in Spades, 76
  in War, 109

ranking Poker hands
  flush, 124–125
  four-of-a-kind, 124–125
  full house, 124–125
  low hands, 126
  no pair, 126
  in Omaha/8, 177–178
  one pair, 125–126
  royal flush, 124–125
  in Seven-Card Stud, 154–155
  straight, 124–125
  straight flush, 124–125
  three-of-a-kind, 125–126
  two pair, 125–126

ranking suits (in Bridge), 386–387

Razz, 123, 194

red/black bets (in Roulette), 509

redeals (in Solitaire), 16

reneging. See revoking

renouncing. See discarding

reserve (heel) (in Canfield), 22

responder (in Bridge), 384

response (in Bridge), 384

Reverse Martingale system, 512–513

revoke cards (in Oh Hell!), 61

revoking (reneging)
  defined, 11
  in Euchre, 74
  in Hearts, 97
  in Spades, 87

Rigal, Barry, 554

right bower (in Euchre), 68, 70

right hand opponent (RHO; younger hand), defined, 7

ring games
  in Internet Poker
    disconnections, 311–312
    Five-Card Draw, 324
    Five-Card Stud, 324–325
    Omaha High, 317–318
    Omaha High/Low, 319
    Pineapple, 323–324
    player's choice, 325
    Seven-Card Stud, 320–323
    Texas Hold'em, 316–317
    timers, 290
    wild card games, 325
  in Texas Hold'em, 207, 214

river (in Omaha/8), 173, 185–186

river (fifth street) (in Texas Hold'em), 164–165, 203, 249–252, 255–256, 316

river (seventh street) (in Seven-Card Stud), 150, 154–155, 319

RNG (Random Number Generator) technology (in slot machines), 517–518

rolls (in Craps), 483

Romanian Whist
  bidding, 62
  dealing, 62
  game play, 62
  requirements for game play, 62

turn (fourth street) (in Texas Hold'em),
164–165, 202, 241–247, 316

21. *See* Blackjack

two pair

in Omaha/8, 175

in Poker, 125–126

in Seven-Card Stud, 154–156, 162

in Texas Hold'em, 230

U

UIGEA (Unlawful Internet Gambling Enforcement Act),
284

unbalanced (distributional) hands (in Spades), 81

undertricks

in Bridge, 399

in Spades, 85

Unlawful Internet Gambling Enforcement Act (UIGEA),
284

Up the Creek without a Paddle. *See* Oh Hell!

up-card, defined, 8

V

Video Poker, 423, 444

vigorishes (vigs), 405, 424

voids (in Bridge), 367

W

War, 109–110

waste-piles

in Calculation, 20–22

in Solitaire, 16

wheel (bicycle)

in Omaha/8, 177

in Poker, 123

in Texas Hold'em, 232

Whist, 11

wild cards

in home Poker games, 189

in Internet Poker, 325

in Rummy, 39–40

Williams, Terry, 522

Winning at Internet Poker For Dummies
(Derossi and Harlan), 2

World Poker Tour (television program), 199, 208

World Series of Poker, 256

wrong-way bettors (in Craps), 491–492

Y

younger hand (right hand opponent; RHO), defined, 7

Z

zero expectation bets, 426

About the Authors

Kevin Blackwood: Growing up in a conservative small town in Maine, Kevin Blackwood never anticipated visiting Sin City. With aspirations of becoming a college professor, he earned bachelor's and master's degrees in religious education and biblical history.

While working on his doctorate at the University of Oregon, he learned how to count cards and started playing blackjack on weekends. One day, he bagged his plans to teach church history, quit school, and headed to Las Vegas.

Since then, Kevin has lived what many would consider the American dream, earning big bucks winning consistently at blackjack tables all over the world. He also jumped on the Texas Hold'em bandwagon and has several Poker tournament wins under his belt.

Kevin is the author of *Play Blackjack Like the Pros* (HarperCollins), the most comprehensive guide to becoming a winning blackjack player.

Chris Derossi: Chris Derossi is a technology geek and a serial entrepreneur. Having started his first company at the age of 14, he has worked at myriad corporations since (creating several along the way). Among other positions, Chris has been the chief architect of the Macintosh Operating System at Apple Computer, the founder of ePeople, and the CEO of Trading Technologies. Chris was a founder of *MacTech* magazine and has written extensively for the computer industry. Chris is an avid Poker player and is often found clutching the first-place trophy in the tournaments he enters.

Mark "The Red" Harlan: Mark "The Red" Harlan was born in Rawlins, Wyoming. At the tender age of 8, he won a pinewood derby competition in the Cub Scouts, giving him his first heavy swig of victory that would forever warp his oh-so-soft-and-pliable mind. Under the influence of this experience, he started playing Poker that same year ("might as well win money if you're going to win") and became good enough by 2005 to be a net money winner in that year's World Series of Poker.

Red's professional experience includes human-interface work at Apple Computer, development of the bidding schema used by eBay, and co-founding CyberArts Licensing.

Red is a member of the American Society of Journalists and Authors.

Lou Krieger: Lou Krieger learned Poker at the tender age of 7, while standing at his father's side during the weekly Thursday night game held at the Krieger kitchen table in the blue-collar Brooklyn neighborhood where they lived.

Lou played throughout high school and college and managed to keep his head above water only because the other players were so appallingly bad. But it wasn't until his first visit to Las Vegas that he took Poker seriously, buying into a low-limit Seven Card Stud game where he managed — with a good deal of luck — to break even. Then he noticed a Texas Hold'em table. He sat down, played for an hour, and decided that was the game for him.

Richard Harroch: Richard Harroch is an attorney with more than 20 years of experience in representing start-up and emerging companies, entrepreneurs, and venture capitalists. He is a Phi Beta Kappa graduate of U.C. Berkeley and graduated from UCLA Law School, where he was managing editor of the Law Review. He has written a number of legal/business books, including *Small Business Kit For Dummies; Start-Up and Emerging Companies: Planning, Financing and Operating the Successful Business;* and *Partnership and Joint Venture Agreements.* He also spearheaded the development of a premier legal-agreements website.

Richard is an avid Poker player and has participated a number of times in the World Series of Poker in Las Vegas.

Bar   nd. Having started
wit   loved on to Bridge
at   he captained the
Bri   years in the world
of   tor on card games.

Publisher's Ackn

Compiler: Victoria M
Senior Acquisitions   tockphoto
Project Manager: Ch
Technical Editor: Jen
Art Coordinator: Ali